Islamic Art

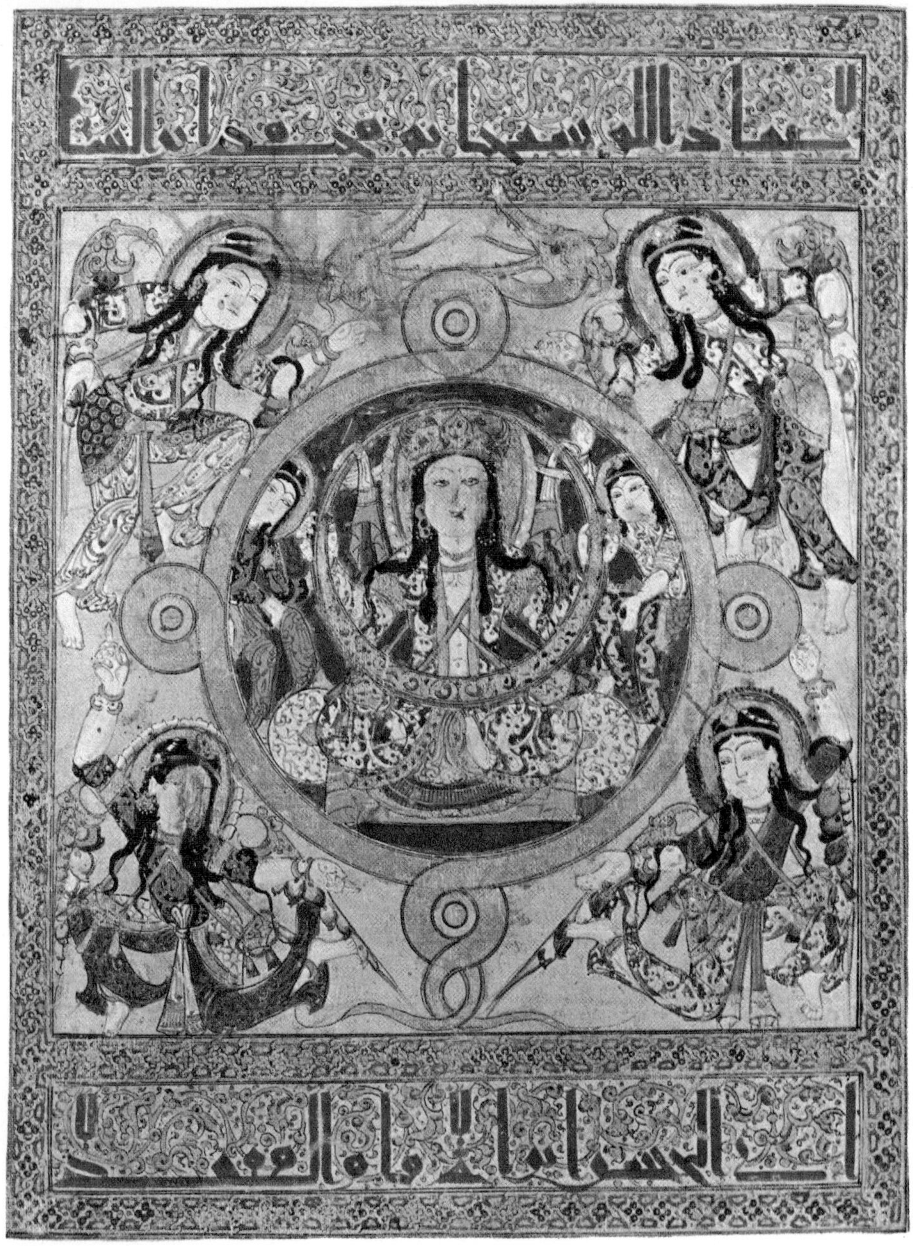

1 Frontispiece to a medical treatise, 'Book of Antidotes' of Pseudo-Galen, showing a central figure holding a crescent-shaped halo and surrounded by four other figures. Probably painted in northern Iraq, 1199

Islamic Art

David Talbot Rice

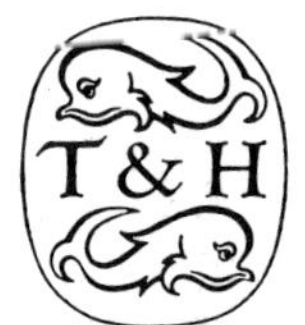

LONDON
THAMES AND HUDSON

REVISED EDITION 1975
PRINTED IN GREAT BRITAIN BY JARROLD AND SONS LTD NORWICH

Contents

Introduction

One of the most striking things about Islamic art is the way in which a completely definite style, a whole repertory of motifs, and a distinct architectural system became, quite early in the era of the Hegira, associated with an idea and a faith. Islamic art is, in this respect, quite distinct from Christian, where diversity rather than uniformity was the characteristic. The arts of the various phases of Christendom – Byzantine, Carolingian, Romanesque, Gothic, Renaissance – were wholly different, and there was great diversity between the regions; indeed, variety was the very essence of the art. In the Islamic world, on the other hand, there was much greater uniformity, both with regard to time and to space. In the first place the artists did not seek the new and unfamiliar in the way that the Renaissance artists did, but rather remained attached to the model whose merit had been sanctioned by time and convention, seeking to renew its appeal, rejuvenate its character, by subtle variations of detail. In the second, the adoption over the whole area from India to Spain of a particular script which also served as a basic form of ornament in art exercised a tremendously unifying effect.

Because of these factors Islamic art has, at first glance, a certain degree of sameness for the Western eye; it seems hard to assign its products to a locality, harder still to date them. Closer acquaintance, however, dispels this first impression, and the aim of the writer in compiling this book has been to present the works first according to their period and second according to their geographical provenance, in order to illustrate both the developments that took place over the ages and the variations for which the different regions were responsible; for the Islamic world was of vast extent and its population was drawn from virtually all the known races of man.

This aim has necessitated a division of the chapters quite distinct from that in most other books on Islamic art, where it has usually been determined either on purely geographical lines or on the basis of material, the text being devoted to a particular region, or the pottery, metalwork, painting or whatever it may be being treated for itself in separate chapters. It is hoped that the arrangement followed here may help to indicate both the nature of the developments that took place at different periods throughout the regions, as well as the factors that distinguish the arts of one region from those of another.

It has been by no means easy to cover the whole sphere of Islamic art within the compass of a small book; to do so certain rather artificial bounds have had to be set up, with regard both to time and to space. In respect of the former, the story has been brought virtually to a close with the early seventeenth century, even if, because of this, it proved impossible to say more than a few words about such things as the carpets of Persia or the rugs of Asia Minor, which for many people probably constitute the best known field of Islamic art. In respect of the latter, India has been omitted from the survey, because the art which developed there on the basis of what was introduced from Persia around 1400 followed very distinct lines, different from those taken elsewhere. Similarly it has been impossible to say anything about arms and armour, jewellery, bookbinding or lacquer, though products in these spheres were often very fine; nor has it been possible to treat of certain specialized aspects of Islamic art such as costume, heraldry or calligraphy, despite the very considerable importance of these subjects. So far as the last of these, calligraphy, is concerned, we can do little more than call attention to the outstanding importance of script as an essential element of decorative art; any more detailed analysis either of the formal *kufic* or the more fluent *naskh* proved unfeasible in the space available, though such an analysis must be regarded as an essential preliminary to any truly penetrating study of Islamic art. Much has thus been omitted, but the major problems have, it is hoped, all been noted and the principal styles defined, with the object of bringing before a wider public a mass of material which has been a source of delight and interest to the writer through many years; more important, much of it may also, in all justice, claim to hold an outstanding place in the story of the art of the past.

Early Islamic Art

The Islamic era is counted from the year AD 622, the date of Muhammad's migration to Medina. Within little more than twenty years of that date Syria and Egypt had been wrested from the Byzantine empire and Iraq and Persia from the Sassanian. The great Byzantine state, heir of Roman territory and Roman glory, was thus brought to its knees by the loss of two of its most important provinces, while the mighty power in Persia that had halted the progress of the Roman advance in an easterly direction for some four centuries was wholly subjugated.

But though the rise of Islam marked the inception of a new and extremely important phase in the world's history, the conquered Byzantine provinces and the old Sassanian empire left a cultural and artistic heritage which was to affect the world of Islam for many a century; indeed so far as art was concerned, this dual heritage was fundamental, and its importance was only equalled at first by the influence exercised by Semitic thought and, rather later, by the role played by the non-figural style of the East. These divergent trends, unified by the universal adoption of the Arabic script which, in one or another of its forms, became more than anything else the factor which made the art of the Islamic world into a distinctive style, the distribution of which coincided with the bounds of the faith, and not with those of any particular ethnic or political element within it.

The earliest caliphs were established in Medina, but it soon became apparent that this city, however desirable as the centre of an unworldly religious faith, was not suitable for the administrative capital of what had, in two decades, become a great political empire; nor could the old life of the Arabs, depending as it did for variety and to a great extent for income on the raiding of more prosperous neighbours, continue, now that a mass of peoples, who were already accustomed to a settled and cultural life under urban

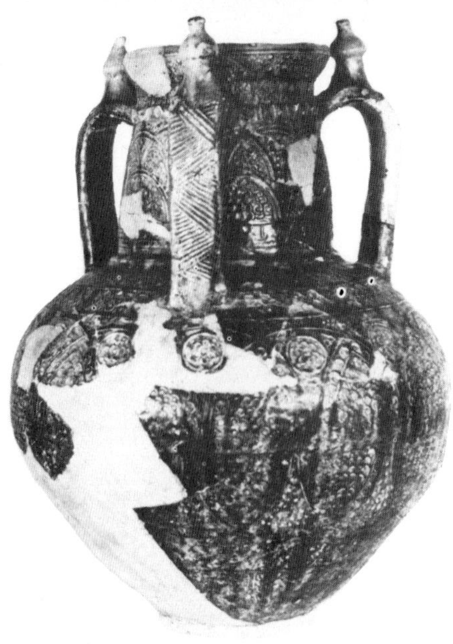

2 Glazed pottery vessel. A date in the eighth century has been established on the basis of archaeological evidence, though the form and glaze belong to a type common from Parthian times. It bears one of the earliest known *kufic* inscriptions

conditions, had been brought within the fold. A new capital had to be chosen and a new way of life developed.

For a century or so this new capital was established at Damascus, in what is today Syria, and it was in this area that the earliest developments of an art which can truly be termed Islamic took place. The earliest phase take its name from that of the first dynasty of Islam, the Umayyad, which sponsored it. It continued until about 750, when the capital was transferred from Syria to Mesopotamia and a new dynasty, the Abbasid, came to power. Thereafter a new style was rapidly developed under the patronage of the eastern caliphs.

We know at present practically nothing of the arts of metal working, textile weaving, or manuscript illumination in Umayyad times – the very arts which were later to become so characteristically Islamic – while with regard to pottery the only vessels, other than purely utilitarian unglazed wares, that can be attributed to Umayyad times are the fairly large jars covered with a blue or green alkaline glaze which had first been developed by the Parthians. It is hard to be sure of the date of many of these. One example (*Ill. 2*), in the Damascus Museum, bears a *kufic* inscription and is dated to the eighth century on archaeological evidence. In architecture the situation is different, for quite a number of buildings do survive, both religious and secular. The most important of them are the Dome of the Rock and the mosque of al-Aqsa at Jerusalem, the Great Mosque at Damascus, a few towns and forts, and a series of palaces on the fringe of the desert which were erected by the caliphs or their sons. To these palaces they could retire to escape not only from the cares of state but also from the ties of settled urban life which still seemed to them oppressive and hampering, even after several generations of residence in the luxurious lands of Syria, away from the harsh atmosphere of desert Arabia.

The Dome of the Rock was founded by the Caliph Abd al-Malik in 687 and completed in 691 (*Ill. 6*); the al-Aqsa mosque was also founded by Abd al-Malik, but it was thereafter rebuilt several times, and little of the original structure survives today. The Great Mosque at Damascus was begun in 705 by the Caliph al-Walid and completed in 715 (*Ill. 10*). All these monuments are interesting, the mosques for their architecture and their decoration, often in mosaic, the towns for their layout, and the palaces for their stucco work and their paintings, as well as for the light that they throw on the nature of contemporary life and conditions.

The Dome of the Rock is octagonal on plan, or rather it consists of an outer solid octagon enclosing two open octagons composed of columns. Above the innermost of these stands a dome on a tall circular drum. The plan represents an elaboration of one which had previously been developed in the Byzantine world in Justinian's day, in such churches as SS Sergius and Bacchus at Constantinople (526–37) and San Vitale at Ravenna (526–47). The interior again owes a great deal not only to the Christian art of Syria and Palestine, but also to that of the Byzantine world proper; the columns, the capitals and the marble revetments of the walls are therefore hardly distinct from those which might have been found in a church in Constantinople. Some of the acanthus designs on the metal coverings of the tie-beams are often closer to local than to purely Byzantine forms, while other decorative motifs on these, as well as those of the mosaics (*Ill. 4*), owe as much to Sassanian Persia as to Byzantine art. The double-winged motif follows Sassanian prototypes (*Ill. 3*)

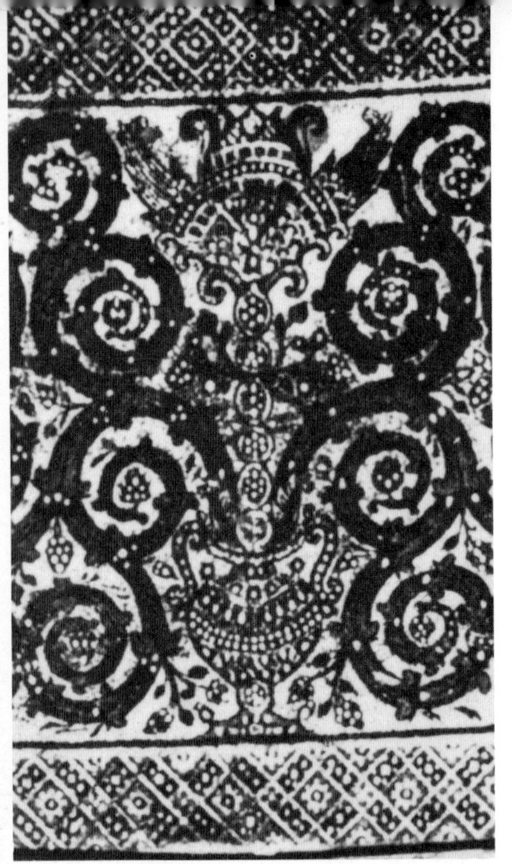

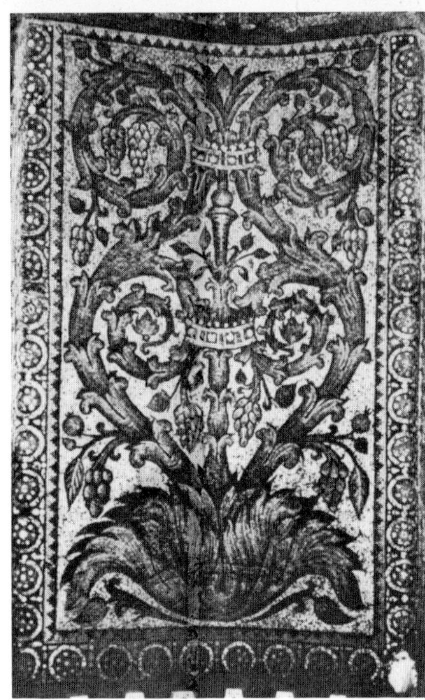

3, 4 Mosaics in the Dome of the Rock, Jerusalem, 691. The stylized scrolls belong to a Hellenistic repertory, but the double-wing motif at the top of one of the panels is wholly Sassanian

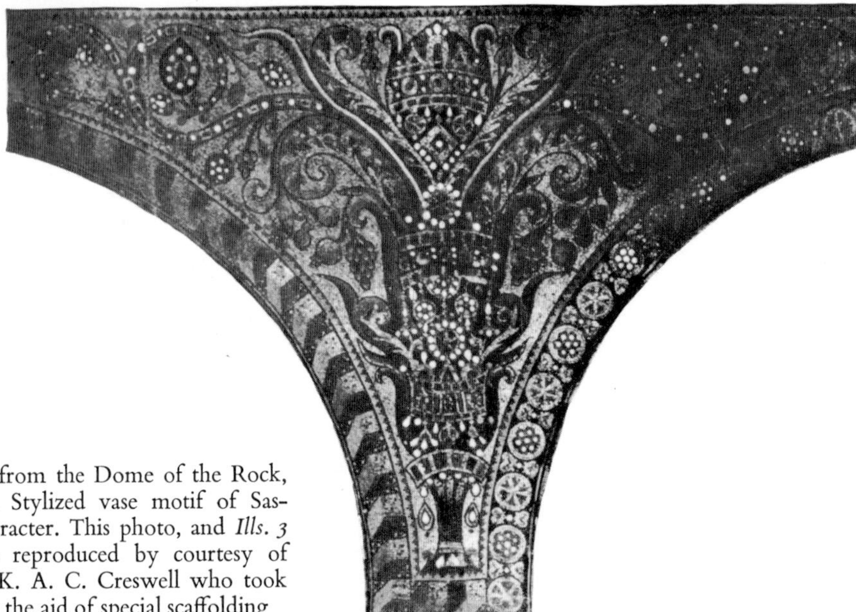

5 Mosaic from the Dome of the Rock, Jerusalem. Stylized vase motif of Sassanian character. This photo, and *Ills. 3 and 4* are reproduced by courtesy of Professor K. A. C. Creswell who took them with the aid of special scaffolding

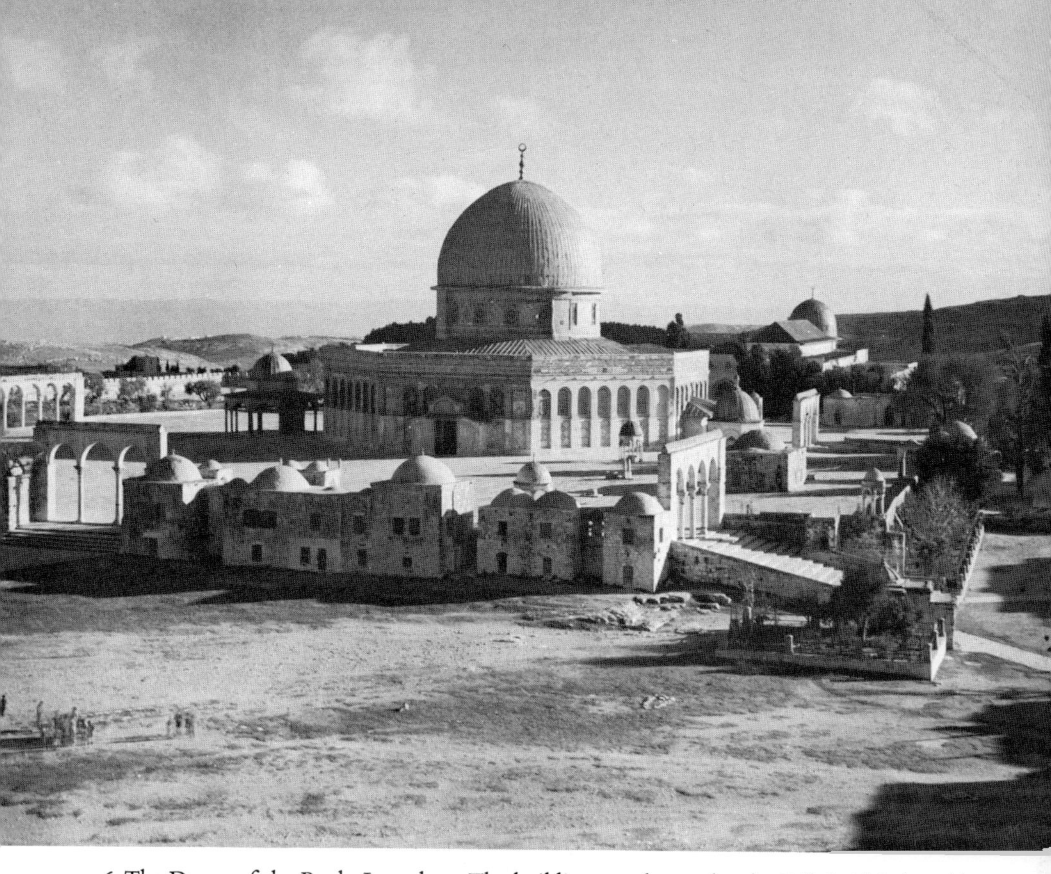

6 The Dome of the Rock, Jerusalem. The building was begun by the Caliph Abd al-Malik in 687. Its plan represents a variation on that of the centralized buildings of the Byzantine world such as San Vitale, Ravenna, or SS Sergius and Bacchus, Constantinople

closely and the love of representing jewels and precious stones as essential elements of the decoration is wholly Eastern. The great composite vase patterns again are completely oriental in character and spirit (*Ill. 5*). They are just as severely formal as some of the trees are naturalistic. The art is in many ways eclectic, but in its very diversity it is also new and original and fully justifies its appellation as Umayyad. The unification of the Arab-speaking world under the Umayyads had certainly opened up the frontiers to numerous diverse influences, but it had also provided the *raison d'être* for the birth of a new art.

The mosque of al-Aqsa at Jerusalem appears originally to have

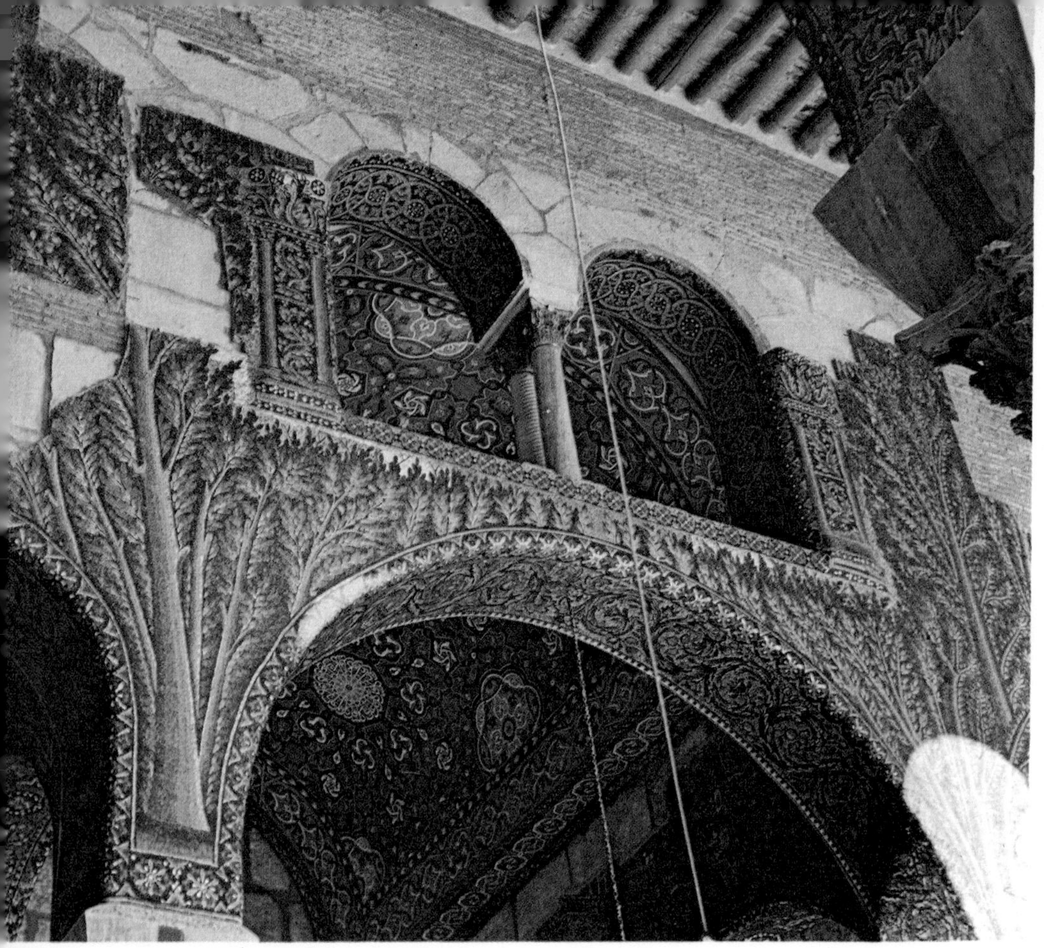

7 Mosaics of the Great Mosque of Damascus, 715. They adorn the walls and arcades of the court. On the former are great architectural compositions and on the latter trees which are admirably suited to the shapes of the spaces they fill

had the form of a great columned hall, and represented a new conception in Islamic architecture, though its columns and capitals were Byzantine. They were re-used when the building was reconstructed by al-Walid, but most of what we see today is later still, for it was repaired by either al-Mansur in 765 or al-Mahdi in 780, and again by the Fatimid az-Zahir in 1035. The Great Mosque at Damascus has undergone fewer changes and in spite of restorations retains its original form. It therefore approaches closely a normal Christian basilica, though the building has been re-orientated, so that the

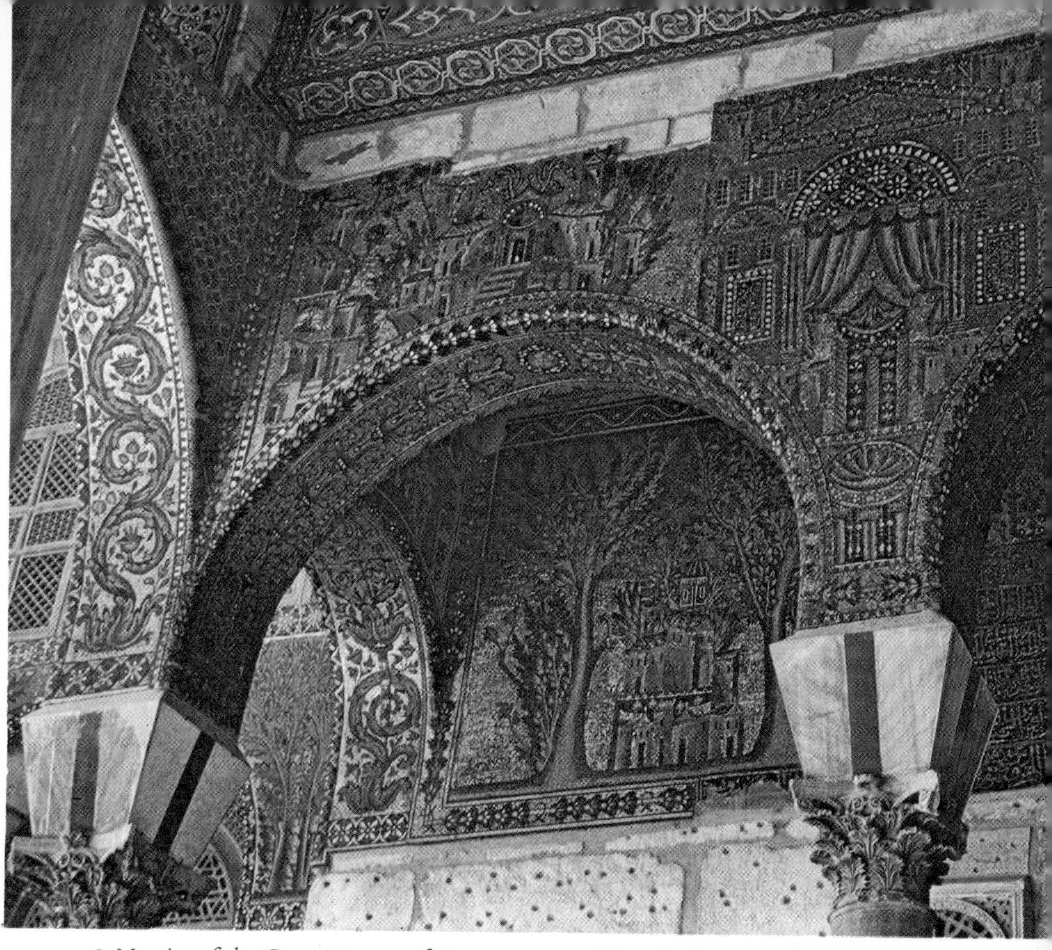

8 Mosaics of the Great Mosque of Damascus, 715. Though there are no figures here, the trees show a penetrating observation of nature. Many of the architectural compositions derive from classical prototypes such as those in the wall-paintings of Pompeii

shrine, the *mihrab*, is at the centre of one of the longitudinal sides and not at the end, and the great forecourt, derived ultimately from the classical atrium, is opposite the *mihrab*, so that one of its sides is formed by the long façade of the mosque itself. Once more the capitals and marble revetments are of Byzantine type and the mosaics (*Ills. 7, 8, 9*) would seem to owe a more marked debt to Constantinople than do those of the Dome of the Rock. They are more naturalistic, less formal, but once again no living figures are included, though both trees and villages are depicted in an entirely naturalistic manner.

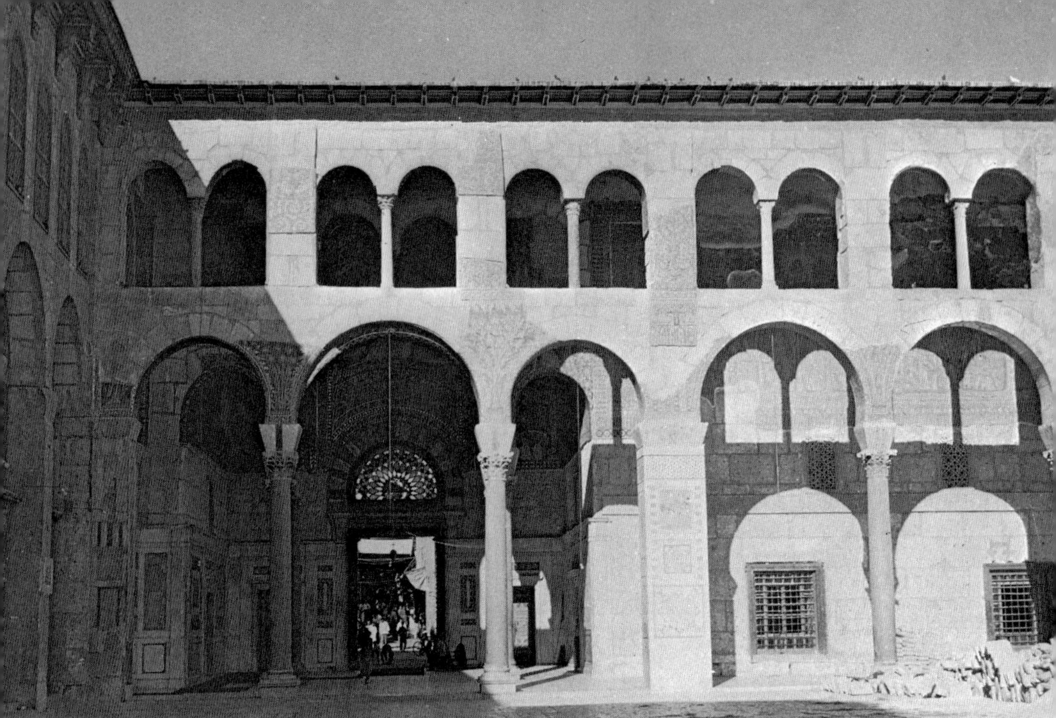

9 Courtyard of the Great Mosque of Damascus, 715, looking towards the principal entrance. Some of the mosaics can be seen above the arcades and on the rear wall which encloses the courtyard

The stylized architectural compositions in many cases depict façades like those of the rock-cut temples of Petra, whereas others would seem to be the figments of the imagination of the artist rather than true depictions, although they derive from an old classical tradition which first made itself felt in the wall-paintings of Pompeii. In the fantasy and delight of their compositions, however, the Damascus mosaics far surpass any similar works of Roman, Hellenistic or Byzantine art that survive, and they undoubtedly constitute not only one of the greatest glories of all Islamic art, but also one of the most delightful mosaic decorations known to the world. In technique they are superior to any other work in Syria and on this account suggest comparison with the floor mosaics of the Great Palace at Constantinople. Certain details of the work are also more closely paralleled there than anywhere else, especially the way in which the green

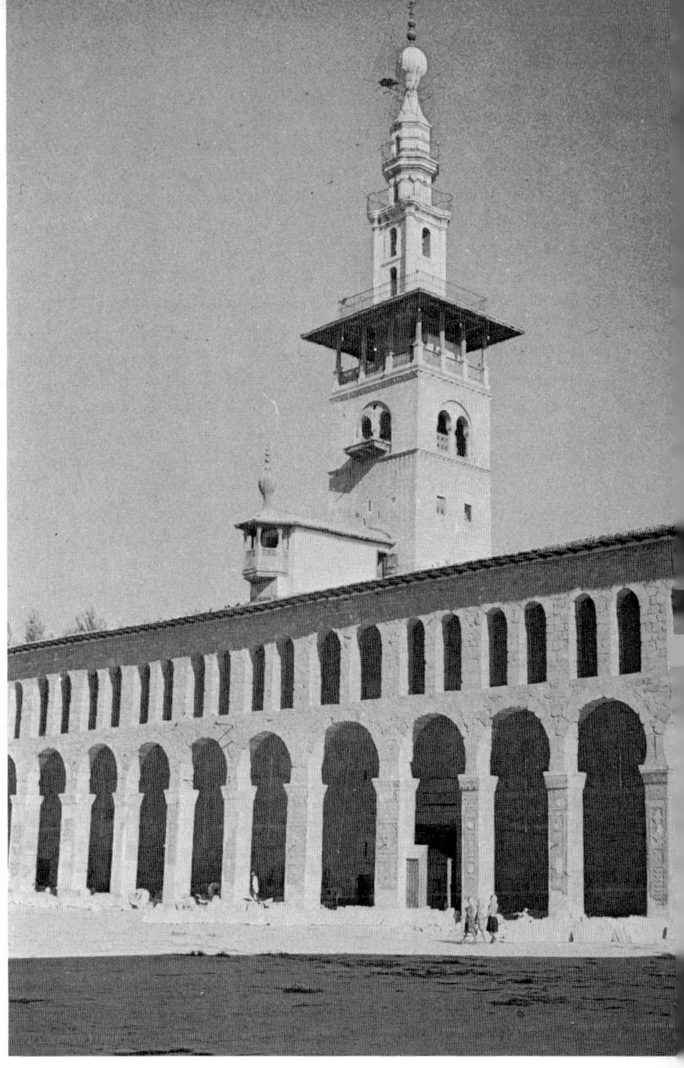

10 Court of the Great Mosque of Damascus, 715, with the minaret behind. Square minarets such as this follow the form of earlier church towers in Syria

leaves of the trees are set before an indigo-coloured background following the same outline like a foil.

The aniconic character of these mosaics gives rise to an interesting question – when did the ban on representation of living figures, which is generally believed to be characteristic of Islamic art, arise? The subject is one which has been argued and discussed by numerous authorities, but it would seem that in the early days of Islam there was no widespread veto; there is certainly no passage forbidding representational painting in the Koran itself. The *Hadith* or Traditions on the other hand did take up a hostile attitude, though it is questionable whether this hostility was actually formulated before the ninth century. It certainly did not affect the secular art of the period, as witness the paintings at Qasr al-Hair, Qusayr Amra and Khirbat al-Mafjah, which will be discussed below, nor was it ever universally enforced with regard to secular art in later times. But the fact that no figures whatsoever are included in the mosaics either of the Dome of the Rock or at Damascus does suggest that in mosques the dictum was already in force by about 690.

Many other mosques of importance must have been set up under the Umayyads, and the records tell that those at Aleppo and Hama closely followed the plan of that at Damascus. Nothing else, however, survives in Syria with the exception of part of the great mosque of Harran which dates from the time of the last Umayyad caliph, Merwan II. In Iraq there were mosques of these early years at Basra, Baghdad and Kufa. The latter was founded in 639; it was adorned with mosaics, and had a gallery supported on marble columns; it was rebuilt under Muawiya, but was subsequently destroyed entirely. Remains of an important mosque have, however, been excavated in the now deserted city of Wasit on the Tigris, about half-way between Baghdad and Basra. It had a great court and the roof was supported by massive piers like those we find at a rather later date at Damghan in Persia; both must have been inspired by Sassanian prototypes. The mosque at Medina was built under al-Walid about 708, and as workmen and materials were collected from all parts of the world to forward its construction, it was perhaps more like those of Syria. The mosques at Tunis, Qairawan and Cordova are also perhaps to be counted as Umayyad foundations, but all were considerably altered subsequently, and in the two former only small areas of wall of a more or less featureless type can be assigned to the original structures. Both were restored on a new plan in the ninth century. The mosque at Cordova now bears little resemblance to anything Syrian, for its affinities are mainly Persian; as it was not begun until 785, it is hardly to be counted as Umayyad from the point of view of art history.

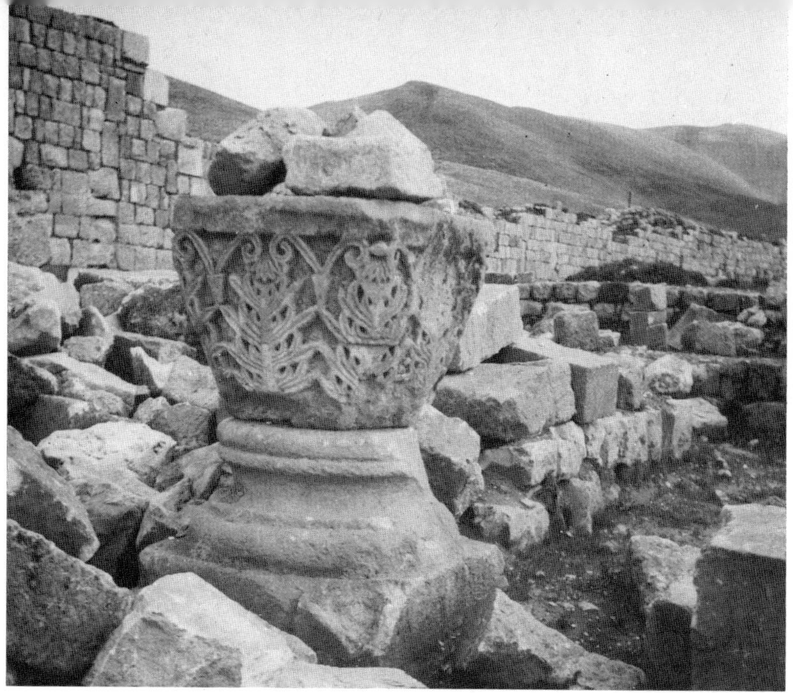

11 Column capital at Anjar, Lebanon, about half-way between Damascus and Beirut. It is rectangular in plan, with a massive enclosing wall. A section of it was occupied by a palace, its sculptured decoration wholly Umayyad in style

Of secular architecture rather more survives. A whole city, which would seem to be of Umayyad date, has recently been discovered at Anjar (*Ill. 11*) on the frontiers of Syria and the Lebanon, close to the road from Damascus to Beirut; no doubt it served as a half-way stage along this important trade route. Like a Roman camp it is rectangular in plan, with an entrance at the centre of each of its four sides. These are linked by streets meeting at a tetrapylon at the centre. In one of the quarters so formed is a palace, the entrance façade of which rose to a height of three storeys. The city walls are strengthened at regular intervals along the outside by solid semi-circular towers. The streets were bordered by columned arcades, most of the columns and capitals being taken from a neighbouring Roman site, but in the palace some of the sculptures are clearly Umayyad and though less extensive resemble in style those on the façade of Mshatta. Other such walled cities no doubt existed and may well be discovered in the future; a palace at Minya on Lake Tiberias is rather similar in plan.

The fortresses and palaces presented in many cases a similar aspect from outside, for the palace walls too were reinforced by semi-circular buttressed towers, but the enclosures were, of course, smaller. There was usually but one entrance, and the layout inside was different. Apart from their artistic and architectural interest the palaces have an additional significance, for they clearly reflect the desire on the part of the patrons who were responsible for their construction, the early caliphs, to maintain their contacts with the desert and at least to continue the sport of hunting, even if the speed of their conquests had brought to an end the frequent raids or 'razzia' which had previously been as much a sport as a means of acquiring wealth. Many of these palaces were elaborately decorated both outside and in, and were on quite a large scale, capable of accommodating a considerable retinue; others were comparatively small, but were nevertheless extremely luxurious.

The most important of them, in all probability, was the palace of Mshatta (*Ill. 12*), for its exterior walls were elaborately sculptured, whereas those of the other palaces were plain. When it was first discovered in the early years of this century it was assigned to the third or fourth century, and though a few writers still believe that it is of early date, the case for an Umayyad origin cannot now be seriously disputed, and a date in the eighth century and reign of al-Walid II seems much more likely. The palace is of considerable size; on plan (*Ill. 13*) it is a square measuring about 144 metres internally, with semi-circular bastion towers like those at Anjar along the sides; but there is only one entrance which leads to the living quarters. These were arranged in three sections, separated from one another by great rectangular courts, which no doubt served to stable camels and horses and to stack up goods. One of the chambers has, on good evidence, been identified as a mosque. The carved façade flanked the entrance gate; the other walls were plain. Each of the bastions was adorned with sculptures up to a height of some five metres, but the motifs of the decorations varied from bastion to bastion and the work of several distinct hands is to be discerned. Some of the motifs are essentially Hellenistic, while others show the influence of Sassanian Persia; it would seem, indeed, that Persian motifs such as

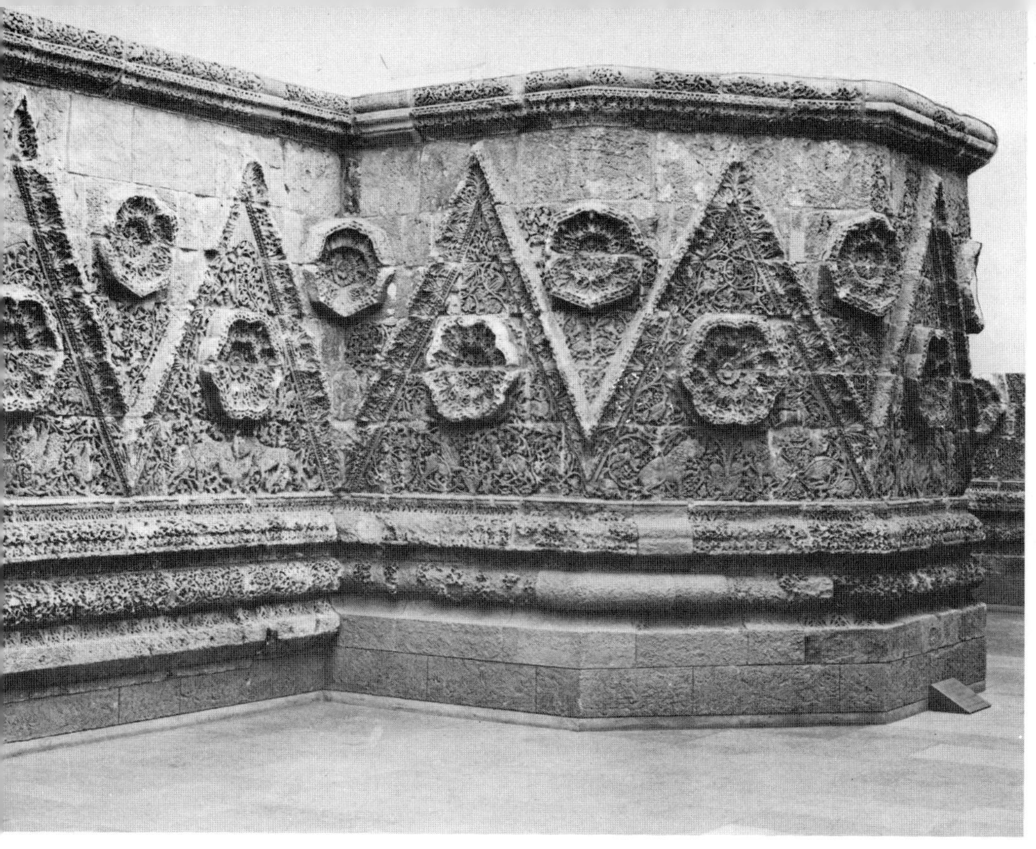

12 The main façade of the palace at Mshatta, probably *c.* 743. The date was formerly disputed, but it is now generally accepted as an Umayyad structure. It is rectangular in plan, with a strong defensive wall. The entrance façade is now preserved in the East Berlin Museum

confronted animals, candelabra forms or double wings, found even greater favour with the sculptors of Mshatta than with the mosaicists who decorated the Dome of the Rock. The whole of the sculptured façade was presented to Kaiser Wilhelm II of Germany by the Sultan of Turkey, and is now reconstructed in the archaeological museum at Berlin (East).

The general layout of Mshatta was closely paralleled in another palace, Qasr at-Tuba, which Creswell assigns to the same date. The same basic plan was broadly followed, if on a smaller scale, in most of the other palaces built by the Umayyads in Syria; it even reached Iraq, where similar palaces were built by the early Abbasids (see p. 29).

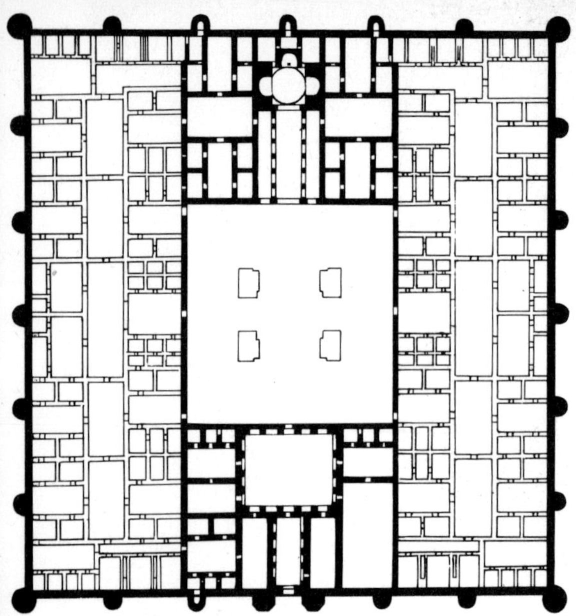

13 Plan of Mshatta. The layout is similar to that of several other desert palaces, all built for caliphs of the Umayyad dynasty. They stand on the fringe of the desert and were presumably used as hunting palaces

If Mshatta is outstanding because of its sculptures, the palace of Khirbat al-Mafjah is equally important on account of its mosaic floors (*Ill. 15*) and the profuse stucco decoration (*Ill. 14*) which once adorned its interior. The mosaic floors are of two types. Most of them are formal and severe, and use geometric patterns of Roman origin, though they are disposed in a new and rather distinctive manner. One section, however, is more naturalistic, for a tree is depicted, of much the same type as those in the mosaics of the Great Mosque at Damascus, and there are animals beneath its branches. Though this mosaic is similar to those at Damascus and finds its origins in the floors of early Byzantine times at Antioch, and even more, in those of the Great Palace of the Byzantine emperors at Constantinople, the animals below savour of the East. The motif of the lion eating a gazelle which appears on one side of the trunk reproduces a theme which had been extremely popular in Persia since Achaemenid times.

The wall-paintings that decorated some of the rooms were so fragmentary that it is impossible to say much more than to state that the motifs comprised both formal decorative patterns and the figures of living persons, and that Sassanian elements were nearly as much to the fore as Hellenistic. The stuccos, though also very fragmentary,

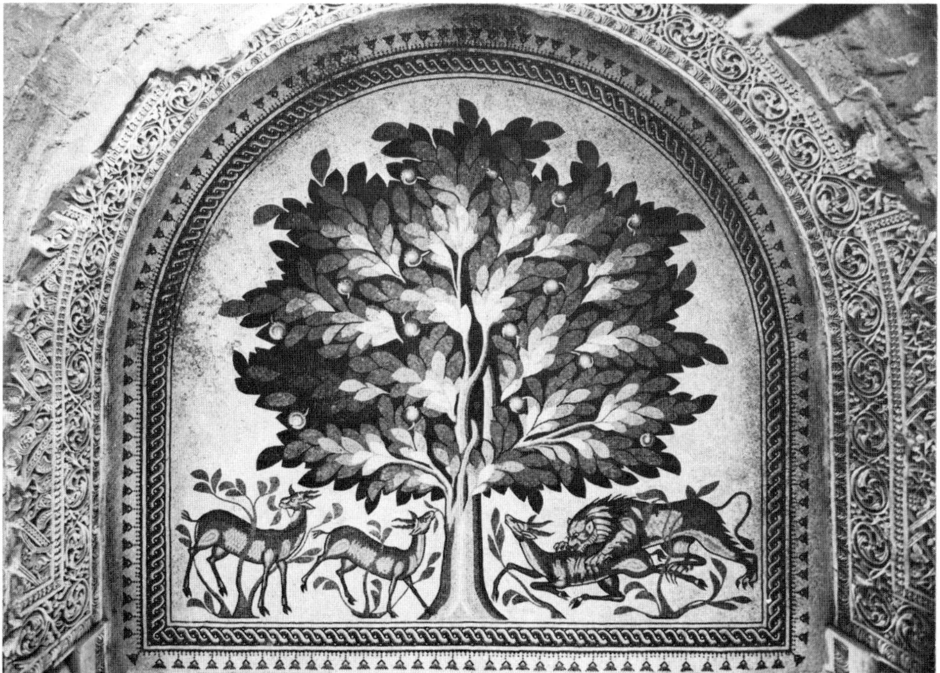

14, 15 (*right*) window grille and (*below*) mosaic floor from the bath of the Palace of Khirbat al-Mafjah, *c.* 743. The palace is in many ways similar to that at Mshatta, but the sculptures that adorned it were in stucco and not stone. Numerous fragments of painted plaster were found during the excavation, many of them bearing figural compositions

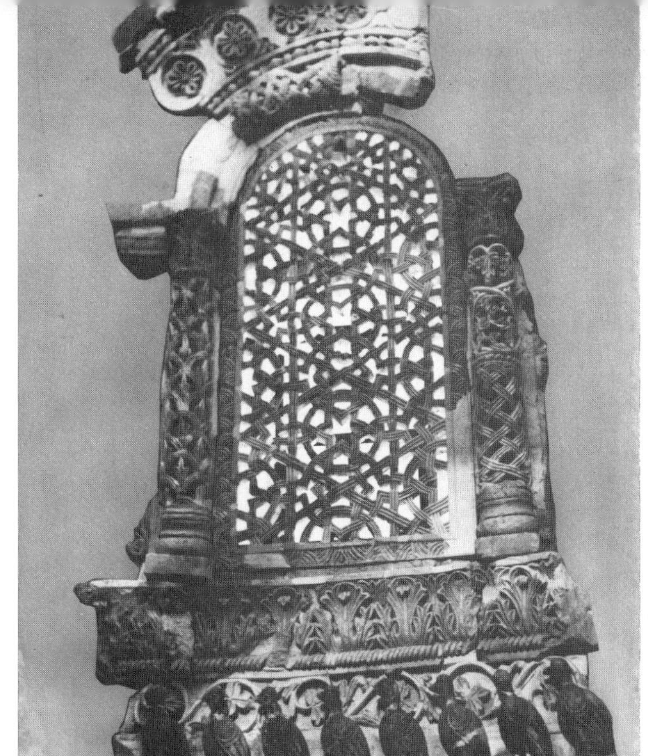

could, however, be reconstructed sufficiently well to convey a very clear idea of the character of the original decoration. The work was in all probability done by locals who drew both from the Hellenistic and the Sassanian repertory; some of the figure subjects are very Sassanian in style, others close to those of Coptic art. The most important feature of the decoration, however, is the way in which motifs that were later to be developed as typical of Islamic art as a whole were anticipated. This is especially true of the geometric window grilles in plaster; similar grilles of marble were used in the Great Mosque at Damascus. These grilles are delicate and restrained, whereas the rest of the stucco work at Khirbat al-Mafjah is rather vulgar. Yet the decoration is important, for the style is distinctive and reflects the influence of a single and rather strong personality. Hamilton, who with Baramki excavated and published the palace, suggests that its builder was the athletic, poetic and forceful but eccentric Yazid III, who reigned for only one year (744).

Though it dates from about 728, the palace of Qasr al-Hair ash-Sharqi (*Ill. 16*) is similarly prophetic, for in its construction it heralds developments in military architecture that were to take place in the eleventh century and were to be transmitted to the West by the Crusaders. Most notable is the use of machicolation, that is, of a gallery projecting over the entrance with holes in its floor, through which boiling oil or other substances could be poured on to the heads of assailants. Its very remarkable façade has now been reconstructed in the Damascus Museum, and much of the stucco work that adorned it is also to be seen there; it is rather more restrained in style than that of Khirbat al-Mafjah. But not only is the great castellated entrance impressive. Two large painted panels of particular interest were also discovered, one representing the earth goddess set in a jewelled roundel of Sassanian character, the other showing a hunting scene (*Ill. 17*) clearly derived from a Sassanian prototype such as those known on many of the famous silver plates in Teheran or in the Hermitage Museum at Leningrad. The colours, however, are not those usual in Sassanian art, where red and blue predominate, but show a preference for pale browns and yellow, colours which were especially popular in Egypt.

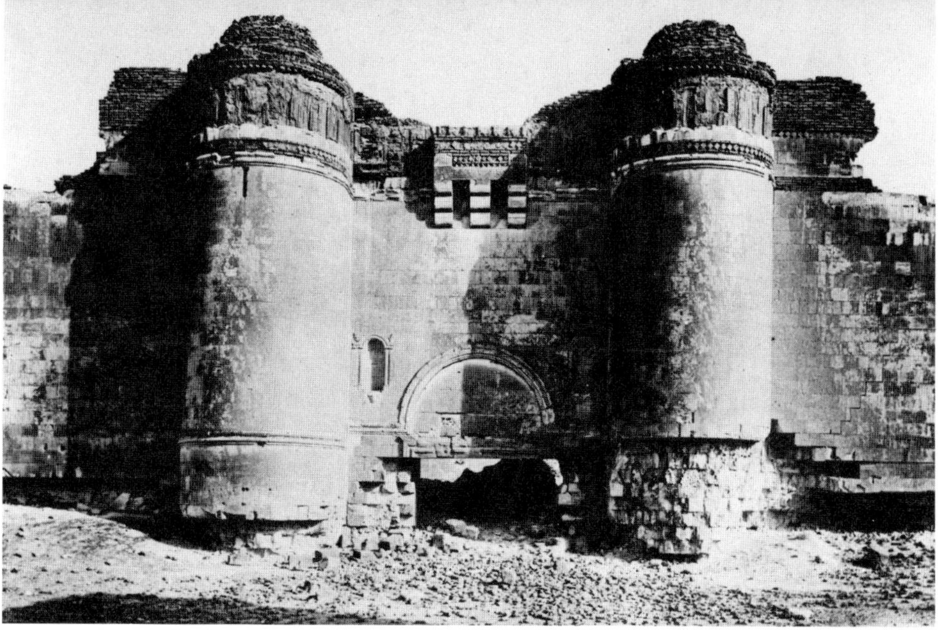

16 The palace of Qasr al-Hair, *c.* 728. This is probably the most spectacular of the desert palaces. Its defensive works, notably the machicolations, were later to be taken over by the Crusaders

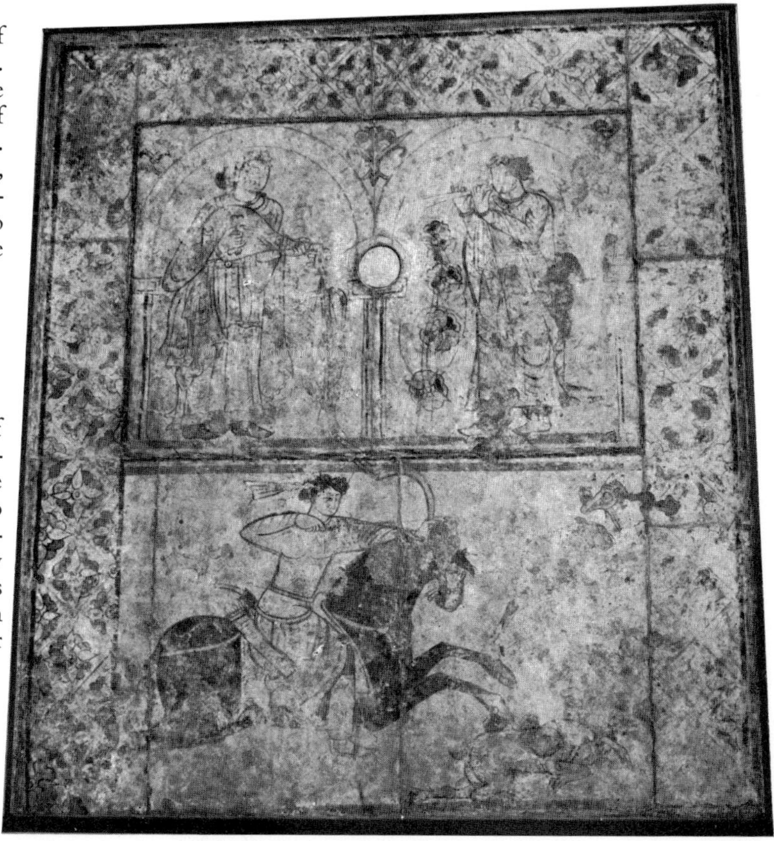

17 Wall-painting of musicians and huntsman from the palace of Qasr al-Hair. Two paintings were discovered there a few years ago, this one is rather Sassanian in character, but another is Hellenistic in style

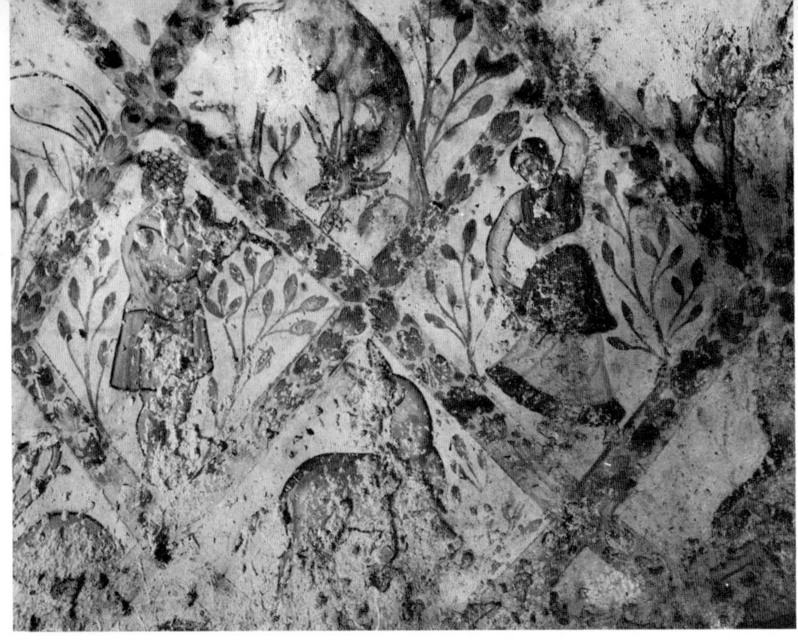

18 The palace of Qusayr Amra, 724–43, was adorned with wall-paintings, mostly of a very Hellenistic character. Some show nude figures, some animals and human figures in a diaper pattern

Of all the secular paintings of Umayyad Syria that have survived, however, the most important are those at Qusayr Amra. The palace there was on quite a small scale, but several of the rooms were decorated with paintings, which varied considerably in character. The roof of one room was domed and adorned with the constellations and signs of the zodiac; on the roof of another was a diaper pattern (*Ill. 18*) with an animal or similar motif in each of its diamond-shaped compartments. On the walls of another room were depicted hunters and allegorical figures, while in yet another there were nude figures of bathers, some of them male and some female. The former derive from Hellenistic prototypes, but it has been suggested that the plump figures of the women reflect the Arab ideals of female beauty as expressed in the verses written by poets at al-Hira before the days of Islam. Probably most interesting of all is a panel showing a number of figures who are to be identified as the kings overcome by the advance of Islam (*Ill. 19*).

The group comprises the Byzantine emperor, in a rich costume of woven silk, the Sassanian ruler, Roderick, King of the Visigoths, the

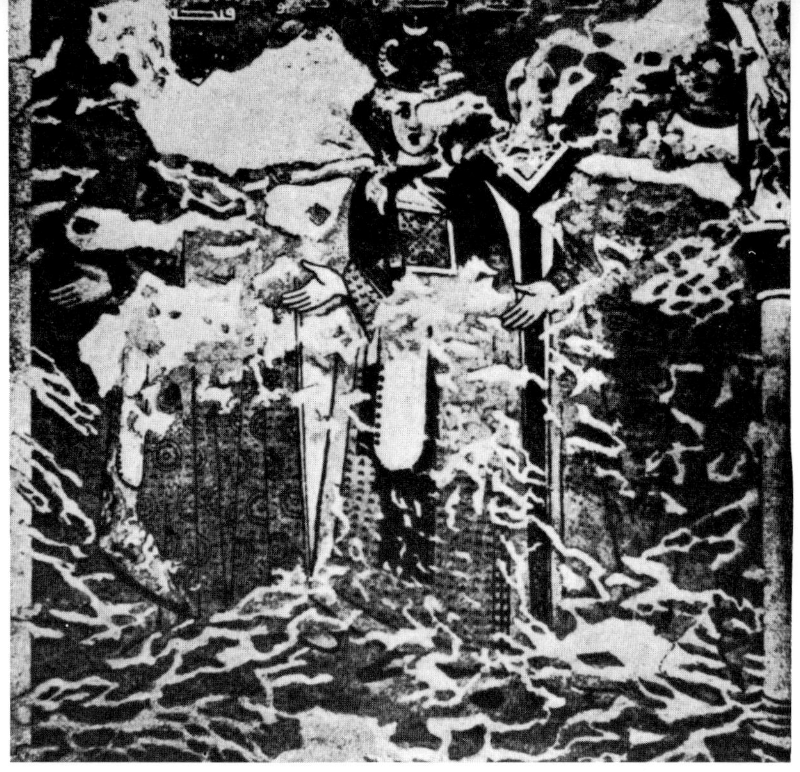

19 This painting also from the palace of Qusayr Amra, 724–43, shows the Kings conquered by Islam. The style is distinctly Sassanian and the figures represent the Byzantine and Sassaman emperors, the King of the Visigoths and the Negus of Abyssinia

Negus of Abyssinia and two figures on a smaller scale who cannot be identified. The names of the figures are written above their heads in Greek and Arabic. The style of the painting is much more Oriental than that of the other compositions at Qusayr Amra, which are broadly Hellenistic, with figures shown side or three-quarter view, carefully modelled and treated naturalistically. The kings, on the other hand, are shown full face, in rigid poses, their limbs hidden by their heavy costumes, originally done in rich, bright colours. The style is in fact that which is generally associated with Sassanian art, and the work must surely have been done by a painter who had been steeped in the Sassanian tradition.

When Qusayr Amra was first discovered, the conservative character of most of the paintings gave rise to the suggestion that the work was of quite an early date; subsequently, however, it was attributed to the eighth century. The presence of Roderick makes an early date impossible, for he only came to the throne in 710, and the paintings must clearly have been done after his accession; he died in 711. There is reason to date them before the fall of the Umayyad dynasty in 750; therefore a date between 710 and 750 is certain. One of the very fragmentary inscriptions that accompanies the paintings refers to a prince, and it would seem that one of the younger Umayyads, and not an actual caliph, was the patron who was responsible for the work. Of the princes the only possible ones are the men who were to become the future caliphs al-Walid II and Yazid III, and this being so, a date in the reign of Hisham, between 724 and 743, is indicated. The palace of Qusayr Amra and its paintings would thus seem to be one of the last works built for an Umayyad patron before the dynasty came to an end and the capital was transferred to Iraq. After that the construction of such a palace would have been most improbable, for a local governor could hardly have been responsible for a decoration of the character we see there. Moreover, with the departure of the Umayyads, Syria declined in importance and several centuries were to elapse before the area once more became significant in the story of Islamic art.

The last of the Umayyad caliphs was Merwan II, who made Harran in northern Mesopotamia his capital and was killed in 750. The great mosque which survives there was partly begun by him, but most of what now stands above ground is of later date. More no doubt remains to be discovered there, for the site has never been fully excavated; work begun by Professor Storm Rice was unfortunately brought to a close by his untimely death in 1962. Only further excavations there or at other Umayyad sites will be able to tell us more about the minor arts of the period. Yet the nature of the mosaics, the stuccos and the paintings does suggest that already a style had been born. Eclectic though these works are in many ways, there is none the less something that marks them as Islamic rather than as Hellenistic or Sassanian, Nabataean or Ghassanid, and it was on the basis established in these early years that the future development of Islamic art was founded.

The Abbasid Period

We know from the texts that mosques were built during Umayyad days at Basra, Wasit, Kufa and elsewhere, but although the capital was moved to Mesopotamia in 750, and soon after established at Baghdad, there are very few monuments on a major scale which can be attributed to these early years. True, mosques still stand on many of the early sites, but they are all of a later date, while al-Mansur's famous round city of Baghdad, founded in 762, has entirely disappeared, and as a part of the modern city now covers the site where it stood, it will probably never be excavated. Its plan was, however, broadly followed at Raqqa, where the walls can be traced, and portions of the original town survive above ground, notably the Baghdad Gate (*Ill. 21*), an impressive structure adorned with lovely ornamental brickwork. The defensive work there is of special interest because, in spite of subsequent additions, it would seem certain that the original layout has been preserved. Some of the methods of defence, including the oblique approach, were later brought to the West by the Crusaders, and represent one of the many legacies which the West owes to Islam. The quality of the architecture is shown by a number of carved limestone capitals dating from about 800, examples of which are preserved in various museums.

More spectacular than Raqqa, however, is the magnificent hunting palace of Ukhaidir, near Kerbela, some 120 miles to the SSW of Baghdad (*Ill. 20*). Its plan is rectangular, and the high external wall, supported by semi-circular bastion towers, has an entrance at the centre of each side. It therefore follows the same plan as the Umayyad city of Anjar, but because it is preserved almost up to roof-level it is possible to gain a clearer idea of its character. Progressive ideas in defensive architecture were carried even further in its construction than in the Syrian structures or at Raqqa. There was an elaborate *chemin de ronde* along the top of the wall, from which an attacker

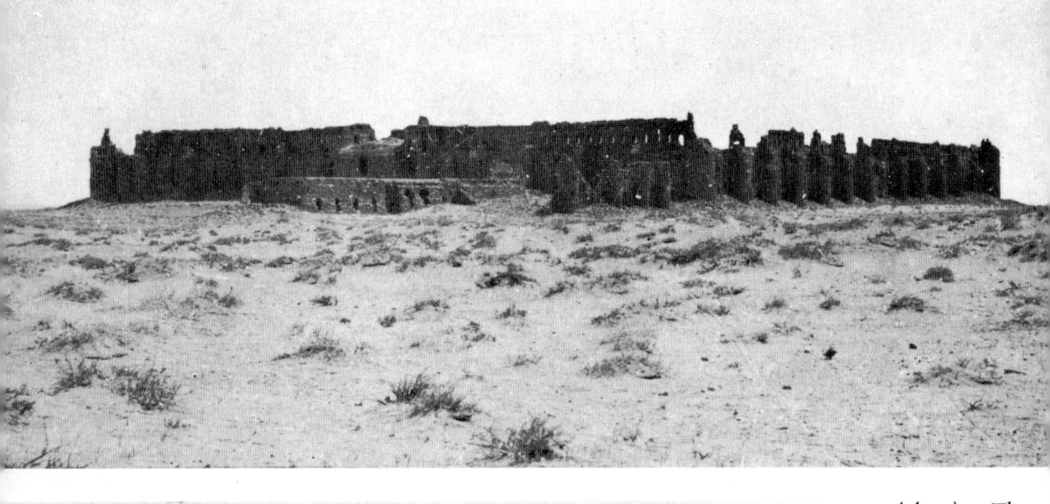

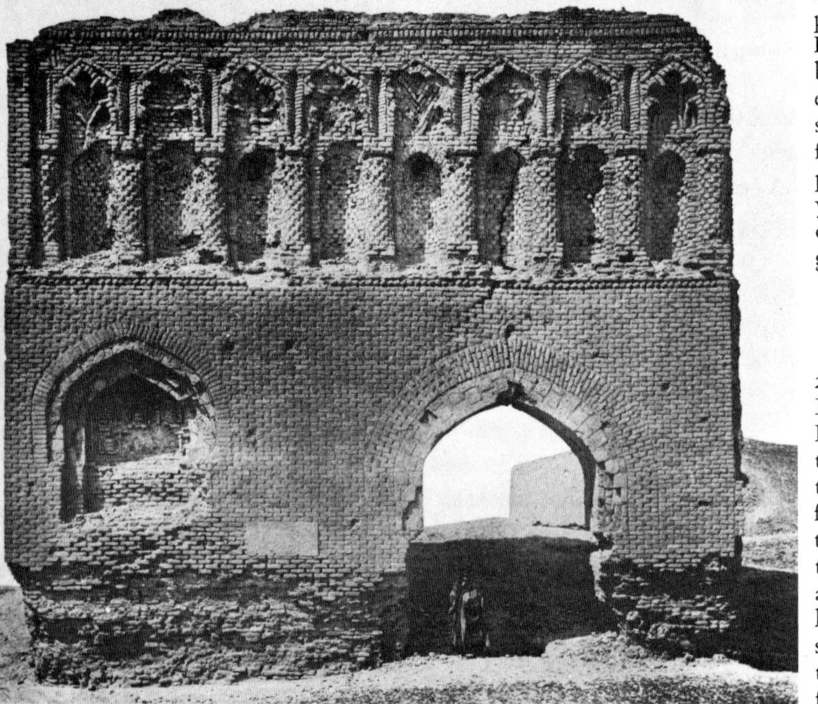

20 (*above*) The palace of Ukhaidir, Iraq, *c.* 780. The building was set up early in the Abbasid period, but follows the general plan of the Umayyad palaces on the opposite side of the great desert

21 (*below*) The Baghdad Gate, Raqqa. Eighth century. The fortifications of Raqqa date from early Abbasid times, and those of the Abbasid capital at Baghdad must have been very similar. Photo by the courtesy of Professor Creswell

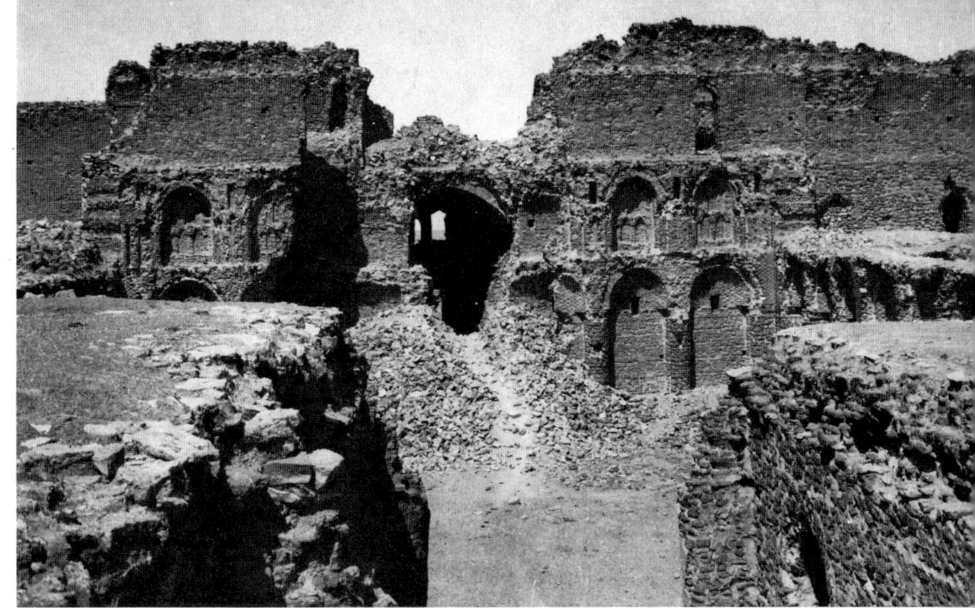

22 The great court of the palace of Ukhaidir, *c.* 780. The palace was rectangular in plan, and was surrounded by a high wall. Within it was divided into a series of courtyards with chambers opening off. These chambers are called *bayts* by Creswell

could be menaced from above, while the four gates consisted each of a chamber bounded by an inner door and an outer portcullis which could be lowered if the door was assailed, trapping attackers in a chamber where they could be exterminated at leisure.

The building itself is astonishingly impressive, standing as it does in isolation in the desert, far from any habitation. It is no less important in the history of Islamic architecture than it is spectacular as a ruin, for we see there in good preservation not only features of defensive architecture which are entirely new, but also a layout of the living quarters within the walls which was to be followed for many centuries all over the Islamic world. The main residential area was divided into a series of courtyards, each surrounded by narrow chambers, which Creswell calls *bayts*. At Ukhaidir these were covered with vaulted roofs and there was an impressive vaulted entrance hall (*Ill. 22*) at the western end, with pillars at its sides and with two upper storeys. The vaults and arches were all of elliptical form – the pointed version, although known in Syria, had not yet been developed in Mesopotamia. The elliptical arch had been used

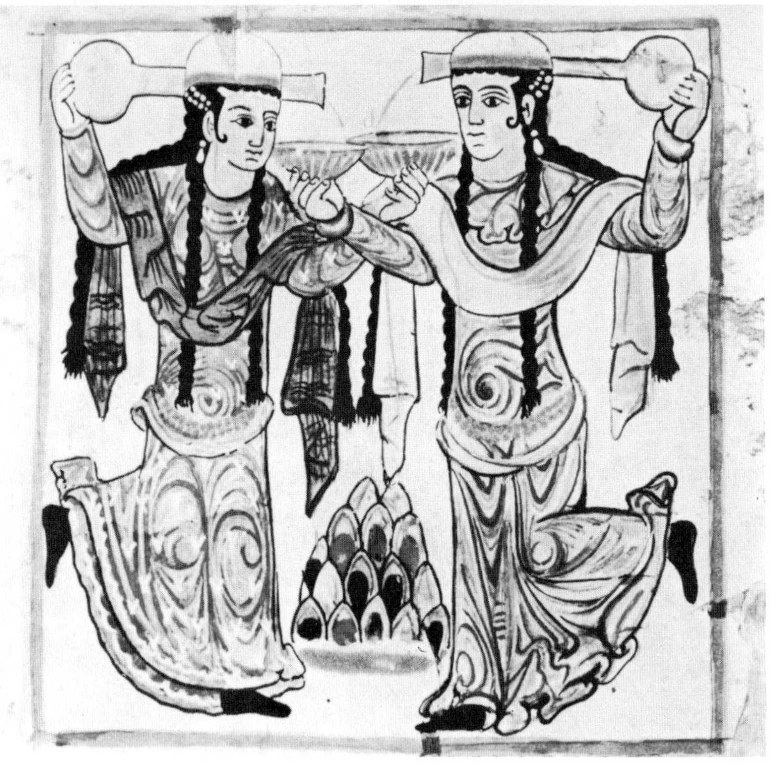

23 Reconstruction of a wall-painting from the harem of the Jausaq Palace at Samarra, 833–41. The harem was decorated with paintings, of which many were figural, but in an eastern style

extensively by the Sassanians, and the whole palace had a very Sassanian character; indeed it was regarded as Sassanian until the discovery that one of the chambers on the ground floor was actually a mosque. Subsequent study has shown that it should probably be associated with Ibn Musa, a powerful court official who was exiled and made Governor of Kufa in 778. A similar but smaller castle, Atshan, marks a half-way stage between the two places, and was probably also built by Ibn Musa to serve as a resting place when he moved out to his desert palace.

We know nothing of the internal decoration of Ukhaidir, for neither stucco nor traces of paintings survive, but thanks to the German excavations conducted at Samarra just before the First World War and to those carried out more recently by the Department of Antiquities of Iraq, our picture of these arts is a fairly complete one. At Samarra the remains of extensive wall decorations in stucco were found and also fragments of some extremely interesting wall-paintings (*Ill. 23*). These had adorned part of the harem in the first palace built by the Caliph al-Mutasim (833–41) and known as the Jausaq al-Khagani. Most impressive was a great scroll enclosing birds, and animals. Birds and animals were also shown individually, usually within medallions adorned with dots representing pearls – a favourite Sassanian motif frequently used for textiles. There were also large figures of nereids and dancing girls, some of them in arcades similar to those which appear on Sassanian silver vessels. The figures were nearly all posed frontally, in the Sassanian manner, even though many of the motifs must ultimately have been derived from Hellenistic art. The rather heavy style of the paintings and the colours, with red and bright blue predominating, were also essentially Sassanian.

The stuccos (*Ills. 24, 25, 26*), which were used not only in the palace, but in many of the houses as well, were better preserved than the paintings, and often stood almost to roof height, covering the entire wall-space of the rooms. They have, for purposes of classification, been divided into three groups. In the earliest the decoration was moulded, and five-lobed vine scrolls formed the main theme; in the next group the stems of the scrolls were omitted and only bud-like designs were included. In a third and distinct group, the stuccos were carved as well as moulded; the carving was in low relief, with sloping margins – a technique known as *schrägschnitt* by the Germans, and usually called 'bevelled carving' in English. Prototypes for the first two styles, which Creswell designates A and B, are to be found on earlier sites in Iraq, such as Hira (eighth century) and Iskafir-bani-Junayd (*c.* 697), and similar stuccos have also been found at Varaksha near Bokhara, where they are probably to be assigned to the seventh century. Style B served as the basis from which the stucco work, which was later to become so important for the decoration of mihrabs all over Persia, was developed. The third, style C, appears to have been evolved at Samarra itself, though the technique was probably brought from Central Asia, where it had long been popular. It has been suggested that the Turkish troops, who formed the royal bodyguard of the Abbasid sultans, may have introduced it.

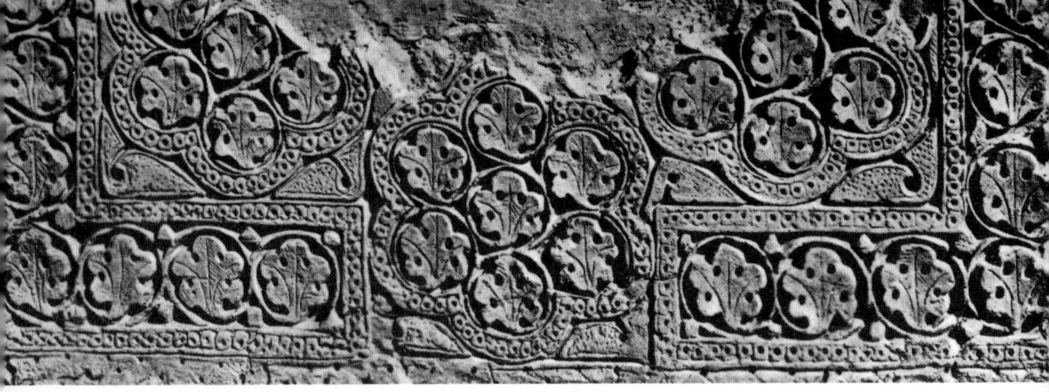

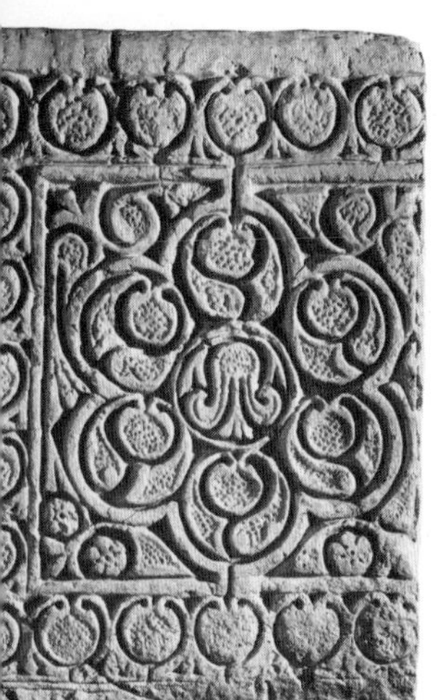

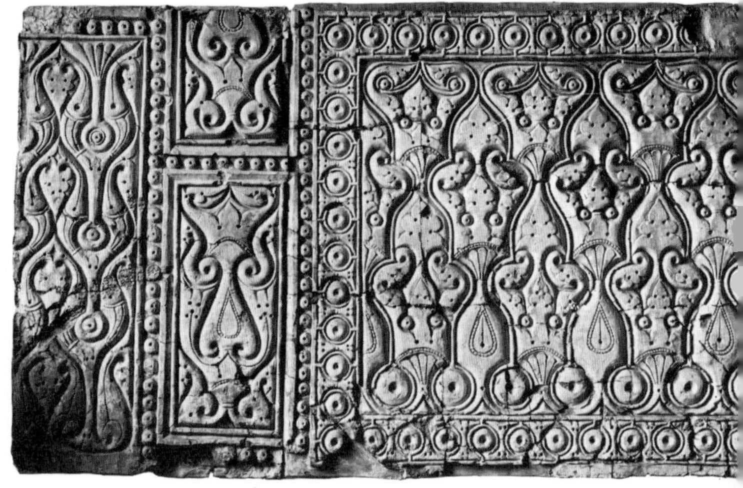

24, 25, 26 Stucco wall panels from Samarra. Ninth century. Three styles of stucco have been distinguished. In the first (*Ill. 23*) the decorations were moulded and five-lobe vine scrolls were popular. In the second (*Ill. 24*) buds supplanted the scrolls. In the third (*Ill. 25*) the decoration was carved in the style usually known as 'bevelled' carving; the technique was probably introduced from Central Asia

The rooms, adorned with stuccos, were single-storeyed, with walls of mud brick, and flat mud roofs. These and the upper parts of the walls had fallen in when the place was deserted and had filled the small rooms up to a height of some six feet, so protecting the stuccos until the day they were excavated. Since the excavation of the palace, most of the stuccos have been removed to museums and today the palace ruins are not very impressive.

The Great Mosque begun in 847 by the Caliph al-Mutawakkil, which was built of burnt brick, is far more spectacular (*Ill. 27*). Its plan (*Ill. 28*) was that usual in early times, namely, a great court, with a covered sanctuary at one end and a smaller roofed area at the other; in the sanctuary there were twenty-five aisles, and the roof was supported on twenty-four rows of columns. The outer walls may have been decorated with mosaics, as tesserae were found in the course of excavations, but nothing survives *in situ*. Outside the enclosure and at its northern end was a circular minaret with a spiral ramp outside reaching the summit, and following the scheme of the temple towers or ziggurats of ancient Assyria. Soon after Mutawakkil had built the Great Mosque, he decided to move the site of the capital a few miles to the north-east, and a new palace, the Jafariya, and a second mosque, the Abu Dulaf, were built around 860. The mosque was on the same plan as that at Samarra itself, with a similar minaret with spiral ramp, but it was a little smaller. In use for a very short time, it is, today, an equally impressive ruin.

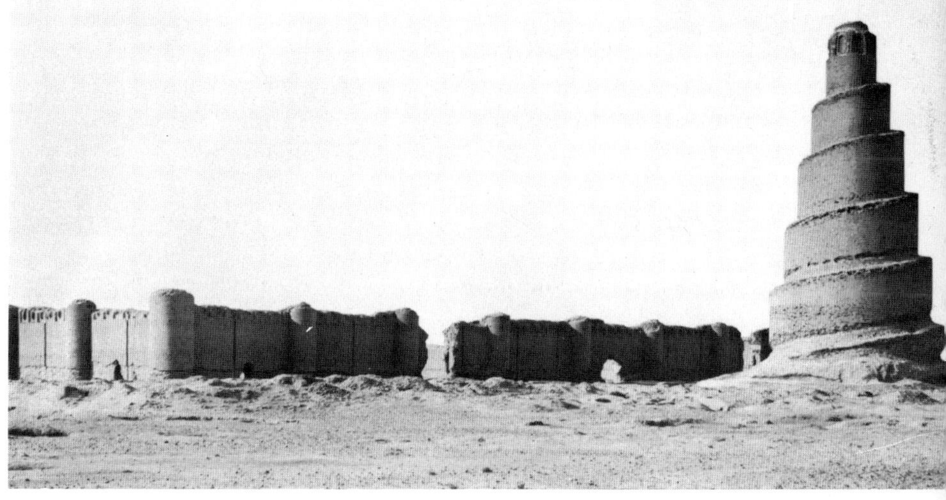

27 The Great Mosque and minaret, Samarra, begun by al-Mutawakkil in 847. The mosque is the largest in the Islamic world. The staged minaret was added about 848. Nearby is an identical one associated with the mosque of Abu Dulaf, and a somewhat similar one in the court of Ibn Tulun's mosque in Cairo

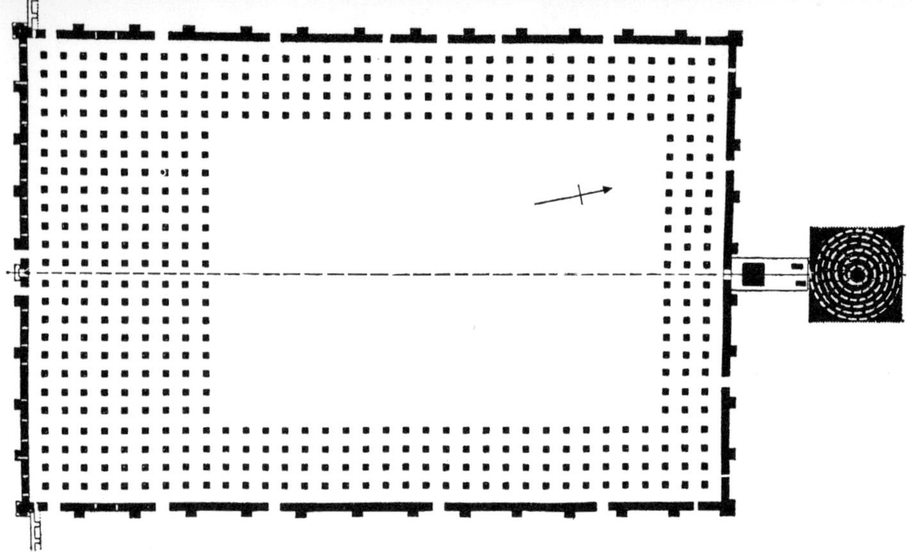

28 Plan of the Great Mosque, Samarra. The outer wall is still more or less intact, but most of the columns of the interior have perished and the whole building is roofless

From the archaeological point of view, Samarra is of the greatest significance, because it was inhabited for so brief a space of time – from 838 until soon after 883 – and though squatters may have continued to live there for a time after the capital was transferred to Baghdad, it is unlikely that any building of significance was done after it was deserted. The pottery and other small items which have been found in the ruins can therefore be dated exactly. Nor were craftsmen idle. We know that superb silks were woven (*Ill. 29*), and wall-paintings in the Jausaq palace reproduce the patterns of the silks and have helped to date textiles found elsewhere. Metalwork was no doubt produced, and quite a few wooden panels (*Ill. 30*) carved in a style close to that of the stuccos have come down to us. But most important was the pottery and it was on the basis of finds from Samarra that the classification of Islamic pottery in Mesopotamia was first undertaken. The evidence made available from there has subsequently been supplemented as a result of scientifically controlled excavations at Susa, Hira, Nishapur and elsewhere, and a fairly exact system of classification has now been established. Quite a considerable number of different groups may be distinguished, some of them common to all the sites, others of a more local character.

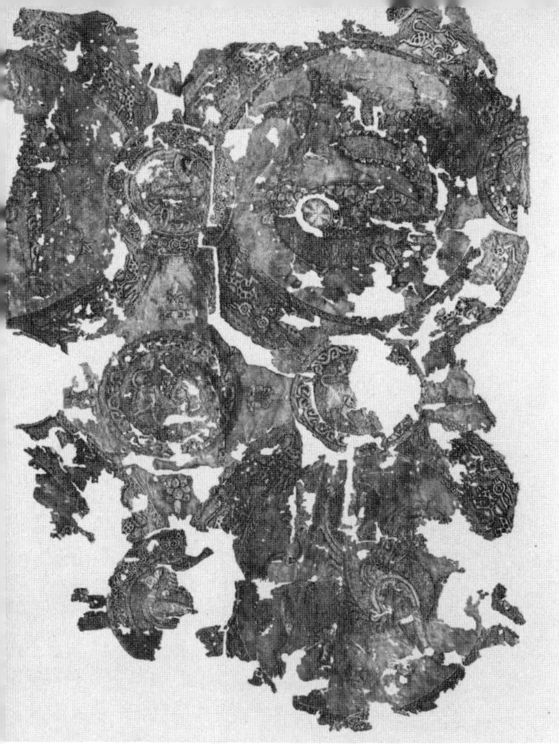

29 Silk of Mesopotamian workmanship, probably dating from the tenth century. The design is close to some of the paintings from Samarra

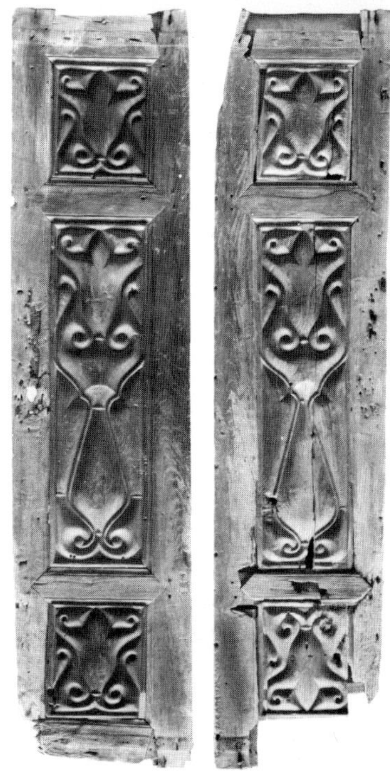

30 Panel of carved wood from Takrit. The style is similar to the stucco of group C at Samarra, and like them it is probably to be assigned to the ninth century.

One of the most widely spread types of pottery in early times was that with the decoration standing out in relief. Two variants exist. In the first, known as Barbotine ware (*Ill. 31*), the vessels are usually unglazed and the decoration was applied in the form of a thin paste, in much the same way that icing sugar is applied to a cake. In the second (*Ill. 33*), the decoration was moulded, and is rather more precise and delicate than in the first type. Geometric and stylized floral patterns were usual, and a few examples bear inscriptions. Of special interest is a bowl in the Damascus Museum bearing an inscription stating that it was made at Hira in Mesopotamia; fragments of a similar vessel were discovered at Hira itself. In this case the lettering is still significant for its content rather than for its appearance, but before long inscriptions were to play a leading role in Islamic decorations and were to become things of great beauty in themselves.

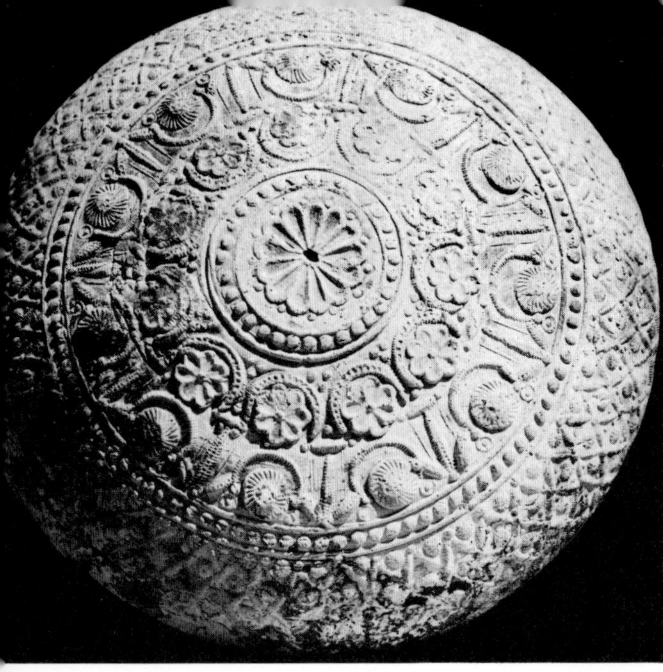

31 Cover of a pottery jar from Susa. Ninth century. The decoration is moulded and stands up in quite high relief. Sometimes relief decorations were applied to the surface like icing sugar. Both techniques were very popular in Mesopotamia at the time

Vessels decorated in the moulded technique were also sometimes covered with green or yellow lead glazes and even lustre. Examples have been found at quite a number of sites, and Egypt was a centre of production as well as Mesopotamia. They may have been inspired by Chinese wares, for some of the designs are very Far Eastern in character, though others are of a more conservative, indigenous style. The delicate precise patterns were often very lovely and served to make of this group a really significant type of early Islamic pottery.

An ultimate Chinese inspiration is also to be assumed in the case of another type of pottery which was equally popular at Samarra and Susa and which also made its appearance rather earlier at Hira (*Ill. 32*). Here there is no relief, the fine white body being covered with a thick creamy tin glaze with a rather bold decoration in cobalt blue and green and sometimes also manganese brown or yellow. Wares that were closely akin were made in the uplands of Persia, and though comparatively simple, they constitute one of the most satisfying groups of early Islamic pottery. The colour schemes that we see here were later developed in Persia in association with a moulded design, to produce yet another important, and from the artistic point of view, particularly lovely group (see p. 68).

32 Bowl from Samarra with decoration in cobalt blue and green on a white ground. Ninth century. This technique was also popular throughout Mesopotamia and Persia, and some of the most lovely wares of the ninth and tenth centuries belong to this group

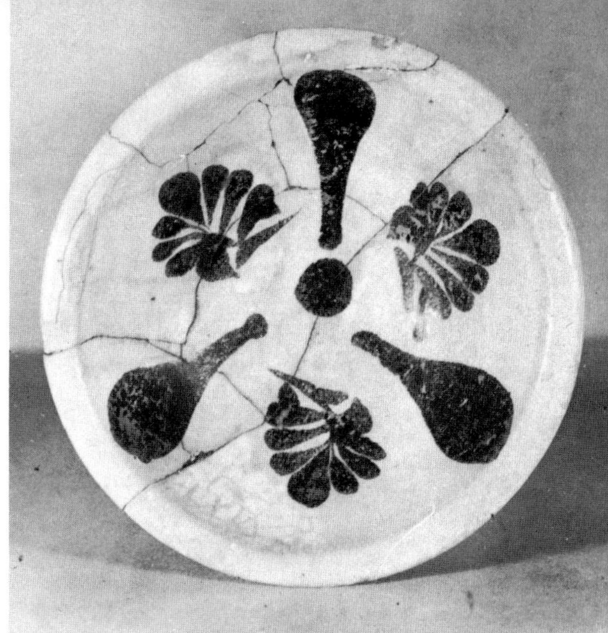

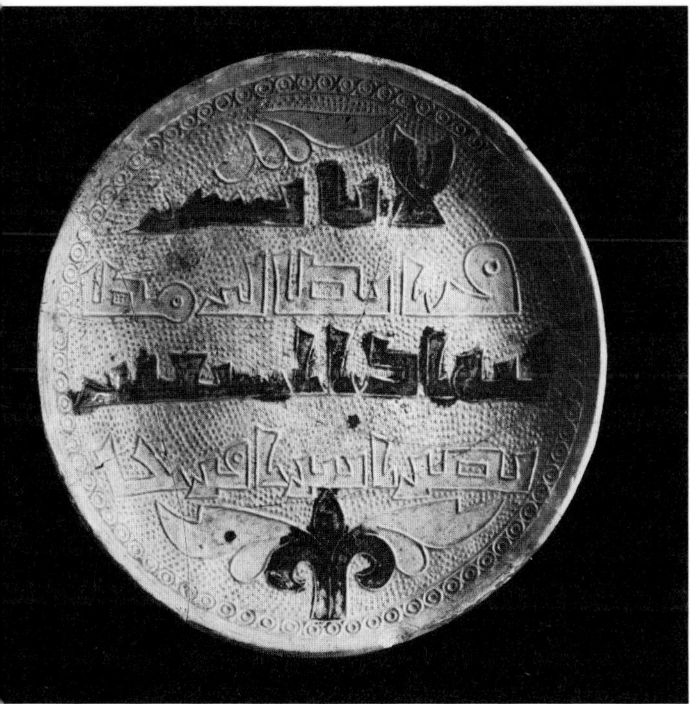

33 Dish with decoration in relief and a *kufic* inscription. The decoration was made by means of a mould but was enlivened by the addition of coloured glazes. Such glazes were usually green or yellow

Quite distinct from this, but even more popular, was a type where the body was red or buff instead of white, and where the decoration was accomplished partly in coloured glazes and partly by the technique known as *sgraffito* (*Ill. 61*). The body was first covered with a white slip and the design executed by scratching through this with a thin point, so producing what is virtually a line drawing. The whole was then covered with a thin yellow lead glaze, which when fired left a dark tone above the exposed body and a pale one above the slip. Splashes of coloured glazes were also added, most often green, manganese or yellow. Sometimes the area adorned was limited by the engraved design, more often the two techniques had little actual relation to one another. The association together of the two techniques and the colours of the glazes at once suggest a comparison with the T'ang potteries of China, and the question arises as to whether this sgraffito ware was originally inspired by imports from the Far East. So far as the polychrome version is concerned, the answer is probably in the affirmative, but the simple sgraffito wares, where the scratched design was used alone, are quite distinct. These wares were so numerous and occurred over so wide an area that in this case an independent development in the Islamic world seems more likely (see p. 64ff).

If an ultimate Chinese origin is to be suggested with regard to some of the above groups, another important type found at Susa and Samarra is wholly Islamic, though there has been considerable dispute among the pundits as to which part of the Islamic world was responsible for the invention of this technique – lustre (*Ill. 34*). Mesopotamia, Persia and Egypt have all had their ardent supporters, but in recent years opinion has tended to harden in favour of Mesopotamia. The earliest lustre ware was polychrome, a rich ruby colour predominating, together with shades of yellow and brown. The motifs of decoration were mainly of a Sassanian type, and the Sassanian palmette and the double-winged motif were especially popular; no figures, animals or birds appear on the earliest examples. The fabric, usually of a fine texture and white in colour, was covered with a thin coat of transparent glaze, and then fired. On to the prepared surface the designs were painted in metallic glazes and the

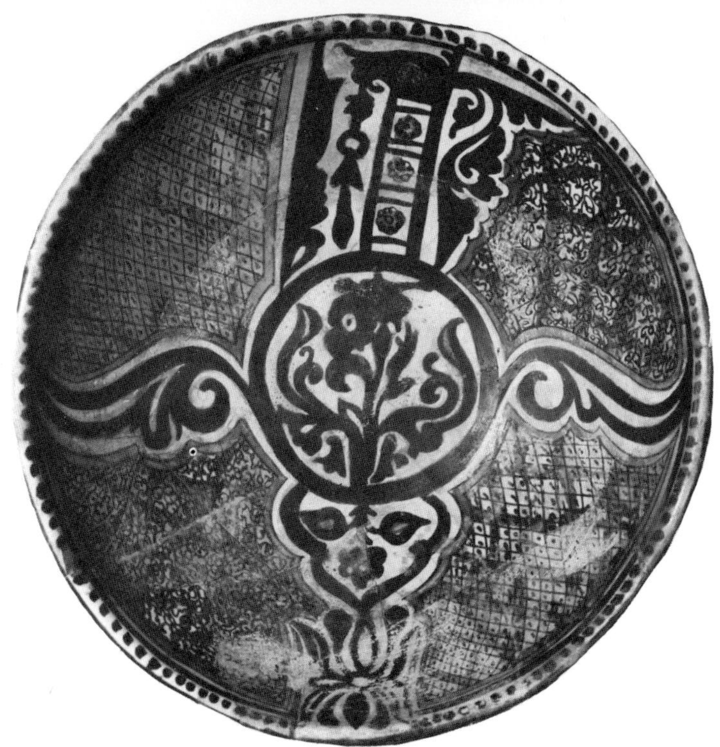

34 Gold and brown lustre bowl from Samarra. The so-called Sassanian palmette plays a prominent part in the decoration. Ninth century

pots refired in a muffled kiln at a low temperature. The result was a delicate lustre surface, which was in itself attractive, over the designs, which were also usually of great beauty in themselves.

Some of the earliest and finest examples we know come from Samarra and for that reason Kuehnel and others have attributed the invention of the technique to Mesopotamia, suggesting that the vessels were made to satisfy the luxurious tastes of the Abbasid caliphs, even if they admit that in the late tenth century much of the finest work was done either in or for Egypt, under the generous patronage of the Fatimid caliphs. Others think that the earliest examples were actually made in Egypt, where they believe that the technique was discovered by chance in late Roman times. It is true that certain vessels of this period have glazes of a lustrous kind, but a long gap separates them from the earliest examples where the lustre was intentional and assumed its colour-changing character.

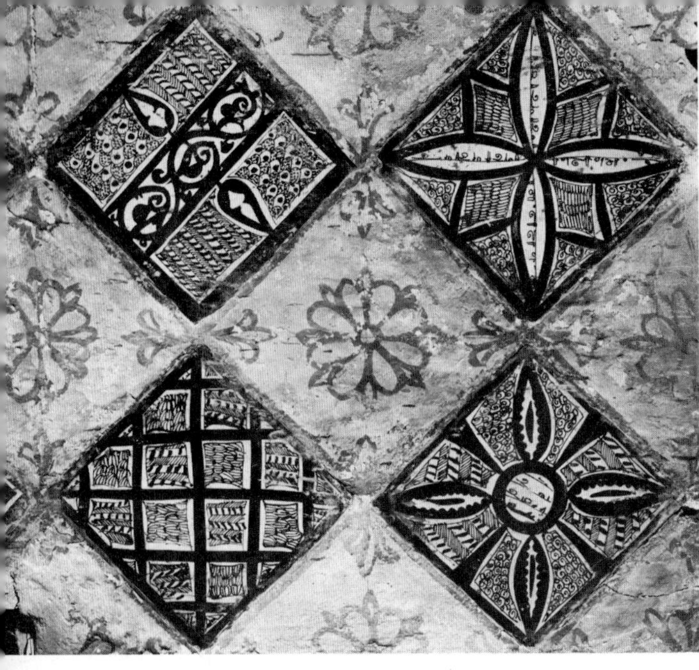

35 Lustre tiles built into the mihrab of the Great Mosque at Qairawan, *c.* 862. Most of these tiles were imported from Mesopotamia, though some are local imitations

Moreover, some of the earliest examples of lustre in North Africa, the tiles of the mihrab at Qairawan (*Ill. 35*), dating from 862, are mostly Mesopotamian, even if a few of them are local copies. On the whole therefore an eastern origin for the technique seems most likely.

More recently, however, another group of scholars have sought to deprive the Arab world of the honour of inventing this technique and have attributed the distinction to Persia. Undoubtedly much fine lustre pottery was made there at a later date, and greater originality and a more profound sense of decoration and of feeling for the technique was shown by the Persian craftsmen than by those of any other region. But whatever the situation was to be later, in the ninth century Persia was neither as important nor as rich as Iraq. The main source of patronage was in the hands of the caliphs, and it was thanks to their munificence that the first developments of this expensive technique were undertaken. It was not really until the twelfth century that Persian lustre pottery began to become important.

The Qairawan tiles serve to show the regard in which Mesopotamian pottery was held elsewhere, and there is evidence to indicate that other Mesopotamian arts were equally highly esteemed. The

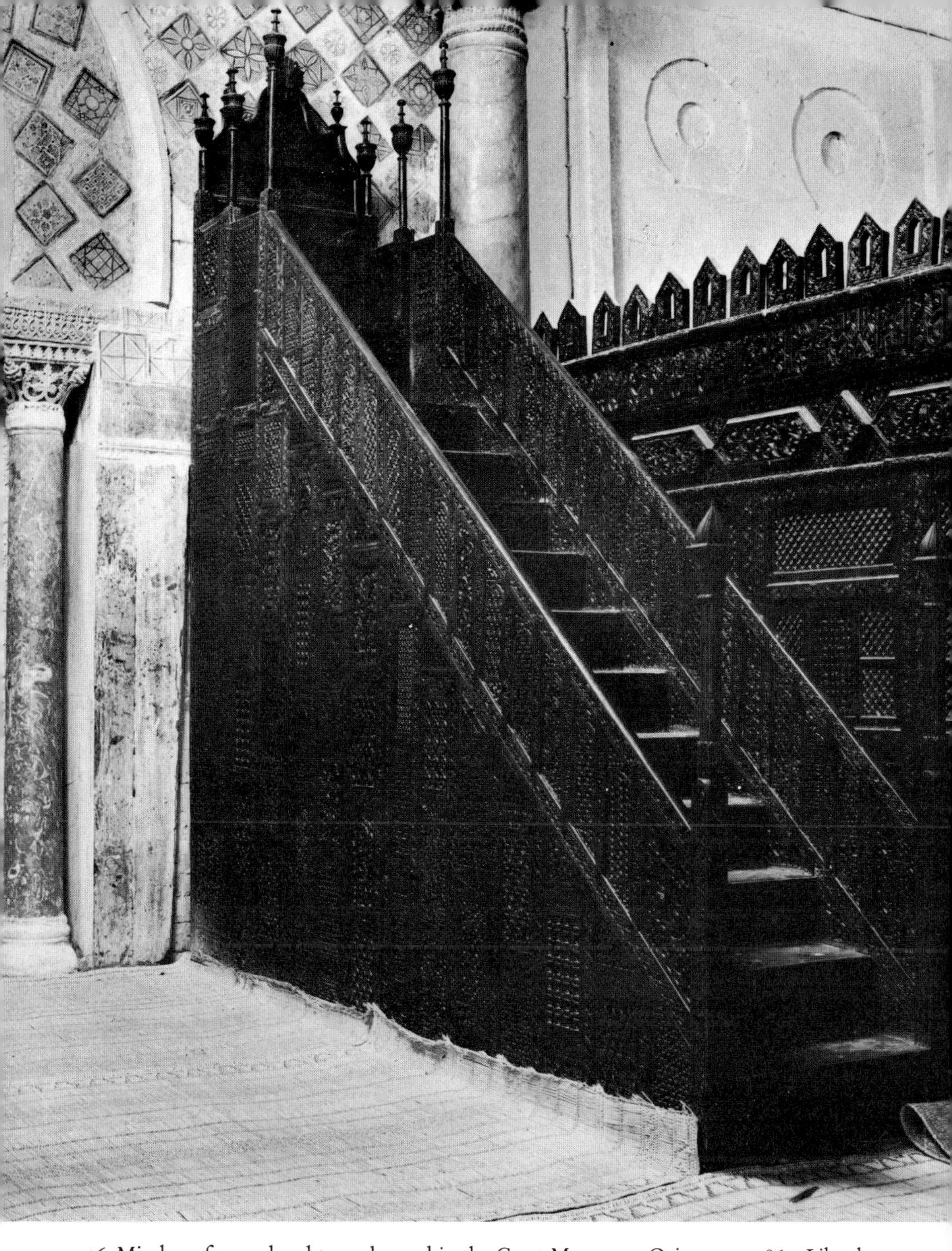

36 Mimbar of carved and turned wood in the Great Mosque at Qairawan, *c.* 862. Like the tiles of the mihrab, the mimbar is probably to be attributed to Mesopotamian craftsmanship

wooden *mimbar* or pulpit at Qairawan was also the work of Mesopotamian craftsmen (*Ill. 36*). Set up in 862, it was therefore made during the period when Samarra was the capital. It is of turned wood, and constitutes one of the earliest examples of such wood work that have come down to us; it was a craft which the Islamic world was later to exploit with great distinction.

The most important of all the Mesopotamian works overseas is, however, undoubtedly the Great Mosque of Ibn Tulun at Cairo (*Ill. 37*), whose patron was the son of a Turkish slave who was made Governor of Egypt by the Abbasid caliph. He soon became virtually independent and reached a position of great power which he used to enlarge and beautify the city, building a whole new suburb, together with a palace, a hospital and a mosque; the latter was begun in 876 and completed in 879. The houses, the hospital and the palace have disappeared, but the mosque remains, and has changed little despite extensive repairs done after a severe fire in 986. Its plan follows that of the earlier courtyard mosques of Mesopotamia, such as those at

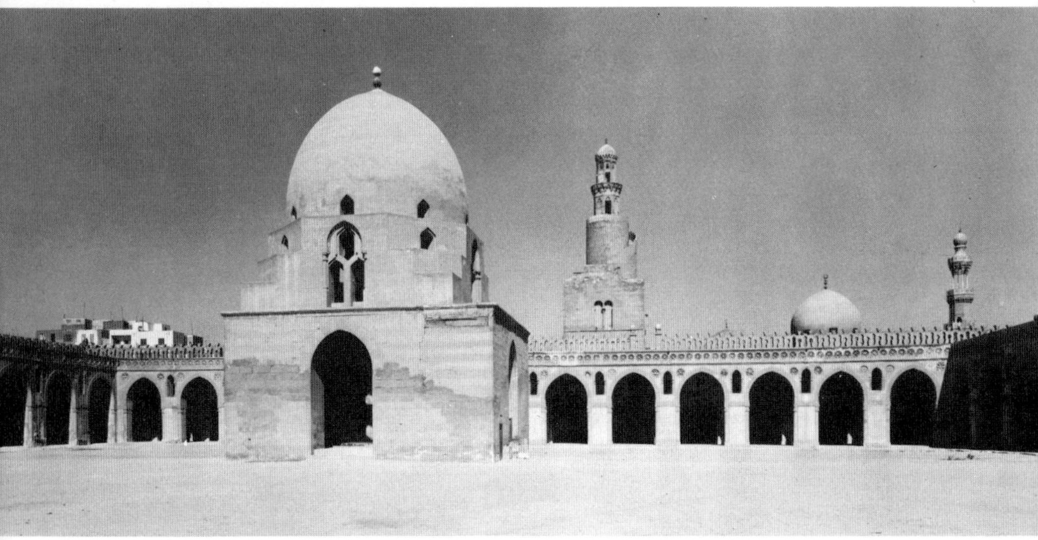

37 Courtyard of the mosque of Ibn Tulun, Cairo. 876–9. The building is of considerable beauty. Extensive use has been made of the pointed arch almost three centuries before it was developed in the West

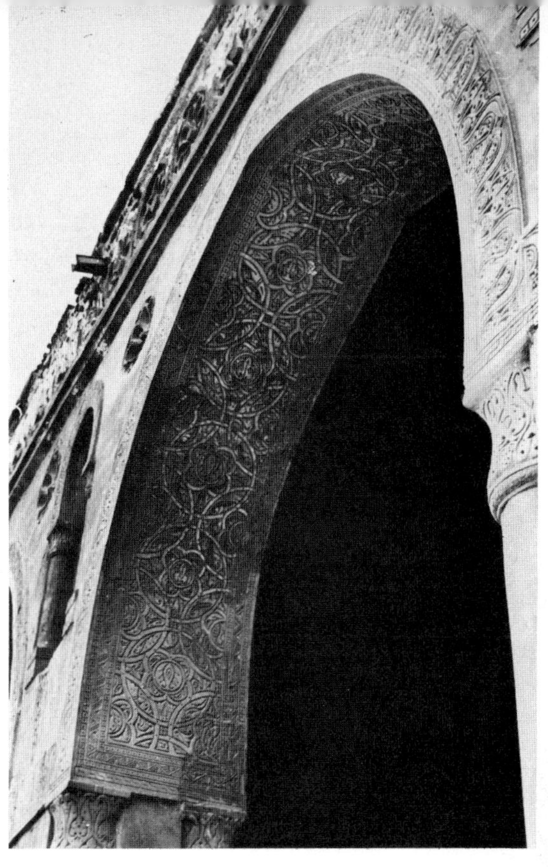

38 Extensive use was made of stucco wall covering for the decoration of the mosque of Ibn Tulun, Cairo. 876–9. The designs are related to those of Samarra in Mesopotamia, but the relief is rather lower and the style more linear

Samarra, but there are only five aisles on the *qibla* or sanctuary side. In place of the columns there are great rectangular piers, the roof is supported by pointed arches instead of horizontal timber beams, and the walls are ornamented with low-relief stucco work of very high quality (*Ill. 38*). The pointed arch had already been used in Syria, but in the mosque of Ibn Tulun we have one of the earliest examples of its use on an extensive scale, some centuries before it was exploited in the West by the Gothic architects. And it was used with extraordinary skill and understanding, for the arcades of Ibn Tulun are things of very great beauty, and the rather severe, formal lines of the stuccos that adorn the walls are equally satisfying. If in the ruins of the Great Mosque and Abu Dulaf at Samarra we can realize something of the grandeur of Abbasid architecture, in the mosque of Ibn Tulun it becomes possible to appreciate the style in all its beauty. It is astonishing to think that in the twelfth century it was for a time abandoned. But happily it was brought into use again, and it would seem that the curious form of its minaret is to be attributed to a restoration done in 1296. The minaret is square and has three storeys of diminishing size, with outside stairs, which, again, recall the ziggurats of ancient Mesopotamia, but is different from those which inspired the minarets at Samarra.

Though Mesopotamia was to remain the main centre of power and culture until the arrival of the Seljuks in the twelfth century, no other site of importance equal to that of Samarra has been excavated, and our knowledge of the period from the close of the ninth century until around 1200 is much more complete with regard both to Egypt on the one hand and Persia on the other than it is with regard to Mesopotamia. In both these areas local styles were developing along independent lines. In the East, for instance, a dynasty called the Samanid ruled at Bokhara (874–999) and an art of a very distinctive type was developed under its patronage, while in the West direct descendants of the Umayyads of Syria were carving out an empire of their own in North Africa and Spain, which owed little to Mesopotamia and the Abbasids. It is the story of art in these more peripheral areas that must therefore now concern us, rather than that of developments in Mesopotamia itself.

Art in Persia until the Mongol Conquest

The course of developments in Persia during the early centuries of Islam was differentiated from that in Mesopotamia, Syria or Egypt by the fact that the inhabitants of the region were not of Arab stock and because the area was in close contact with the regions to the north, Turan, and to the east, Central Asia, and therefore subject to influences from these areas. These influences – but little felt in the more westerly parts of the Islamic world – were of very great importance in the East, and we shall have more to say of them as we proceed. Also, the development was different. The Persia of the Islamic age was not only the most direct cultural heir of the great Sassanian empire, but was also divided into separate kingdoms, ruled by a series of independent dynasties from early in the Islamic era. The most notable of these dynasties were the Tahrids in Khorasan, with their capital at Merv and then at Nishapur, from 820 to 872, the Saffarids in Seistan from 867 to 903 and the Samanids, whose capital was at Bokhara in 874. Later, they extended their rule from Transoxiana controlling most of northern Persia from soon after 900 until 999, when Mahmud of Ghazni (999–1030) brought the whole of the area from central Persia to farthest India under his sway. At much the same time a people of Turkish origin, the Ghuz, had begun to exert influence in western Transoxiana and in the eleventh century one of these tribes, the Seljuk, was established first at Bokhara, then at Merv (1037), then in central and western Persia, and finally at Baghdad (1055). By the last quarter of the century the Seljuks controlled the whole of Western Asia. One branch remained in firm control of Iraq and Persia, while another, which came to be known as that of the Seljuks of Rum, followed up a victory over the Byzantines at Manzikert in 1071 by ousting them from most of Asia Minor.

Though the age of Seljuk supremacy was to be one of the most glorious in the history of Persia, those that preceded it, though less well known, were by no means insignificant so far as art was concerned, as a few buildings of considerable importance, and some truly outstanding groups of pottery which are to be assigned to these years, survive to show. Moulded and cut glass of great beauty was made. The designs were strong and bold, suggesting the inspiration of Sassanian prototypes, and this same influence was also prominent in the textiles, which were made in a number of different centres. Work in both materials went on anyhow until the thirteenth century without any very marked changes of style.

Of the buildings the most important is a mosque at Damghan in northern Persia known as the Tarik-khana (*Ill. 39*). It was built between 750 and 786, and its great circular columns, topped by elliptical arches, are extremely impressive. The plan was a simple square, with a columned arcade on three sides and a three-aisled structure on the fourth. The whole conception of the building clearly owes a great deal to Sassanian architecture and such buildings as the palaces of Sarvistan and Firuzabad.

Very few monuments of the next two centuries survive, and it is only from the tenth century that enough buildings become available to permit a proper study of the architecture; thereafter the monuments are reasonably numerous. Thus the next example in point of time that is well enough preserved to be classed as a work of art rather than a piece of historical evidence is the Mausoleum of Ismail

39 The Tarik-khana mosque, Damghan, Persia. 750–86. Its arches are elliptical, but approach the true pointed form closely. The massive circular piers are distinctive and very impressive

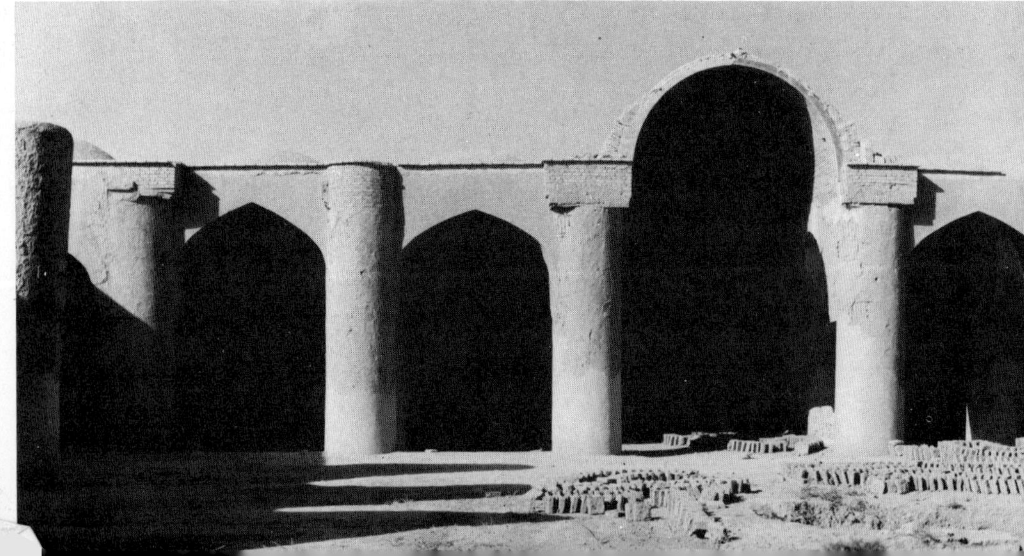

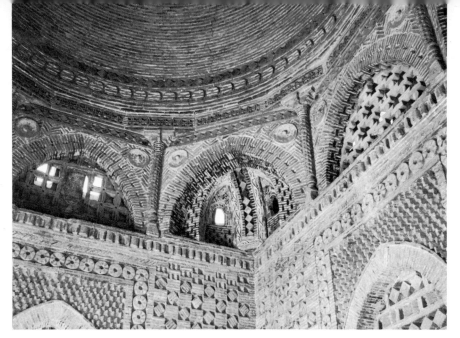

40 The Mausoleum of Ismail the Samanid, Bokhara, *c.* 907. Most imaginative use is made of ornamental brickwork. It was popular all over Persia as well as to the north of the Oxus

the Samanid (d. 907) at Bokhara (*Ill. 41*). The decorative brickwork of the setting for its dome is of great quality and originality (*Ill. 40*); it is the earliest example we have of a technique which was to become very popular in Persia and in which work of great beauty was to be executed.

41 Exterior of the Mausoleum of Ismail the Samanid, Bokhara. *c.* 907. Here the patterns of the brickwork seem to have been inspired by basketwork

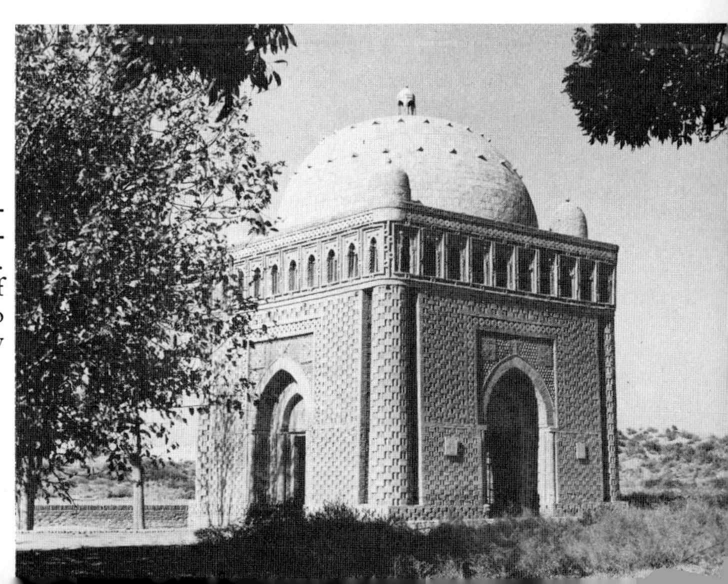

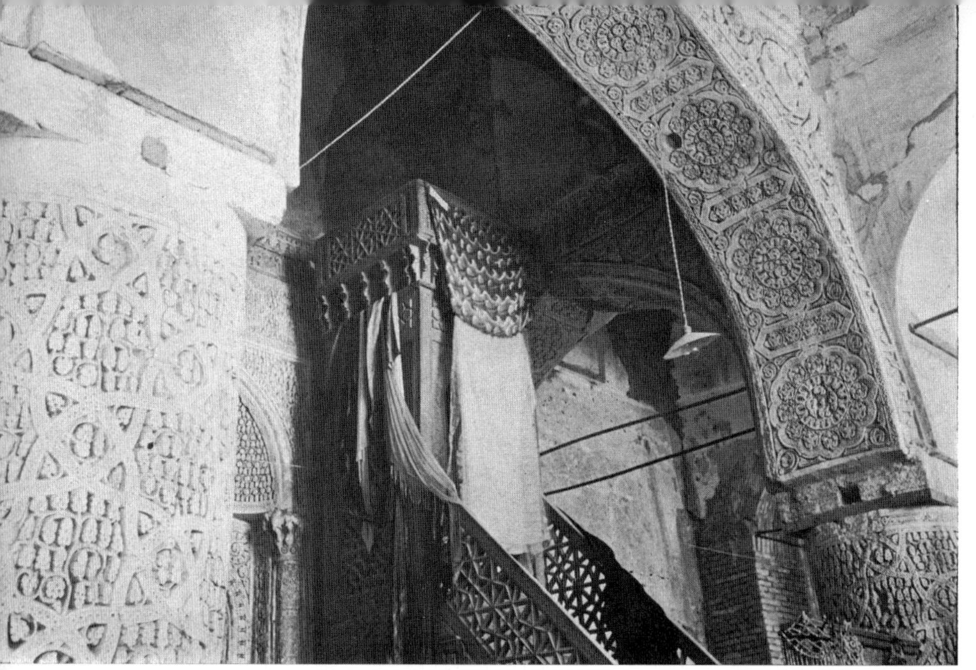

42 The Masjid-i-Jami at Nayin, Persia, *c.* 960. Its stucco decoration, though ultimately related to that of Samarra, shows the development of a new and more flowing style

The next example in chronological sequence, the Masjid-i-Jami at Nayin, was built around 960. The same basic plan of a square court surrounded by arcades was followed, but at the centre of each side there was an arch of slightly larger size, which represented in embryo an idea which was later to be developed as the characteristic mosque form in Persia, namely, that of a great porch or *iwan* at the centre of each side of the central court. The stuccos that adorn the building show much the same sort of progressive development as the architecture (*Ill. 42*). The dark and light effect achieved by deep undercutting was considerably intensified, the designs being more minute than they were a century earlier at Samarra, and the *horror vacui*, or insistence on filling every available space with ornament, is more advanced. But there is still a certain majesty of conception which tends to disappear in subsequent work, where figures came to be included and where the artists tried to do in stucco things that could have been done better in paint. Some important examples dating from between 961 and 981 were found at Nishapur.

The stuccos of the tenth, eleventh and twelfth centuries, however, are hardly of the same artistic quality as the pottery. In this art the craftsmen seem never to have put a foot wrong, whatever technique they adopted. Similar motifs to those used on the stuccos were employed from time to time as the basis of the relief adornment of the plain unglazed wares, but they seem more balanced, more beautiful on the smaller scale, and on the glazed wares a wholly new repertory of figural motifs of great originality and variety appears.

As stated above, one of the most important centres during these early centuries was Nishapur in Khorasan, capital for a time of the Tahirid dynasty, though it was most important under the Samanids. Fortunately, unlike most sites in Persia, it is one at which scientific excavations have been undertaken, so that we know something of its artistic history. The houses were quite elaborate and the walls decorated with paintings which included trees, views, animals and figure subjects of basically Sassanian character. Most important, however, were the pottery finds, which included wasters and even actual kilns. Wares of several distinct types were made, the most distinctive of which had a red or buff body and designs in several colours, black, green, tomato red and bright yellow being the most usual, under a colourless glaze (*Ill. 43*). The bowls were mostly thin, with widely flaring sides, but a few vessels of more elaborate

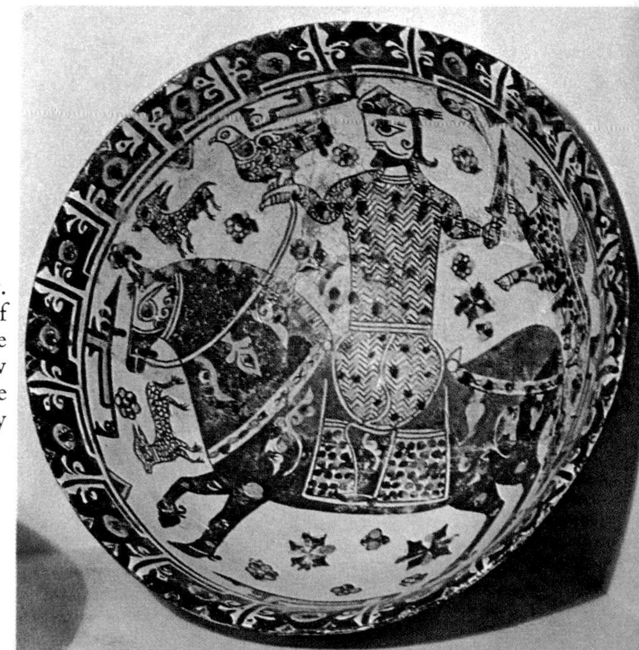

43 Pottery bowl from Nishapur. Tenth century. As a result of excavations at Nishapur by the Metropolitan Museum of New York, it is now possible to associate this very distinctive type of pottery with the city of Nishapur

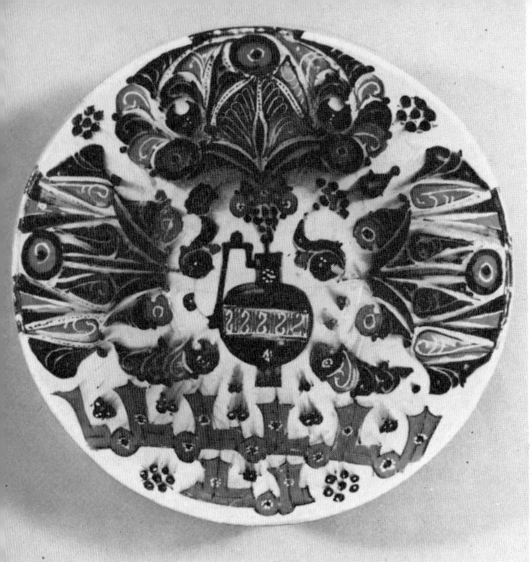

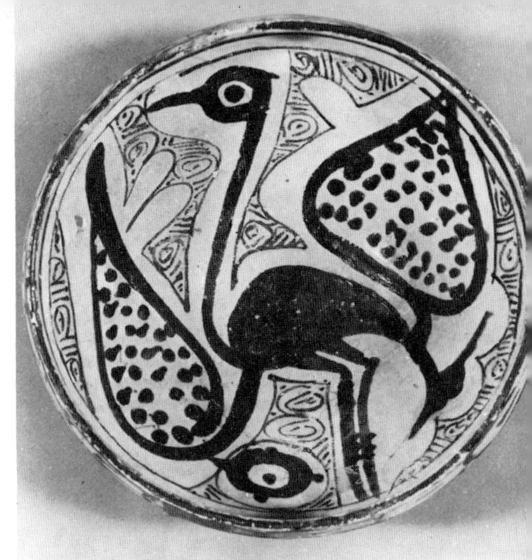

44, 45 (*left*) Bowls, probably from Samarkand and (*right*) Nishapur. Wares that are somewhat similar were made in both these places. Their decorations are invariably severely stylized. That of the former, made up of script, vase and floral motifs, is in pale red and deep brown, that of the latter, a stylized bird in black

form were also found, notably a ewer, with the neck ending in the shape of a bull's head; it must have been inspired by a Sassanian metal prototype. In another group the decorations were in black on a smooth white ground (*Ill. 45*), while another was distinguished by its dark brown glaze with a decoration of flowers with white petals and tomato-red centres (*Ill. 44*); both types are paralleled at Samarkand. At Nishapur, however, examples can be dated on archaeological evidence to the eighth and ninth centuries.

In addition to these very distinctive wares, examples of sgraffito ware, the engraved designs strengthened by painting in manganese brown, were found; yellow and green glazes were also used. The vessels resemble examples from Rayy, Saveh, Hira and elsewhere but date from the eighth rather than from later centuries. Sometimes they are close to T'ang prototypes, and evidence for relations with China is further supported by the presence of a few sherds of celadon. At a somewhat later date contacts with Mesopotamia were proved by the finding of pieces of lustre ware of Samarra type, and another type of local ware, with a decoration in very deep brown on a cream slip, seems to have imitated lustre. Wares of the characteristic

Nishapur type, with decorations in black and yellow, have also been found in Afghanistan, so providing further evidence of the great extent of trade and cultural interchange at this time.

Across the Oxus, in the region of Samarkand, other groups of pottery were developed which were related to those of Nishapur, though the designs were in general less harsh and angular. These types of pottery are usually known by the name of Samarkand wares (*Ill. 46*), though they were probably manufactured in a number of different centres, and remained in use over a very long period. Indeed, the peasant wares which were made at Samarkand, Bokhara and elsewhere in Turkistan down to quite recent times belong to the same family. The bodies of the vessels were red or pink, and were covered with a white, red or black slip, over which the designs were executed. The result comprised patterns in white, red, black, brown and yellow, under a thick colourless transparent glaze. The forms were mainly restricted to simple plates and bowls, though a few jugs and jars are known also. The designs were in general of a basically geometric character, but were balanced and sophisticated; kufic script was freely used, with very fine effect.

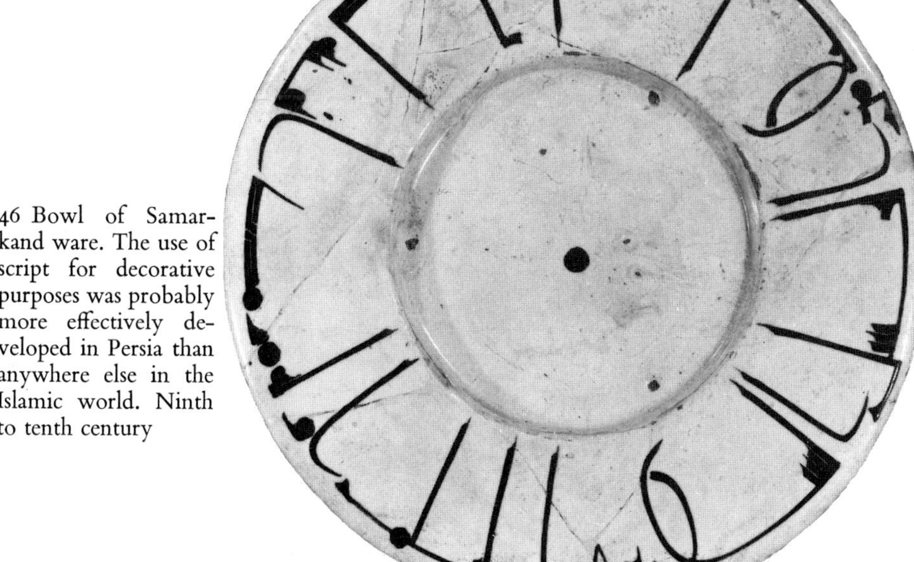

46 Bowl of Samarkand ware. The use of script for decorative purposes was probably more effectively developed in Persia than anywhere else in the Islamic world. Ninth to tenth century

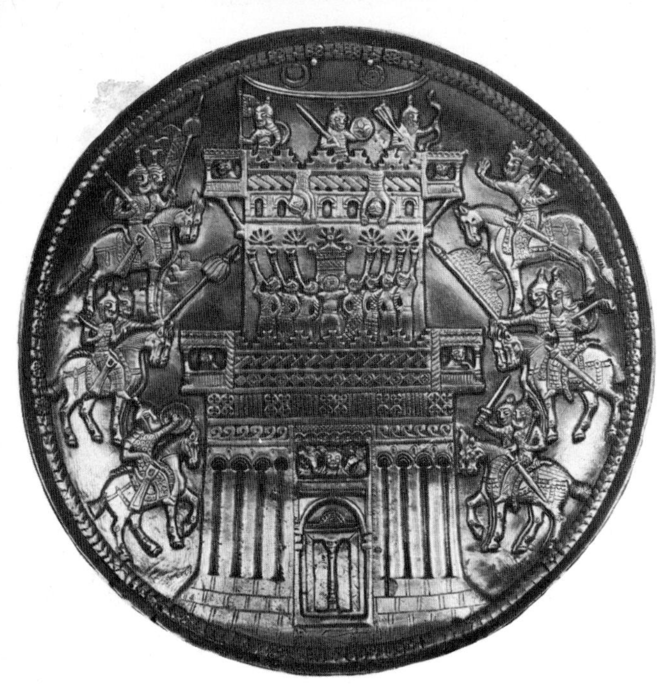

47 Silver plate depicting the siege of a castle. Vessels of this type were very popular in Sassanian times, but they continued to be made for a century or so after the Islamic conquest. Ninth or tenth century

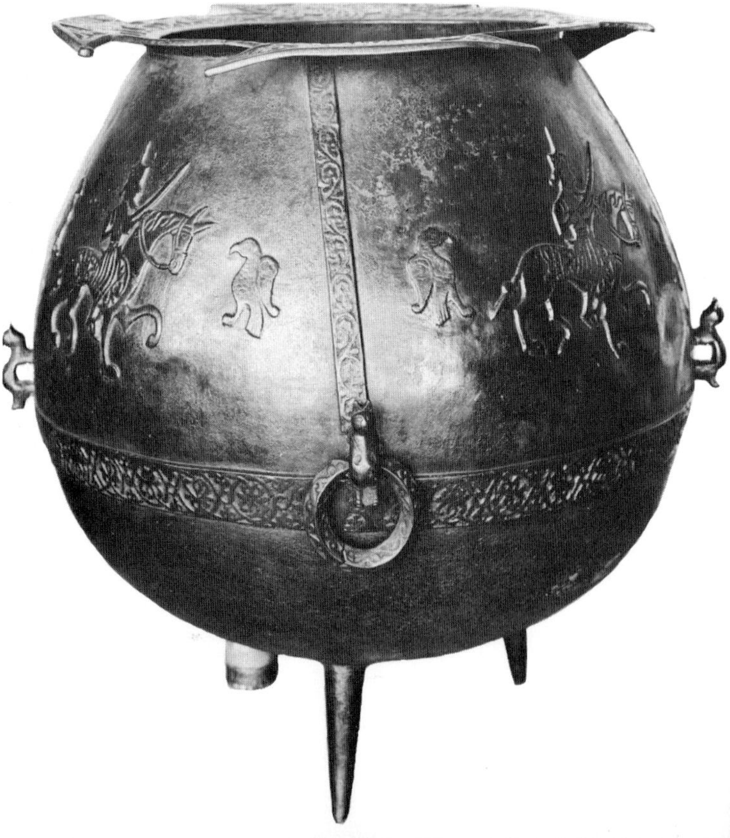

48 Bronze cauldron from Daghestan decorated with equestrian figure and two eagles. The rim is decorated with horses and lions. It is probably to be dated to the twelfth century, though the style is very conservative and in many ways recalls Sassanian work

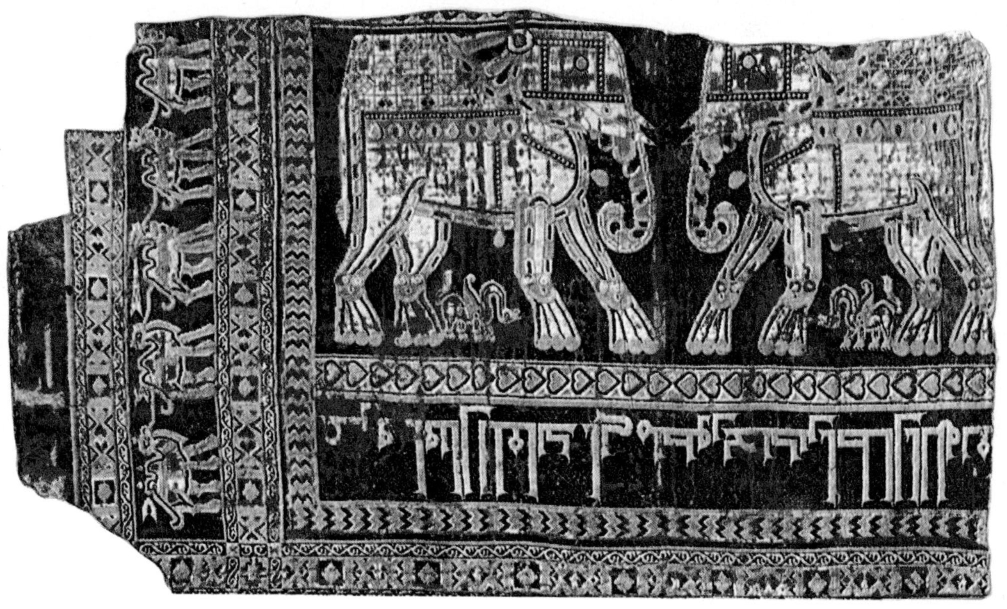

49 Woven silk bearing an inscription 'Glory and happiness to the Commander Abu Mansur Bukhtakin, may God prolong his prosperity.' Tenth century

Other arts of this age were characterized by the same vigorous, rather violent traits, though in the metalwork the influence of Sassanian prototypes is very clearly apparent. A dish in the Hermitage (*Ill. 47*), depicting an attack on a fortress, may serve as an example. It is probably to be dated to the ninth or early tenth century, yet it is still in a purely Sassanian style. This kind of figure-work remained popular for a long time, especially in the Caucasus area, and its legacy is to be seen in a group of stone sculptures from Daghestan, examples of which are now in the Hermitage, as well as on metalwork. A particularly interesting example in the latter material is a bronze cauldron (*Ill. 48*) now in the Victoria and Albert Museum, which is probably to be dated to the twelfth century.

Many of the textile designs show the influence of the same trend, notably the famous elephant stuff from Josse sur Mer in France, now in the Louvre (*Ill. 49*). Its style is distinctly Sassanian, and were it not for the inscription on the border, in a fine, majestic kufic, it might well have passed as a Sassanian piece. Yet an atmosphere of change is in the air, for the gryphons between the elephants' legs show hints of China and indicate that Far Eastern elements were already beginning to make themselves felt. The textile is to be dated to *c.* 960, and assigned to Khorasan, which was an important centre of manufacture.

In addition to Khorasan there also seems to have been a flourishing textile industry in Soghdia, and recently D. G. Shepherd and W. B. Henning have shown that a number of silks with stylized, confronted birds or animals can with reasonable certainty be assigned to that area and are dated to the eleventh century or earlier. A well-known textile in the Musée Lorrain at Nancy, another in the treasury at Sens and a number of related examples in various museums (*Ill. 50*), are assigned to the group. In the south of Persia a more delicate type of work, with linear designs and very full – almost finicky – backgrounds was being developed. Work seems to have begun in that region during the tenth century, though few of the actual examples that have come down to us are earlier than the eleventh.

In the later years of the tenth century, however, it was in Afghanistan rather than in Persia itself that the principal source of patronage was centred, thanks to the rise to power of the Ghaznavid dynasty, first under Sabuktagin (976–97) and then under Mahmud of Ghazni (999–1030). Except for the two great towers of victory, one set up by Masud III (d. 1114) (*Ill. 52*) and the other dating from the reign of Bahram Shah (d. 1152), little survives at Ghazni itself, but excavations are now being conducted there by an Italian expedition under the direction of Professor Tucci, and results may be

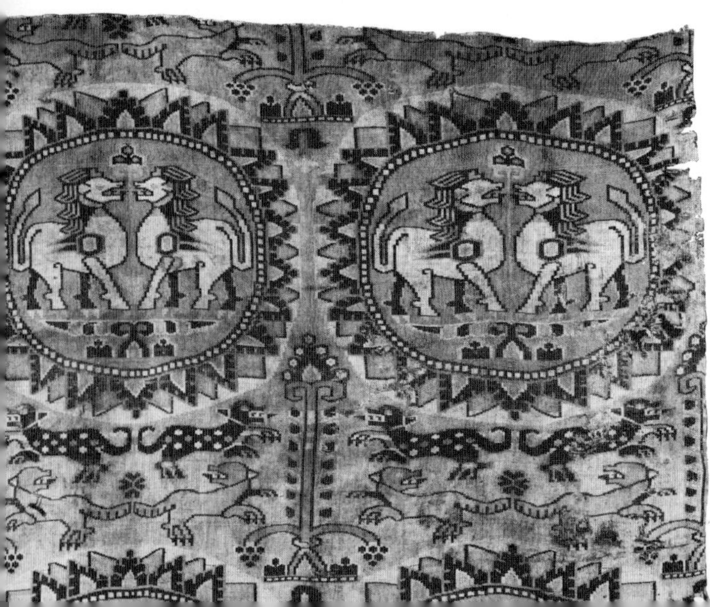

50 This woven silk in the Victoria and Albert Museum belongs to a distinctive group which probably came from Soghdia. The earliest examples are assigned to the seventh century, although the style continued for a long time

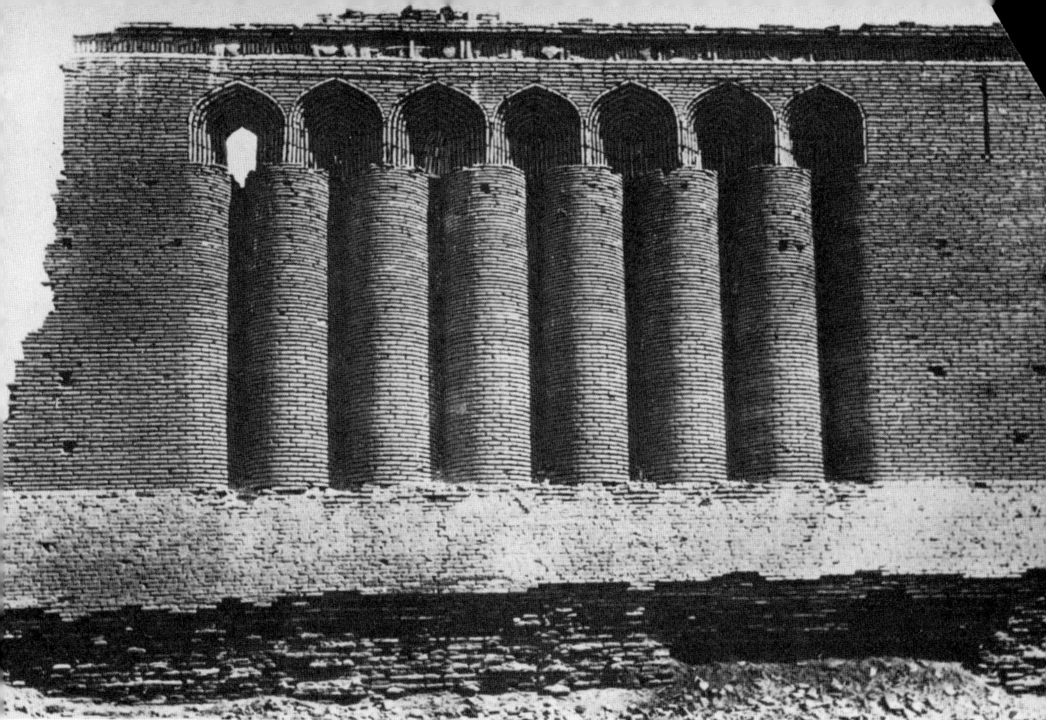

51 The Rabat-i-Malik, Persia, which is strangely modern in its lines and proportions. Nowhere was plain brickwork used to better advantage than in Persia. Second half of the eleventh century

expected in the near future. Some remarkable paintings of the early eleventh century which appear to depict the royal guard have, however, been excavated at Lashkari Bazaar in southern Afghanistan. The Ghazni Towers today terminate in great bands of inscription; originally another storey rose above, as can be seen from the somewhat later tower, or rather minaret, at Jam (*Ill. 53*), built by Ghiyath ad-din Muhammad (1163–1203) of the Ghurid dynasty. The minaret is well preserved, though the mosque which it served has perished. It stands in isolation in a narrow gorge, one of the most impressive structures that time has left to us. The famous Qutb minaret of Delhi must have been inspired by it. Here, as on so many buildings from the eleventh century onwards, script forms the main basis of the ornament.

In the region farther to the west the Seljuks crossed the Oxus into Khorasan and established themselves in power there after their victory near Merv in 1040. It is from this period that date some of the

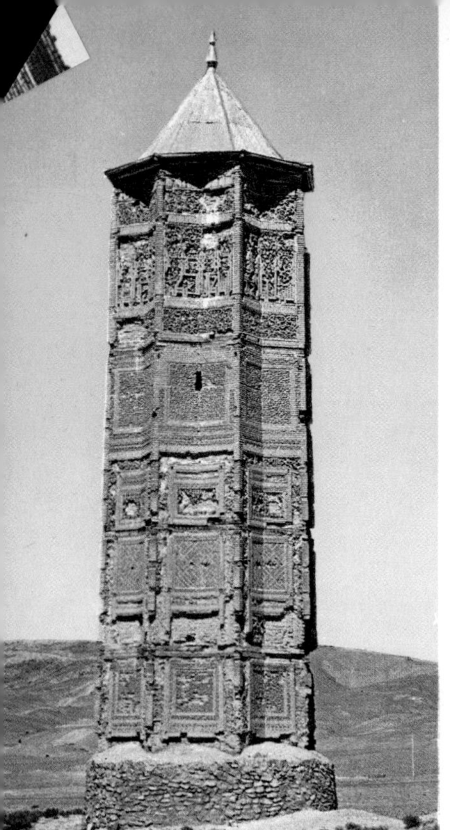

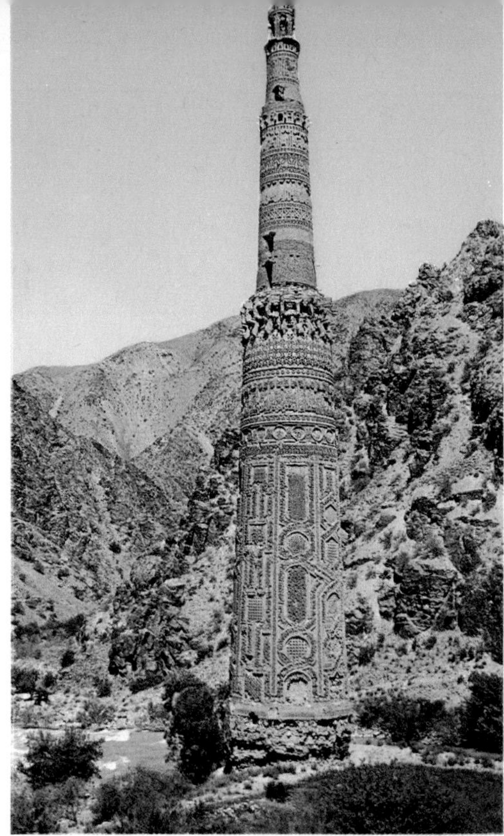

52, 53 (*left*) the tower of Masud III (1099–1115) at Ghazni. This tower and a similar one set up by Bahram Shah are all that is to be seen of the once great city. Originally they had two storeys like the minaret of Jam (*right*), 1163–1203, which stands alone in a gorge

most remarkable buildings in Persia, for it was an age of very great activity. We perhaps know it best through its architecture, for a number of outstanding buildings survive, some of which seem strangely modern in appearance (*Ill. 51*). They are mostly in brick, and the craftsmen all had an astonishing feeling for that material, which they invariably used to the very greatest advantage, especially in the treatment of main façades. It was, however, in the construction of the domes that their greatest achievements were made, both inside, in their manipulation of the transition from the square base below to the circle of the drum above, and outside, in the form and proportions of the domes themselves. Sometimes the exterior faces

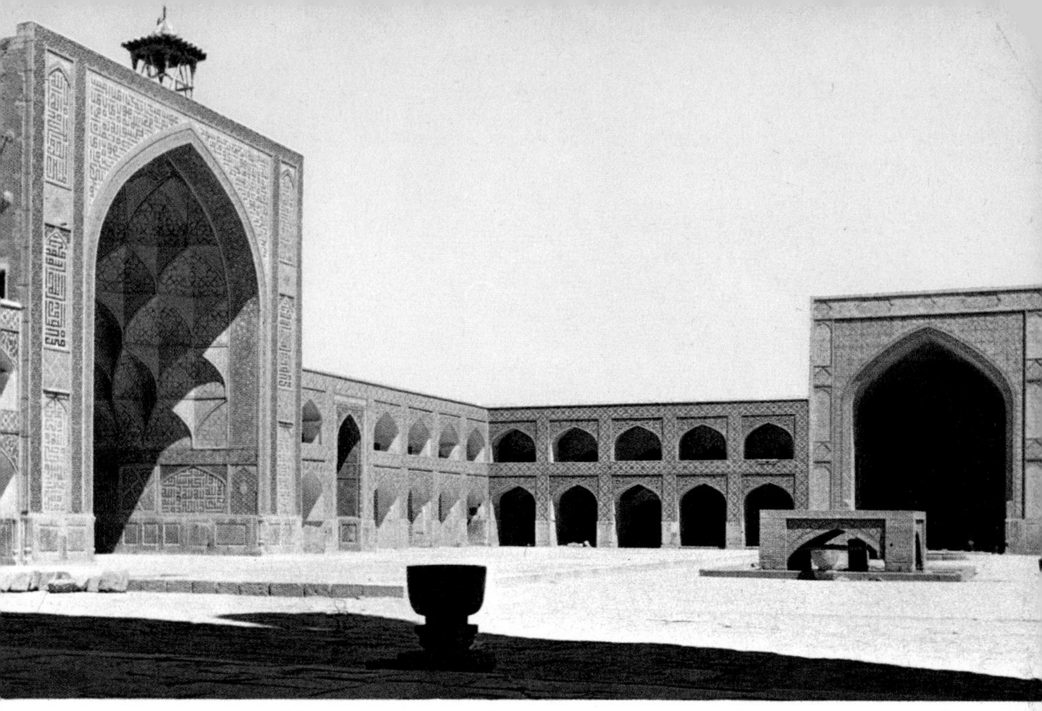

54 The main court of the Masjid-i-Jami, Isfahan, 1088. Each side of the courtyard is bounded by a great *iwan*, their vaults supported by a system of ribbing which heralds a similar development in Gothic architecture in the West

of the domes were plain, sometimes adorned with geometric patterns in coloured tiles, as in the Masjid-i-Jami at Qazvin (1113) (*Ill. 55*). Inside, the proportions and decoration in monochrome brick were particularly outstanding and the dome chambers were often of supreme beauty; those of the Masjid-i-Jami at Isfahan (1088) (*Ill. 54*) are numbered among the finest products not only of Persian but also of all architecture. The system of building, however, was not only beautiful, it was also creative, for it would seem to represent an ingenious exploitation in brick of an idea first tried out in wood, where a square compartment was roofed by setting beams across the corners, so forming an octagon, then across the corners again, until the whole area was covered; the brick-vaulted ribs (*Ill. 56*) thus cross and recross in a manner similar to that of the beams of the wooden prototypes, and the way that ribs were used as frames on which the masonry of the domes and vaults was supported anticipated developments in the Gothic world by some centuries.

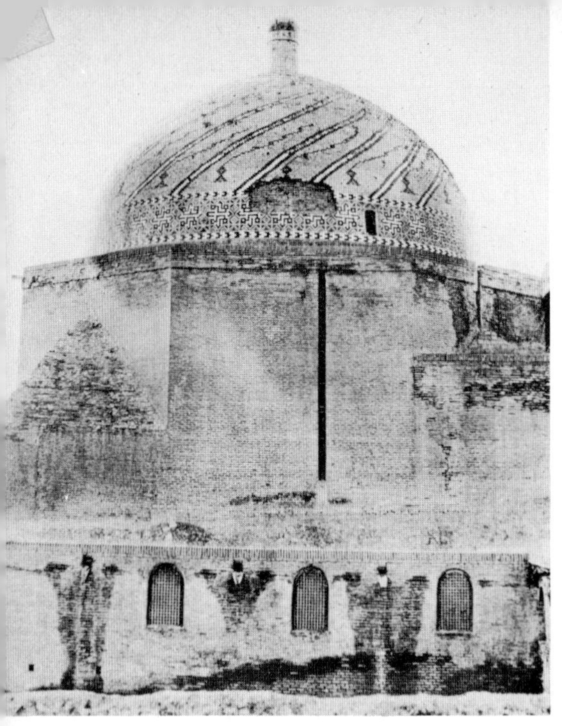

55 The Masjid-i-Jami, Qazvin. 1113. The mosque is typical of many built in Persia at this time, and shows the use of coloured tiles for the decoration of the exterior of the dome

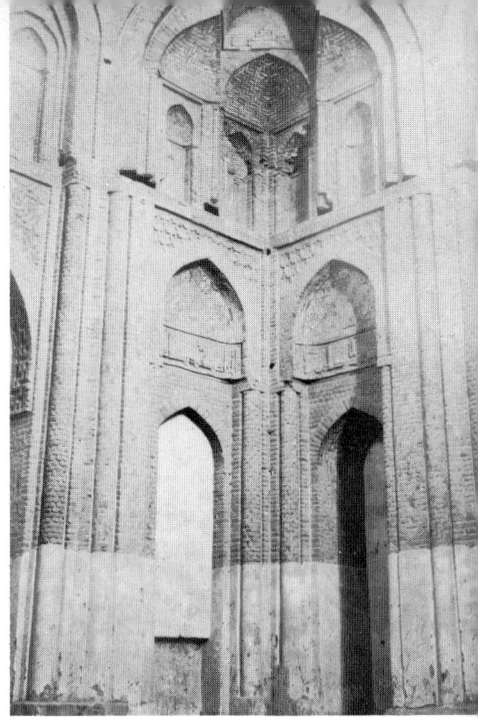

56 The Masjid-i-Jami, Isfahan. 1088. The interior of one of the dome chambers, illustrating the skilful use of plain bricks to achieve a sober but impressive decoration

Lovely though the brickwork was in itself, the Persian builders were not always content to leave it in its natural state. As at Qazvin glazed tiles, usually blue and black, were frequently applied over the brick, while for interior decoration stucco work like that used in earlier centuries at Nayin was considerably developed, especially for the adornment of mihrabs. Some of the best of these date from the twelfth century (*Ill. 57*). The detail of the background areas is perhaps over-minute while the main designs are sometimes rather heavy, but technically the work was extremely proficient and it was an art that was much admired.

Apart from the magnificent mosques that they built in Persia, however, the Seljuks were responsible for the development of another and very individual type of building, the *gumbat*, *türbe* or tomb tower. These were usually circular in plan, though sometimes there were star-like projections all round and the later examples were

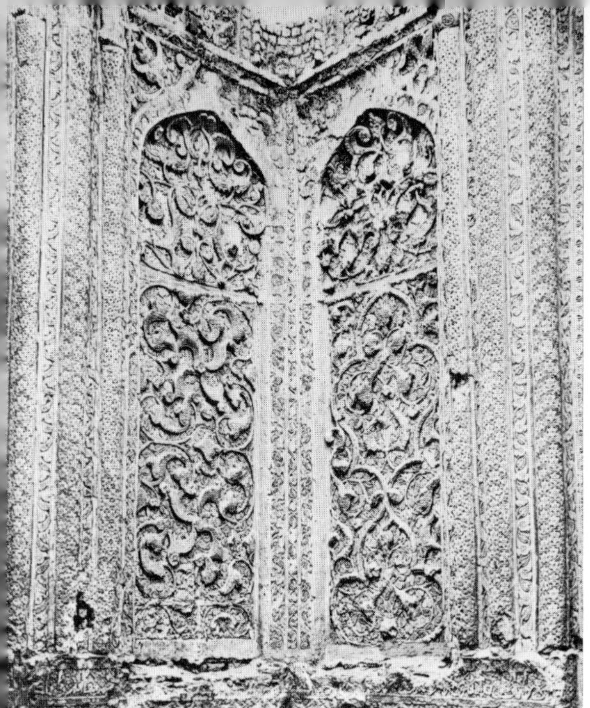

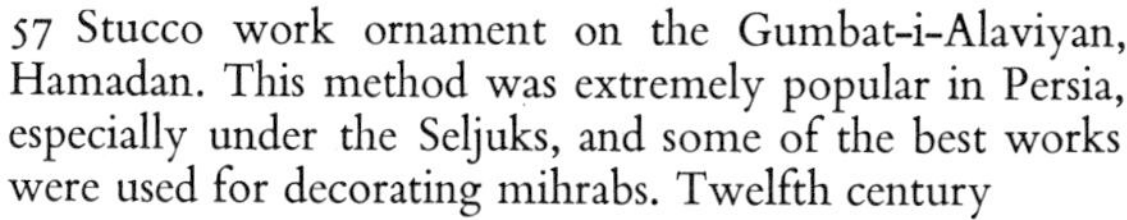

57 Stucco work ornament on the Gumbat-i-Alaviyan, Hamadan. This method was extremely popular in Persia, especially under the Seljuks, and some of the best works were used for decorating mihrabs. Twelfth century

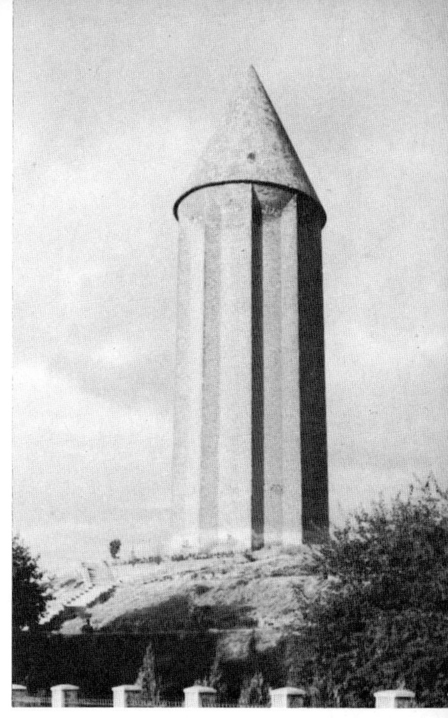

58 The Gumbat-i-Qabus, northern Persia, 1006, is one of the finest examples of the *gumbat* or *türbe* first developed for burial purposes by the Seljuks

sometimes polygonal. Nearly always there was a band of decoration and usually an inscription at the top, irrespective of the shape of the plan. The Gumbat-i-Qabus (*Ill. 58*), in the north of Persia not far from the Caspian shores, is perhaps the most spectacular and certainly one of the most beautiful of these structures. It was set up as a burial tower for the Emir Shamas al-Ma'ali Qabus about 1006, and is built of brick, with a conical roof and a band of inscription at the summit. This may serve as the type example of a group which was to constitute one of the principal architectural forms, first in Persia and then in Asia Minor, for the next three centuries.

Inside there were usually two storeys, the burial, in a sumptuous coffin, set in the upper one, with wives of the deceased sometimes buried in smaller sarcophagi beside the principal one. Outside the niched façades produce a particularly delightful effect in the bright sunlight of the Middle East, especially in the simple unadorned form

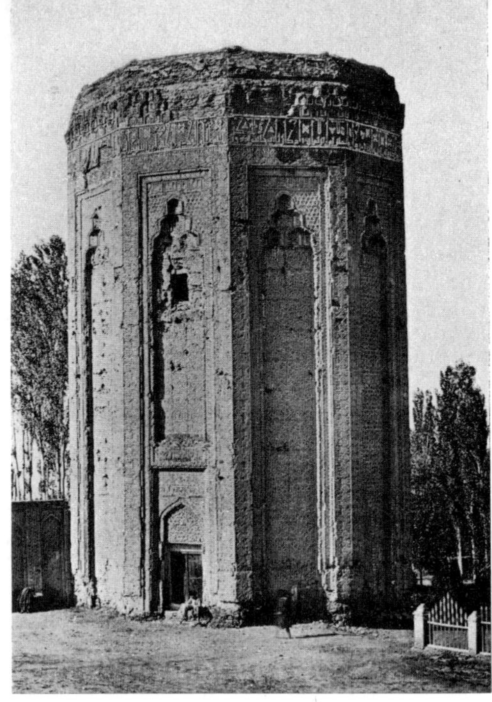

59 The Gumbat of Mumina Khatun, Nakchevan. 1186. The earlier gumbats were usually circular in plan, only later did the polygonal form become usual. The circular form was carried westwards by the Seljuks and greatly developed in the Caucasus region and Anatolia

that was usual in early times. Later, in the Caucasus and in Anatolia, the gumbats became more ornate (*Ill. 59*). But the simple unadorned brickwork of some of the Persian examples of the eleventh century, offset by an impressive inscription at the top, often produces an effect of very great beauty, and the gumbats are to be counted as a really important contribution to Islamic architecture.

Diez, in his *Die Kunst der islamischen Völker* (p. 71), suggests that the towers were derived from pre-Islamic prototypes, and cites in proof of his thesis, an example at Vahneh, which has now perished. But it is to be questioned whether this structure was really pre-Islamic, for it might equally well be a rather more primitive version of the popular Seljuk type, and it seems more likely that the development of this important architectural form was due to Seljuk patronage. But whence was it derived? The classical form of the martyrium, as we see it in what is now the church of St George at Salonica or in a more barbaric variant in the Mausoleum of Theodoric at Ravenna, at once springs to mind. But we know of no earlier examples in the Middle East, and if the form was carried from

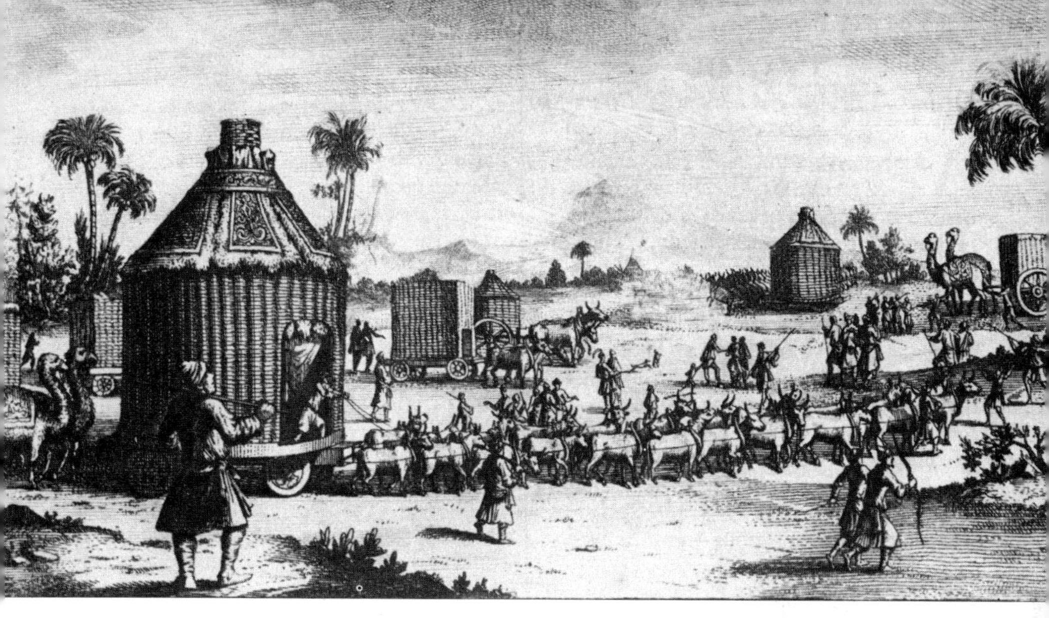

60 Engraving of a drawing made in Central Asia by Friar William of Rubruquis in 1253. It shows typical Mongol tents and it is possible that the stone and brick built gumbats were inspired by this form

northern Persia to Anatolia by the Seljuks and was not derived from a classical prototype, a source in the East must be found. We have it in the conical tents or *yurts* (*Ill. 60*) so exactly, that one may conclude that these towers are to be regarded as a transformation of the fragile abode of the living into a more lasting accommodation for the dead, set up in a more substantial, more permanent material. The fact that the earliest of these buildings are to be found in northern Persia and the regions closest to Transoxiana, where the Seljuks first settled, supports this suggestion.

The Seljuks were not only considerable builders, but also great patrons of the minor arts. As is always the case where excavations have to be depended upon for the provision of the evidence which is available for the study of an art, pottery must play a role which is perhaps out of proportion to that which it performed originally, for it has survived whereas more fragile materials have perished. The great variety of pottery techniques that were in common use and the quality of the wares serves nevertheless to attest the brilliance of the Seljuk age, while the excellence of the figure drawing gives some

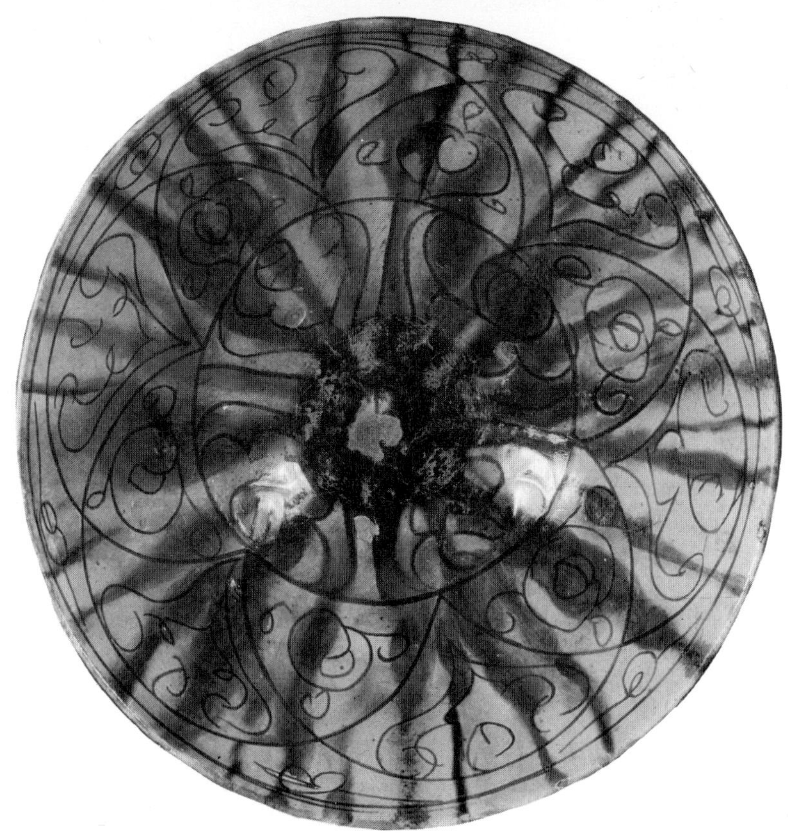

61 Bowl of splash-glazed ware with foliate and scroll patterns. The decoration is thinly incised through a white slip under pale yellow and green glazes. It was probably inspired by the T'ang wares of China. Eighth or ninth century

idea of what the paintings that adorned the palaces and some of the richer houses must have been like. We know from the records that these paintings were highly prized, but very few examples have come down to us.

Of the types of pottery, sgraffito wares of various types, following on from those encountered at Susa and in Mesopotamia, were still perhaps the most popular, but the variations on the technique had become more numerous. A number of groups may be distinguished. The first, the least common, consisted of wares where a thinly engraved design played a very subordinate role, the main decoration

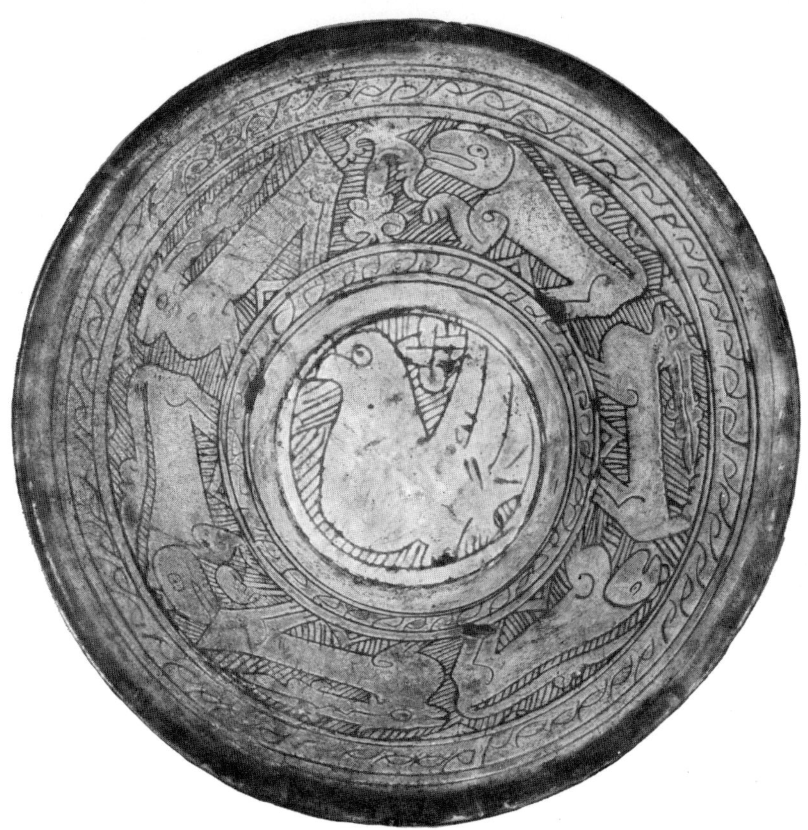

62 Bowl with a bird, stags and lions. The decoration, in the technique known as sgraffito, is engraved through a white slip to the red body beneath. This technique may have been inspired by Chinese wares or developed independently in Persia. Ninth or tenth century

being splashed on in green and yellow glazes (*Ill. 61*). As in Mesopotamia, this ware was made in direct imitation of imports of the T'ang ware of China, and in this most purely T'ang form it was comparatively short lived, for it was especially popular in the eighth and ninth centuries, but tended to disappear after that.

The next group belongs mainly to the tenth century, and is represented by vessels of a red body, covered with a white slip, and with a thinly engraved design under a colourless lead glaze (*Ill. 62*). Thinly engraved designs which are very similar appear on metalwork of the period. The designs often represent birds, usually against a fully

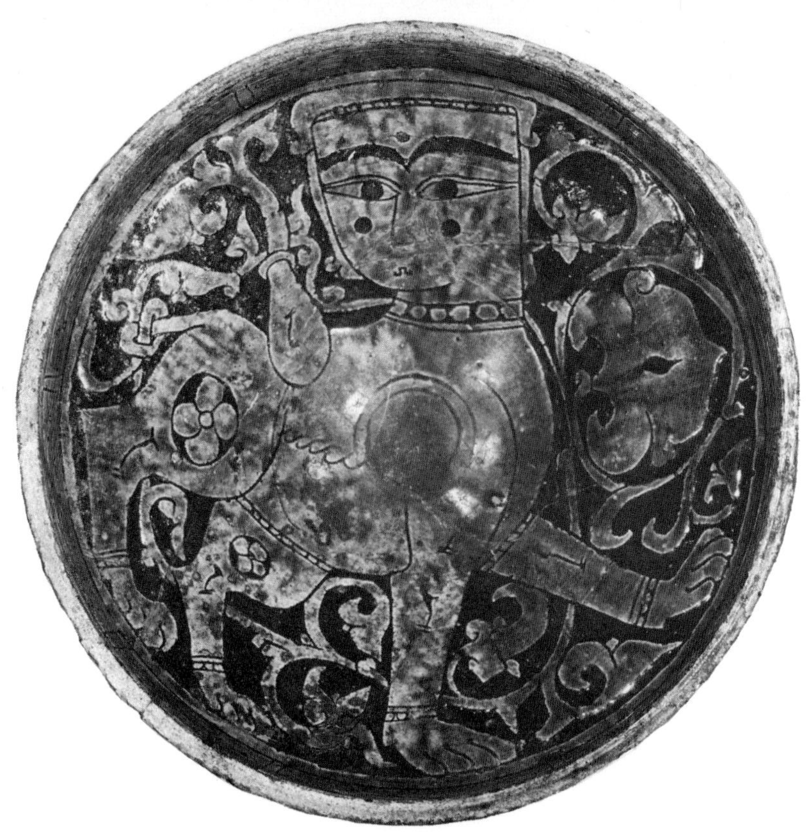

63 Bowl with human-headed quadruped and floral scrolls in deep green. Large areas of the slip have been removed to produce what is termed champlevé decoration. Eleventh century

charged background. In a related group, which was developed in the thirteenth century, and which is sometimes associated with Agkhand, the incised lines coincide with a carefully painted design in green. Later still, another variant (*Ill. 67*), with scribbled engraving and careful painting in brown and green, was also developed; the type is associated with the place-name *Amol*.

Finally, a group may be distinguished in which large areas of the slip were removed to produce a champlevé design, usually under a deep green glaze (*Ill. 63*). Heavy, flat-footed bowls, with curved rims and jugs with necks like birds or animals, were most usual. The

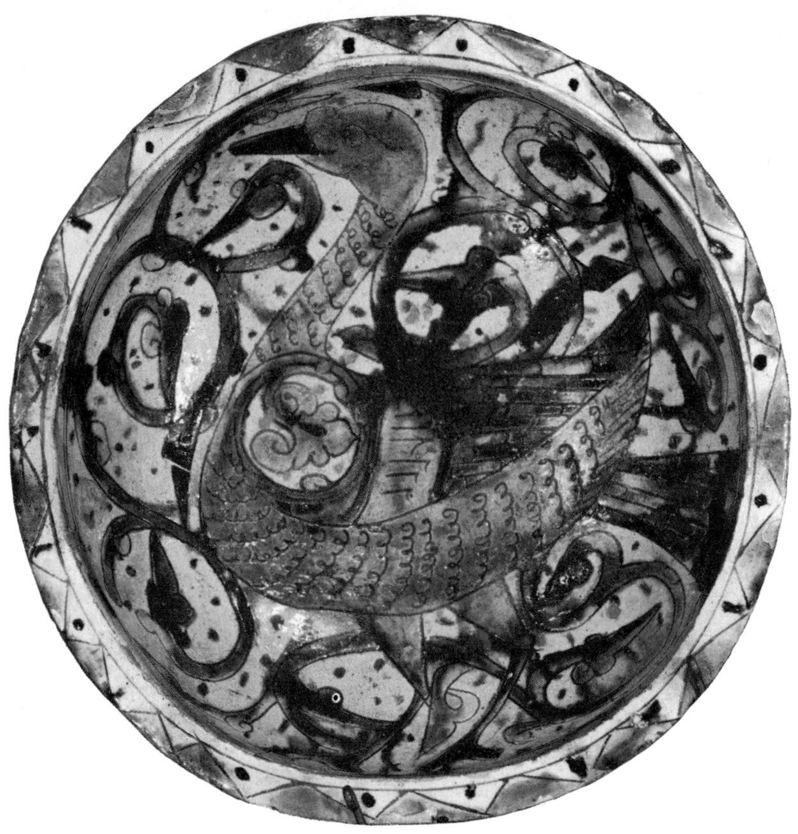

64 Bowl depicting a duck among sprays and scrolls. The decoration is in sgraffito and painted in green and brown under a cream coloured glaze. Spirited birds of this type were popular in Persia. Eleventh century

name *Gabri* has come to be associated with the type. There were numerous variants both of technique and ornament from vessels where the designs were grand and majestic to those where the designs were delicate and flowing. Generally the latter are perhaps a century later than the others. The place-names – Agkhand, Yasukhand, Amol and so on – associated with all these groups have varied with the years and are not to be regarded as very reliable, for most of the examples that are known have been named by dealers and they cannot always be relied on as indicating the correct localities where the vessels were found, still less those where they were made

(*Ill. 64*). More scientifically controlled excavations concerned with the Islamic period in Persia are badly needed.

Bowls with a fine white body and a decoration in cobalt blue or green, like those already encountered at Samarra, were made in Persia from the ninth to the eleventh century, and another family with white body must have been related. Here the decoration was either moulded or carved, sometimes being pierced right through the body, which then assumed the character of a semi-porcelain. Chinese models no doubt had a role to play in the evolution of the technique. Vessels usually take the form of beakers; they date from the twelfth and thirteenth centuries, and seem to have mostly been made at Rayy. In a closely related ware, glazes of deep blue or brown were substituted for the cream-coloured ones of the other group, and the technique was elaborated for the decoration of objects of considerable size, which even included small coffee stands or tables; it was exploited both at Raqqa in Syria and also in Egypt.

Moulded decorations also characterize another group which is usually known as *Lakabi* ware (*Ill. 68*), but the areas in relief were also coloured, blue, yellow, purple, green and pink being used to pick out the designs against white or cream grounds. Flat plates or dishes ornamented in this technique were often extremely beautiful, although the potters never mastered the art of preventing the colours from running in the vertical position. Kashan was probably the main centre of production. The designs of the silhouette wares, which were painted in black on a fine white body under a transparent ivory or turquoise glaze, produced a somewhat similar effect, for their margins were so clearly defined that they almost look as if they were in relief as well as in black. This technique has been associated with Rayy.

However, Rayy potters seem to have excelled, especially during Seljuk time (1037–1256), in the production of two other groups of luxury ware, namely, lustre and the so-called *Minai* or polychrome painted ware (*Ill. 69*). Both techniques were difficult and complicated. In the Minai wares the bodies, of a fine white consistency, were painted in pale blue, green or purple under the glaze, and fired. Black outlines and details of the designs were then added in

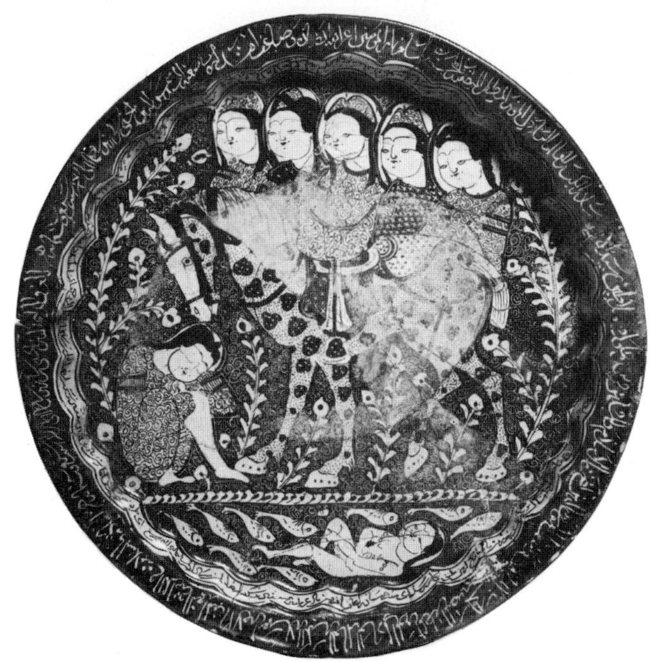

65 Lustre dish, Prince Khusraw discovers Shirin bathing. Signed 'Sayyid Shams ad-din al Hasani'. Kashan, *c.* 1210

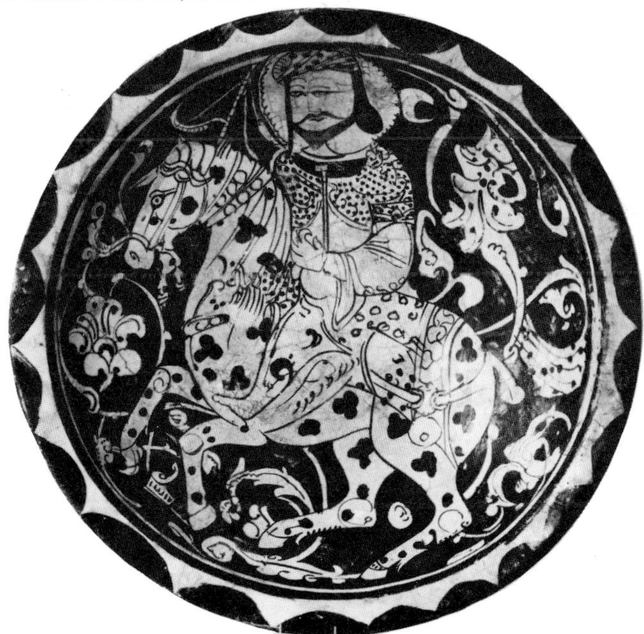

66 Dish with horseman painted in brownish-gold lustre. Rayy, late twelfth century

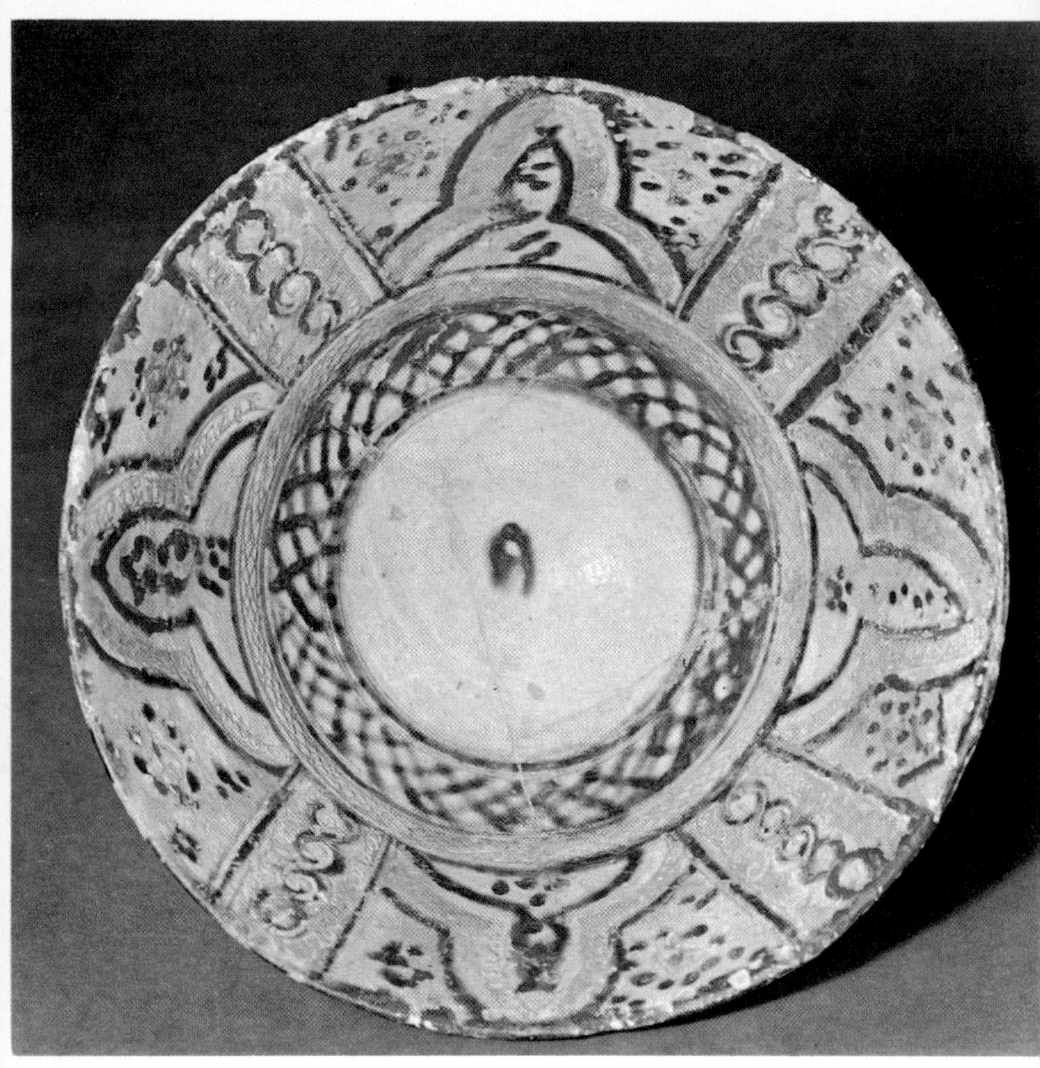

67 Amol ware bowl, from the author's collection, is characterized by a thin sgraffito decoration with delicate green line. Twelfth or thirteenth century

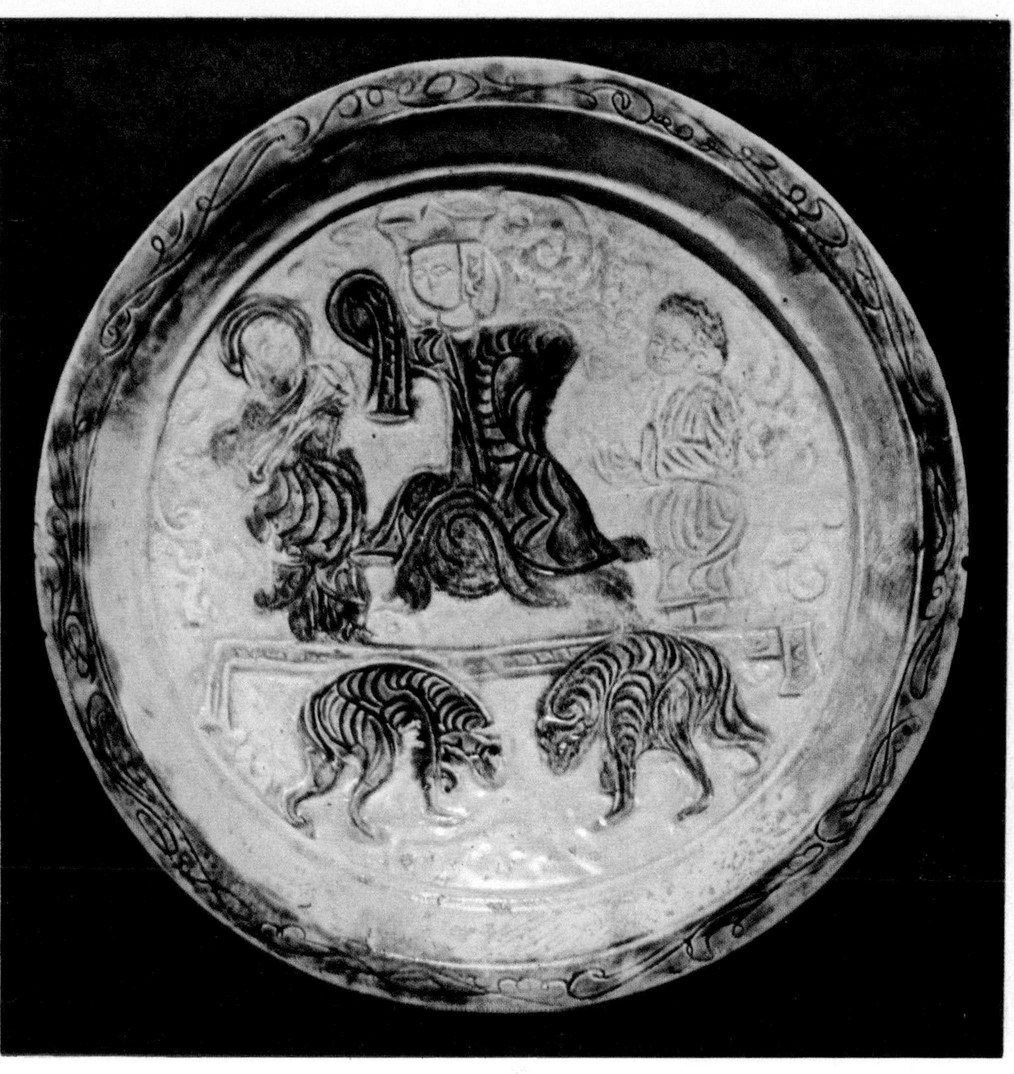

68 Dish, depicting dancers and hyenas, decorated in relief under polychrome glazes. This type of ware is usually known as Lakabi and was a luxury ware restricted to the use of rich patrons, and examples were probably always rare

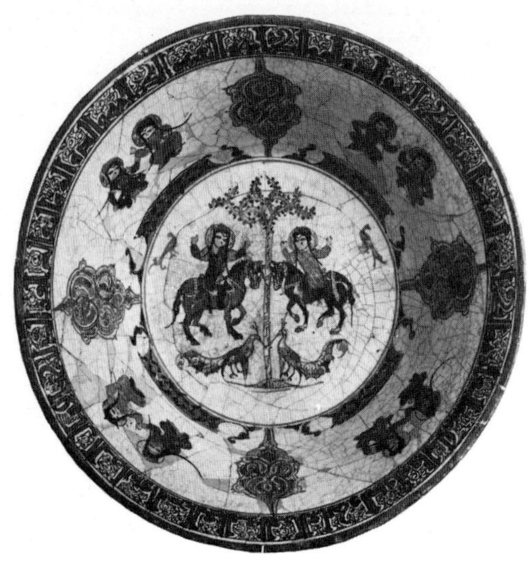

69 Bowl with confronted horsemen of Minai type. Miniature paintings such as this serve to give an idea of what the manuscript illustrations of the period must have been like. Twelfth or thirteenth century

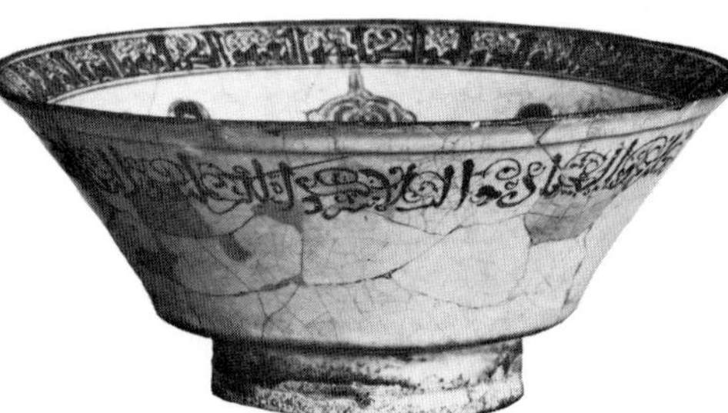

vitrefiable colours which were of great variety, comprising blue, grey-blue, turquoise, green, yellow, brown, black, red and gold, and the variety was intensified by the fact that the grounds were sometimes coloured also, lilac or turquoise-blue being usual in addition to white. The colours were then set by a second firing. The painting was in a delicate, miniature-like technique, and figural subjects, often of a narrative character, were favoured. Very similar drawings characterized the lustre wares from the later twelfth century onwards and the designs of the two groups are often so alike that one may conclude that the same artists worked in both techniques. Their drawings on this durable material serve to give an idea of what works on more fragile materials like paper or plaster which have now perished might have been like. The Minai pottery was perhaps made at Kashan and Saveh as well as Rayy.

The introduction of lustre into Persia took place at a comparatively late date; the earliest example we know that can be definitely dated is a bottle of 1179, now in the British Museum. The technique was fully mature at the outset, so that it must have been introduced from outside, and both Mesopotamia and Egypt have been suggested as the immediate source of inspiration. As time went on, however, the work became more fluent, reaching an apex in the twelfth century. As stated above the designs were delicately and beautifully painted in ruby, carmine or gold, sometimes singly, sometimes combined, and included in addition to arabesques and leaf-forms very vivid human figures (*Ill. 65*). Horsemen (*Ill. 66*) seem to have inspired the painters particularly, and this composition was admirably suitable. Sometimes the backs of these were coloured blue and occasionally the lustre was on a blue ground. The best of the bowls seems to have been made at Rayy, while the potters of Kashan and Sultanabad specialized in the production of lustre tiles and large vessels. Work continued, in any case at Kashan, until the fifteenth century, whereas at Rayy it does seem to have been resumed after the Mongol conquests of the early thirteenth century.

Around 1200 another type of pottery came into fashion – the blue and black (*Ill. 70*). Kashan was the main centre of production, but work was also done at Sultanabad, Saveh and Sultaniya. Sometimes the surface of vessels of this type were moulded or engraved, sometimes the colours were used without a relief background, the decoration being painted on in black and the whole covered with an attractive deep blue glaze. Moulded designs of very similar character were also used alone, without the black, under turquoise or other glazes.

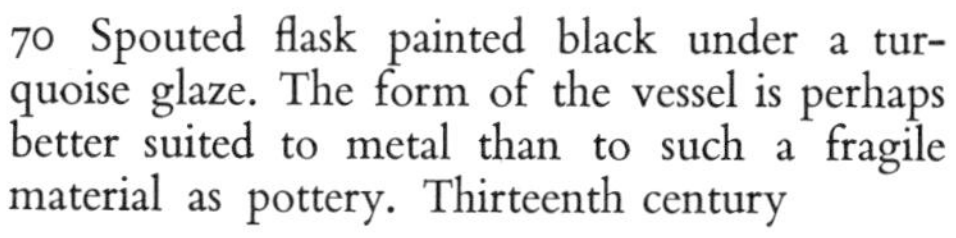

70 Spouted flask painted black under a turquoise glaze. The form of the vessel is perhaps better suited to metal than to such a fragile material as pottery. Thirteenth century

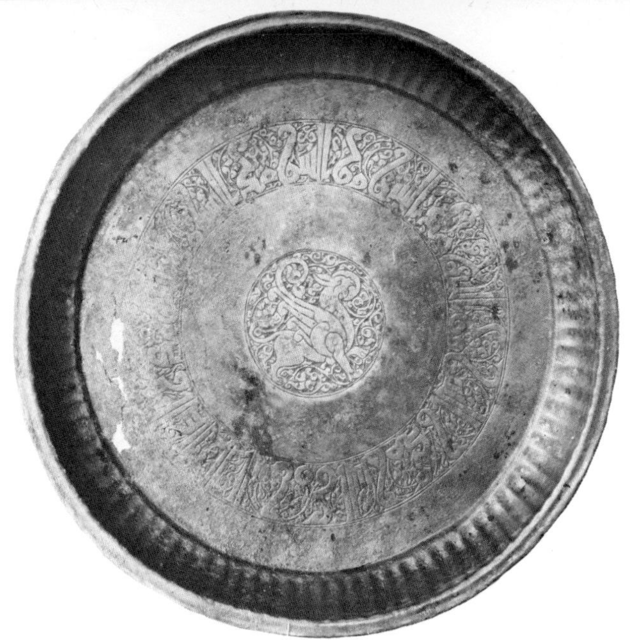

71 Bronze tray with a design similar to the type also used on the sgraffito pottery. Twelfth or thirteenth century

The Minai technique, as well as those where a moulded or pierced decoration predominated, was essentially Persian and these methods were never developed elsewhere. Other techniques, like lustre, blue and black, and above all sgraffito, were popular all over the Islamic world. The problem of where they were all invented is, however, very complicated, and though we know that there was a great deal of interchange, there was also probably a good deal of independent invention also. Only when we find fairly advanced techniques appearing suddenly in an undeveloped area, as was the case with certain types of sgraffito and moulded wares of Persian type that occur in Afghanistan in the twelfth century, can we be sure that a technique was introduced from outside.

In addition to the pottery, a few examples of metalwork of the Seljuk age in Persia are available. Heavy mortars in bronze with inscriptions round the rim were in common use. Jugs and ewers which were close to Sassanian prototypes continued to be made; sometimes their necks were in the form of birds or animals, and metal vessels like these inspired some of the types of pottery (*Ill. 70*).

The pottery was also similarly influenced in the twelfth century by the designs engraved on large flat plates or trays (*Ill. 71*) similar to those still in everyday use all over the Islamic world. Mirrors and weights with a decoration in relief on the back were common, while incense burners in the form of birds or animals, and especially lions, were apparently more of a luxury product. There is a particularly attractive one in the Hermitage (*Ill. 72*) in the form of a lion with a curly tail and a cheeky face; it is signed: Ali ibn Muhammad as-Salihi. They seem to have inspired the water vessels in the form of lions, known as aquamaniles, which were so popular in the West at much the same time. Small, rather fine, vessels of silver were also made, but most important of all were bronze vessels with the decoration in silver or copper inlay, very similar to those frequently associated with the name of Mosul. This indeed was the type *par excellence* of the Persian metalworkers, and the technique was probably first developed in eastern Persia. The finest of them is a

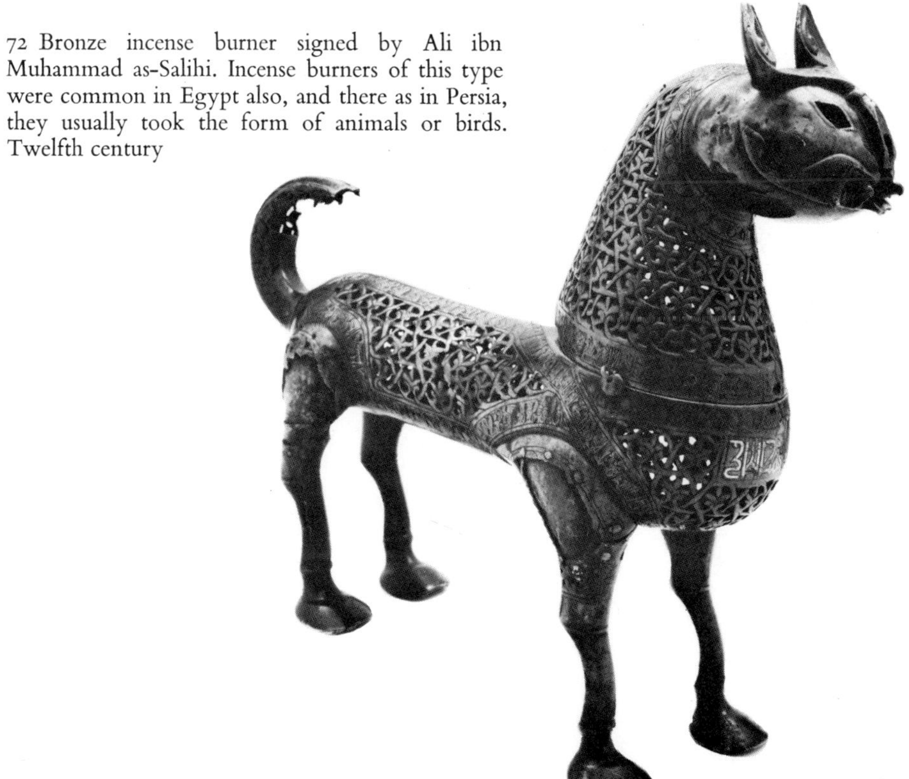

72 Bronze incense burner signed by Ali ibn Muhammad as-Salihi. Incense burners of this type were common in Egypt also, and there as in Persia, they usually took the form of animals or birds. Twelfth century

cauldron in the Hermitage, signed Muhammad ibn 'Abd al-Wahid and Masud ibn Ahmad, done at Herat in 1163 (*Ill. 73*). It remains unsurpassed in the story of Islamic metalwork. A dozen or so other signed and dated pieces of inlaid work of this age survive which can also be assigned to Persia rather than to Mesopotamia.

Some very fine jewellery was made at this time, and the rulers were great patrons of fine weaving, rather linear, all-over designs being especially popular. Glass, though it never equalled that of Syria, was also made and adorned with gold and bright enamel colours from the thirteenth century onwards.

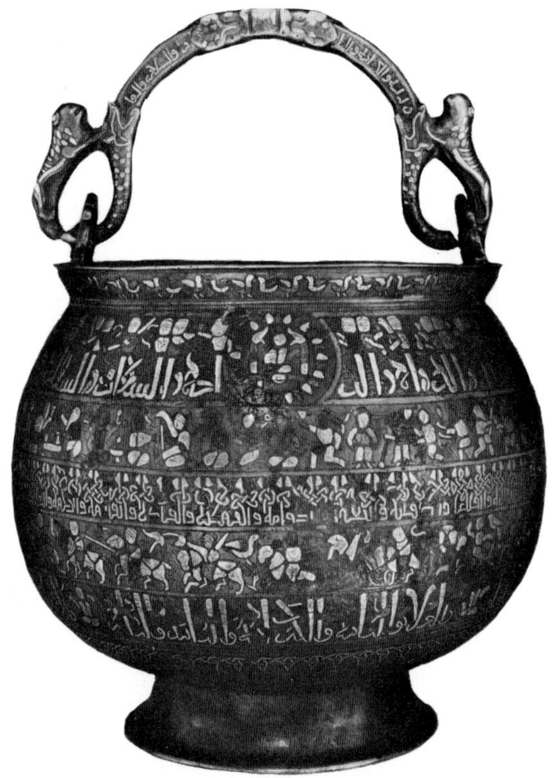

73 Bronze kettle with inlaid design, signed by Muhammad ibn 'Abd al-Wahid and Masud ibn Ahmad. Inlaid work of this type was at one time all attributed to Mosul, but it is now known that the technique was practised in Persia, Syria and Egypt. Herat, 1163

Spain, Egypt and North Africa until *c*. 1200

The conquering zeal of early Islam was not confined to the eastern world. The Byzantine province of Egypt fell before the Arab attacks about 641, and during the following century the armies of Islam moved across North Africa, destroying their enemies, yet founding cities and mosques as they went. From Africa the attackers moved up into Spain, and though they had penetrated as far north as Tours in France by 732, the capture of Toledo about 711 marked the real limit of their control. At much the same time that the new Abbasid dynasty was rising to power in Iraq, a member of the Umayyad family, Abd er Rahman I (756–88), succeeded in establishing himself as an independent ruler in Spain, and founded a line which was to remain in control there, and at times in North Africa also, for some three hundred years. One of his successors, Abd er Rahman III, even claimed the title of caliph in 929. Abd er Rahman I was a great supporter of art, as were many of his successors, and under their patronage there grew to fruition a very distinctive and original style which is usually known as the Hispano-Mauresque. Its greatest monument was the mosque of Cordova, begun in 785 and added to at various periods until the fifteenth century, when it became a Christian church (*Ill. 75*).

In its earliest form it was a courtyard mosque of rectangular plan, with a sanctuary of eleven aisles akin to that of the original al-Aqsa mosque at Jerusalem and with horseshoe arches like those at Damascus topping the arcades. It was enlarged in 833 by Abd er Rahman II and again in 965 by al-Hakam II (961–76), when the great dome in front of the mihrab was completed (*Ill. 74*). This is a very remarkable structure and represents something quite new, for the dome is supported on a series of intersecting ribs. The system of ribbing is paralleled on a less elaborate scale at Toledo, as well as in Armenia and in the lovely Masjid-i-Jami at Isfahan. It is probable

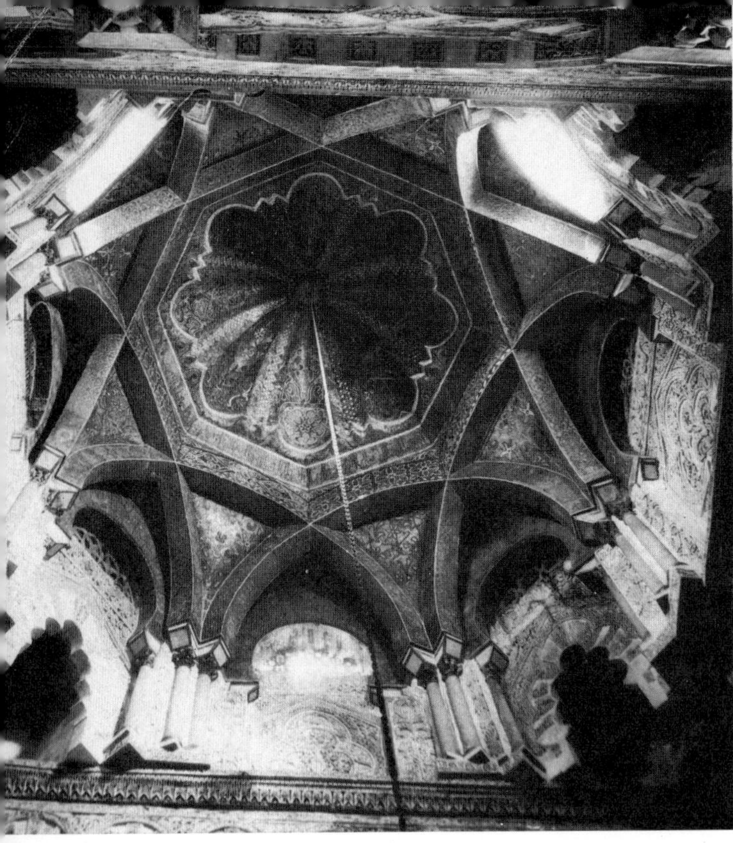

74 Central dome of the Great Mosque at Cordova. The supports of the dome, a series of intercrossing arches, are similar to those in the dome chambers of the Masjid-i-Jami at Isfahan. 961–8

that the system was actually evolved in Persia, even though the domes of the Masjid-i-Jami are later in date than that at Cordova. The Isfahan domes are remarkable because of the beauty of the brickwork, but at Cordova decoration was added which is somewhat over-ornate. It included mosaics supposedly done by craftsmen brought from Constantinople for the purpose, but there is nothing very Byzantine about the character of the work. The horseshoe mihrab and the tiers of hexafoil arches that bound the mihrab chamber show a degree of elaboration not reached elsewhere in the Arab world, yet they are typical of the ornate Hispano-Mauresque style.

A minaret was added by Abd er Rahman III (912–61) and further additions were made by al-Mansur in 987. Today the area that formed the sanctuary has nineteen aisles, and is the third largest mosque still extant, being exceeded in size only by the Great Mosque

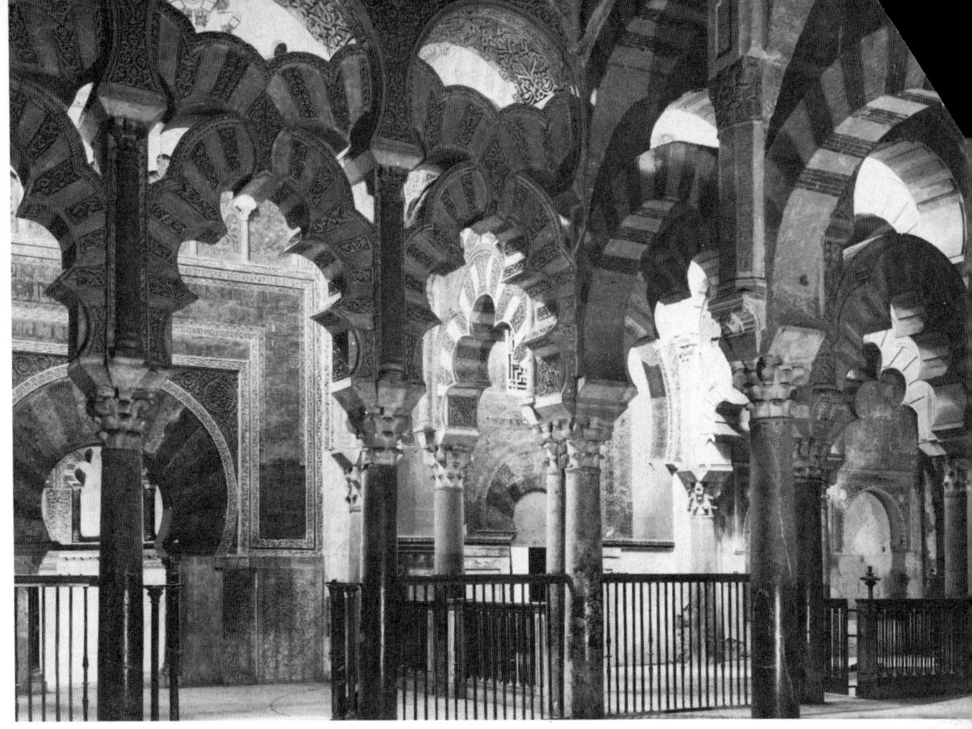

75 Sanctuary of the Great Mosque at Cordova. The mosque was begun in the eighth century but was frequently added to, especially during the tenth century. The hexafoil arches in two tiers represent a new and original departure in Islamic architecture

of Samarra and that of Abu Dulaf near by. It is enclosed by a great stone wall, and in the structure itself, stone and brick courses alternate in the same way as in the Byzantine world or as in the great Umayyad city of Anjar in the Lebanon; the system was probably inspired by an Umayyad example in Syria. The double arches, one above the other, however, constitute an unusual structural feature; the idea was perhaps suggested by one of the Roman aqueducts, of which there are several fine examples in Spain.

Except for the mosque there is little that survives from Islamic times in Cordova, but there is a small mosque at Toledo, the Bab Mardoum, and a whole city, Medinet az-Zahra, founded by Abd er Rahman III in 936 and subsequently deserted, available as a more or less unencumbered archaeological site. Excavations there have not only produced important finds but have also made possible a fairly thorough reconstruction of what a city of tenth-century Islamic

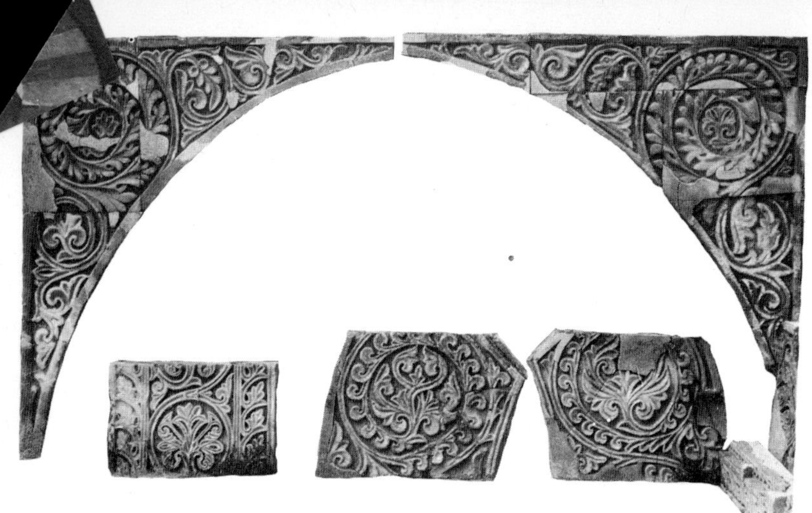

76 Stucco decoration from the palace of Abd er Rahman III at Medinet az-Zahra. 936

Spain was like. The city stands in terraces on a sloping hill-side, surrounded by walls, but the layout was irregular and the houses are of little architectural interest. The houses were built mainly of stone, and, as in Mesopotamia, stucco was liberally employed for decorating the wall surfaces (*Ill. 76*). This stucco and a number of brick floors set in geometric patterns are the only constructional features of artistic interest that the city has to offer. Elements of Byzantine art are more obvious here than in Mesopotamia, and the stuccos, plainer and less elaborate than those of Samarra, are easily identifiable as Spanish. However, the flat ceilings of the houses – they occur again in the mosque at Cordova – and perhaps also the multiple lobed arcades, are features that may well be of Mesopotamian inspiration.

The finds of minor works at Medinet az-Zahra were less numerous and interesting than those from Samarra; no fragments of frescoes have appeared, and the pottery was limited to barbotine wares – mostly jugs – and vessels with a painted decoration in green and brown on a yellow ground. Both types owed their basic inspiration to Mesopotamia, but were developed locally very rapidly. The results were, however, of a very provincial character, and it was not until several centuries later that any really high-class pottery that was distinctively Spanish began to be made, in the form of a particularly rich and accomplished lustre ware. The first mention of this occurs in 1066, when reference was made to the 'golden pottery of

Toledo'. In 1154 Calatayud in Aragon was mentioned as a centre of its production, but potteries also seem to have existed at Manises, Paterna and Valencia, and there were probably factories in North Africa also, though their products seem to have been confined to rather simple wares with a two or three-colour decoration. The typically Spanish pots, distinguished by their great size and by the elaboration of their forms, are all of rather later date.

Of the other arts the most important and distinctive was probably that of ivory carving (*Ill. 77*). Rectangular and, more particularly, circular caskets, with a very profuse decoration of exuberant palmette scrolls, birds and animals, were most usual. One of the earliest, now in Madrid, is dated 964 and examples of the later tenth century are comparatively numerous. Their style is akin to that of Fatimid work in Egypt, but has a distinctively Spanish flavour and it is not difficult to tell the products of the two countries one from the other. A little later, however, a new centre grew up in Sicily, producing work which was very like the Spanish, both in the method of ivory carving and textile weaving. In this case it is not always easy to be sure which works are Sicilian and which Spanish (see p. 150).

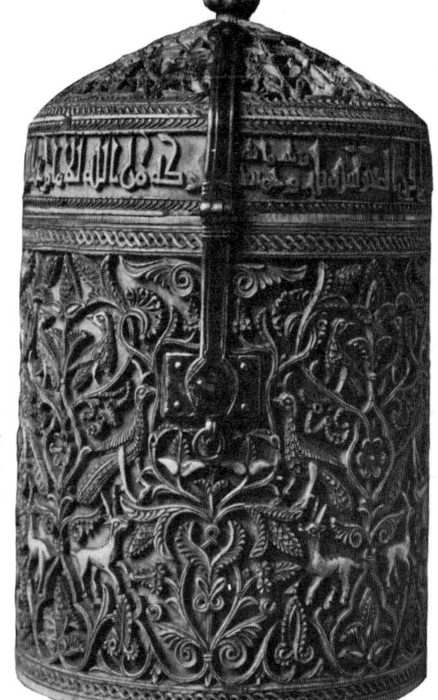

77 Ivory casket made at Cordova and dated 964. Ivory carving of the type, in comparatively high relief, was much in favour in Muslim Spain. Rather similar work was done in Sicily, though most of it is somewhat later in date

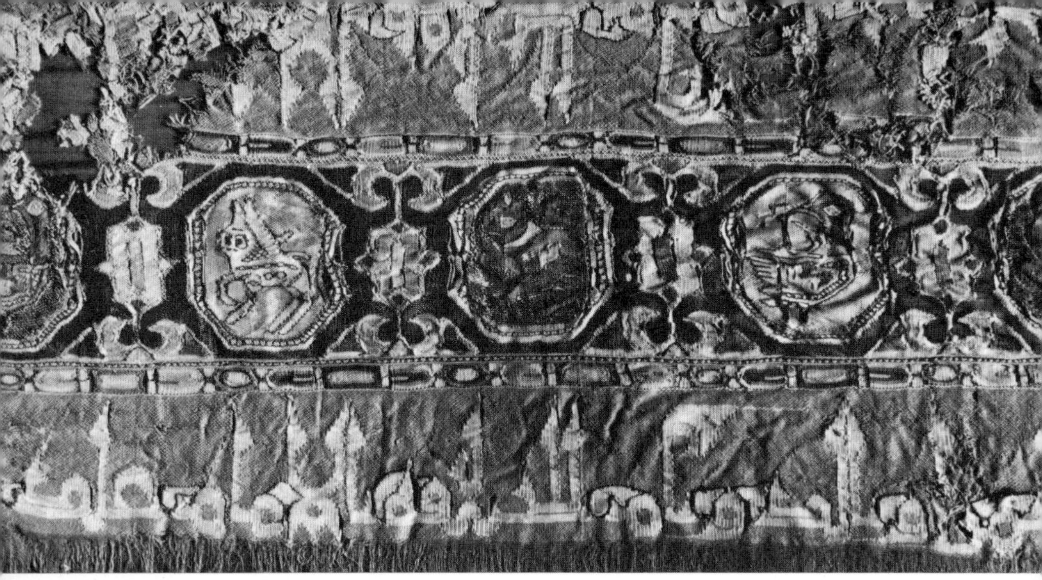

78 Textile known as the 'Veil of Hisham' in silk and gold. Tenth century. Woven textiles of very similar type were also produced in Egypt at the same time, and there is little that can be regarded as characteristically Spanish about this example

As was usual in the luxury-loving world of Islam, the manufacture of fine textiles was also much in favour in Spain and seems to have begun immediately after the Islamic conquest. Andalusia was the most important centre, and Idrisi notes that there were as many as eight hundred looms there; in the tenth century there were looms at Almeria and soon after they existed at Malaga, Seville, Granada, Balza, Murcia and Alicante also. One of the earliest of their products that survives is the so-called 'Veil of Hisham' (*Ill. 78*), now in the Academy of History at Madrid, which is identified by an inscription in fine large-scale kufic letters. But when no inscriptions or historical records are available it is not easy to distinguish the early Spanish work from that executed in Egypt. Only after the tenth century did the Spanish style become more clearly marked.

During these early centuries North Africa enjoyed a considerable degree of independence. Morocco was ruled by the Idrisid kings from 788 to 974, with the capital at Fez, and around 800 an independent dynasty was set up under the Aghlabids in Tunisia, with its capital at Qairawan, which rapidly became one of the holiest cities of Islam. Its famous mosque was founded by Hisham in 724, and the

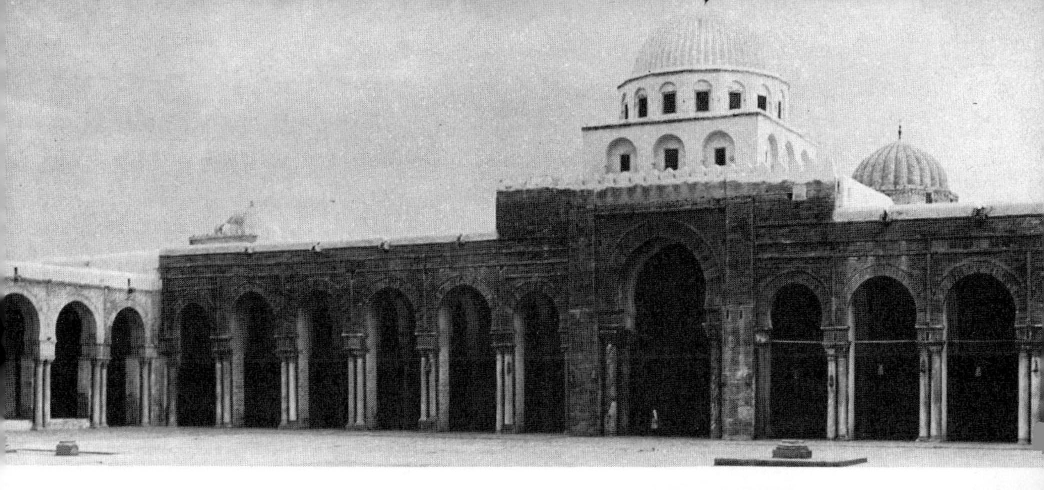

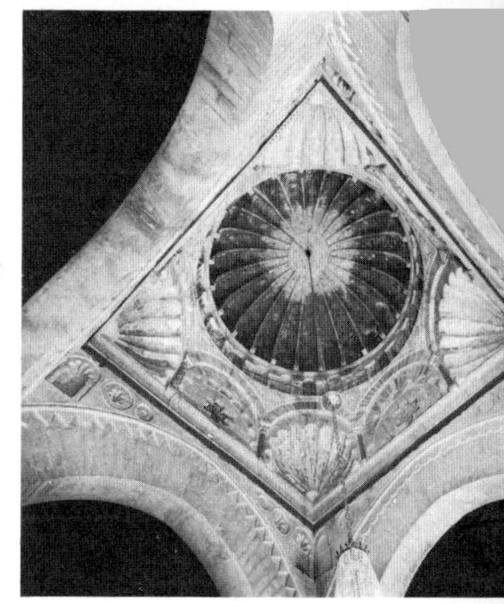

79, 80, 81 The Great Mosque at Qairawan, Tunisia. The plan was laid out in 836 by Ziyadat Allah on the site of an earlier mosque. The courtyard (*Ill. 81*), paved with marble, is irregular. The pointed arches of the court probably represent part of the reconstruction done in 862. The lowest part of the minaret (*Ill. 81*) is dated to 724, but the upper portions are of the same period as the courtyard and most of the rest of the mosque, including the dome above the mihrab (*Ill. 80*)

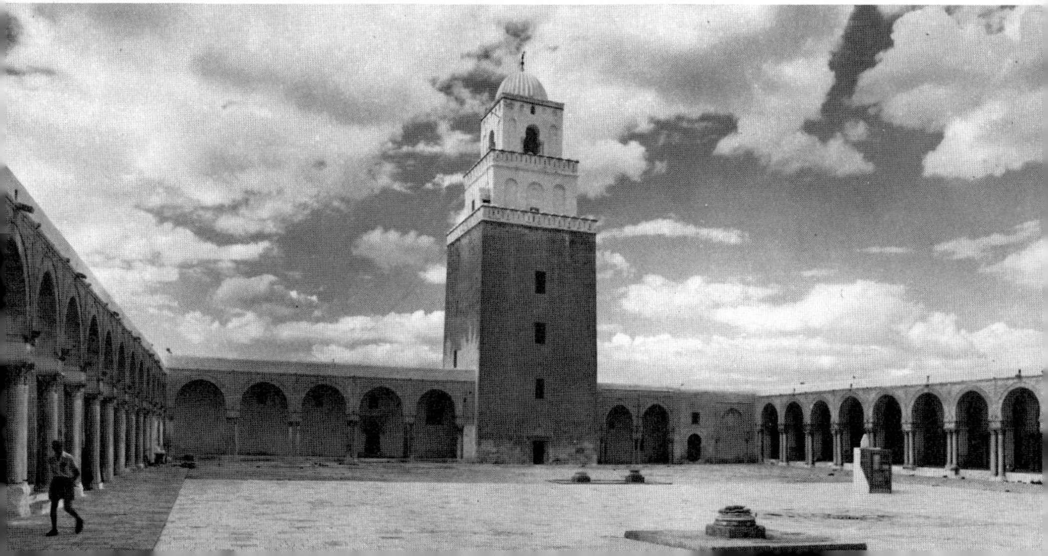

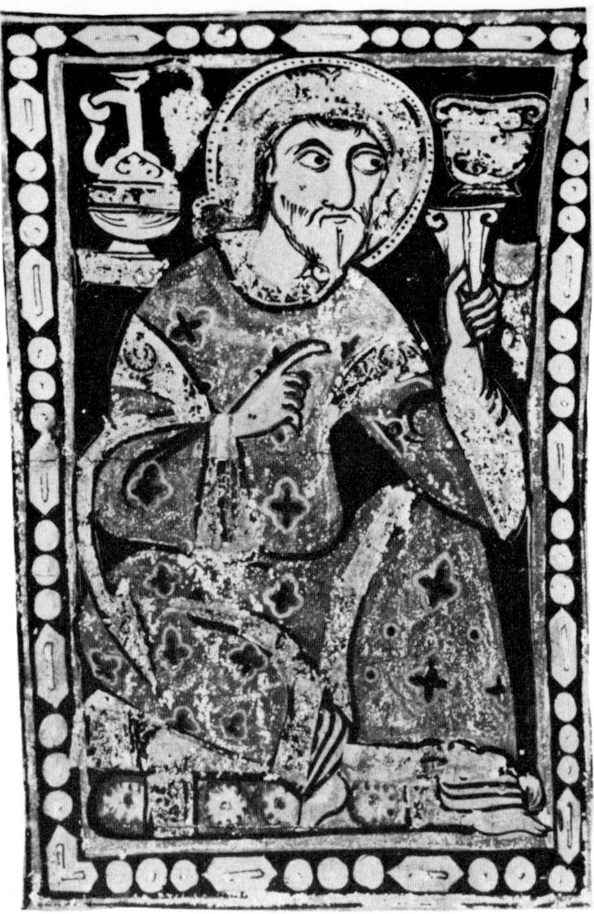

82 Detail from the painted ceiling of the Palatine Chapel at Palermo. 1154. The chapel was built for the Norman king, Roger, between 1132 and 1140 in the Byzantine style, but the ceiling is wholly Islamic and represents the heritage of the island's connections with Egypt from 902 until 1061

three-storeyed minaret (*Ill. 81*) dates in part at least from this period, though the earliest parts of the mosque itself and the layout of its plan belong to 836. The work of this century also includes the famous tiled mihrab and carved wood mimbar or pulpit which have already been mentioned (see p. 43). They are probably to be dated to 862, as are the pointed and horseshoe arches (*Ill. 79*) of the arcades and the dome in front of the mihrab (*Ill. 80*), which recalls Umayyad work in Syria. A few of the capitals belong to this period also, but most are earlier ones re-used. The mosque was severely damaged when the town was sacked in 1054, but it was restored then and on more than one subsequent occasion, notably in 1294, when the spectacular gates were added.

At Tunis itself two important mosques were set up under the rule of this same dynasty (800–909), that of Sidi Okbar, restored by Ziyadat Allah in the early ninth century, and that of Zaytun, also rebuilt in the ninth century. There is also an important mosque at Sousse dating from 850.

In 902 the Aghlabids captured Sicily, which thereafter became a Muslim outpost and an important centre for the production of textiles and ivory carving, though we cannot associate any fine pottery with the island and no mosques of importance survive there. But the link with Egypt was more significant than that with Tunisia, for in 909 the Fatimids came into power at Qairawan and later established themselves in Egypt. Sicily became loosely connected with Egypt, and Arab control of the island really only ended with its conquest by the Normans in 1061. Even then contacts were maintained, and the ceiling of the Palatine Chapel at Palermo, painted in 1154, is an essentially Fatimid work (*Ill. 82*). Its paintings may be compared with some perhaps a century earlier recently discovered in a bath building near Cairo (*Ill. 83*) and now in the Museum of Islamic Art there.

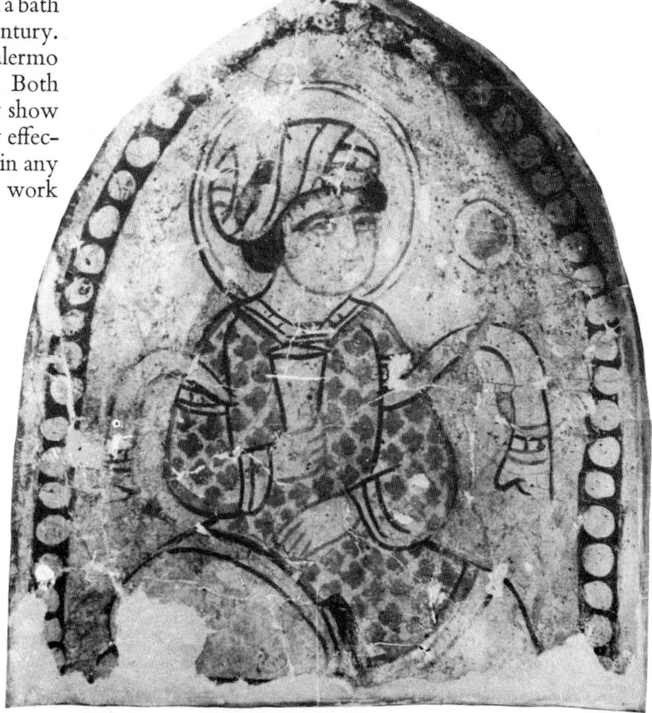

83 Wall-painting from a bath near Cairo. Eleventh century. The style of the Palermo ceiling is similar to it. Both are interesting for they show that there was no very effective ban on figural art, in any case so far as secular work was concerned

Though Egypt was one of the first areas to be conquered by Islam, and though there are records that mosques and other buildings were founded by the governors who represented the Umayyad caliphs there, nothing now survives from those early years. Indeed, although the great mosque of Amr at Fostat was founded at the time, there is no part of it that can be dated to before 827, when its size was doubled at the orders of the Abbasid Caliph al-Mamun, and there are only a few small areas of masonry that can be assigned even to that date, for most of the building, as it stands today, is to be associated with a restoration accomplished in 1407 and much of the actual construction is as late as the nineteenth century. The mosque of Ibn Tulun (*c.* 868) must, as we have shown, be counted as a Mesopotamian work, due to the close association of its patron with Abbasid Mesopotamia. But the more or less contemporary Nilometer (861) (*Ill. 84*) is wholly Egyptian and retains its original form. Its style is already distinctive from anything of the same age elsewhere, and we find there stone masonry of great excellence and precision which heralds that of the later Cairene mosques. A very clearly marked style of low-relief carving, quite different from that of the stuccos of Ibn Tulun's mosque, was used for its ornament; the pointed arch was already fully developed, in a form quite distinct from the elliptical type that was used at an early date in Persia. True pointed arches had, however, already been used in Syria and Palestine, as in the cistern at Ramlah (789). Indeed, though the mosque of Ibn Tulun was basically Mesopotamian and though

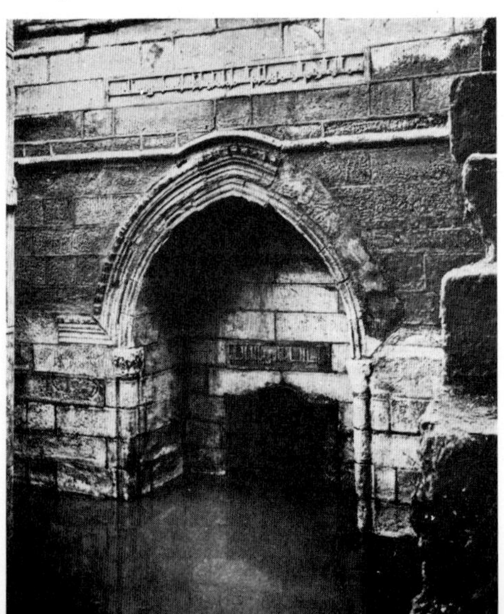

84 The Nilometer, Rhoda Island, Cairo. 861–2. The use of pointed arches here, at a very early date, may be noted. Its importance was first recognized and it was first adequately photographed by Professor Creswell

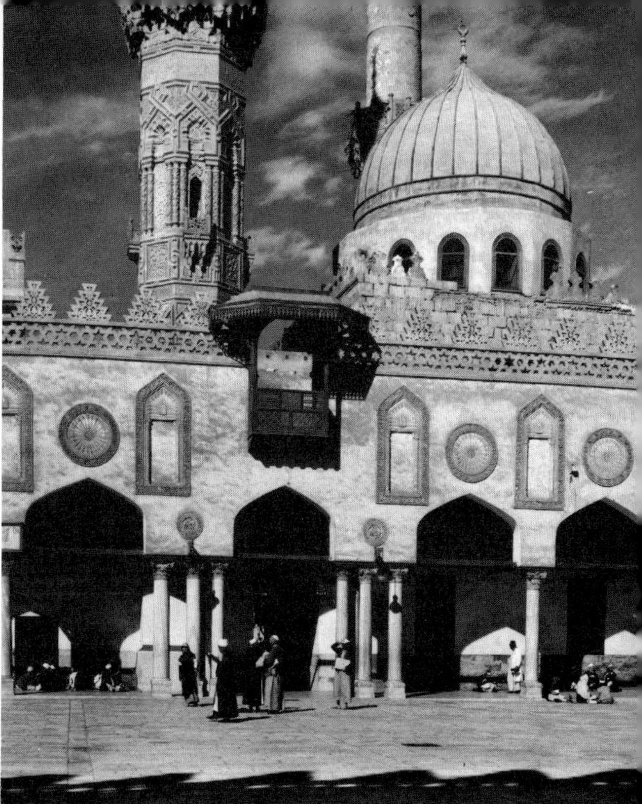

85 The mosque of al-Azhar, Cairo. The mosque was founded in 970 and is one of the earliest and finest examples of the Egyptian style in Islamic architecture. It has, however, undergone numerous alterations

political relationships with Mesopotamia were close during the second half of the ninth century, cultural links between Egypt and Syria were even closer. When once he had established himself as independent ruler of Egypt, Ibn Tulun soon assumed control of the whole area as far north as Antioch.

The Tulunids remained in power until 905, but after that date Egypt was once more brought under the sway of the Abbasids for a time, and it was not really until about 970, when the city of Cairo was founded near to the old Fostat as the capital of the new Fatimid dynasty, that Egypt became truly independent. The Fatimid dynasty was to survive until 1171, and though the sultans of the dynasty were not always very successful or admirable, the two centuries of their rule were from the artistic point of view perhaps the most glorious in Egyptian history. During this period there was a great deal of building, and it was a Fatimid patron who was responsible for the famous mosque of al-Azhar (*Ill.85*), founded about 970, though

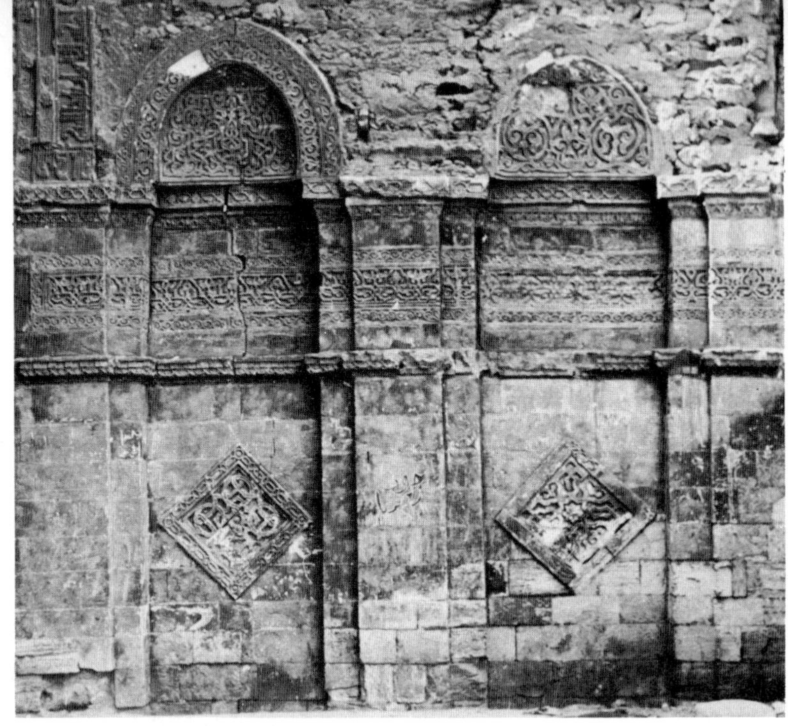

86 Façade of the mosque of al-Hakim, Cairo. 990–1013. The stone carving to the north of the entrance is especially fine. To some extent it follows the style of the earlier stuccos

there have been various additions since, notably that of the main gate in the twelfth century. The central portion of the sanctuary is, however, original, as is the decoration in low-relief stucco work, which represents a development from the style of that used by Ibn Tulun. The wooden door of the mosque, now in the Museum of Islamic Art (*Ill. 87*), was presented by al-Hakim in 1010, and shows something of the same rather rounded manner as the stuccos; the stone work, both in al-Azhar's and in al-Hakim's mosque (*Ill. 86*) which was built between 990 and 1013, is rather more monumental. Al-Hakim's mosque has a large court and a fine, though small, brick dome over the mihrab, probably original, though most of the rest of the building is to be assigned to a period of reconstruction under Beybars.

Several other important mosques were built under Fatimid patronage, notably that of al-Mustansir (1036–94), one of the most active patrons of the dynasty, but there is no finer example of the art of this

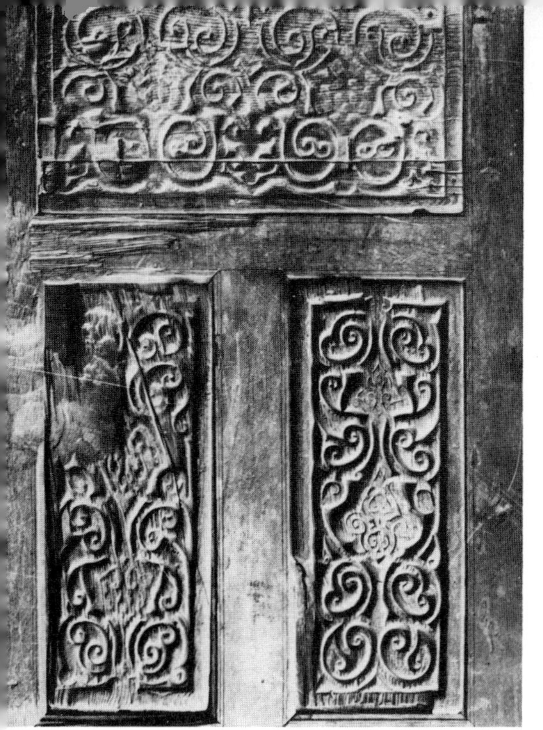

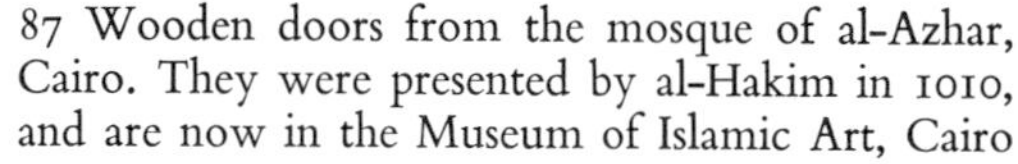

87 Wooden doors from the mosque of al-Azhar, Cairo. They were presented by al-Hakim in 1010, and are now in the Museum of Islamic Art, Cairo

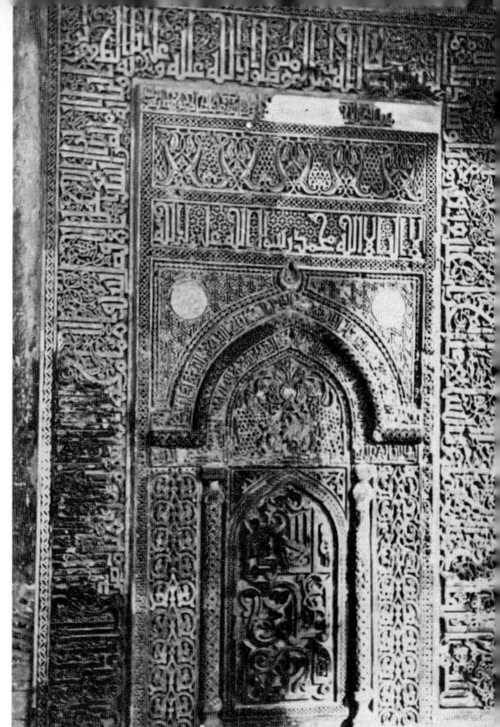

88 The mihrab of al-Afdal in the mosque of Ibn Tulun, Cairo. 1904. It is a work of great beauty, and worthy of a place in this building

age than the stucco mihrab which was added to the mosque of Ibn Tulun in 1094–it is known as the Mihrab of al-Afdal (*Ill. 88*), and served as the prototype for a great deal of carving in later times.

Secular work of the period was no less superb, for it was during the last quarter of the eleventh century that the fortifications of the city were re erected in stone and that the magnificent gates were built, of which the Bab el-Futuh is perhaps the finest (*Ill. 89*). Their construction was no doubt stimulated by the capture of Jerusalem by the Seljuks in 1071, and the rulers must have felt all the more content with these strong defences when soon after a new foe appeared on the scene in the guise of the Crusaders, who entered Jerusalem in 1099. The fine stone masonry, the pointed arches, the elaborate voussoirs and the defensive conception of these structures all represent developments which were to follow in Romanesque and Gothic architecture a generation or so later. Palaces were no

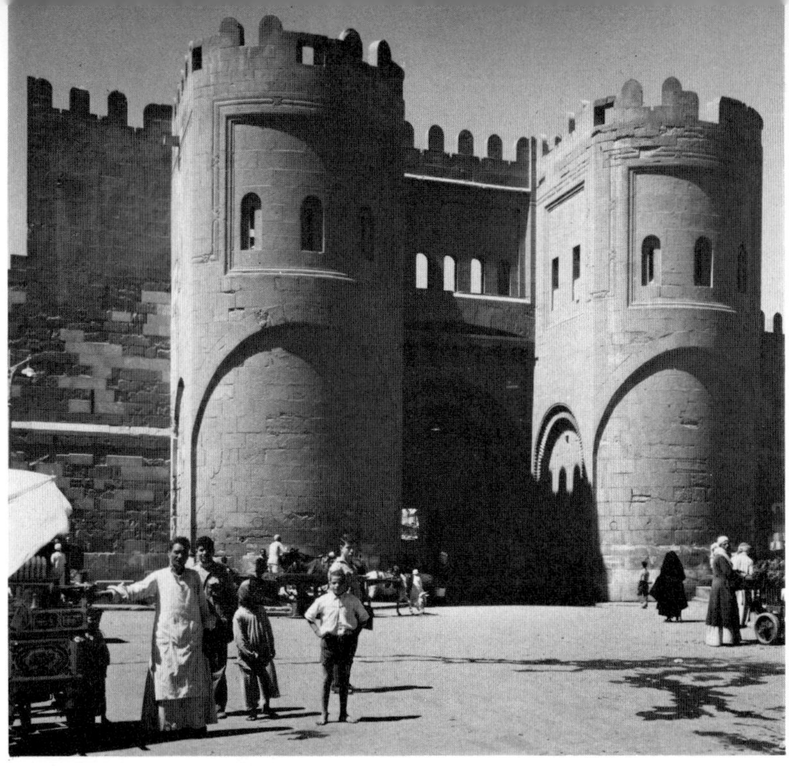

89 The Bab el-Futuh, Cairo. The gate forms part of the impressive fortifications erected during the last quarter of the eleventh century. These embody various features which were later taken to the West by the Crusaders

doubt important also; ruins of some, as at Mahdia, have been excavated in other parts of North Africa.

Production of the arts on a minor scale was no less important than developments in architecture and good work was done in pottery, even more so perhaps in the sphere of textile weaving. Very good carvings in ivory and wood and fine works in metal were also produced. But perhaps most outstanding of all were a series of very distinctive rock-crystal ewers decorated with designs of birds or fantastic animals in a bold, extremely effective style (*Ill. 90*). Some of these found their way to the West, where they have been preserved in cathedral treasuries ever since. The records state that work of the type was done at Basra, but all the examples that have survived – some 170 are recorded – are Egyptian. Fragments bearing similar high-relief decorations which were found during the Samarra excavations were actually of cut glass, not crystal. In addition to scrolls, birds and animals of a very Sassanian type, these vessels sometimes bear inscriptions also. In three cases these inscriptions provide dates; one vessel, in St Mark's Treasury at Venice, is of the tenth and the others are of the eleventh century.

The earliest examples of Islamic pottery that we know from Egypt would appear to have been imported from Mesopotamia, but the local potters soon turned to the new styles and the importance of the art grew with the rise of the Fatimids. We know of it mainly from fragments; whereas in Persia excavations have produced large numbers of complete vessels, finds of whole pots in Egypt have been few and far between, though the rubbish-heaps of Fostat have produced literally hundreds of pieces, especially the bases of bowls. Vessels with a white body and an incised decoration under alkaline glazes appear to have served in more day-to-day needs, but lustre was also developed at an early date.

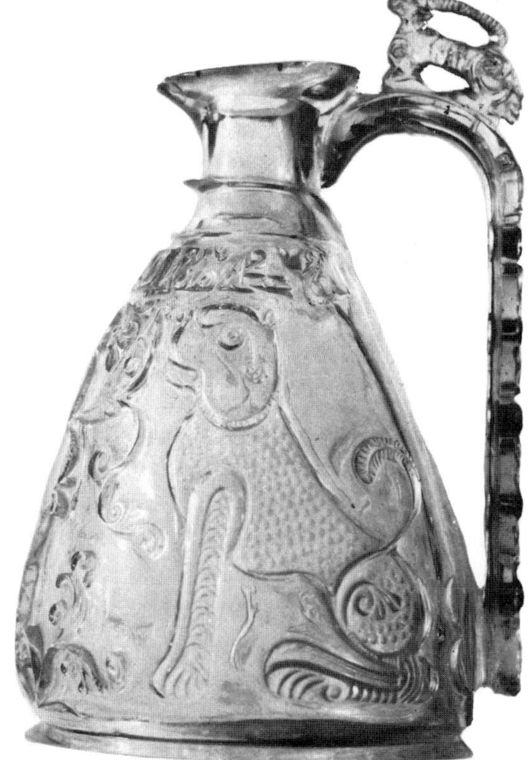

90 Ewer of rock crystal inscribed with the name of Caliph al-Aziz. Rock-crystal ewers with carved decoration of scrolls and fantastic animals constituted one of the most important products of Fatimid art. Many subsequently found their way into cathedral treasuries in the West

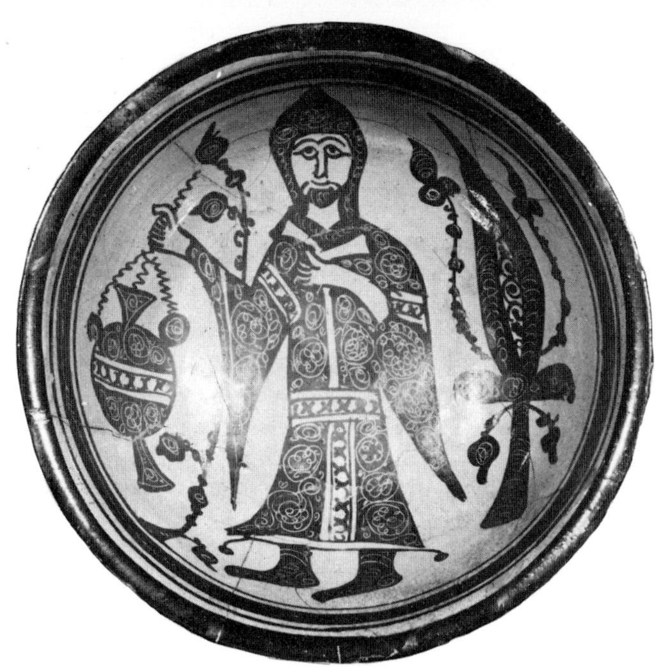

91 Bowl of lustre ware. It is signed by a potter named Sa'ad, who was presumably a Muslim, though the design depicts a Christian priest swinging a censer. First half of the twelfth century

Though the craftsmanship was less skilful than in Mesopotamia and Persia, the bodies coarser and more sandy, and the shapes somewhat lacking in refinement, the lustre was of high quality and the designs skilful and varied. Formal patterns, fish and human figures of a very Hellenistic character, were favoured, and flowing calligraphic patterns were considerably developed. Two types are known, one monochrome, the other polychrome, and the technique was spoken of in especially glowing terms by the traveller Nasr i-Khosrau when he visited Egypt between 1046 and 1050. It would seem that some of the pieces were made for Christian patrons, for Christian subjects appear, and there is a particularly fine example of the early twelfth century in the Victoria and Albert Museum, which bears the figure of a priest swinging a censer (*Ill. 91*). It was signed by the potter Sa'ad, whose work is characterized by a habit of scratching through the lustre ground with a thin point. Another famous potter was called Muslim. If the numerous signatures in Arabic which

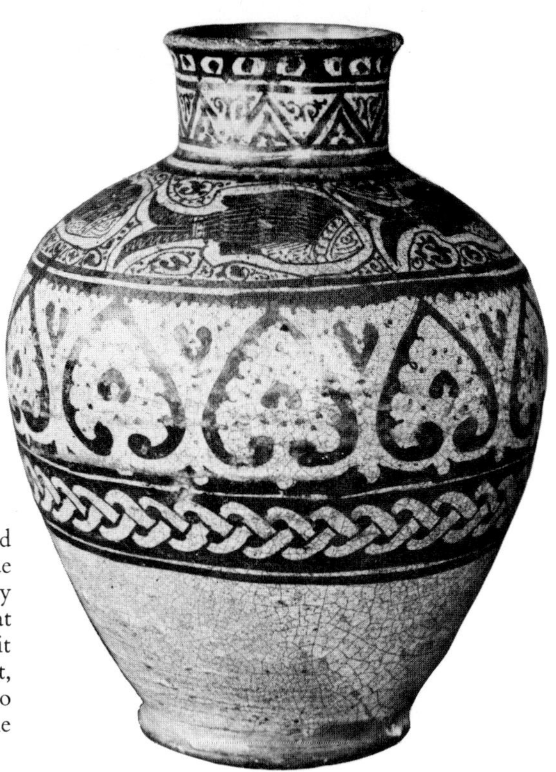

92 Earthenware jar decorated in yellow lustre over an opaque white glaze. Like the majority of the Egyptian ceramics that have come down to us, it was probably made at Fostat, though Butler assigned it to Upper Egypt. First half of the twelfth century

appear on the bases of fragmentary bowls from Fostat are to be taken as a guide, it would seem that the potters were mostly Arabs.

The most important kilns were situated in the neighbourhood of Cairo, but it is possible that work was done in Upper Egypt also, and a particularly fine vase with a decoration in gold lustre, also in the Victoria and Albert Museum (*Ill. 92*), has been attributed to that area by Butler; his dating to the ninth or tenth century is, however, too early. With the end of the Fatimid dynasty in 1171 the centre of production moved to Damascus and links with Raqqa which had perhaps existed in very early times were renewed. But one type remained important in Egypt, the unglazed water jugs with perforated filters in the necks, often of very ornate character.

If the pottery of the Fatimid age is mostly fairly distinctive and easy to recognize as Egyptian, the same can hardly be said of the metalwork, for incense burners, aquamaniles and other vessels which are closely akin to the Persian ones seem to have been made in quite large quantities both in Syria and Egypt. The largest and most spectacular of these incense burners is in the form of a gryphon and is now preserved in the Campo Santo at Pisa (*Ill. 93*). The birds and animals whose forms these vessels take are similar to those carved on the rock-crystal jugs, and belong to the old animal repertory of the Near East so popular in all the arts from Sassanian times onwards. Sometimes they appear again on the textiles, but in general inscriptions were tending to come into favour in Egypt as a decoration for the woven stuffs rather than figural patterns. Though script was everywhere being developed as an ornament, it was probably never so popular as it was in Egypt, where it soon became the distinguishing feature not only of Egyptian textile weaving, but also of embroidery.

Egypt had been a very important centre of the textile industry since Pharaonic times, though it is possible that the fact that more has been preserved there, due to the dry climate, than elsewhere has led to something of an over-estimation of the role of the Egyptian looms as against those of Syria, Persia or the Byzantine world. Be that as it may, there is a mass of material which is to be classed as Coptic, even if it is not all Christian, and a good deal also that was produced for Muslim patrons, whatever may have been the religion of the workmen who made the textiles. The typical Coptic stuffs, with small-scale figural designs usually depicting Christian scenes, continued to be produced long after the Islamic conquest, and many of the examples in our Western museums were probably executed during the days of the Fatimid caliphate. It is, however, the purely Islamic textiles that concern us here and not the Coptic ones, and many of them were not only of great technical excellence but also of very great beauty. Both silks and linens were in favour for high-class work, and they were probably made at a number of different centres. Akhmin, which had been important in early times, was certainly one of them. Some of the designs are purely decorative, some are figural, and some consist only of inscriptions, which in many instances are most beautiful, because of their delicacy and the reticent balance of the designs. Also they are useful for they often contain names and so help to date the textiles. Silver thread played a significant part, and its presence serves to distinguish a group

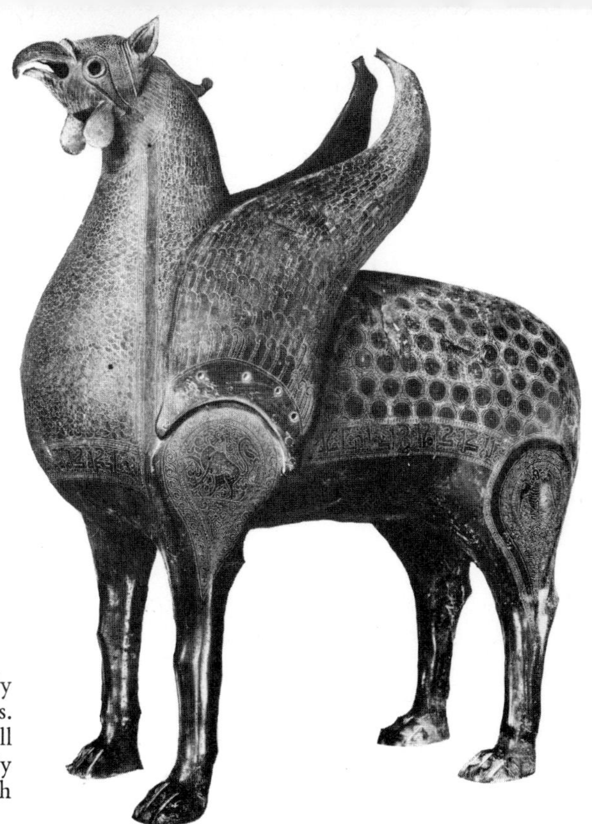

93 Bronze gryphon probably made in Egypt in Fatimid times. In style it is akin to the small incense burners, but it is actually almost a metre high. Eleventh century

usually known as the 'Tiraz' stuffs. Like the rock-crystal ewers, these textiles, even when they bore inscriptions giving the name of a caliph of Islam or a dedication to Allah, often found their way into Western cathedral treasuries, where they have been preserved ever since. The so-called 'Veil of St Anne' at Vaucluse may be noted (*Ill. 94*), because it bears an inscription stating that it was made at Damietta on the Nile Delta in 906/7.

In addition to the woven stuffs, which were of great importance, textiles with a pattern produced by resist-dyeing were also made. The technique, which had been in use since late classical times, consisted of covering parts of the material with a resist, such as wax, and then dipping it into a dye, so that the design was produced either in the dye colour or by its absence, as the case might be. Embroideries, characterized by the richness and multiplicity of the colours used, were also important from Fatimid times onwards.

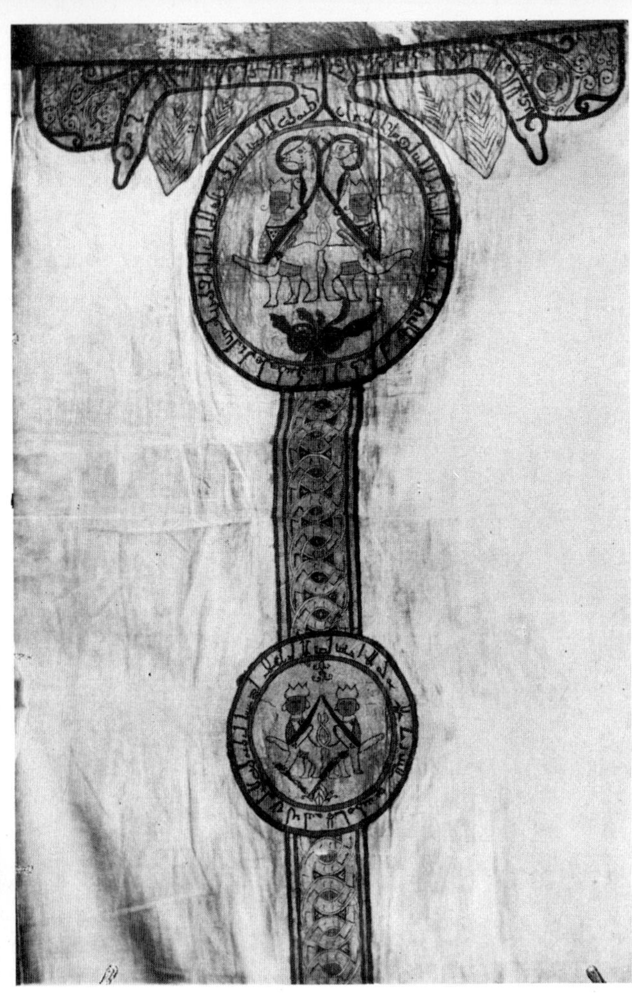

94 Textile known as 'The Veil of St Anne', now at Vaucluse. It is actually a typical Fatimid work, and is dated by an inscription to 906/907

It is very likely that painting also grew in importance under Fatimid patronage, for a few fragments of papyri bearing pictures have been unearthed from the rubbish dumps at Fostat; most of them are now in the Archduke Rainer Collection in Vienna. More recently scientific excavations not far from Cairo have disclosed fragmentary wall-paintings in the ruins of a bath building (*Ill. 83*) which are to be attributed to the eleventh century. Two drawings in the Museum of Islamic Art at Cairo may also be noted, one of which at least appears to be a sketch for a ceramic decoration; they too are to be assigned to the eleventh century.

Mesopotamia: Tenth to Thirteenth centuries

The period of Samarra's supremacy (836–83), so far as art was concerned, was one of the most brilliant in Islamic history; at no time before had so much been built in so short a space of time or had such elaborate decorations been devoted to so large a number of houses as well as to mosques and palaces. As one wanders over this immense field of ruins one can but marvel at the age which was responsible for such lavishness and at the callous way in which the city was deserted almost as rapidly as it had been constructed. In 883 Baghdad once more became the capital, and remained so until it was sacked by the Mongols in 1258. But it would seem that the period between its reinstitution and its sack saw nothing like the same profusion of expenditure as the earlier age. Indeed, the power of the Abbasid caliphs was at this time nothing like as great as it had been, for they had become virtually puppets in the hands of their ministers the Buvayhids, and though much was no doubt sponsored in the arts and there was certainly a good deal of building, the ruins of old Baghdad are inaccessible and no other large city of the period has so far been excavated in Mesopotamia.

Curiously enough, the most important work of art that has come down to us from these years that can be assigned to Baghdad with certainty is of the most fragile of all materials – paper. It is a koran now in the Chester Beatty Collection which was copied and decorated in Baghdad in the year 1000 (*Ill. 96*). It is written in very fine *naskh* lettering, and on quite a number of folios there are ornamental frames for the text which take the form of octagonal or similar compartments. At the sides of the pages are projections of stylized floral form, like the motifs which appear on some of the Sassanian silver plates. The geometric ornament, however, savours of the art of Central Asia, which was later to be so effectively developed by the Seljuks in the tile mosaics of their mosques in Asia

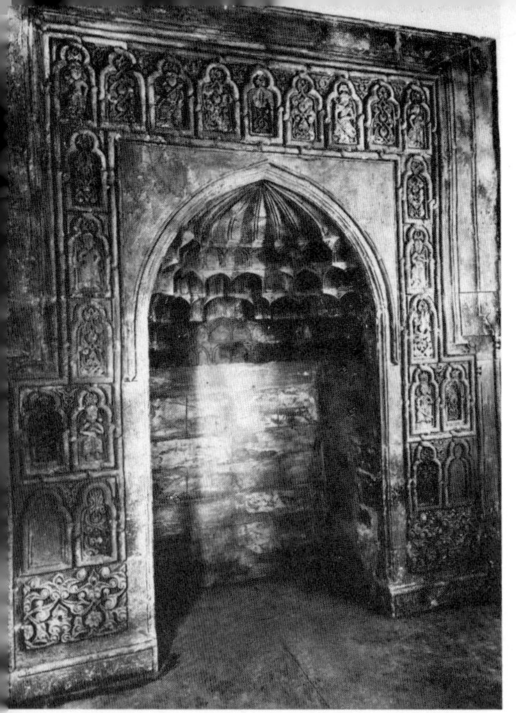

95 Stone carvings with human figures were common in churches in the Mosul region, but it is exceptional to find human figures used in the decoration of a mihrab. Eleventh century

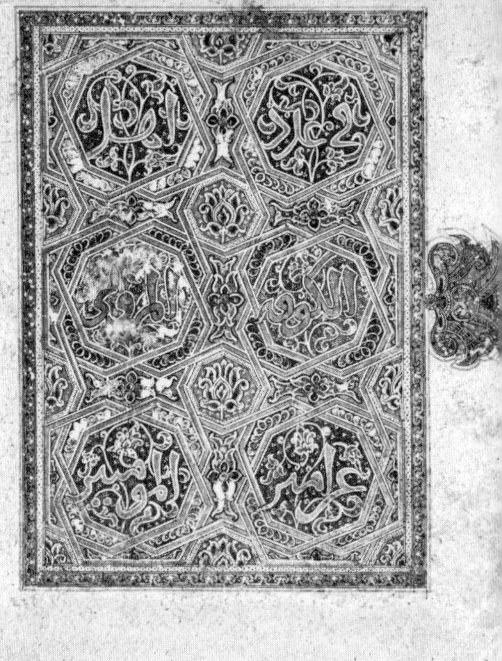

96 Leaf from a manuscript of the koran painted at Baghdad about 1000, probably by a calligrapher named Ali ibn-Hilal, showing the octagonal frames for the fine *naskh* lettering

Minor. Illuminations of a similar geometric character were to be used in numerous later korans, but few are as majestic as this early example, which is also the first book that can be assigned to Baghdad, a city which was later to become important in the story of secular book illustration.

We know rather more about the art of the north of Mesopotamia than about that of the south, however, for there good stone was available, and even if no excavations have been made and not much survives in the way of architecture, there is quite a lot of stone sculpture lying above ground. It was all carved in an independent, individual style. A series of extremely interesting mihrabs are available to illustrate it; some of them are now installed in the old Abbasid palace at Baghdad which has been turned into a museum, others are still *in situ* in Mosul and its region. On one of the most interesting mihrabs, dating from the twelfth century, human figures have quite a part to play in the decoration (*Ill. 95*). Attention may also be called to the stone sculptures which adorn the Armenian cathedral on the Island of Achthamar on Lake Van, built between 904 and 938 for, as Professor Otto-Dorn has shown, they reproduce many of the motifs that were used in the Samarra wall-paintings. Contacts between Armenia and northern Mesopotamia were close, and were maintained for some centuries; some two hundred years later Badr ad-din Lulu, ruler of Mosul and its region from 1233 to 1259, though a Muslim, was actually an Armenian by birth.

Motifs that are allied both to the Samarra paintings and to the sculptures of Achthamar are also to be found on ivory carvings done in Mesopotamia between the tenth and the twelfth centuries; the most important of them are the drinking horns, known as oliphants, of which there is a particularly fine example in the Royal Scottish Museum at Edinburgh (*Ill. 97*). Even in the tenth century the Mosul area stood to some extent apart, for it was under the control of the Hamdanids from 929 to 991 who were of the Shia persuasion and maintained themselves in independence through the days of Abbasid decline. Later it became a more or less independent emirate.

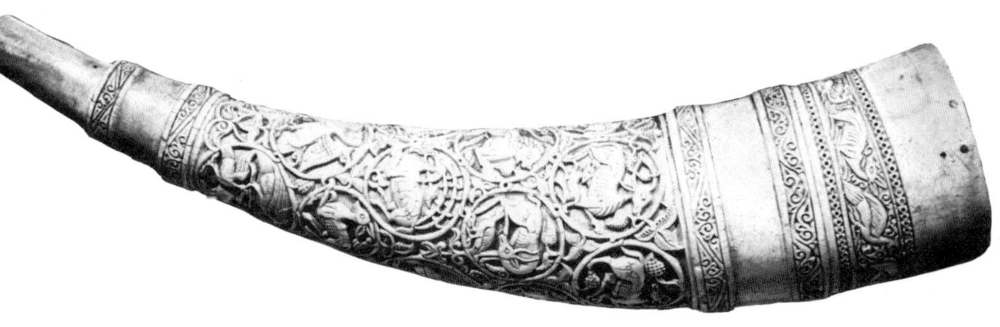

97 Ivory oliphant or drinking horn. These great horns seem to have been especially common in Mesopotamia. Eleventh century

In the middle of the eleventh century Baghdad was captured by the Seljuks, and their arrival marked a continuation of the caliphs' eclipse as effective rulers, though their political power was to revive in the following century. The names of three of the Seljuks stand out, Tügrül Beg, the conqueror of Baghdad, Alp Arslan (1063–72) who penetrated into Asia Minor, and Malik Shah (1072–92). Alp Arslan is commemorated for us by a lovely silver plate which was made for him in 1066; it is now at Boston (*Ill. 99*). The most important figure of this age, however, was the grand vizier, the Nizam al-Mulk, who virtually controlled all the affairs of the state until his death in 1092. He was a truly remarkable personality: learned, balanced, a keen supporter of literature and patron of the arts, in Persia as well as in Iraq. In Persia, for example, he was responsible for the lovely domed chambers (*Ill. 56*) and for other parts of the great Masjid-i-Jami at Isfahan which were finished in 1121/22. It was he too who set the state on a sound basis and restored the fortunes and reputation of its capital Baghdad, which was to stand firm until the arrival of the Mongols soon after the middle of the thirteenth century. This was no mean task, for it was an age of turmoil and disorder for western Islam which began with the conquest of Jerusalem in 1099 and only ended with the victories of Saladin around 1170.

Although firmly dated works are rare, it may be concluded that production in every sphere continued in Mesopotamia during the tenth and eleventh centuries, but that the differentiation between Mesopotamian and Persian products became less considerable. In the present state of our knowledge a distinct Mesopotamian school is only to be distinguished towards the end of the twelfth century, and this primarily with regard to miniature painting. Then there were produced throughout Mesopotamia a number of secular book illustrations of really outstanding quality; they may be grouped together under the heading 'Mesopotamian school'. Some of them can be assigned to Baghdad, others are to be attributed to Mosul and its region, and it would seem that there were also important workshops at Basra and Kufa, as well as at certain places in Upper Mesopotamia, like Diyarbakir, and in northern Syria, in the region of

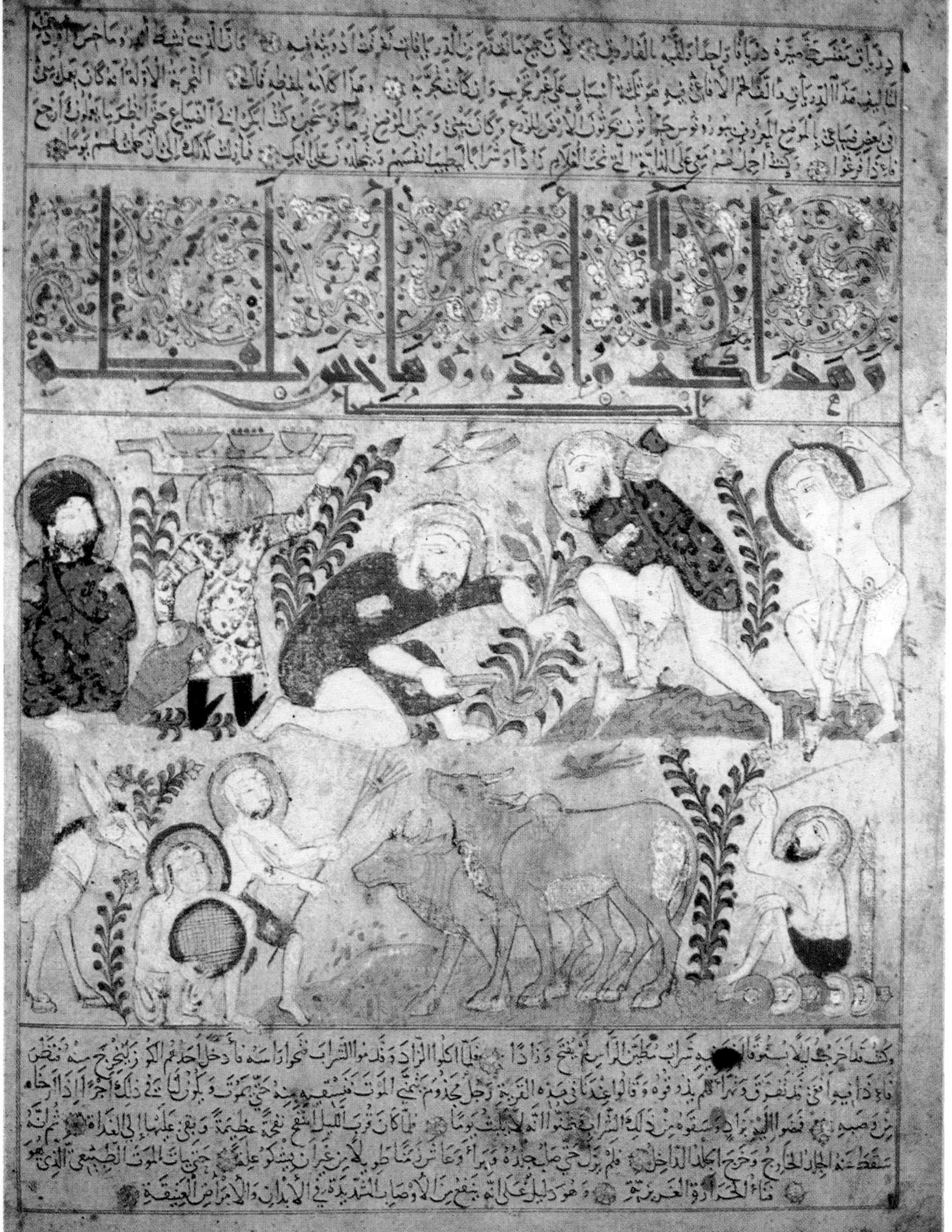

98 A page from the 'Book of Antidotes' showing labourers at work on the cultivation of plants which were grown for their medical properties. Medical manuscripts were much valued in Iraq and quite a number dating from the early thirteenth century have survived. Probably northern Iraq, 1199

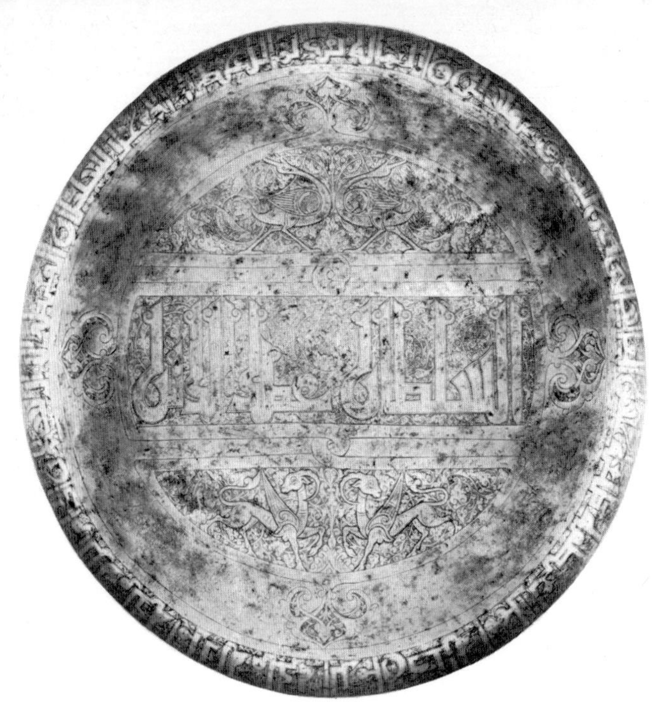

99 Silver dish made for the Seljuk sultan, Alp Arslan, in the year 1066. The linear design is typical of the Seljuk age and its restraint and balance distinguishes the dish as a work of outstanding quality

Aleppo. It is not always very easy to tell the products of the different centres apart.

The types of book that were illustrated were comparatively limited; they comprised medical treatises, books about animals, a few volumes of lyrical poetry and, most important of all, books in which were recorded the adventures of the hero in al-Hariri's so-called *Maqamat* or 'Assemblies'. The examples of this last book are particularly attractive because the subject-matter called for a satirical approach and for a liveliness of portrayal, and the painters of the school were past masters in both these veins.

The earliest of this school that can be definitely dated is a copy of Galen's works now in the Bibliothèque Nationale in Paris. It was copied in 1199 for a certain Mahmud, but unfortunately the colophon does not say where. Its frontispiece (*Ill. 1*) is a truly remarkable work, depicting a figure surrounded by a halo like a crescent moon and framed by a serpent, both motifs which stem from an old Mesopotamian repertory; the serpent was repeated in relief on the lovely Talisman Gate at Baghdad (*Ill. 100*), built in 1221, but unfor-

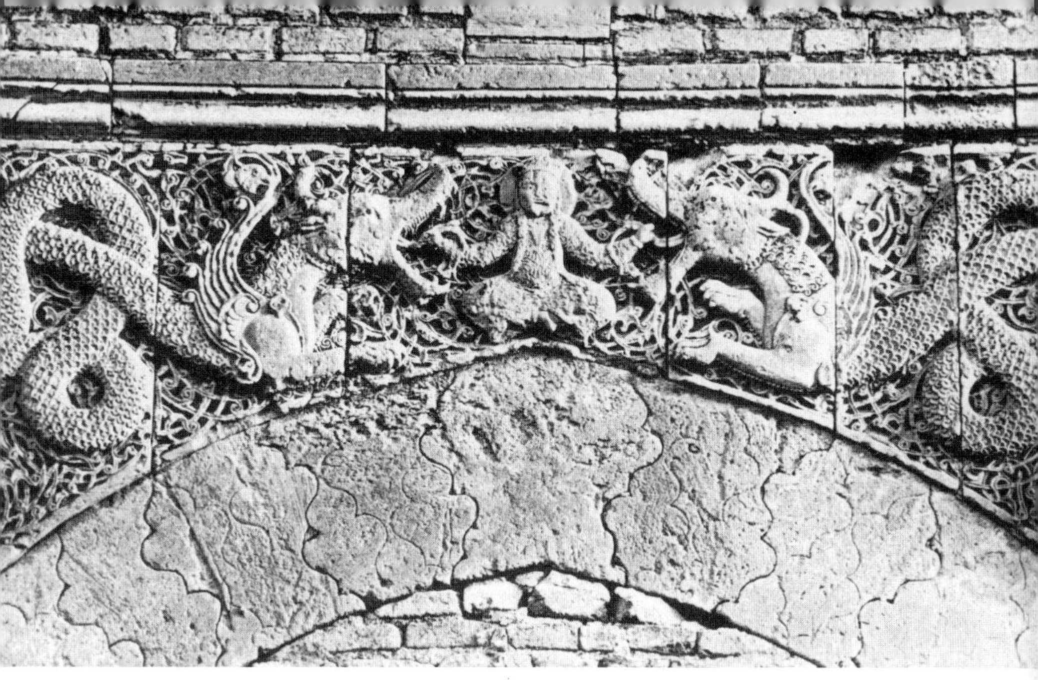

100 Detail of the serpent decoration above the archway of the Talisman Gate at Baghdad, built in 1221. It formed a part of the fortifications of the city, but was blown up in 1917. Part of another gate still survives, but it lacks decoration

tunately blown up in 1917. But there are numerous other illustrations in the book, some concerned with medicines and the method of their preparation, and some with the cultivation of the herbs from which they were made. In some illustrations agricultural labourers are shown at work (*Ill. 98*), and many of the scenes are vivid and delightful, in spite of the two-dimensional convention they follow, according to which all the figures are shown on the same plane and look as if they are silhouetted against an open background. There is another copy of Galen's works at Vienna, closely akin but perhaps rather less spirited; it is probably of slightly later date. Both would seem to have been done at Mosul, for many of the figures are close in style to those of two Syriac gospel books which were illuminated there around 1220; one is in the British Museum (Syr. MS. 7170), and another in the Vatican (Syr. MS. 559).

Another work which is akin and which is also to be assigned to Mosul or its region is a copy of the *Kitab al-Aghani* or 'Book of Songs', copied in 1217. There were originally twenty volumes in this

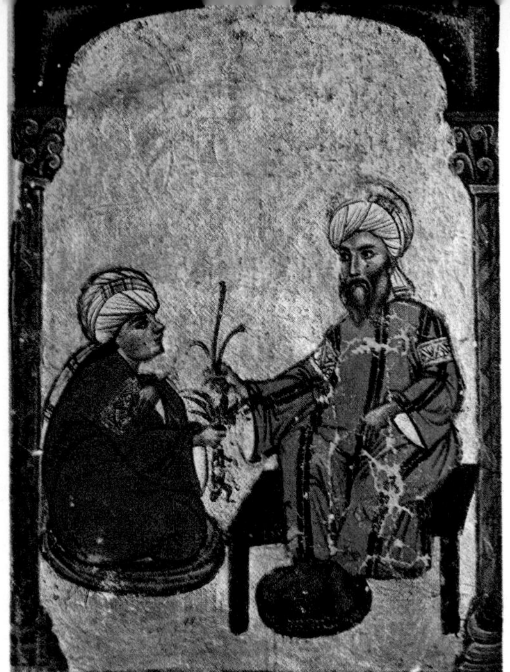

101 Page from *De Materia Medica* of Dioscorides, showing Dioscorides and a student. It was probably made in north Iraq, 1229

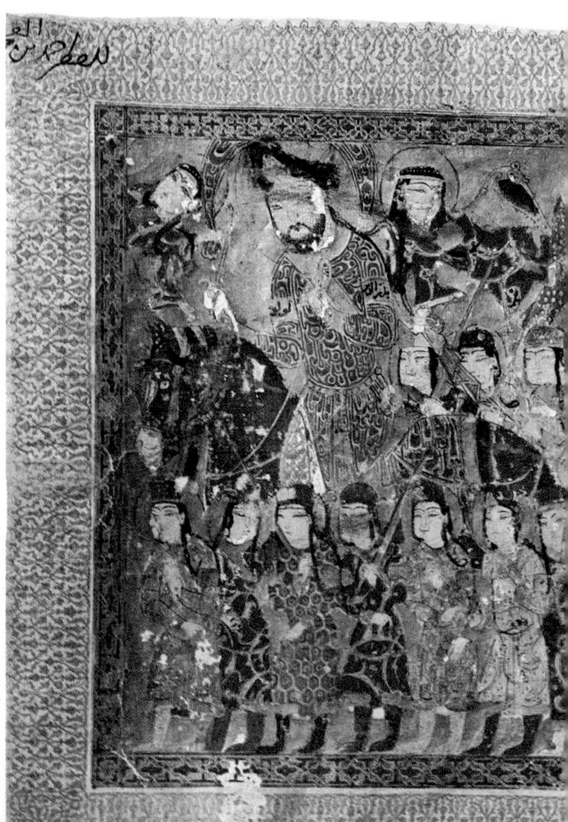

102 Page from an illuminated manuscript known as 'The Book of Songs' of Abu'l Faraj al-Isfahani. There were originally twenty volumes, but only six of this series survive, each with a fine frontispiece

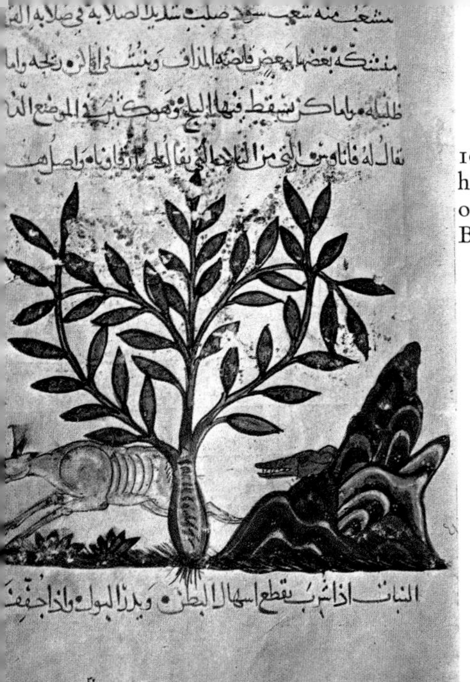

103 (*left*) The plant 'Astraghalus' and a hunting scene. Another page from a copy of *De Materia Medica* of Dioscorides. Baghdàd, 1224

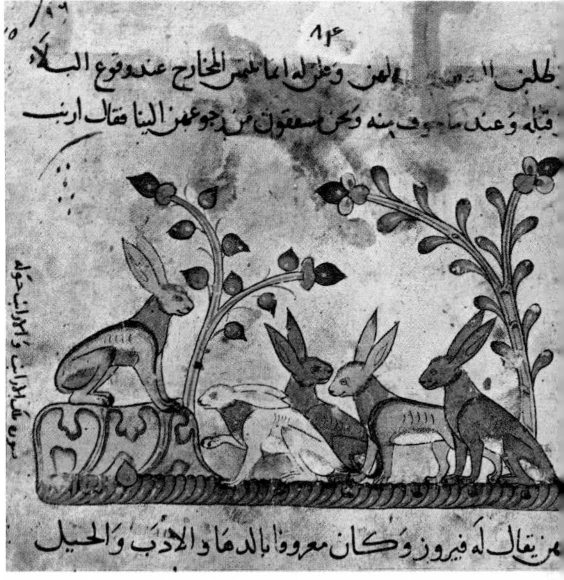

104 (*right*) The king of the hares interviews his subjects, from a copy of the Fables of Bidpai. Although this manuscript is a work of the Mamluk school, it follows closely one illustrated in north Iraq *c.* 1222

set, but only six now survive, one at Copenhagen, two at Cairo and three at Istanbul (*Ill. 102*). Each has one illustration, a frontispiece, which in two volumes represents a mounted figure, in two others the same person is shown enthroned, in another he is approached by two suitors, while in the last a group of females who have been identified as nuns engaged in ritual dances and lustrations are depicted. In every case the work is grand, majestic and impressive, and great attention has been paid to the pattern of the textiles of which the costumes were made, with the result that the effect is at the same time both decorative and monumental.

The style of these paintings may be contrasted with that of those in a copy of the medical treatise of Dioscorides at Istanbul (Ahmed III,

2127) (*Ill. 101*), where the figures have clearly been copied from a Byzantine model. Another copy, now divided between the Aya Sofya Library, Istanbul (No. 3703 – now in Süleymaniye Library) (*Ill. 103*), and a number of private collections, is dated to 1224. It was probably executed at Baghdad – in any case the figures are taller than those in manuscripts executed at Mosul, and more attention has been paid to the modelling of the costumes and less to rendering the decorative patterns that adorned the textiles of which they were made. This is to be seen in those of the illustrations depicting individuals or subjects such as chemists' shops or drug manufacturies; others depict medicinal plants, simply and in two dimensions only, but with considerable realism, while the animals shown with them on some of the pages are similar to those which appear in the animal picture-books.

It is in these that some of the most enchanting of all the miniatures of this school are to be found, especially in the illustration of the Fables of Bidpai (*Kalila wa Dimna*); the finest copy is one in the Bibliothèque Nationale in Paris (MS. arabe 3465) (*Ill. 104*), to be dated to about 1222. It contains as many as ninety-two miniatures, all of them extraordinarily expressive in spite of the wholly two-dimensional approach. In all the pictures the artist seems to have penetrated to the very soul of the animals he is rendering, while the rocks, trees and other accessories are imbued with a strange charm and delight. In these books the subject-matter is in the main confined to animals; in other works the same brilliant powers of characterization were dedicated to the depiction of human beings and to the expression of their emotions.

As stated above, one of the favourite books of the age was that known as the 'Assemblies' (*Maqamat*) of al-Hariri, in which were recounted the adventures of his hero Abu Zayd as-Saruji in various regions and in very diverse circumstances. Three outstandingly important copies of this book survive, all in the Bibliothèque Nationale in Paris although a fourth copy exists in Leningrad and a fifth, very damaged version is in Istanbul. The earliest of them, which is probably to be dated to the early thirteenth century, is known as the St Vaast Hariri (MS. arabe 3929) (*Ill. 105*). Its miniatures are by three distinct hands, but all their work is closely akin. All of them paid considerable attention to pattern. They probably worked in the Mosul area, and certainly owed a considerable debt to the Christian painters of the region who were responsible for the illustrations of the Syriac gospel books mentioned above. The figures throughout have haloes of a Byzantine type, but the style is fundamentally distinct from that of Byzantine art in the narrow sense of the term – that is to say the art of Constantinople and its dependencies – as is clearly shown if the illustrations are compared with those of the volume of Dioscorides at Istanbul mentioned above, where the figures are tall and elegant, the costumes rendered in a classical manner, and the gold backgrounds wholly Byzantine; only the turbans worn by the figures serve to mark the miniatures as Islamic.

The next of the Hariris in the Bibliothèque Nationale (MS. arabe 6094) (*Ill. 106*), which is to be dated to 1222/23, is rather more polished than the earlier St Vaast Hariri and has departed further from a Christian prototype in that none of the personages have haloes. The faces too are rather more Persian and greater attention has been paid to detail. More important still is the fact that the artist was also more concerned with an attempt to set his figures in a three-dimensional background, and this aim is carried further in the last manuscript of the series, the famous Schefer Hariri (MS. arabe 5847) (*Ill. 108*), which is dated to 1237. It is signed by Yahya-ibn Mahmud al-Wasiti, and was certainly done in southern Mesopotamia, probably at Baghdad. The work is of outstanding quality. The figures are extremely expressive, the compositions are often very beautiful in themselves, and the colours are gay, brilliant, and remarkably effective. The rather formal trees, the way in which the figures are confined to two planes, and the nature of the facial types attest its heritage, but there is in some of the pictures, like that of the Eastern Isles (*Ill. 107*), a new complexity, a new outlook, and this page at least is to be counted as marking a very important stage in the development of landscape painting in Islamic art.

Though the manuscript illuminations constitute the most interesting and original products of this age in Mesopotamia, outstanding metal objects were also made, especially in the north. At Innsbruck

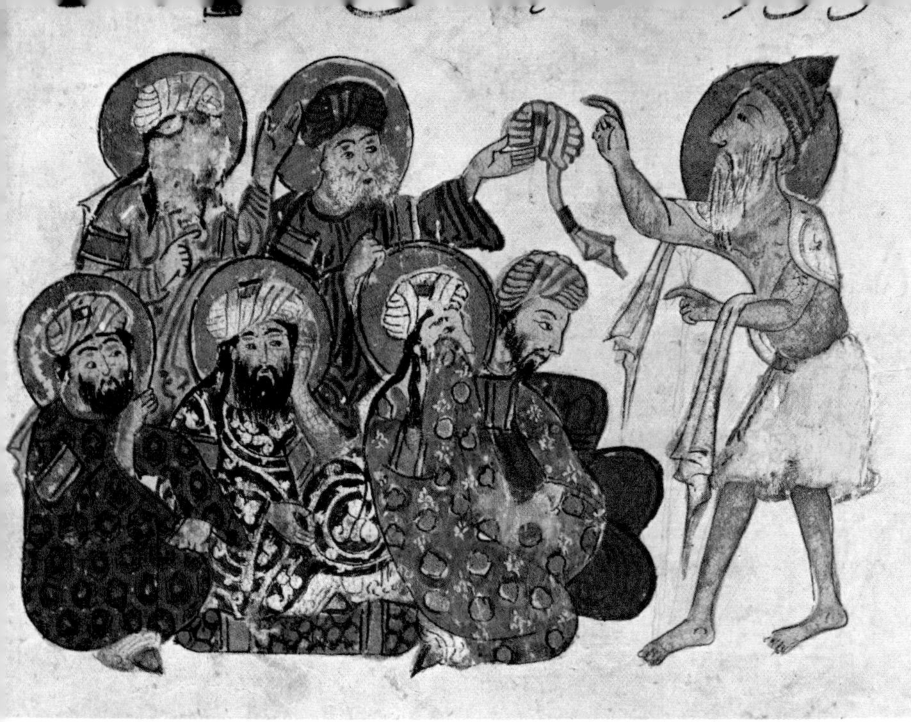

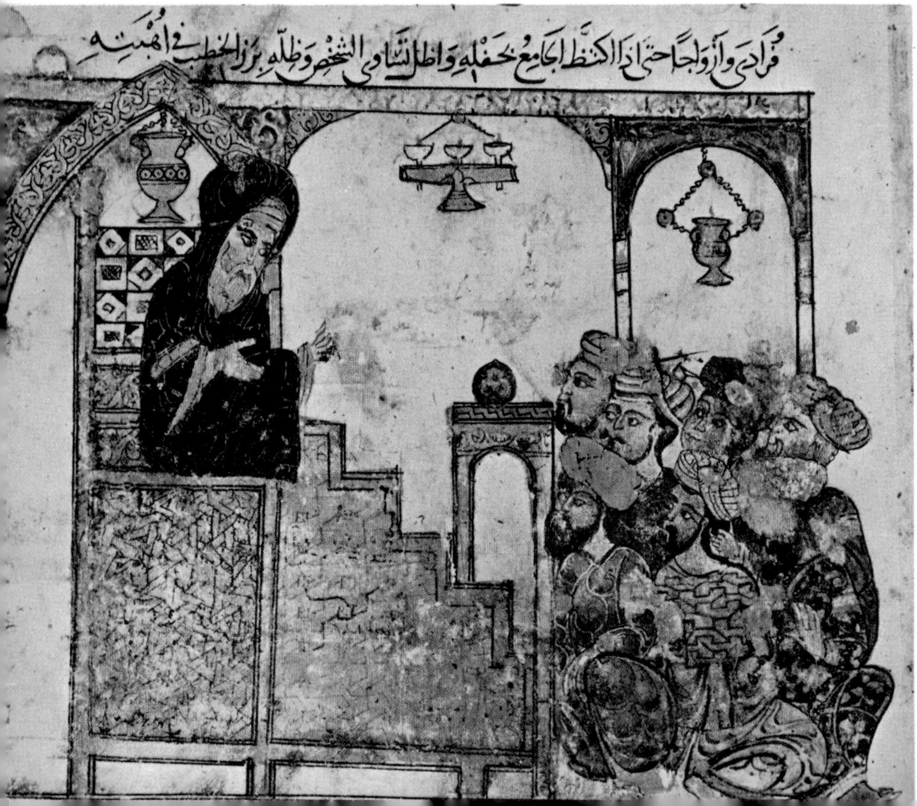

فرادى وازواجا حتى اذا اكتظ الجامع بحفله واظل تساوي الشخص وظله برز الخطيب في اهبته

105 (*above left*) Leaf from a manuscript of the 'Assemblies' of Hariri, known as the St Vaast Hariri. Here Abu Zayd is seen with a half-naked, old man who speaks to him in verse. Late thirteenth century

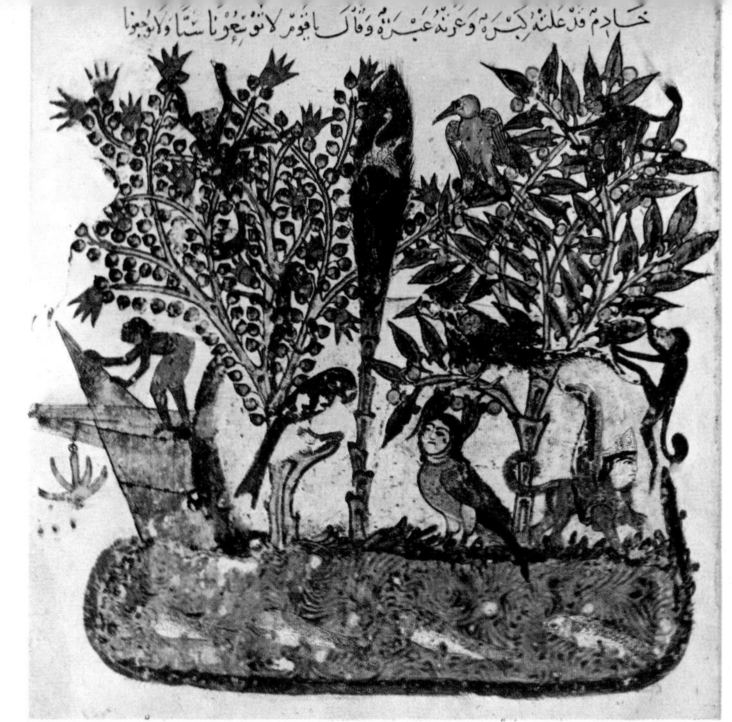

106 (*below left*) Illustration from the 'Assemblies' of Hariri, a sermon in a mosque. This copy is rather more polished and finished than the St Vaast Hariri and was probably written in northern Iraq in 1222/3

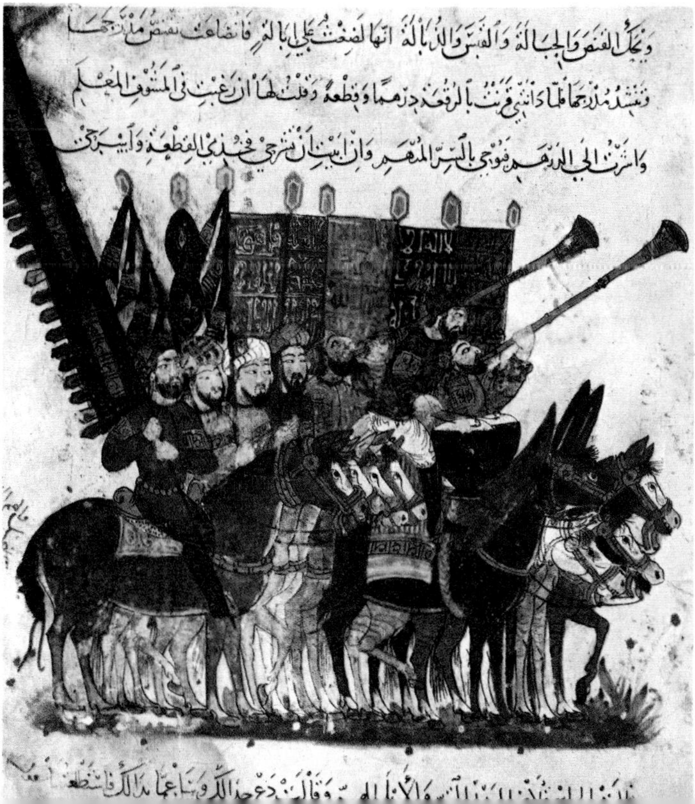

107, 108 (*above right*) The Eastern Isles; (*below right*) The standard bearers of the caliph. Two miniatures from the 'Assemblies' of Hariri, known as the Schefer Hariri. This is probably the finest of all the Hariris. Baghdad, 1237

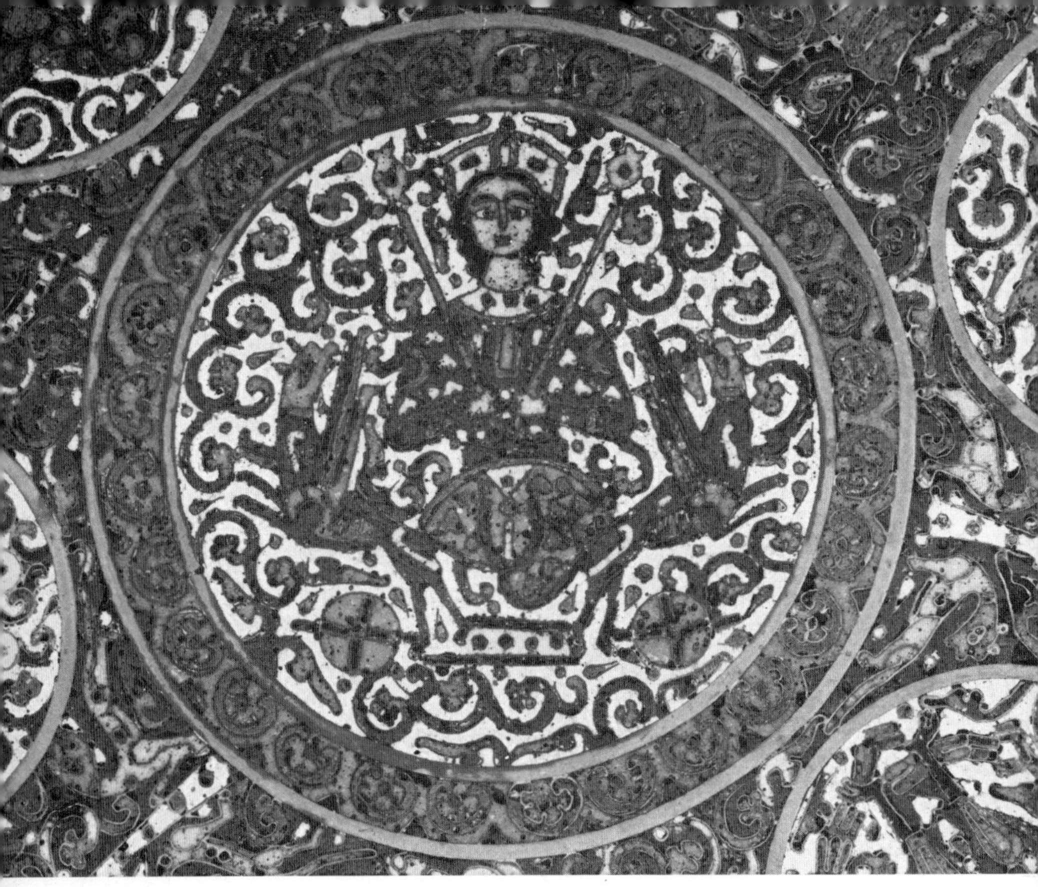

109 Detail from a bronze dish inlaid with champlevé enamel with the name of an Ortokid prince of Mosul, Suleyman ibn-Daud (1114–44). It was probably made at Mosul, though the design must have been inspired by the Byzantine world

there is a most interesting bronze dish decorated with enamels (*Ill. 109*), which bears the name of an Ortokid prince who reigned in the region of Mosul from 1114 to 1144. It is an isolated example, showing both in its technique and in its decoration a good deal of Byzantine influence, whereas the name of Mosul is associated with another, completely distinct and entirely Islamic group which was to flourish over the whole of the Islamic world, except for Spain and the western parts of North Africa. It was distinguished by the very difficult technique of inlaying a decoration of silver and sometimes also of copper onto a bronze core, and was developed especially for the decoration of tall jugs, ewers and large candlesticks.

Whether or not the technique was first developed at Mosul is hard to say, for in recent times the priority of this city has been questioned in favour of eastern Persia (see p. 75). But Mosul was certainly an important centre, even though very few actual examples can be associated with the place with absolute certainty. The most important of them is a ewer in the British Museum, usually known as the Blacas ewer (*Ill. 110*); it dates from 1232 and is signed, 'Made by Shuja ibn Mana of Mosul'. A jug found at Hamadan in Persia and signed by Ali ibn Hamid of Mosul may also be noted. A number of other vessels bear the name of Badr ad-din Lulu, who was first Atabeg and then independent ruler of Mosul throughout the period from 1218 until 1262, and these again may be assigned to the city with a reasonable degree of certainty. To Mosul or Aleppo are also to be attributed a number of vessels which bear as a part of their decoration medallions containing figures either directly modelled on Christian prototypes or close in style to those which appear in the illuminations of Syriac gospel books.

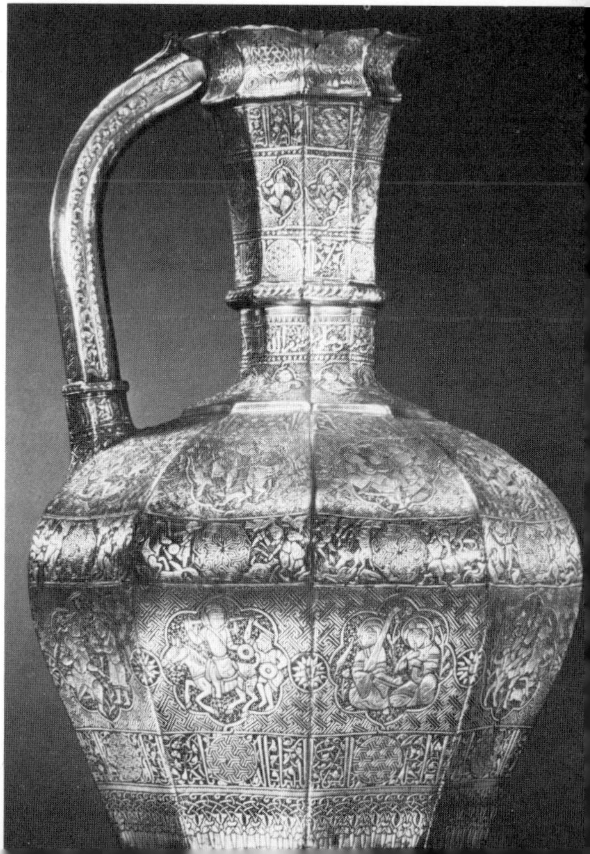

110 Brass ewer inlaid and inscribed 'Made by Shuja ibn Mana of Mosul'. It is the most important example of the technique known as Mosul work which is both definitely dated and which can be associated with Mosul itself

The technique was also very popular in Syria and it was probably from there that it spread to Egypt, and the signatures of craftsmen who can be associated with one or other of those countries appear on quite a number of examples. Others can be identified on the evidence of the designs, which are sometimes close to those of Egyptian or Syrian carved woodwork. The stylized scrolls or arabesques and kufic inscriptions are particularly important in this connection.

With the rise to power of the Ayyubid dynasty (1171–1250), Syria had become the primary centre of western Islam. At Raqqa, on the fringe of Mesopotamia, was situated the most important home of pottery manufacturing, while Damascus was the centre of thought and culture. The Raqqa potteries produced sgraffito, painted and moulded wares, and, after about 1170, lustre of a rather distinctive chocolate colour, often on a blue ground. The potters who worked there followed Persian models fairly closely, though the vessels they made were heavier and coarser and the pastes softer and more friable. In 1259 Raqqa was sacked by the Mongols, and little pottery seems to have been made there subsequently; instead Damascus became more important, and there production continued without interruption, for the Mongol advance was halted by Sultan Beybars at Ain Jalut on September 3, 1260 and western Syria escaped the destruction suffered by Persia and Mesopotamia. As a result the old Mesopotamian school of painting which was to a great extent eclipsed in its native land left a heritage which was very fully developed in Syria and thence penetrated into Egypt, where miniatures of very great beauty were produced under the patronage of the Mamluk sultans right down to the latter part of the fourteenth century. Though the revival of painting in Persia, which took place around 1300, owed quite a lot to the work of the old Mesopotamian school, it was in the main a wholly new Persian style that developed there, owing just as great a debt to Central Asia as it did to the old art of the Arab world. The Mongol conquests thus marked for a time the end of Arab art in the east. Thereafter the Arabs of the west and the Persians in the east were to hold the stage, and it is to a study of developments in the east that we must turn in the next chapter.

CHAPTER SIX

Persia: The Mongol Period

The first Mongol invasions of Western Asia began under Jenghis Khan about 1220, when Samarkand and Rayy were devastated; they reached their farthest extent in 1260, when Hulagu's invasion of Syria was halted by the Mamluks. Firm Mongol rule can be said to have dated from the capture of Baghdad in 1258, soon after which Mesopotamia and Persia were united under the control of the Ilkhanid Mongol dynasty, which lasted until 1336. The capital was transferred to Tabriz, but although Baghdad declined, a number of cities in Persia such as Isfahan and Shiraz achieved a new importance in spite of the terrible destructions wrought by the invaders.

It is no doubt true to say that the way had been to some extent paved for the Mongols by the advent of the Seljuks who had also moved westwards from Central Asia, but the effect was very different. The Seljuks had penetrated slowly, their rulers had risen to power gradually and, generally speaking, peaceably, and stable government and prosperity followed their advance. The Mongols came like a hurricane, destroying all before them. Historians have described their passage in terms of the greatest horror, and many years were to elapse before life could once more resume its normal course. But artists were sometimes spared in the general holocaust, and by the end of the century the majority of them had congregated at the capital, Tabriz, which thenceforth became the main centre of cultural activity in the Middle East. Unfortunately no buildings of this age survive there, nor do we know much about the minor arts of the specific period of Ilkhan rule. In contrast, however, we do know quite a lot about the paintings of the age, not, it is true, about those of the first thirty years, but about those done during and after the last decade of the thirteenth century. Quite a considerable number of manuscripts have survived, and their illustrations show the birth of a new and very distinct style.

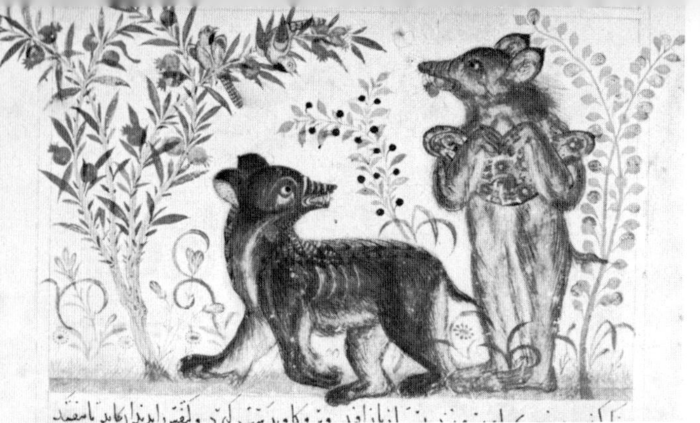

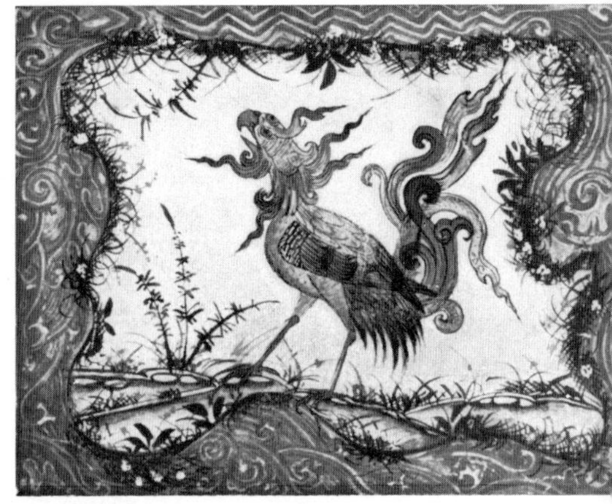

111, 112 Illustrations from a manuscript known as the 'Morgan Bestiary' showing (*above*) two bears, and (*right*) a phoenix. Its illustrations are in different styles, some recalling work of the Mesopotamian school and others being distinctly Chinese in character. Probably made at Maragha, 1294

The first of the manuscripts that may be mentioned is a copy of the *Manafi al-Hayawan* or 'The Usefulnesses of Animals', of Ibn Baktishu now in the Pierpont Morgan Library; it is usually known as the Morgan Bestiary and was probably at Maragha, written and illustrated in 1294. Its illustrations are by several painters, one at least of whom was working in a manner fairly close to that of the old Baghdad school – he must have been schooled in Mesopotamia and have survived the slaughter that followed the Mongol invasion, for his paintings were two-dimensional, his figures heavy and solid, his trees followed the same stylistic convention as the plants of the early Dioscorides manuscripts, while his colours were brilliant and contrasting. Another man who worked on the same volume had, on the other hand, adopted a completely distinct style, linear and three-dimensional, using light, feathery brush-strokes, and employing motifs that were basically Far Eastern. Indeed, some of the illustrations in this book are so Chinese that they might even be attributed to immigrant artists from the Far East. The two styles are absolutely distinct; such a miniature as that depicting a phoenix is wholly Chinese (*Ill. 112*), while one showing two rather delightful bears (*Ill. 111*) is in the solid, two-dimensional homely manner that we met in Mesopotamia half a century or more earlier.

In some manuscripts, like the Morgan Bestiary, the two manners appear side by side, in others they have been blended together, to constitute a new and distinct style. Indeed, as time went on the blend became so complete that it is only by careful analysis that the two lines of inheritance can be separated one from the other. It was this blend that constituted the basis of Persian miniature painting from the mid-fourteenth century onwards, and had it not taken place, the art could never have developed in the way it did.

The blend was, of course, not complete at first, and the miniatures of another important book of the age belong only to the first stage of coalescence. This is a copy of al-Biruni's 'Chronology of Ancient Peoples', dated 1307, and now in the library of Edinburgh University (No. 161). The blend is to be seen very clearly in a miniature showing the temptation of the first man and woman (fol. 48v), where Ahriman, the spirit of Evil, induces them to eat the forbidden fruit by eating it first and so transforming himself from an aged man into a youth (*Ill. 113*). The haloes worn by all three figures and the way in which the folds of the costumes are shown attest an ultimate influence from East Christian art; the bright colours and solid figures derive directly from the miniatures of the Mesopotamian school, like those of the Hariri manuscripts discussed above; the knobbly tree-trunks and the attempt to render the background in three dimensions by multiplying the number of planes are features derived from the Far East.

In some of the other miniatures of the book which are to be attributed to a different hand, the blend was still far from complete, for the old manner of Mesopotamia definitely remains to the fore. But in other volumes, written and illuminated at Tabriz at much the same time, the Mesopotamian style has been almost completely subordinated to the Far Eastern, characterized by its light, feathery

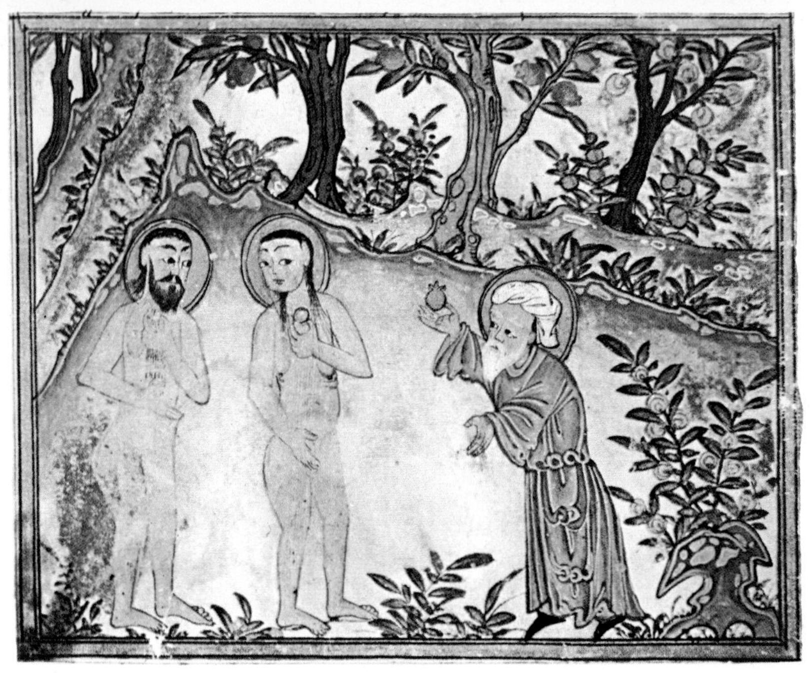

113 Illustration from al-Biruni's 'Chronology of Ancient Peoples' copied at Tabriz dated 1307/8. The illustration shows the temptation of the first man and woman in the garden of Paradise

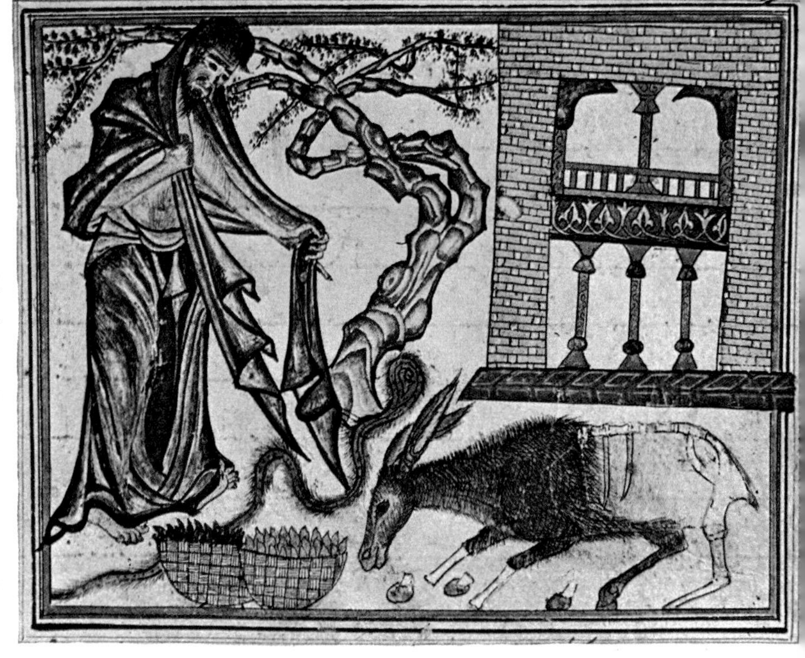

114 Illustration from Rashid al-Din's 'Universal History' copied at Tabriz in 1306 showing the Prophet Jeremiah. God caused the Prophet to die for a hundred years because of his lack of faith and then brought him and his donkey back to life

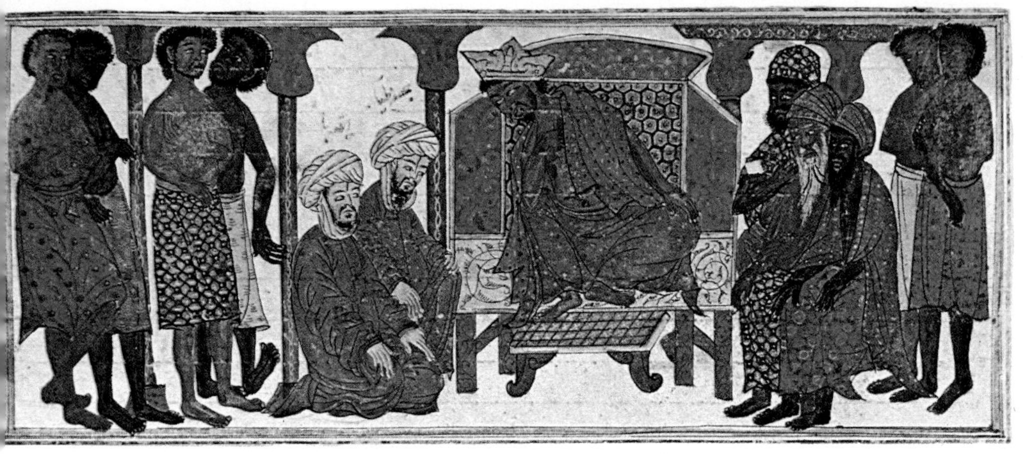

115 Illustration from the Edinburgh Rashid al-Din. A Muslim embassy to the court of the Negus of Abyssinia. Most of the pictures in this work show obvious Chinese influence, but here the solid manner of the old Mesopotamian school is reflected. 1306

brush-strokes and its marked illusionism; even the racial type of the figures is distinct. The old convention of the trees has here been wholly discarded in favour of a new one where the trunks are twisted and knobbly and the branches like those on a willow-pattern plate, the approach is in general three-dimensional, while a gentle colouring in half-tones has been substituted for the brilliant fresh hues of the Mesopotamian work.

The most important examples of the style are some volumes of Rashid al-Din's 'Universal History' (*Jami al-Tanarikh*), and one of the finest of them is at Edinburgh (No. 20) and dates from 1306. Another volume in the same style, done seven years later, is in the possession of the Royal Asiatic Society in London, and another copy is in Istanbul. The book was actually in four volumes and it is said that Rashid al-Din had two copies of the book written and illustrated each year, one with text in Arabic, the other in Persian.

Once again several hands are to be distinguished in both these volumes. One, like the man who did an enchanting picture of the Prophet Jeremiah (*Ill. 114*), worked in an almost wholly Chinese style. The theme illustrated is that of the prophet who had doubted the Almighty's power to raise up Jerusalem after its destruction; he was made to die for a hundred years and then brought to life again; his donkey was resuscitated before his eyes, and we here see its

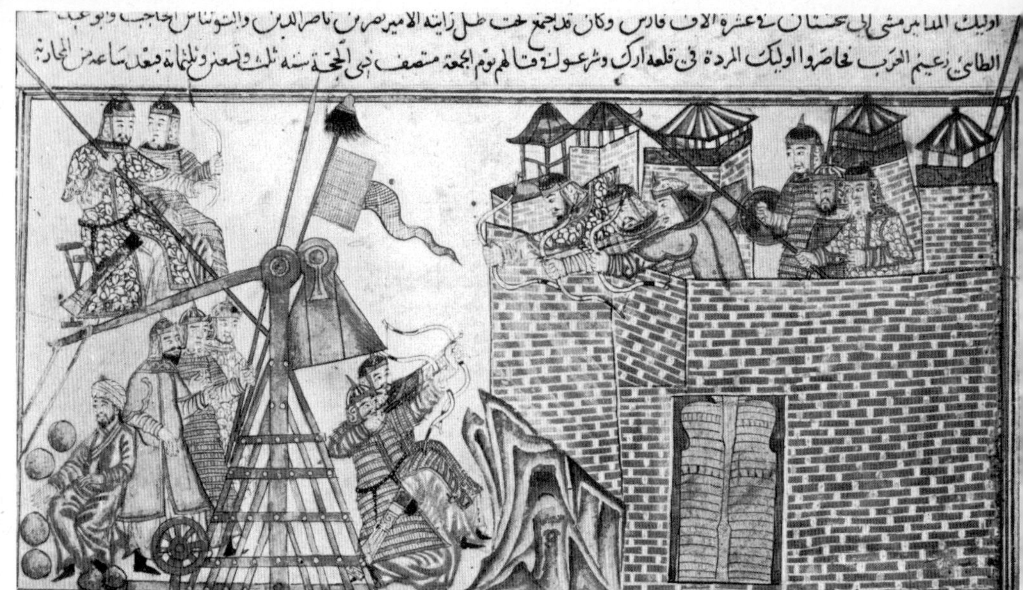

116 A battle scene. Illustration from the Edinburgh Rashid al-Din. There are several similar scenes towards the end of the volume, which represent a diversity of historical events, though the costumes and appearance of the figures clearly depict Mongol warriors. 1306

skeleton gradually coming together. Another painter, who did such scenes as that illustrating an embassy to the court of the Negus of Abyssinia to arrange for the extradition of certain early converts to Islam who had taken refuge there (*Ill. 115*), must have learnt much from the old school of Mesopotamia. Another liked to draw scenes of violence and movement and took great delight in depicting the angular patterns of Mongol costumes and uniforms (*Ill. 116*). There are a whole series of battle scenes by him towards the end of the Edinburgh volume, and he might be described as the man amongst the illustrators who was most able to interpret the spirit and background of the Mongol world.

The most outstanding of all of the painters who illustrated this volume, however, showed something of a blend of all these manners, for his work has the solidity and strength of that of Mesopotamia, the delicacy and charm of the Chinese and the mastery of movement of the Mongol painter – if we may so designate the man who executed the battle scenes – added to all these, he was possessed of a feeling for composition and an imagination and a sense of balance,

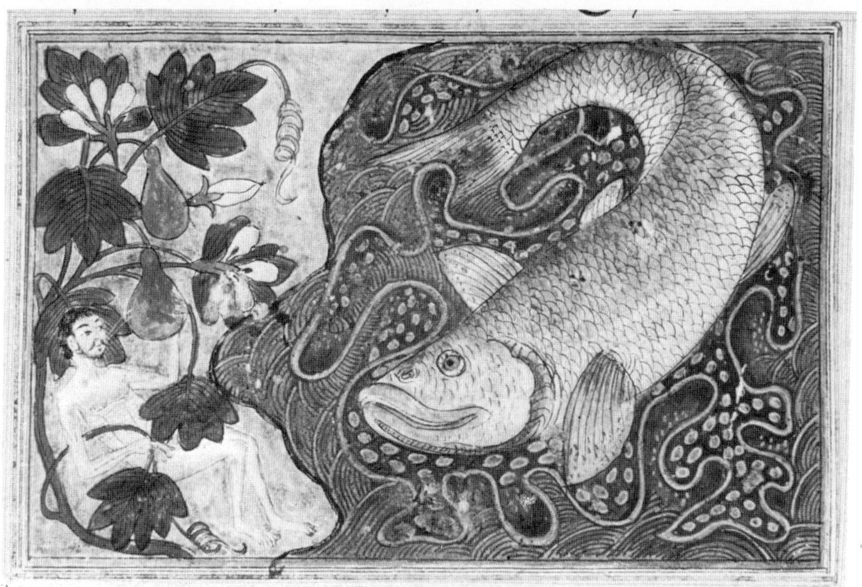

117 Another illustration from the Edinburgh Rashid al-Din depicting Jonah and the Whale. The events recorded in this volume include a number from the Old Testament. This is perhaps the finest painting in the whole book. 1306

which mark him out as a master of very great ability. His picture of Jonah (*Ill. 117*) – for the history contains items from the Bible as well as secular events – though on a small scale, is a painting of very great power and beauty and the swirling movements of the great fish show a truly remarkable feeling for rhythm.

The mastery of movement and the subordination of a convention to the expression of an idea that we see here was soon to become the hall-mark of the school of Tabriz, which reached its apogee at much the same time that the Ilkhanid dynasty, which had given the school its birth, came to an end. It is best represented by a book which has, alas, now been broken up and is divided among numerous collections. It is usually known as the Demotte *Shah-nama*, but would be better called the Great Shah-nama of Tabriz, for never in the whole story of Persian painting was it surpassed in richness, in quality or in the number of scenes illustrated. It must have been done at Tabriz between 1330 and 1336.

The *Shah-nama*, or 'Book of Kings', was composed by the poet Firdausi at the court of Mahmud of Ghazni about 1010 and at once became one of the most popular books in the whole of the Middle East. It was frequently reproduced, but it is only from after the early fourteenth century that any number of copies have survived, and only from that date are there any that contain illustrations; thereafter it was perhaps the most frequently illustrated of all Persian manuscripts. Some of its scenes were included in Rashid al-Din's history, because in Persia there was never any very clear distinction as to where real history ended and fiction began, but most of the scenes are different and depict iconographical themes which must often have dated back for several centuries. Stylistically these illustrations represent a marked development from the manner of the Rashid al-Din volumes, for the Chinese elements have been subordinated to a new, more forceful manner, which owes its character to something more than an affection for the old art of Mesopotamia. In fact, the truly Persian element has here come to the fore at last, and we are for the first time in the presence of a painting which can truly be described as Persian. From this moment onwards the development of the school was to be continuous and uninterrupted. The interest in pure expression, almost approaching caricature, which characterized the Hariris, has given place to a more intimate and profound insight into character; the delight in colour or pattern for its own sake has become absorbed in a feeling for a unified composition which was a basic part of the theme, while the profounder emotions of life have become one of the matters of chief concern for the artist. We see here, in fact, works of art where deep emotions are rendered with real understanding.

Several different painters must have been responsible for the illustrations of the Tabriz *Shah-nama*. One was at his best when movement was involved (*Ill. 118*), one seems to have preferred subjects where majesty and dignity were to the fore, and one at least was a real master of the pathetic. It was he who painted the scene of the Bier of the Great Iskander surrounded by mourners (*Ill. 119*); the conqueror is possessed of a wholly Oriental grandeur, while the prisoner is rendered with a profound understanding of the misery of his plight. This is one of the most expressive pictures in the whole of Persian art.

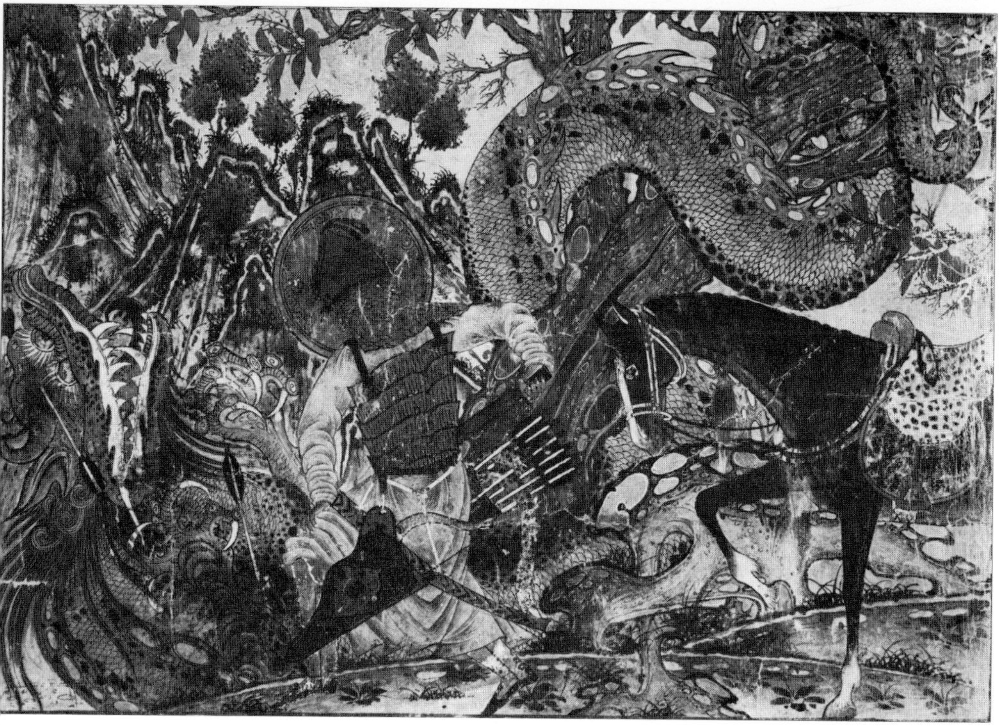

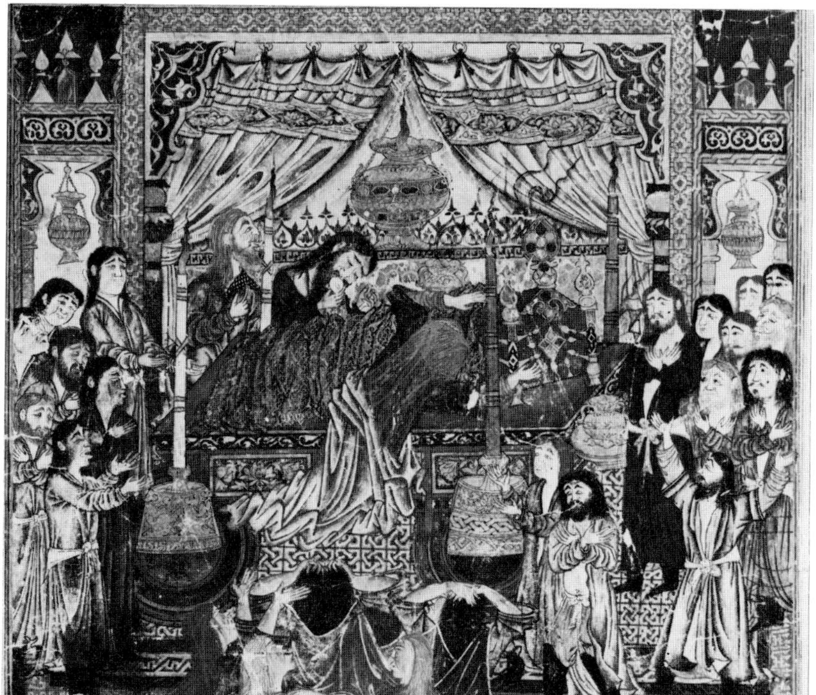

:18, 119 Miniaures from the Shah-nama, or Book of Kings, of Firdausi, known as the Demotte Shah-nama. This book has now been split up, but (above) shows Bahram killling Dragon, and (below) the Bier of the Great Iskander. The illustrations are by several different hands. Tabriz, 1330–6

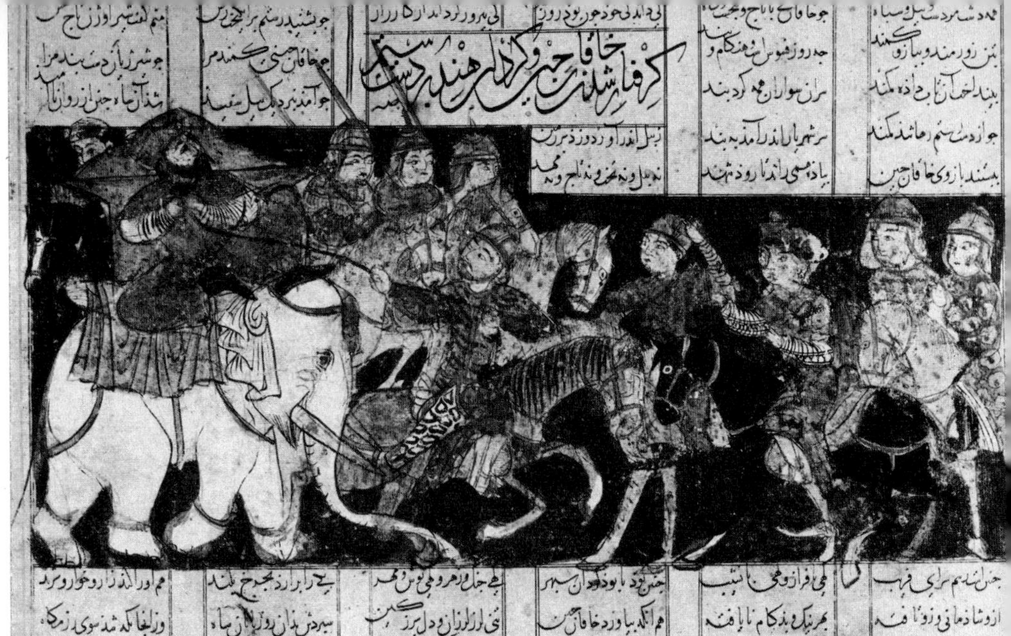

120 Page from a *Shah-nama* showing Rustem dragging the Khakhan of China from his elephant. It belongs to a distinct group known as the Red Ground *Shah-namas*. Mongol, late thirteenth century

With the end of the Mongol dynasty the country was for a time divided, petty rulers rose to power in various centres, and a number of minor schools of painting grew up in different localities. Work continued to be produced, however, in north-west Persia at Tabriz, and probably also at Maragha, and a group of *Shah-namas*, usually known as the 'Red Ground *Shah-namas*' (*Ill. 120*), is probably to be associated with that region; they are usually comparatively small in size and their illustrations are vivid but not very subtle.

Another school, known as the Inju, was centred at Shiraz under the patronage of the Inju dynasty (1335–53); it ended when the city fell to the Muzaffarids soon after the middle of the century. There was much less Chinese influence here, and the work of these painters has been compared to that of those who decorated pottery of the Minai group; it may well be that some of the illuminators turned from time to time to the decoration of pots of one sort or another.

A third school grew up under the patronage of the Jala-irid dynasty which ruled at Baghdad from the mid-fourteenth century

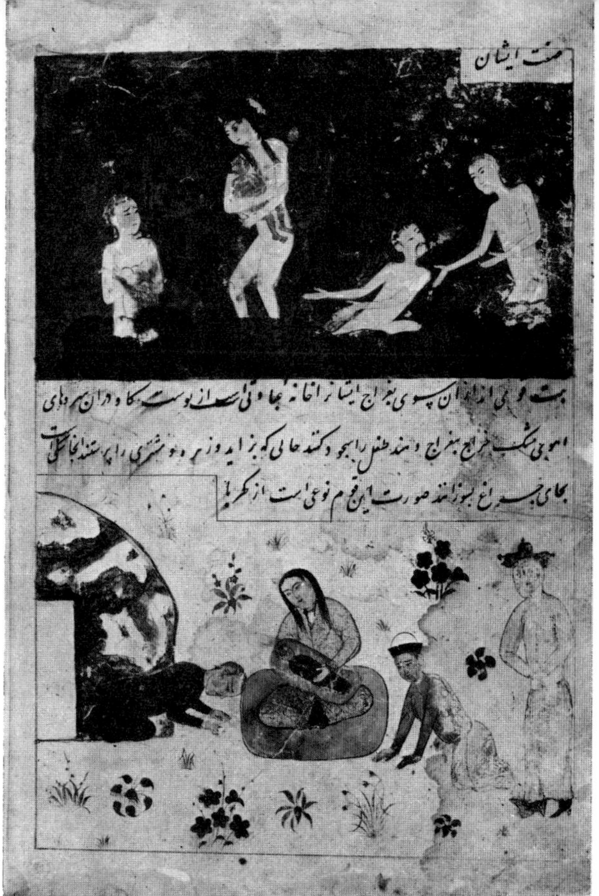

121 Illustration from 'The Book of Marvels' depicting (*above*) Bulgars bathing in the Volga, and (*below*) Tibetans adoring a new-born child. This manuscript was copied in 1388 and belongs to the Jala-irid school which flourished in Baghdad at the end of the fourteenth century

until about 1400. A magnificent book in Paris, the 'Book of Marvels of the World', dated to 1388, is to be assigned to this school (Bib. Nat. supp. Pers. 332). Its style is grand and impressive, showing more of the influence of the old manner of Baghdad than of the Far East. Its pictures are also interesting because of their subject-matter, for many of them depict methods of cultivation or the customs and habits of diverse peoples; thus on one page the planting and cultivation of pepper is shown and on another Bulgars are depicted bathing in the Volga and, below, Tibetans adoring a new-born child (*Ill. 121*).

Though the paintings constitute the most important and most interesting art of the Mongol period, the ceramics of the age are far from insignificant, and though the potteries of Rayy and a number of other centres were destroyed, some, like Kashan, survived and others which had hardly been known before rose to prominence. The mantle of Rayy seems to some extent to have descended upon Kashan, and lustre wares were produced there for a time. Sgraffito wares were still no doubt made in a number of centres, for those above all others were the wares in everyday use. Just as with paintings, new ideas in pottery were introduced from the East, and the imitation of Chinese styles and techniques became all the vogue. The favourite blue and black wares which grew in popularity as the century advanced were made at Kashan; the bodies were thin and fine, in contrast to the rather heavier type of blue and black made at Sultanabad.

During the course of the fourteenth century, however, Sultanabad to some extent supplanted Kashan as the main centre, its products being characterized by rather thick white bodies, with flat, inturned rims and thick glazes forming tear-drops outside and thick pools at the base inside. The decorations were painted under the glaze, either direct on to the body or over a grey slip, which was sometimes so thick that it produced a design in relief. Modelling in low-relief was often associated with the painted decoration. Sometimes the finest of the bowls had fluted sides (*Ill. 123*). The designs were loose and flowing, consisting mainly of leaves or animals of a very naturalistic type (*Ill. 122*). Miniatures of the period, especially those done at Shiraz, often showed a similar affection for flowered backgrounds, with animals or birds among the foliage.

As a result of the discovery of pottery wasters at Sultanabad, the important group with designs in black on a blue ground, above a friable white body, can be associated with Sultaniya as well. Sultaniya is known to us primarily because of a superb building which survives there, the mausoleum of the Mongol ruler Uljaitu Khodabende Shah, begun in 1305 (*Ill. 124*). The basic idea of its plan goes back to the Seljuk gumbat, the mausoleum of centralized plan, which became so important wherever the Seljuks penetrated. But the conventional scheme has been left far behind in this strangely imaginative octagonal structure, which originally had a thin pencil-like minaret at each of the corners of the octagon. It may be somewhat barbaric in its conception, like an immensely enlarged Mongol

122 Bowl with underglaze decoration of birds and foliage in black and turquoise. Fourteenth century. The type of decoration was characteristic of the potteries of Sultanabad, a centre which vied with Kashan in importance

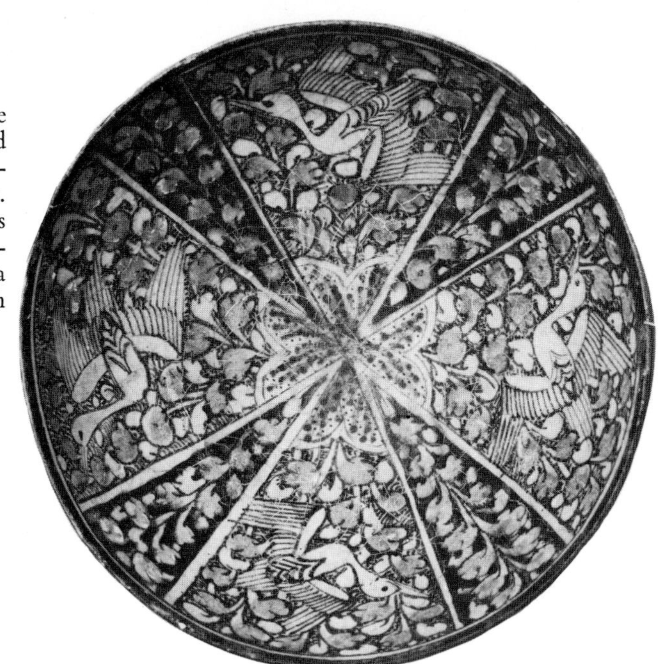

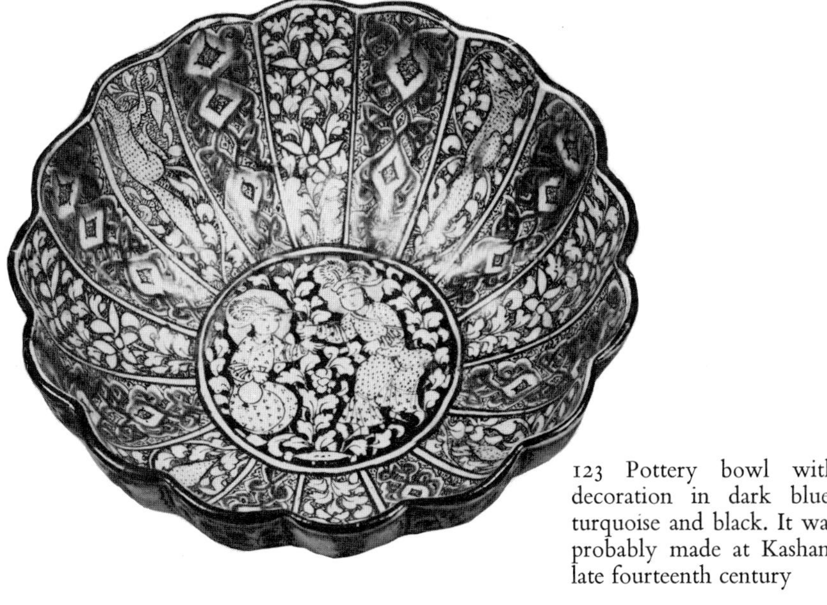

123 Pottery bowl with decoration in dark blue, turquoise and black. It was probably made at Kashan, late fourteenth century

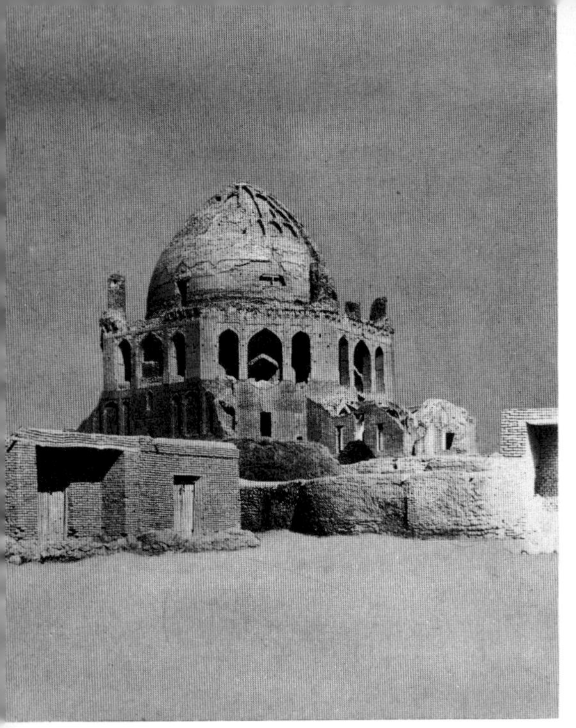

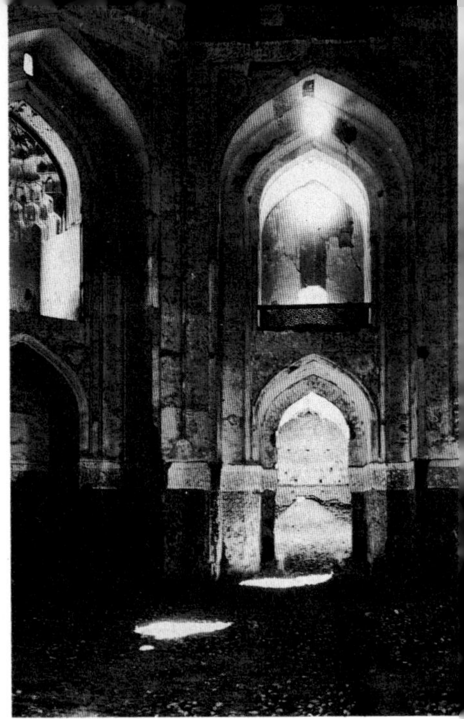

124, 125 (*above*) The mausoleum of Uljaitu Khodabende Shah at Sultaniya. The exterior is very unusual with originally a tall minaret at each of the four corners. The interior (*above right*) is more restrained and conventional. The building was begun in 1305

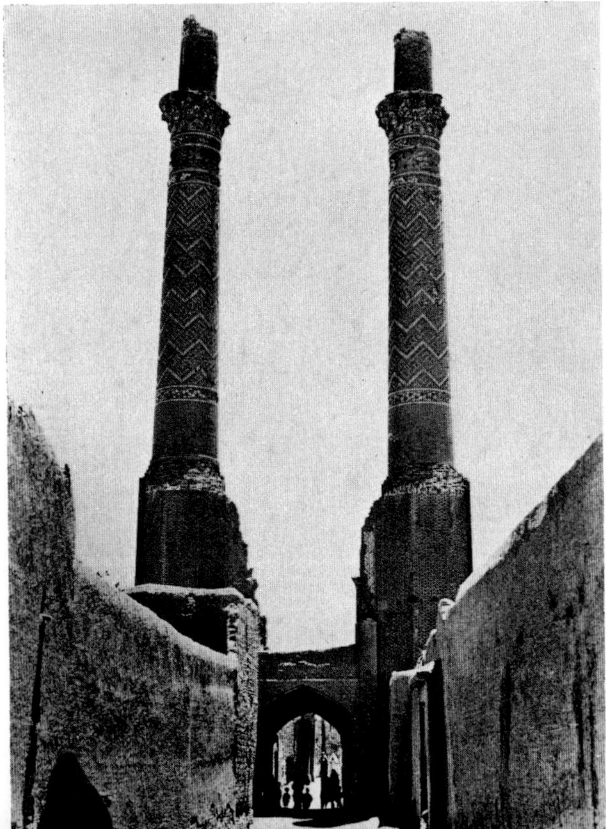

126 (*left*) The twin minarets at Isfahan. Tall, elegant minarets adorned with coloured tiles were typical of the architecture of this time. Sometimes they were set in pairs, as here, more often they were single. Late fourteenth century

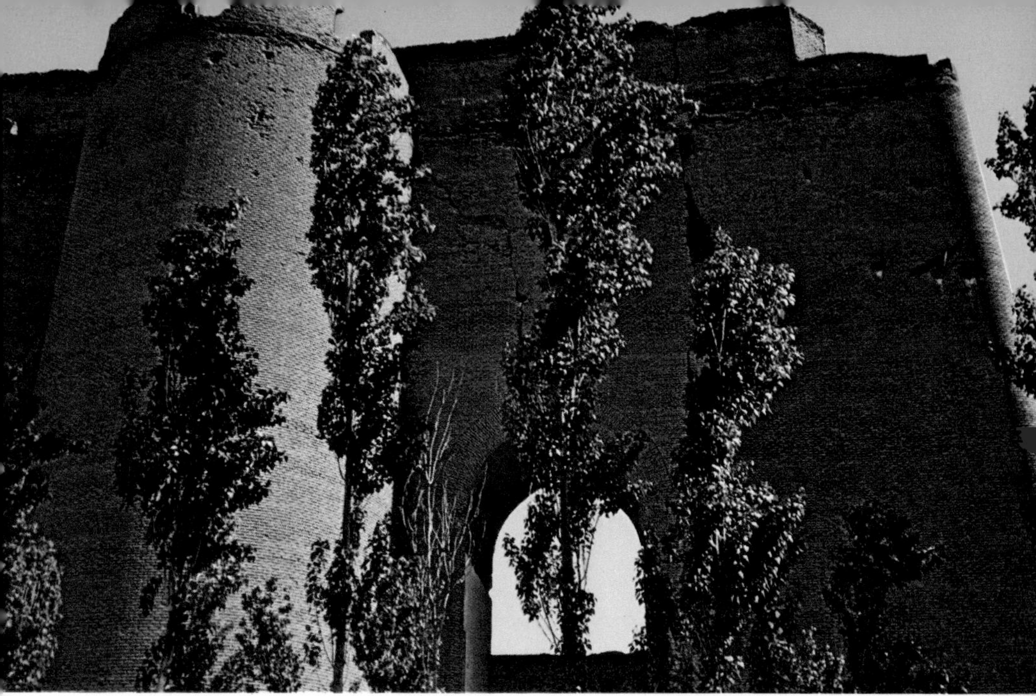

127 The citadel, Tabriz. The tremendously massive walls of this structure contrast markedly with the slender lines of the minarets of the same period. Fourteenth century

tent, yet it is also extremely evocative of the Mongol age, and remains not only as one of the most original but also one of the most striking contributions to the art of that period in Persia and to the Mongol spirit as a whole. If its exterior is experimental and daring, its interior, on the contrary, is almost reticent in the quality of its decoration and elegance of its proportions (*Ill. 125*).

To judge by the other buildings that survive from this age, it was a period of great brilliance in architecture. Tall, elegant minarets (*Ill. 126*), decorated with tiles or brickwork, seem to illustrate the feeling for fantasy that dominated much of what was done, yet the tremendously massive walls of the citadel at Tabriz (*Ill. 127*) indicate a wholly distinct approach, for this immensely solid building cannot have been inspired wholly by functional aims. The architect, one feels, must have rejoiced intensely in the sheer mass of its brickwork. The Masjid-i-Jami at Varamin (*Ill. 128*), built in 1325–6, on the other hand, presents a more conventional conception, though it is none the less of great beauty and fine proportion and boasts some most attractive stalactite work in its interior. Its glazed tiles are impressive and were perhaps made locally, for Varamin was certainly a centre of pottery making, though the characteristic blue and white ware which is usually associated with the place only became really important with the fifteenth century.

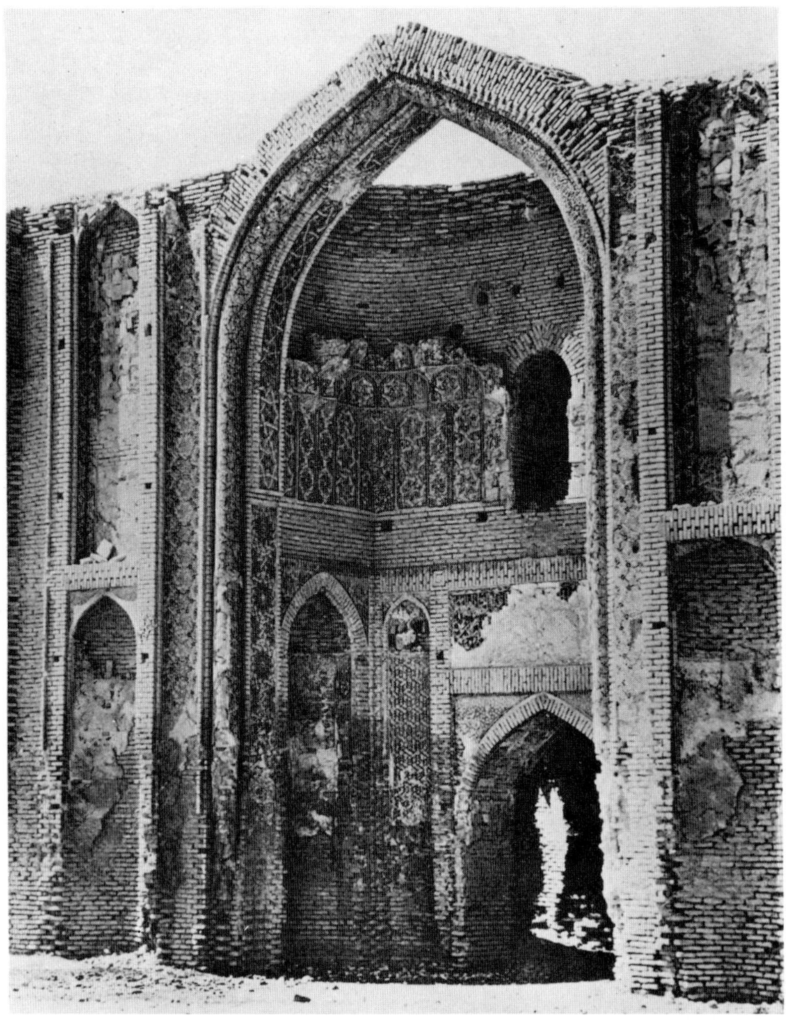

128 The Masjid-i-Jami at Varamin, 1325–6. In spite of the record of destruction wrought by the Mongol invasions, the period of their rule was particularly rich in architecture. The mosque at Varamin is typical of the period

CHAPTER SEVEN

Syria and Egypt: Twelfth and Thirteenth centuries

During the latter part of the eleventh and the earlier part of the twelfth century the situation in Syria was by no means stable. Jerusalem was captured by the Seljuks in 1071 and by the Crusaders in 1099; Aleppo and Antioch were constantly fought over; the coastal fringe was mostly in Crusading hands, and it was not until the arrival on the scene of Saladin in the second half of the twelfth century that anything like unity or stability were enforced. But from then onwards the destinies of Syria and Egypt were closely knit together and the arts of the two countries thereafter developed hand in hand. Under the patronage of the Ayyubids (1176–1250) and, still more, under that of the Mamluks (1250–1517), they flourished very considerably, and though it was at the capital, Cairo, that the finest buildings were set up, it was in Syria that much of the best work on a small scale was done. It was there that much of the most accomplished pottery was made and much of the most delicate glass manufactured, there, as much as, if not more than in Mosul, that metalwork was most intricately inlaid, there that some of the best carved woodwork was produced, many of the textiles most skilfully woven, and there too that some of the miniatures which were so much favoured by the Mamluks were painted.

So far as pottery was concerned the most important centre in early times had been at Raqqa on the Euphrates, on the fringes of Syria and Mesopotamia. Close contacts must always have been maintained between that city and Persia, for some of its pottery was directly modelled on the Persian, especially the lustre and the black and blue wares which were to become so popular in the fourteenth century. The city retained its importance until its destruction at the hands of the Mongols in 1259. Barbotine ware, both unglazed and with a moulded decoration under a green or blue glaze, was made there, though it is not easy to distinguish the Syrian from the

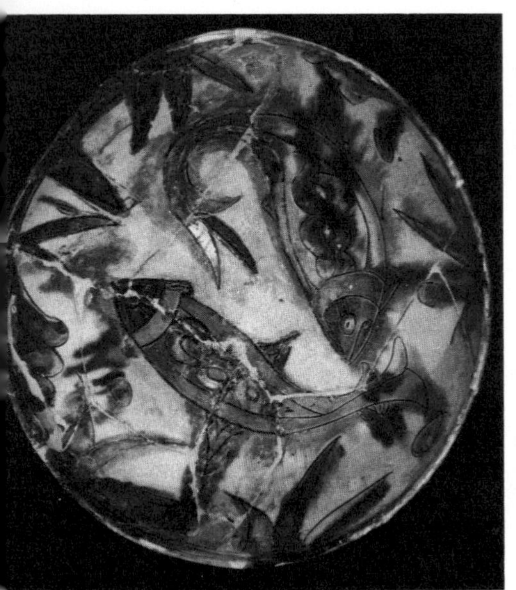

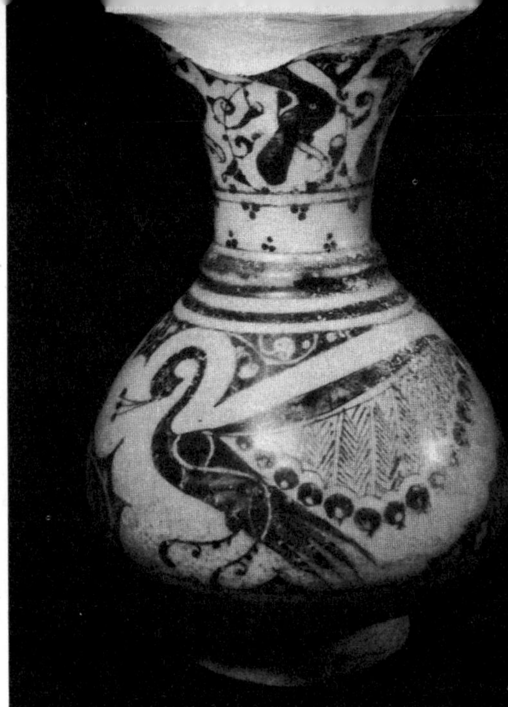

129, 130 Bowl and vase of Raqqa ware. Thirteenth century. Raqqa was the most important centre of pottery production in Syria, but it is not always easy to tell its products from those of Damascus or Egypt

Mesopotamian or Persian variants; lustre was also produced. But most important of all was a ware with a rather sandy white body and a decoration in black, blue or blueish-purple painted under the glaze; large jars with wide mouths were popular. Sometimes a thin sgraffito design was associated with the painted decoration as on a large bowl with two fish in the Damascus Museum (*Ill. 129*). Their swirling movements show a real mastery of design and a similar excellence distinguishes a great deal of the Raqqa work.

It is, however, often rather hard to tell the products of Raqqa from those made elsewhere in Syria or in Egypt, for the Raqqa style was developed both at Rusafa and at Damascus after the original centre had been destroyed, and Raqqa products were also copied at Fostat. A fine, tall vase of the thirteenth century in the Damascus Museum might, for example, almost equally well be a product of Raqqa, Damascus or Fostat (*Ill. 130*).

The problem of attribution to sites is further complicated by the fact that there seems to have been a good deal of traffic in pottery, and it is impossible to be sure that objects found in the various centres were actually made there. This is the case with an exceptionally impressive figure of a horseman (in the Damascus Museum) which was found at Raqqa (*Ill. 131*). It is of fine white paste, and is covered with cream and blue glazes like those on the so-called Lakabi wares of Persia (see p. 68). The costume and facial type of the figure are of a distinctly Eastern type, like those which characterize much Persian work of the early thirteenth century. The Raqqa figure is thus perhaps to be regarded as an import from Persia, made under the patronage of one of the Seljuk rulers of the twelfth century.

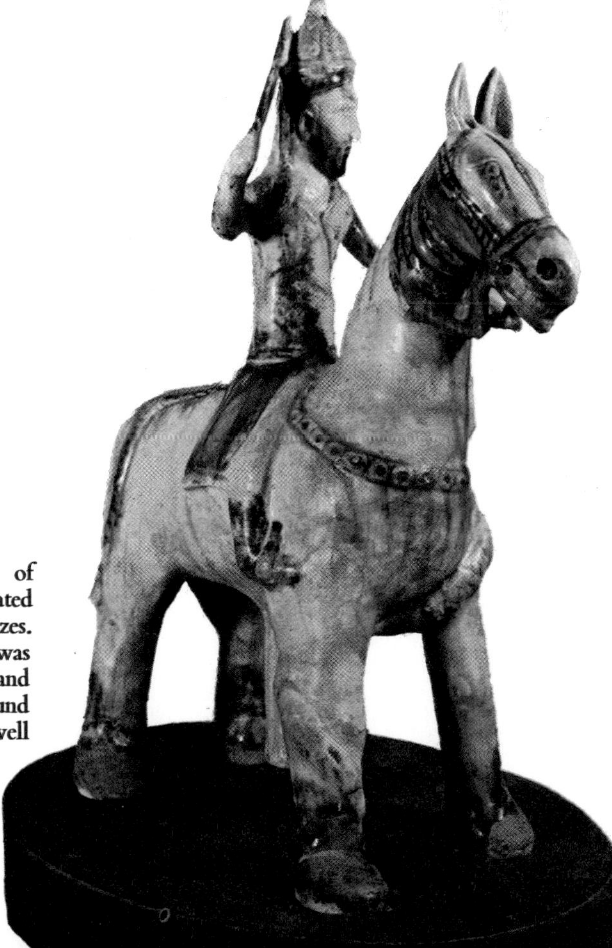

131 Pottery figure of a horseman decorated with polychrome glazes. Very similar work was also done in Persia, and as the figure was found at Raqqa it may well have been an import

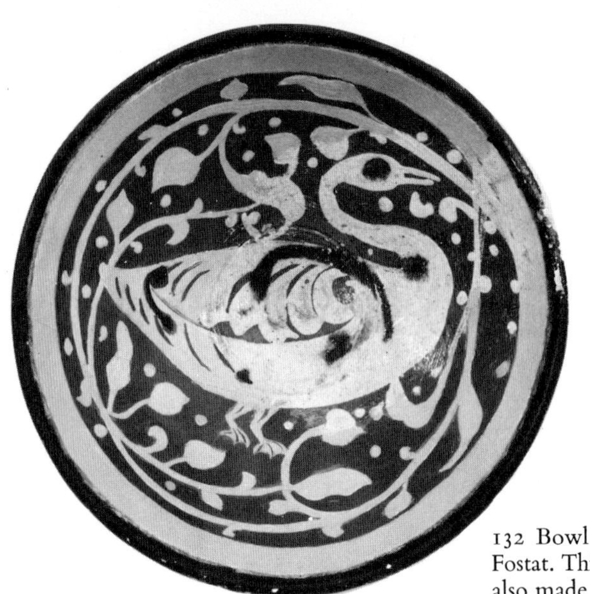

132 Bowl of the thirteenth century from Fostat. This is an Egyptian version of a type also made in Syria

Nevertheless, in spite of these problems, certain types of pottery of the later thirteenth and fourteenth centuries can be associated with Damascus. The products of its kilns are to be distinguished by their heaviness and by the rather coarse bodies. In addition to bowls, wide mouthed jars and *albarelli* were especially popular. The decorations were done both in lustre and blue and black, and consisted of large arabesques, heavily and robustly handled, birds and fish; human figures hardly ever appear. A few pieces are dated by inscriptions to about the middle of the fourteenth century, and in the fifteenth century blue and white wares of a rather Chinese type were also made at Damascus.

Numerous fragments of bowls which are very closely akin as regards the decoration, but which on the whole are rather smaller in size, have come from the rubbish mounds of Fostat. These often bear signatures on the bases, and the names seem to belong to Egyptians, so that the vessels they signed were apparently made locally and so constitute a true Fostat group. Some good lustre was made (*Ill. 132*), with decorations of arabesques or birds drawn in a hard metallic style, while after 1400 blue and white wares were to become nearly as popular as in Persia or Syria.

Another type of vessel can also be associated with Fostat quite firmly and definitely (*Ill. 133*), namely, that characterized firstly by a decoration in the sgraffito technique, secondly by the dark brown, highly fired glazes, thirdly by the high based and deep-sided forms that prevailed, and finally by the thick, heavy bodies. This was really the most characteristic Fostat type, and when we speak of Fostat pots it is usually to these that we refer. The decorations, in addition to depicting the birds and animals which were so frequently used in association with the sgraffito technique elsewhere, also often included birds with spread wings or cups on tall stems, which were used as heraldic symbols during the Mamluk age. They often occur on other works of art also, especially on the enamelled glass vessels. Fish, rare elsewhere, were usual, and very effective use was made of script, treated to show off its decorative qualities.

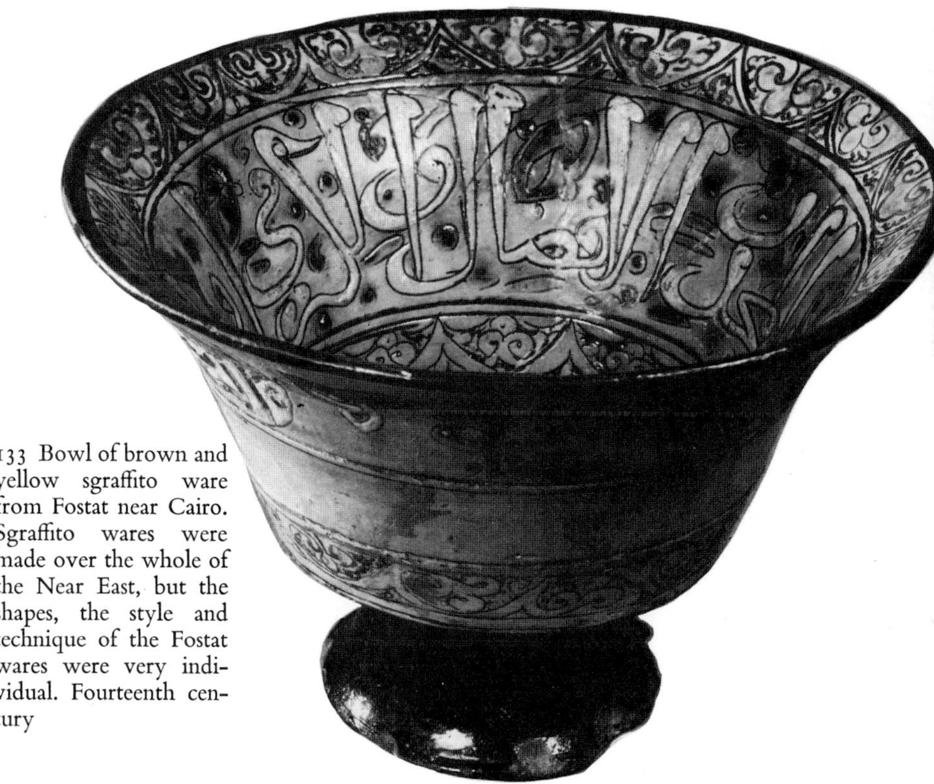

133 Bowl of brown and yellow sgraffito ware from Fostat near Cairo. Sgraffito wares were made over the whole of the Near East, but the shapes, the style and technique of the Fostat wares were very individual. Fourteenth century

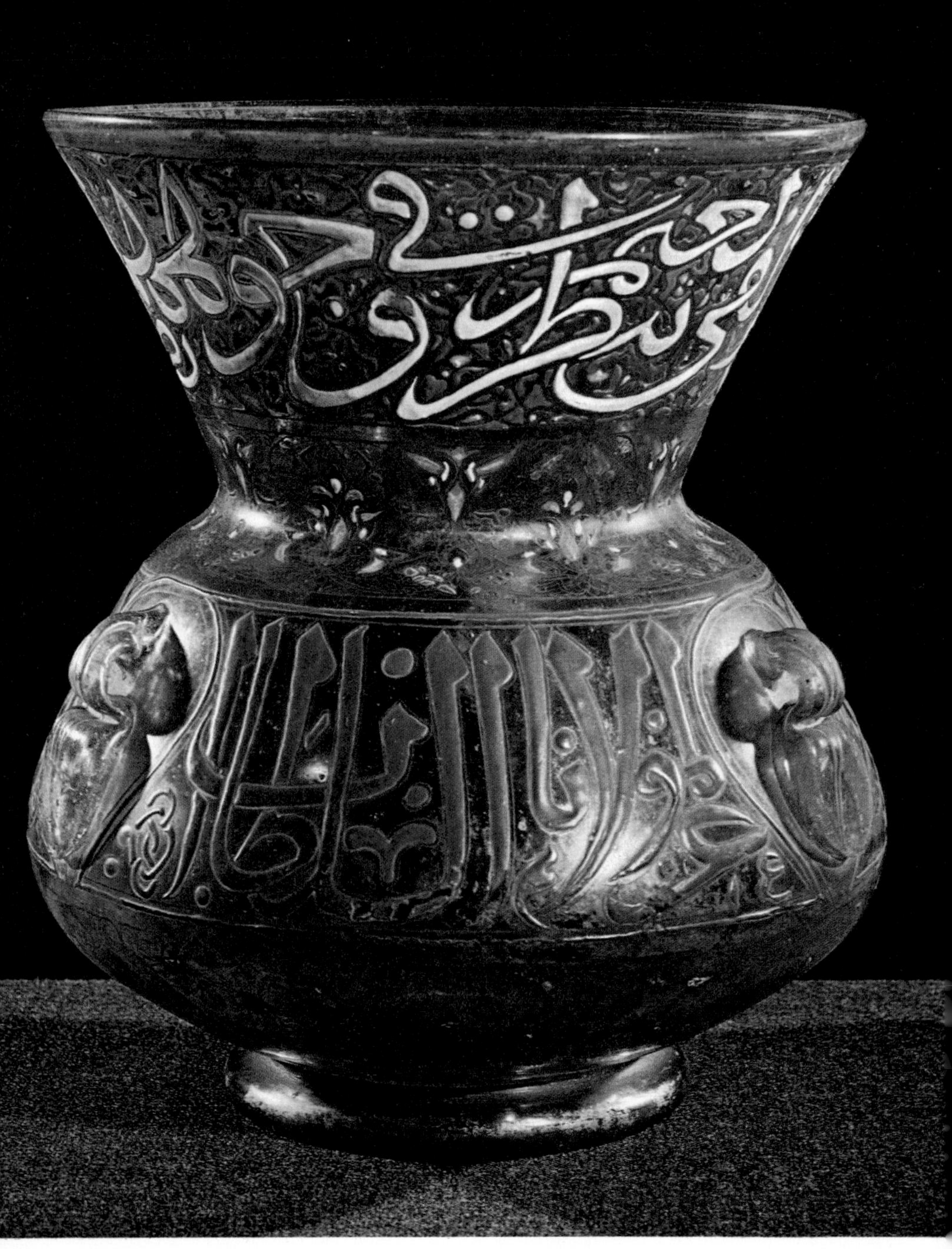

134 Glass mosque lamp with enamelled decoration inscribed with three quotations from the Koran and a dedication to Beybars II. Lamps such as this were made all over the Islamic world, but the finest are to be assigned to Egypt and Syria. Syrian, early fourteenth century

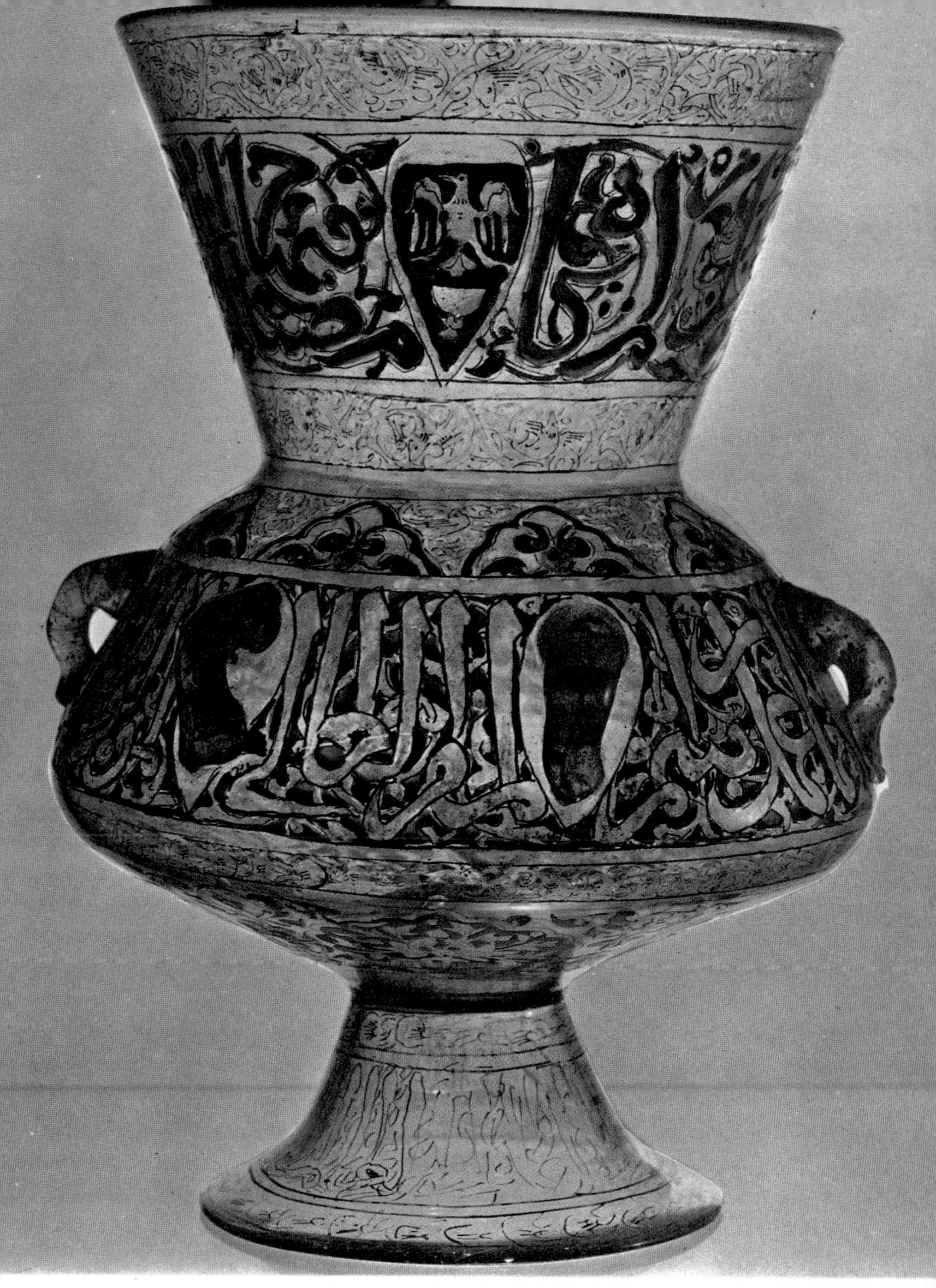

135 Glass mosque lamp with enamelled decoration made for Sayf ad-Din Tuquz-timur, Assessor of Sultan an-Nasir Muhammad. Probably made in Syria, 1340

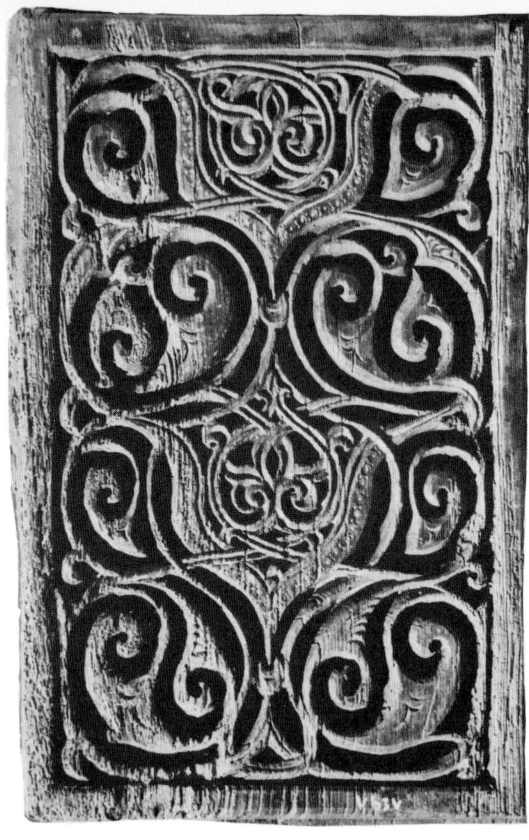

136 Carved wooden panel. Wood carving of this type characterized by elegant, flowing designs was very popular both in Egypt and Syria. It is often hard to distinguish the products of these two countries. Thirteenth century

Syria always seems to have been important as a centre of woodworking and inlaying, indeed the craft flourishes there even today more than in any other part of the Islamic world. Some panels, now in the Damascus Museum (*Ill. 136*), dating perhaps as early as the tenth century, serve to illustrate the simpler style, which depended solely on carving; rather later a method of inlaying the wood with ivory, bone or mother-of-pearl was perfected, and the technique was subsequently developed in Egypt and North Africa. There, however, geometric designs were preferred, and in the earlier work these were usually more flowing and depended on stylized floral forms or arabesques. The wood-carvings of earlier date often show the influence of the third group that we distinguished in the decoration of the Samarra stuccos (*Ill. 25*), for the characteristic slanting or 'bevelled technique' was often used.

Another art which was indigenous to Syria was that of glass-making. The Syrians seem to have been masters of all the various techniques from early times, for much of the best Roman glass was made in the area, and its early development has often been attributed to the Phoenicians who once inhabited the coastal belt. The mastery of the technique continued into Islamic times, for blown, moulded and cut glass were all made for the Muslim patrons. Most important of all, however, was the enamelled glass, a technique which was known in Roman times, but which achieved new glories under the Islamic rulers, more especially for the decoration of a very distinctive form of lamp, with large bulging base and upper section and with a narrow waist in between (*Ill. 134, 135*). The earlier ones are to be assigned to the thirteenth century, but the majority belong to the fourteenth century or later. Tall, narrow beakers and long-necked bottles were also often decorated with similar enamelling; there is an especially fine one of the Mamluk period in Vienna. Kufic or *naskh* script made up the most usual decoration; in Egypt motifs with heraldic significance, like the cup or spread eagle, set in medallions, were often included as a part of the decoration.

Exactly when the technique of inlaying bronze with silver or copper was first developed in Syria, or whether or not it was adopted from Mosul, is hard to say, but it is certain that good work of the so-called Mosul type was done there, especially in Aleppo and Damascus, from the early thirteenth century onwards and from Syria the technique probably spread to Egypt. Basins (*Ill. 137*), ewers and other vessels were usual, but the most common objects to be adorned in this way were the broad based candlesticks which formed an essential part of the furnishing of the finer mosques. One bearing the date 1317, in the Benaki Museum at Athens, is typical and is probably to be assigned to Syria. But the Egyptian craftsmen were just as proficient, and one of the finest examples of the technique, the so-called Baptistry of St Louis, now in the Louvre (*Ill. 138*), is to be regarded as Egyptian work. As on many of the secular examples, stylized human figures set in medallions sometimes formed a part of the decoration of the candlesticks, though on those intended for use in the mosques inscriptions or formal scrolls were

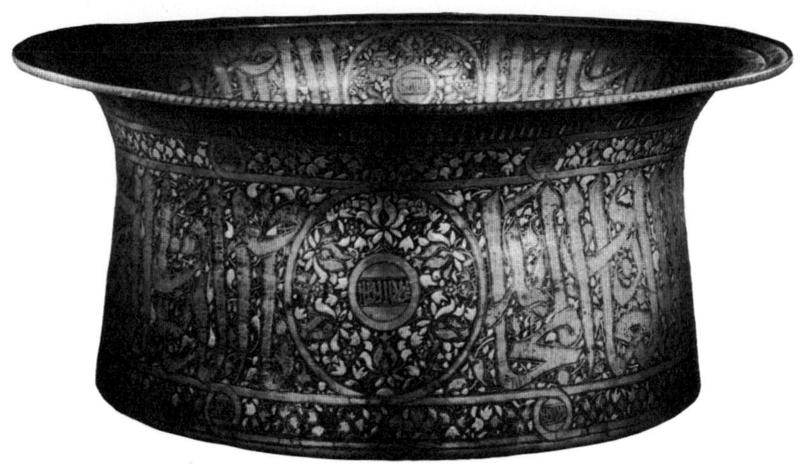

137 Copper basin with inlaid decoration and bearing the name of Sultan an-Nasir Muhammad (1294–1340). It is an example of the technique once associated with Mosul, but must have been made in Egypt

normal. Among the figures on the Baptistry of St Louis is a portrait of a certain Salar, who was captured by Beybars and became a protégé first of Qala-un and then of Khalil, and eventually became viceroy of Egypt; on this evidence the basin can be dated to between 1290 and 1310.

If the glass, the metal and the pottery is all clearly to be classed as art, it may perhaps be questioned whether the textiles and some of the woodwork of this age, especially towards its end, should not rather be designated as craftwork. On the textiles designs on a small scale or inscriptions supplanted the large-scale motifs of earlier times and embroideries gradually took the place of the loom-woven stuffs; fine though all these often are, they lack the magnificence of the earlier work, and attract because of the detail of the craftsmanship rather than because of the grandeur of the compositions. The sculptured and inlaid woodwork, with its love of intricate arabesques or small-scale geometric patterns, though amazingly proficient, again is hardly great art – often indeed it seems somewhat tedious. It is adequate for what it was intended, doors, mihrabs and so forth, but can hardly be regarded in the same light as the glasswork or the pottery.

The question of whether or not the manufacture of carpets was included in the repertoire of the Egyptian textile weavers at this time is a somewhat debated one. Fragments have been dug up at Fostat, one of which can actually be dated to the year 821, while others can be assigned on stylistic grounds to dates from the tenth century onwards. It has, however, been questioned whether these should be regarded as local work or imports, and in the fourteenth century there was certainly a significant trade in imports from Turkey. By the seventeenth century, however, the word 'Cairene' was in common use to describe a special sort of carpet made in Egypt. These carpets were distinguished by very characteristic geometric designs inspired by marble pavements, rather than gardens – like the carpets of Persia, or mosque plans – like those of Turkey. The fact that similar designs inspired the woodwork of the middle period in Egypt, as well as the known competence of Egyptian weavers in other veins in early times, tends to support the existence of a local carpet industry, and that, if it existed at all, it was probably established as early as the eighth or ninth century.

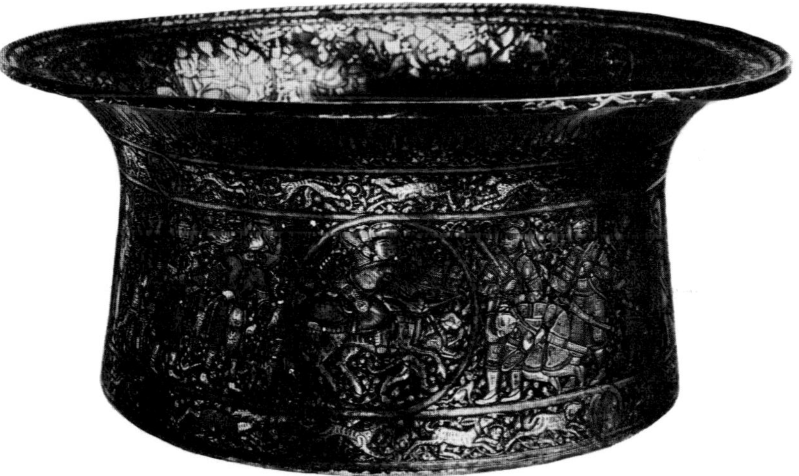

138 Copper basin with inlaid decoration. This, the largest and most important example of inlaid metalwork from Egypt, is usually known as the Baptistry of St Louis. *c.* 1290–1310

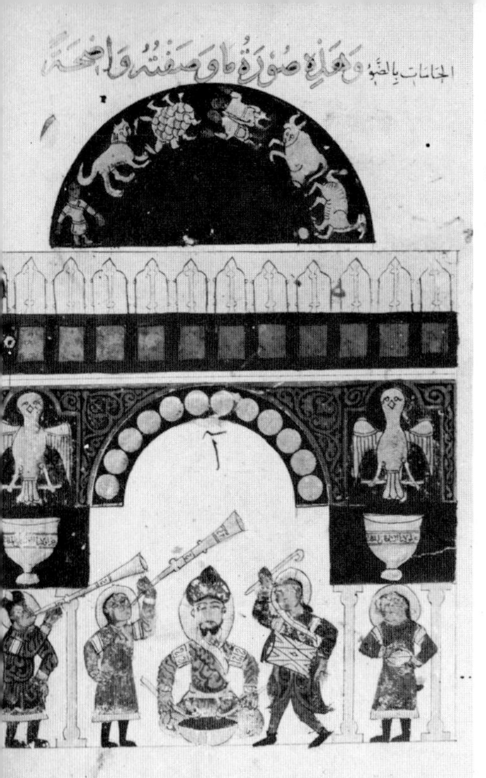

139 Illustration from al-Jaziri's treatise on *Automata* representing a water clock. The book was first written at Diyarbakir between 1181 and 1206, but the copy from which this miniature comes is dated to the mid-thirteenth century

140 The physician wakes from sleep to find a banquet being given in his house. From 'The Banquet of the Physicians' copied in Syria in 1273

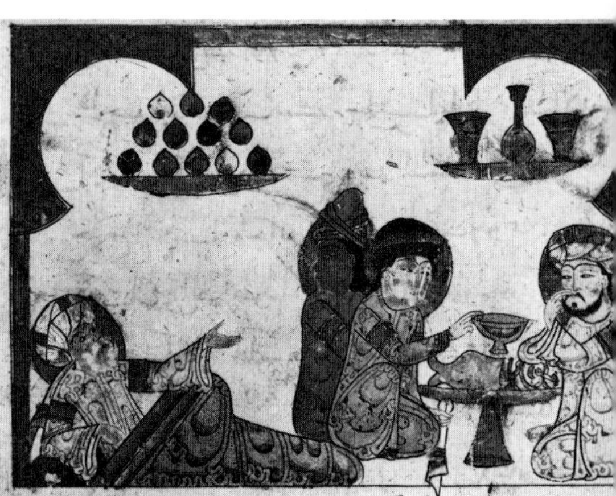

It is perhaps to some extent true to say that the miniature painting of the Mamluk school had a certain dry, wooden character which distinguished it from the earlier work done in Mesopotamia. The figures are somehow like dolls or puppets instead of living individuals, and the renderings are decorative rather than interpretational. But deficiencies in this direction are compensated for by the gay, delightful colouring and the almost Matisse-like conception of some of the designs.

Most important of the earlier Mamluk books are copies done in Egypt and Syria of the famous treatise of al-Jaziri on *Automata*, first written at Diyarbakir between 1181 and 1206 (*Ill. 139*). The original no longer survives; the copies probably follow it very closely, for one in the Saray at Istanbul, done in 1254 (No. 3472) is close to others of a century later, except for the addition of certain motifs which are part of the repertory of Mamluk heraldry. A cup on one of the leaves of a Mamluk volume may be cited, and may be compared with the same heraldic motif on pottery from Fostat or on metalwork. Other volumes that were illustrated belong to the old repertory so popular in Mesopotamia – the 'Fables' of Bidpai, the 'Assemblies' of Hariri and so on. In addition a few other books were illustrated, such as one now in the Ambrosian Library at Milan, entitled 'The Banquet of the Physicians' (*Da'wat al-Atibba*); it is dated to 1273 and was probably done in Syria (*Ill. 140*). The schematic frame, the symmetrical balance, the rippling, wrinkled folds of the costumes and the way that the dishes of fruit or wine vessels have been reduced to a symbolism akin to that of the art of the twentieth century are all characteristic.

The beginnings of the Mamluk school are represented by two copies of the 'Assemblies' of Hariri in the British Museum. One (Add. MS. 22.114) is dated to 1237, and the scene of two figures conversing in a room with looped curtains (*Ill. 141*) is typical. The colours are bright and contrasting, but the faces are much less expressive than those which characterized the Mesopotamian work. The same colouring is to be seen in the scenes with three figures in a tent. The arrangement of the curtains follows a convention which had been current in the Byzantine world since early Christian times. The other (Or. MS. 9718), dated to 1271, is akin, but is rather more stylized and this is carried further in a manuscript in the Bodleian (MS. Marsh 458), which is dated to 1337; some of the pictures seem to have been conceived almost as pieces of pattern. The work is nevertheless of high quality and it is to be counted as one of the finest Mamluk books we know, though it is perhaps surpassed by one at Vienna, dated to 1334, for it has a magnificent frontispiece which as a piece of pure decoration is wholly successful (*Ill. 142*). Though in the main a work of Arab art, Eastern influence has penetrated, for the plumed hats worn by the two musicians are wholly Mongol; the turban of the central figure on the other hand is of a type that was reserved for the Mamluk princes.

A similar change affected the animal picture-books, although owing to the advanced degree of stylization that had been reached in the Mesopotamian models, it is perhaps less striking at a first glance. Indeed, although a copy of the Fables of Bidpai in the Bodleian (MS. Pococke 400), dated to 1354, has sometimes been assigned to Iraq, it is, in fact, probably to be regarded as a close Egyptian copy of an earlier Mesopotamian work. The trees of the Syriac manuscript of the gospels in the British Museum (Syr. MS. 7170) may be compared, and the colouring is less brilliant than in typical Mamluk work. Another copy of the Fables in the Bibliothèque Nationale (MS. arabe 3467), on the other hand, contains miniatures which are more essentially decorative, and fall obviously into the Mamluk group. The ultimate and most extreme development of the style is, however, represented by a copy of an animal picture-book, the *Kitab Manafi al-Hayavan*, in the Ambrosian Library at Milan (A.R. A.F.D. 140). Here the plants, birds and animals are wholly stylized and the greatest quality of the pictures lie in their delightful, brilliant, but wholly unnaturalistic colouring. The book contains thirty-two miniatures and they bring to a logical but delightful conclusion the work of the Arab school of secular book illustration.

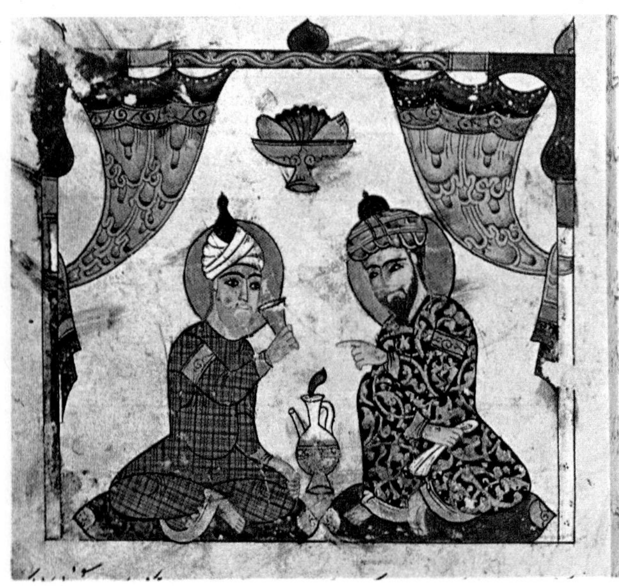

141 Leaf from a copy of 'Assemblies' of Hariri which shows two figures seated. Syrian, 1237. Although most of the manuscripts of this type can be assigned to Mesopotamia, a number were also done in Syria and Egypt, under the patronage of the Mamluks

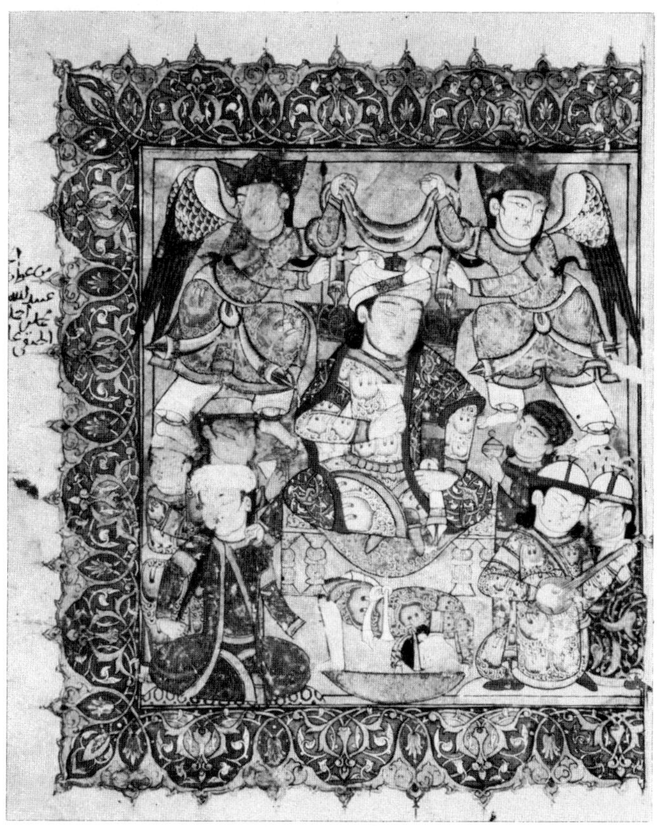

142 Leaf from the 'Assemblies' of Hariri showing a Prince enthroned. It was probably executed in Egypt in 1334 and is one of the finest works of the Mamluk school that has come down to us

Perhaps the most remarkable of all the work done under the patronage of the Mamluk sultans, however, were the buildings for which they were responsible in Cairo. Some of the sultans built a very great deal, nearly everyone built something, for it had become the custom for a fine mausoleum to be erected for burial purposes, and the tombs of the caliphs are one of the glories of Cairo. In addition to a mausoleum nearly every one of them built a mosque – not a great congregational mosque as in early times, but a smaller, more compact structure where there was opportunity for the carver and the craftsman to show their skill.

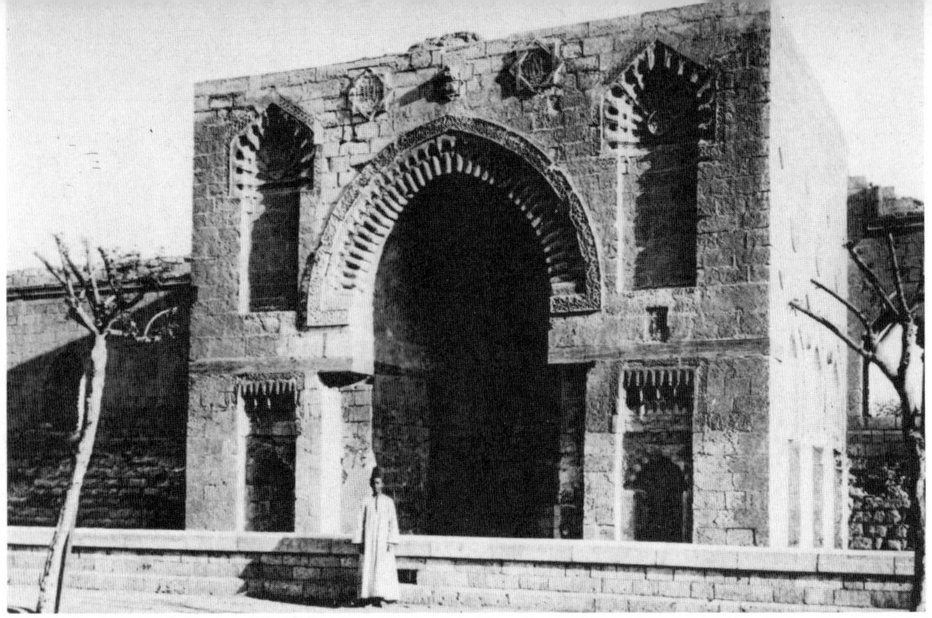

143 The north-west entrance to the mosque of Beybars (1260–77), Cairo. All the sultans of the Mamluk dynasty were great patrons of art and architecture and each of them was responsible for a fine mosque in Cairo. Photo by courtesy of Professor Creswell

The first of the series was the mosque set up by Beybars (1260–77) (*Ill. 143*), outside the city, on the road to Heliopolis. It is the exception that proves the rule, for it is the only congregational mosque of the age. It consists of a great rectangular court with a six-aisled sanctuary and three aisles at the other end and at the sides. Its north-west entrance is particularly impressive and shows the work of the sculptor to good advantage. Qala-un (1279–90) was responsible for a *madrassa* and a mosque in Cairo itself (*Ill. 144*), the two forming a complete entity, with a fine minaret in three stages. Sultan an-Nasir Muhammad built several mosques and palaces including the Nasiriyya College. The twin minarets of one of his mosques, on the citadel, are rather Persian in style, while on the other there is sculpture of very outstanding quality (*Ill. 145*). Finally Sultan an-Nasir Hassan (1347–61), though he was himself a despicable character, was responsible for one of the finest of the mosques which, with its madrassa, was built about 1362; it is very tall, almost like a fortress, and has one of the highest minarets in Cairo and perhaps the finest mihrab and mimbar of the period.

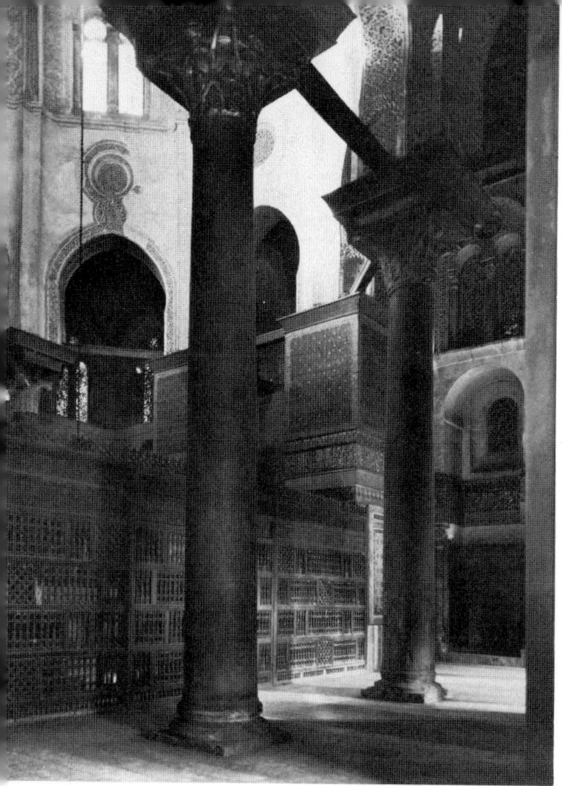

144 Interior of the tomb chamber, Mosque of Qala-un (1279–90), Cairo. All these Mamluk mosques were primarily intended as burial places

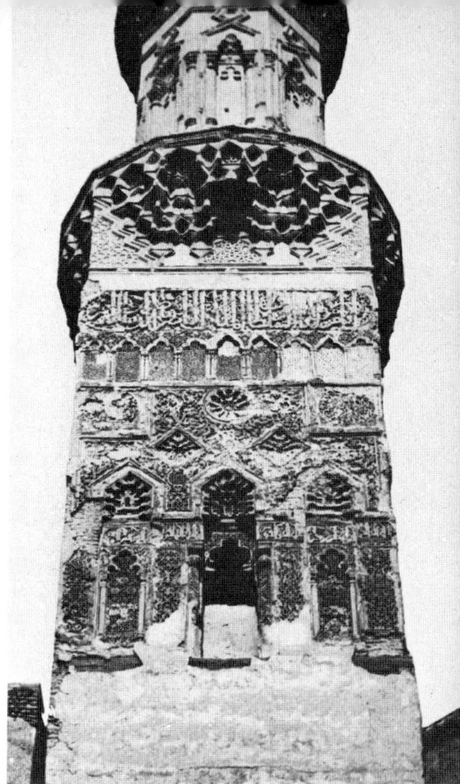

145 Detail of the sculptured decoration on the minaret of the madrassa of Sultan an-Nasir Muhammad (1294–1340), Cairo

The fine building tradition established by the Mamluks was followed by their successors of the Circassian Mamluk dynasty, which was established in 1382 and lasted until the conquest of Egypt by the Ottoman Turks in 1517. Stylistically there is no sharp division between the work of the two periods, and the mosque and madrassa that bear the name of the first Circassian Mamluk sultan, Barquq (1382–99), are close in style to pure Mamluk work, while the stages of the minaret of a mosque built for his son Farag outside the walls recall those of earlier buildings, notably that of the mosque of Ibn Tulun.

In 1400 history was to repeat itself, for Farag once more halted the Mongol progress, this time by defeating Timur (Tamerlane). His victory resulted not only in the continuance of a period of

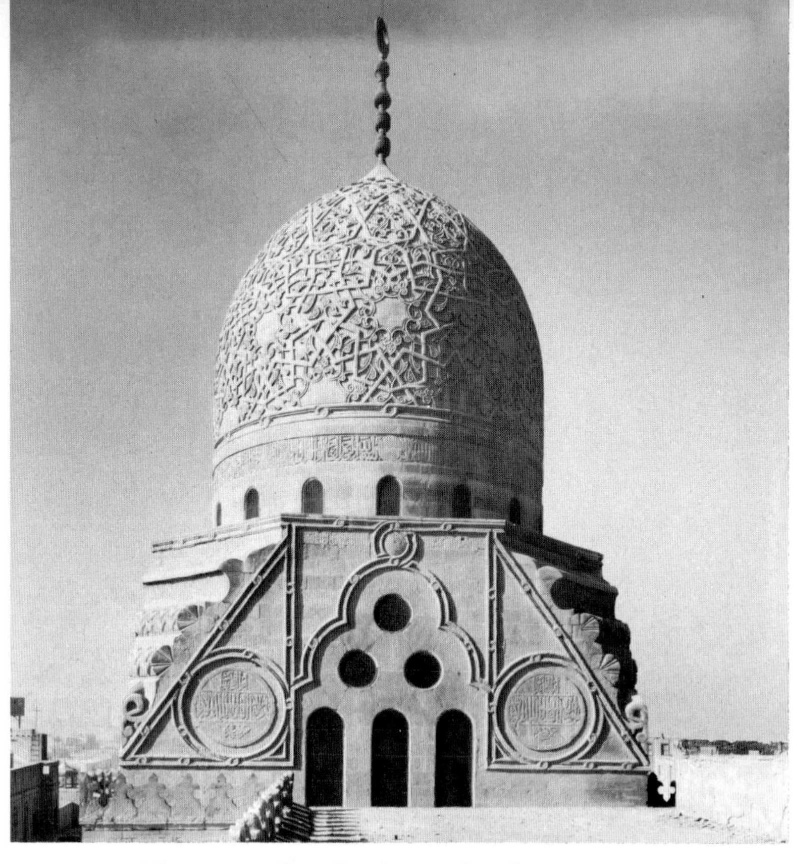

146 Dome of the mosque of Qaitbay (1463–96) in the Eastern Cemetery, Cairo. The tradition of building established by the Mamluks was carried on by their successors, the Circassian Mamluks

wealth and prosperity, but also in the development of a somewhat precious style in art, which lacked the vigour which seems to have resulted from the Mongol invasions in Persia, despite the havoc that was wrought. The Egyptian buildings were all exquisite, notably the famous madrassa and mausoleum of Qaitbay (1463–96) in the eastern cemetery, but they seem almost too perfect and their decoration is so delicate thar it somehow appears to be overdone; this is true, for example, of the geometric reliefs which adorn the outside of the dome of Qaitbay's mosque (*Ill. 146*). In fact, these works, exquisite though they are, represent the limit of a style which could go no further without revolution or violent change. They may be said to mark the end of the story of Egyptian art, for in 1517 the country was conquered by the Ottoman sultan, Selim I, and the last building of consequence to be erected, Süleyman's mosque on the citadel (1550–6), was in a completely new style, based on a Constantinopolitan model which had itself been derived to no small degree from a Byzantine prototype.

Though few other buildings in Egypt or Syria were as completely Ottoman in style as Süleyman's mosque, the last phase of Islamic art there was nevertheless much affected by Ottoman influences, especially in the spheres of architecture and ceramics, and most of the buildings set up were thus very like those of Constantinople. At the same time a new type of pottery was made at Damascus which it is sometimes hard to tell from that of Isnik, in Turkey, though in general the designs tend to be less precise and hard and more

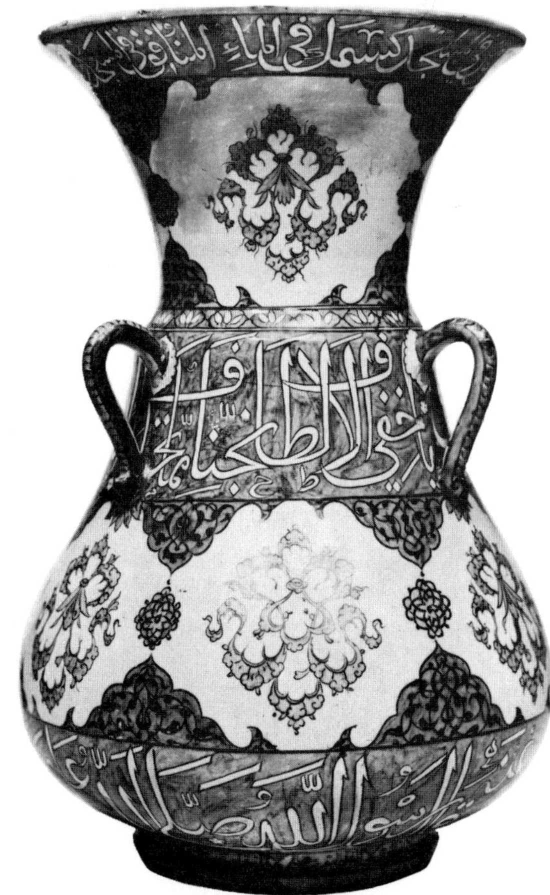

147 Pottery mosque lamp found in the Dome of the Rock, Jerusalem, and dated 1549. It was probably made in Damascus, though the pottery is very closely akin to that done for Turkish patrons at Isnik. The Turkish style was adopted in Syria after the conquest of the country by the Ottoman sultans in the early sixteenth century

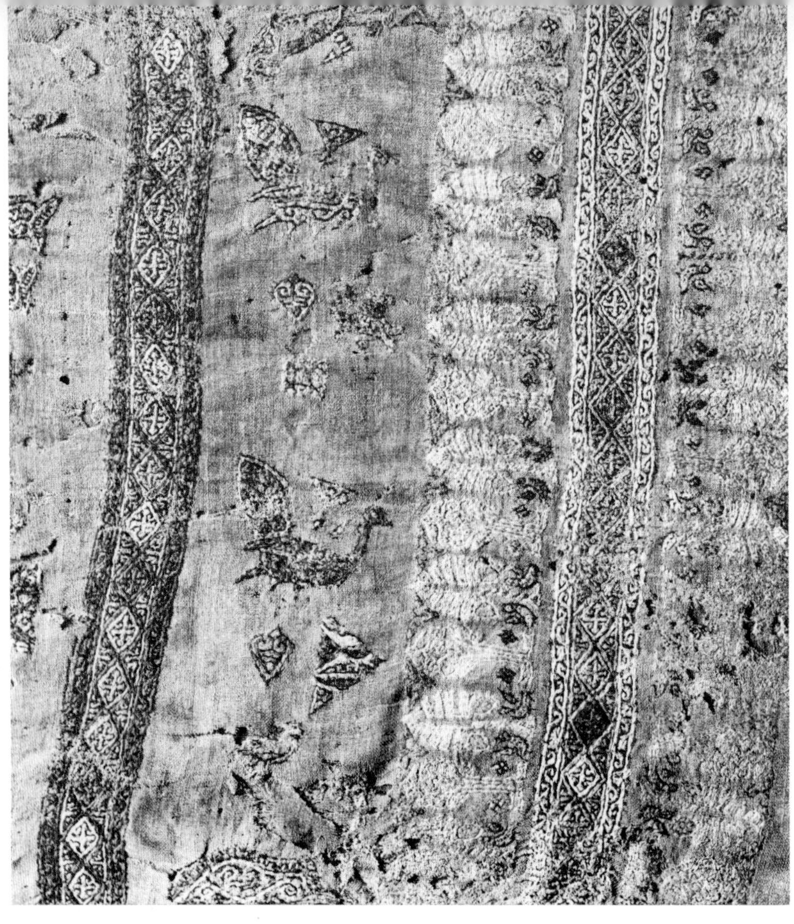

148 Cushion cover embroidered on linen. In later Mamluk times embroidery to a great extent superseded the fine woven stuffs of earlier date. Probably Egyptian, seventh to eleventh century

spontaneous, and manganese purple was a favourite colour. It is distinguished by a very fine white body with a painted decoration of flowers and leaves in apple-green, blue and pale purple, outlined in black against a clear white ground. Lamps, bowls and other large vessels were usual (*Ill. 147*). The best work was produced in the later sixteenth century and much of it is to be classed amongst the finest products of Islamic art. Of the other arts the embroideries were perhaps the most outstanding and they seem to have replaced woven stuffs to a considerable extent (*Ill. 148*).

CHAPTER EIGHT

Later Islamic Art in North Africa, Spain and Sicily

Though there was no very clear division between the earlier and later phases of Islamic art in Spain, the style nevertheless changed very considerably as time went on, and in the later work a wholly distinctive manner was developed which was more decorative and less monumental than the earlier, reflecting very clearly the character of the society which produced it, for the centralized government of Cordova ended about 1090 and the country fell under the control of a number of local rulers. The same was equally true of North Africa. In both areas the buildings became smaller and less monumental, and their decorations more ornate and more superficial, depending for their appeal on elegance rather than grandeur. The Great Mosque at Tlemcen (1082–restored 1136) (*Ill. 149*) is typical of this phase. It is comparatively small yet the ornament is lavish. The horseshoe arch has been evolved to an exaggerated degree and the multi-lobed arches and the pierced stonework of the dome are amazingly intricate; the effect is picturesque and delightful, but it can hardly compare as a piece of creative architecture with such buildings as the mosque at Cordova or the Masjid-i-Jami at Isfahan. The same is true of the pottery and the other arts, however graceful they may be; only the textiles stand out because of the great majesty of their designs.

The first phase of this new age, both in Africa and Spain, is known as the Almoravid dynasty, which was centred at Marrakesh from 1056 until 1148, but also controlled southern Spain. It was succeeded by the more coherent Almohads, lasting until about 1250, when Spain fell under the control of a line of rulers from North Africa who were inspired by profound religious ideals of a basically iconoclast character. Their capital was at Marrakesh, and the Qutubiya mosque there (second half of the twelfth century), in its plainness and restraint, illustrates the character of the religious art of the

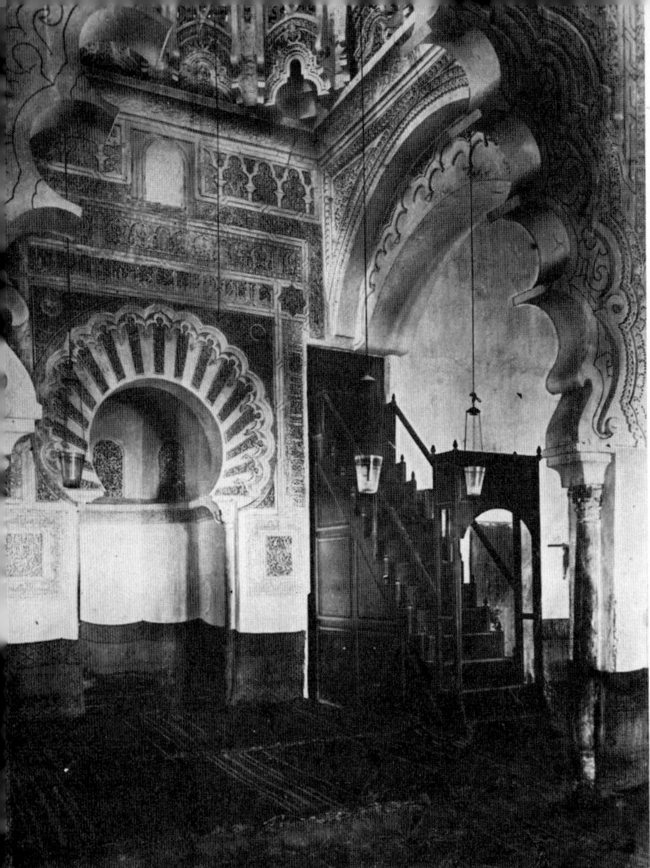

149 The mihrab chamber of the Great Mosque, Tlemcen, Algeria 1082, restored 1136. The multi-lobed arches are typical of the rather ornate style developed in North Africa and Spain from the twelfth century onwards

age as a whole (*Ill. 151*). Anything in the way of greater ornateness was reserved for work in the secular sphere, and here some very outstanding buildings were produced during the later twelfth and the thirteenth centuries. The great city gates of Marrakesh (*Ill. 152*), Rabat and elsewhere show the decorative style of this secular art at its best. They were important, for they served not only to protect the entrance to the cities but also acted as the places from which justice was dispensed and where meetings of importance took place. At a later date the gates even became symbols of the centre of government and sometimes even served to designate a régime – in the Ottoman world the idea survived in the term 'Sublime Porte' which was actually the gateway to the central block of government offices at Constantinople, but the name was applied to the whole governmental machine.

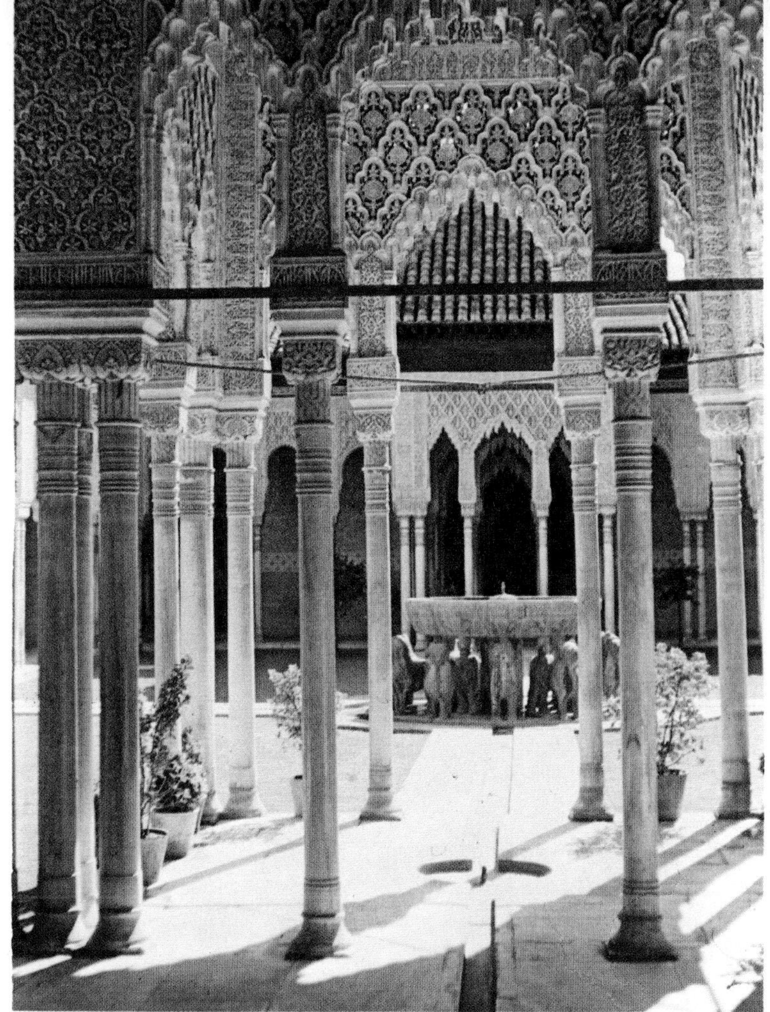

150 The Court of the Lions, the Alhambra, Granada. 1354. This was one of the latest additions to the palace which served the local rulers of that part of Spain

A number of North African cities rose to importance at this time in addition to Marrakesh – the most outstanding of them was Rabat. Pottery was made in many of these cities and there was a certain amount of weaving; taken as a whole, however, no very important products in the minor arts are to be associated with North Africa, and what was done belongs more to the range of folk art rather than fine art (*Ill. 153*).

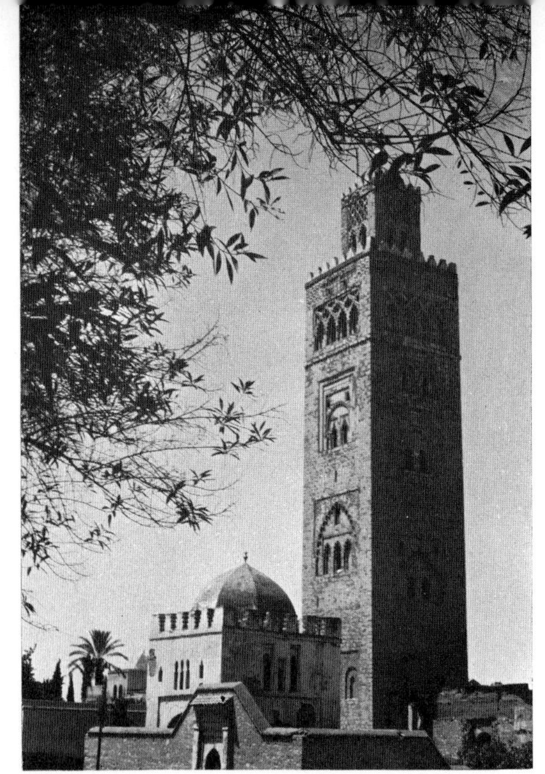

151 (*left*) The Qutubiya mosque, Marrakesh. In the restraint of its decoration it is typical of work done under the patronage of the rulers of the rather austere Almoravid dynasty which was in control at Marrakesh from 1056 to 1148

152 (*below*) The Rabat Gate, Marrakesh. Late twelfth century. It formed a part of the fortifications of the city, but also served as a centre where meetings took place and where justice was dispensed

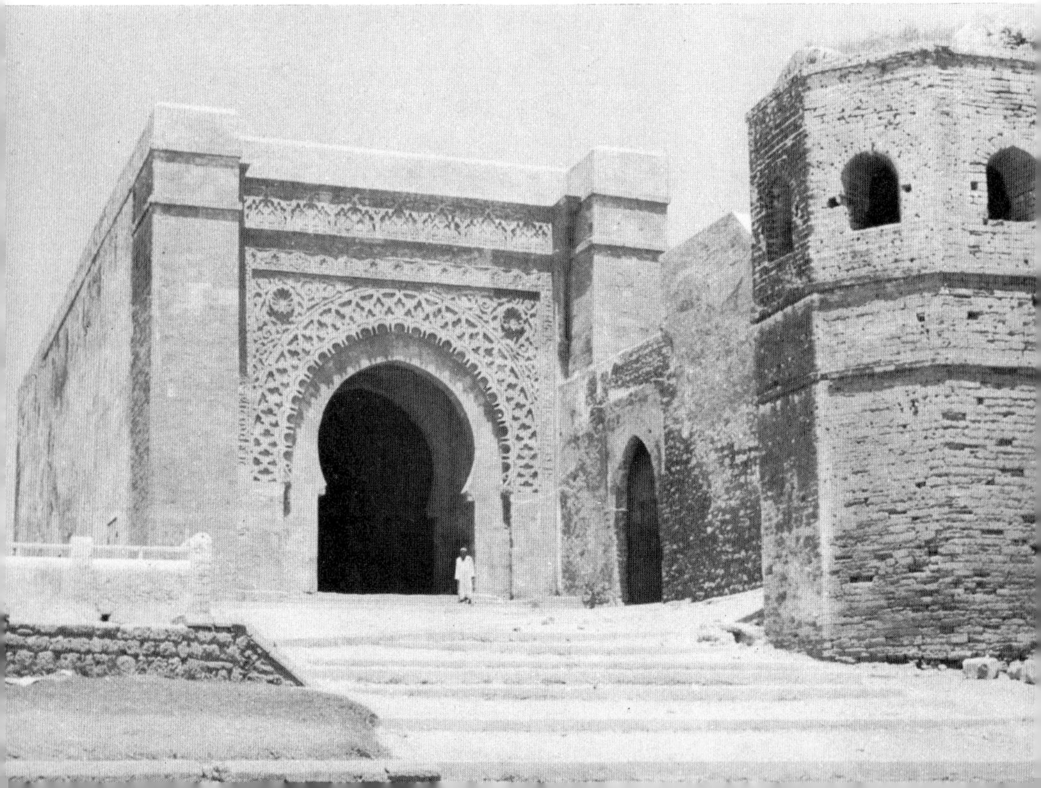

In Spain exactly the opposite situation prevailed, for there the minor arts were more interesting than the architecture. This was, however, to some extent due to the fact that few of the Islamic buildings there survived the Christian conquest, and it is really only in the Alhambra at Granada that anything of architectural consequence is to be seen. Granada served as the capital of a small independent dynasty from 1237 until 1492 when the Muslims were driven out of Spain. The Alhambra was the palace of the rulers and it underwent a number of repairs and enlargements during the whole of this period. The famous 'Court of the Lions', with its lion fountain in the centre, was added in 1354 (*Ill. 150*).

Though there are but few monuments of Muslim architecture in Spain, the ivory carvings, textiles and, at a later date, the pottery were all of high quality. As regards the former, the rather full, ornate style which had characterized the work of the tenth and eleventh centuries continued; the textiles became more elaborate and in the pottery a number of techniques new to Spain were developed. The best work dates from the fourteenth and fifteenth centuries, and is represented by the famous Hispano-Mauresque lustre wares (*Ill. 154*). The technique was first developed in Murcia and Almeria in the thirteenth century, but it was monochrome; polychrome lustre only appeared almost two centuries later, by which time the motifs of decoration were mostly of a definitely Western character and as often as not included Western heraldic emblems. It was a luxury art produced to suit wealthy patrons, and many of the vessels like the great storage jars in the Alhambra were of great size and of not much practical use. The large dishes for fruit which are represented in numerous collections are in closer accord with present-day tastes. More practical were the coarser wares decorated in a bold, simple style, in green (*Ill. 153*). Paterna in Valencia and Teruel in Aragon were two of the main centres of production. The work is closer in style to that of such Italian centres as Urbino than it is to anything produced in the rest of the Islamic world, and it thus stands rather apart. Tiles with a decoration both in relief and in coloured glazes were also made, especially in Andalusia, but they too were more Italian than Islamic in character.

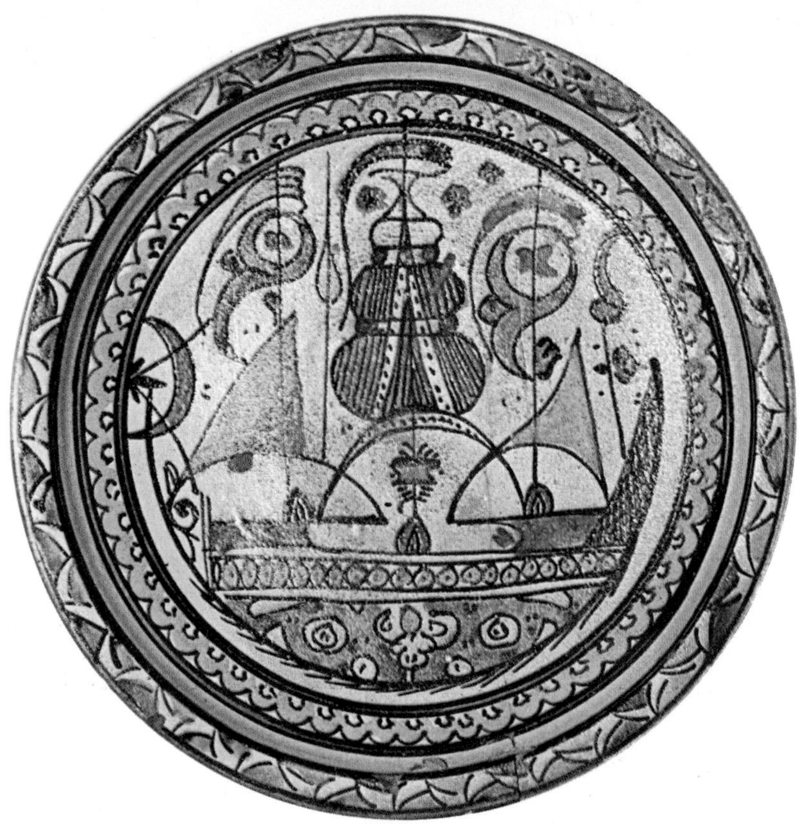

153 Bowl of polychrome ware from Rabat. The potteries of North Africa, though gay and colourful, were never of the same artistic quality as those of Egypt, Syria and Persia. Most of them are indeed to be assigned to the sphere of 'folk' rather than 'fine' art

Except perhaps for the Hispano-Mauresque lustre, the quality of Spanish pottery was rather poor in contrast to that of Egypt and Persia, and the varieties were limited. But the textiles were on the other hand outstanding, and some of the most beautiful products of these later years must be assigned to Spanish looms, or to those of Sicily, where work which was very similar was done. Indeed, it is not always easy to tell the Spanish products from the Sicilian, though the two are distinct from those of the rest of the Islamic world, both in respect of their designs and also with regard to the colouring, which was unusual and distinctive. The grounds were often rather dark, green, brown or black being the favourite colours, and the designs were in cream, red, blue or white. The patterns were again characteristic, being somewhat rigid and severe. An outstanding textile of the twelfth century in the Musée de Cluny (*Ill. 157*), for example, bears confronted peacocks, one row in red and gold, the next in yellow, against a brown ground. A somewhat similar colouring characterizes a textile with a highly stylized bird design in the Museum at Vich (*Ill. 155*); it has sometimes been assigned to Spain and sometimes to Sicily, but it is hard to be sure of its provenance.

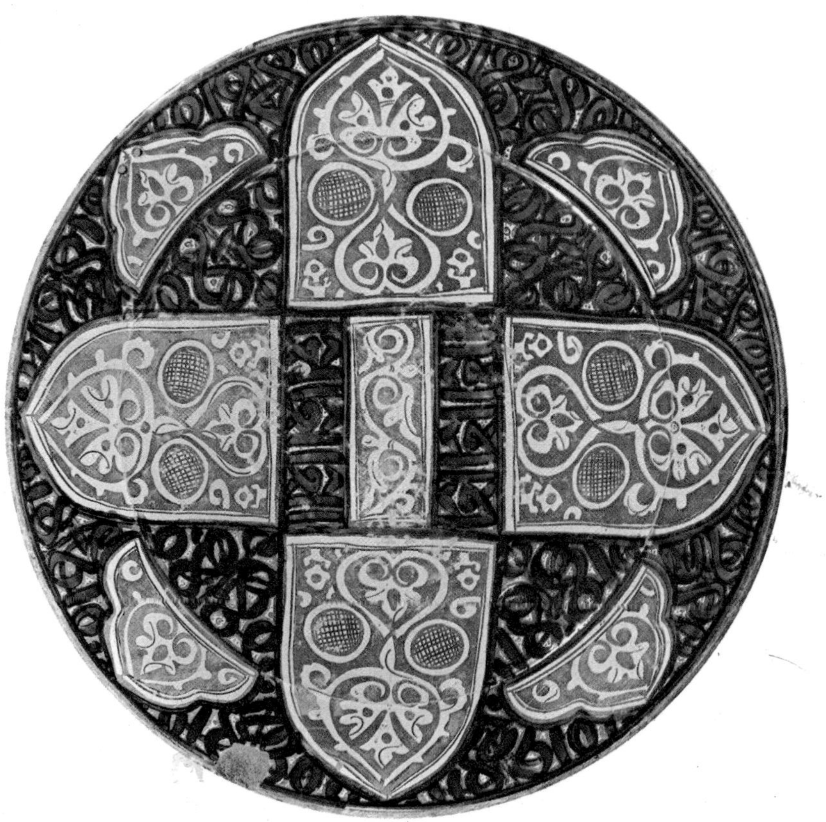

154 Dish of Hispano-Mauresque ware from Valencia. The gold lustre vessels of Spain, though there were many Western elements in their designs, represent in many ways one of the highest peaks of Islamic art. Early fifteenth century

Though Sicily was an important centre of manufacture of purely Islamic textiles – they had no doubt been made there during the period of Egyptian overlordship – others which were more definitely Byzantine in style were also produced in the island. We know that Roger II introduced craftsmen from Greece who presumably worked in a Byzantine manner, and textiles like the Shroud of St Potentien at Sens are probably to be regarded as their work. It is finely woven and carries a design of confronted birds and addorsed gryphons in medallions bordered by kufic inscriptions. The presence of Greek craftsmen did not mean the death of Islamic motifs, and the great Coronation Mantle of the Sicilian kings, now at Vienna, which dates from 1134, is more Islamic than Byzantine (*Ill. 156*). The camels and lions which form the nucleus of the design are thus entirely Eastern, and it also has a border of kufic script. It is actually an embroidery, although the disposition of the design is close to that of the woven silks and the absolutely balanced, confronted beasts would be well suited to weaving on a loom.

Another group of textiles which is undoubtedly to be assigned to Spain contrasts markedly so far as the designs are concerned with these figured stuffs, and the patterns are basically geometric, even if stylized animals or birds are sometimes included. Textiles of this type first appeared in the thirteenth century. The same rather unusual colour contrasts distinguish them. Gold threads were often used in their production, and as time went on delicate brocades replaced the rather coarser, heavier textiles of earlier days. But, as with the lustre ware, European motifs, often of an heraldic character, were then quite often included, and work of this type usually goes under the name of the Mudejar style.

We know practically nothing of Sicilian pottery and nothing was produced that can compare with what was made elsewhere in the Islamic world. But Sicily was an important centre of ivory carving, and there are quite a number of caskets, which are to be regarded as Sicilian rather than Spanish (*Ills. 158, 159, 160*). Most of them bear

155 Woven silk textile known as the Tapestry of the Witches. It has sometimes been assigned to Spain, sometimes to Sicily, but the former is more likely. Twelfth or early thirteenth century

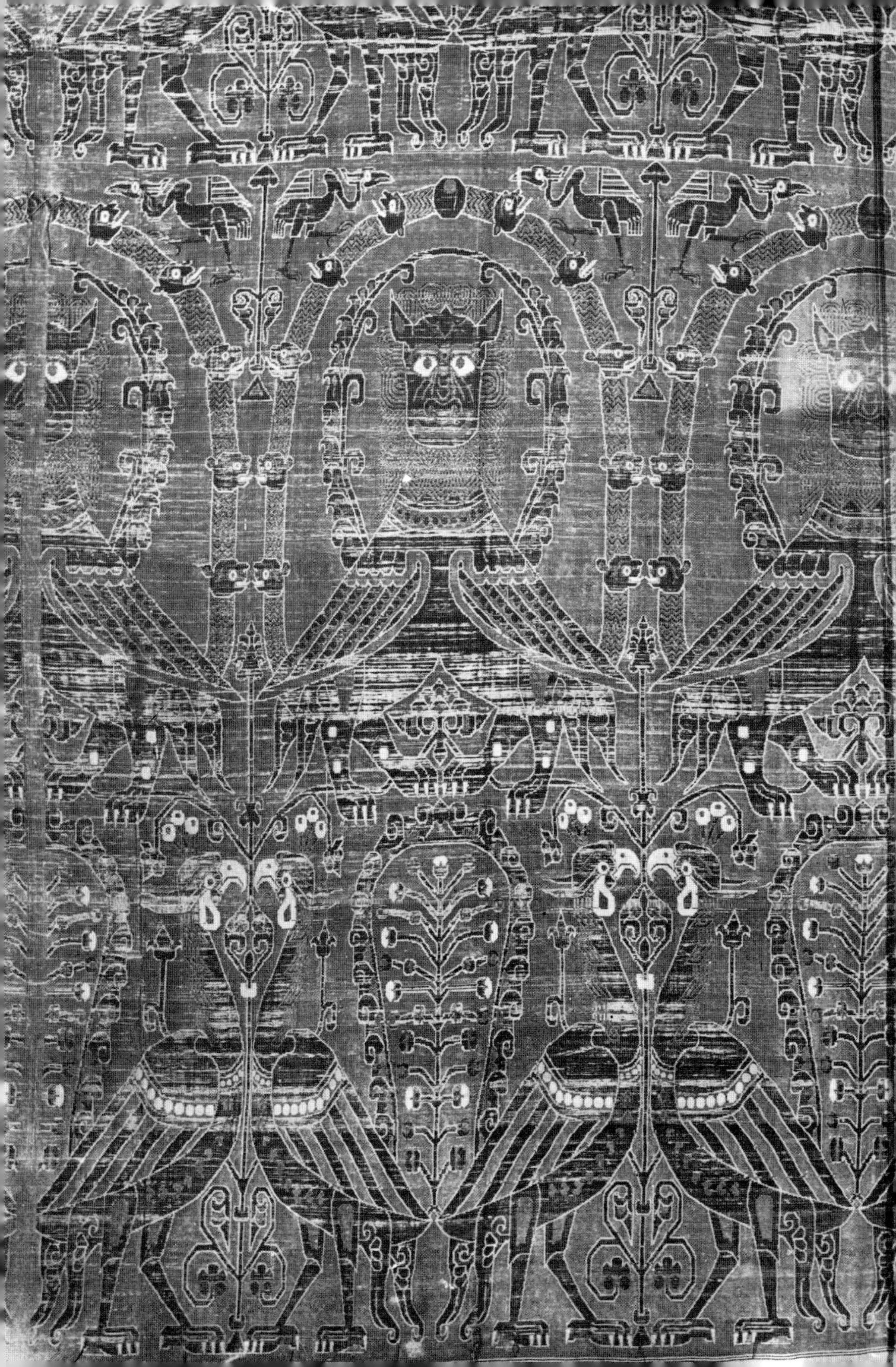

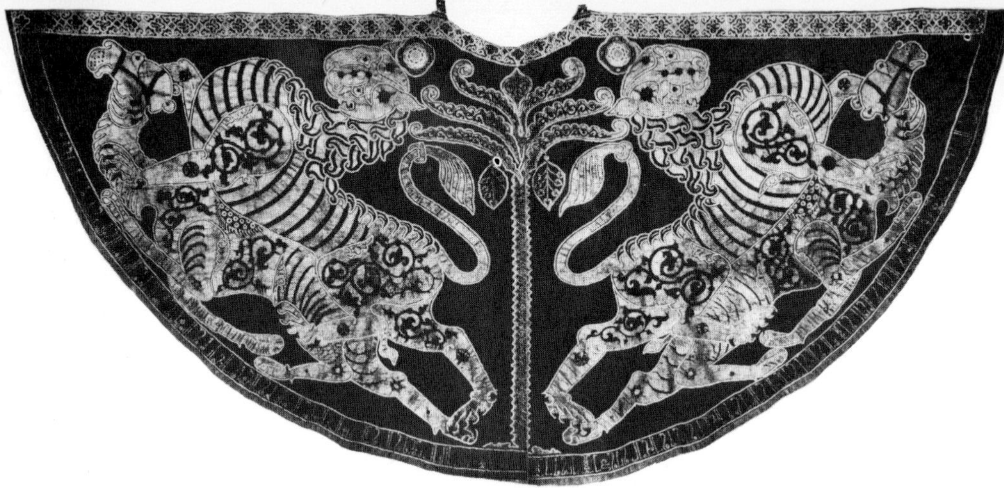

156 The Coronation Mantle of the Holy Roman Emperors, made for Roger II of Sicily in 1134. It is actually an embroidery, but the disposition of the design suggests the inspiration of a woven stuff

inscriptions in *naskh* or kufic and these sometimes give a date. They are distinguished by a decoration which is usually partly painted and partly in lowish relief or engraving; those where the decoration is in high-relief are more probably Spanish. The Sicilian ones are mostly to be assigned to the twelfth century, the Spanish ones to a rather earlier date. Peacocks play an important role in the decoration and stags and hares in foliage are also usual, as well as riders who carry hawks on their arms. The themes of the decorations are in fact closely similar to those of the mosaics which adorn the so-called Norman *stanze* in the Palatine Palace at Palermo. Though Byzantine in technique, these are in a basically Persian style, and would seem to owe a debt to Sassanian art rather than to subsequent developments in Islamic times. The heritage may well have passed by way of Byzantium, for there was a room in the imperial palace at Constantinople known as the 'Persian House' which was probably decorated in a very similar manner.

The Islamic element also made itself felt in the secular architecture of Sicily, notably in several small palaces of which one called La Ziza, at Palermo, is the most important. They were set up for the Norman rulers, but whereas the decorations that these kings sponsored in the churches were wholly Byzantine in character and were done mainly

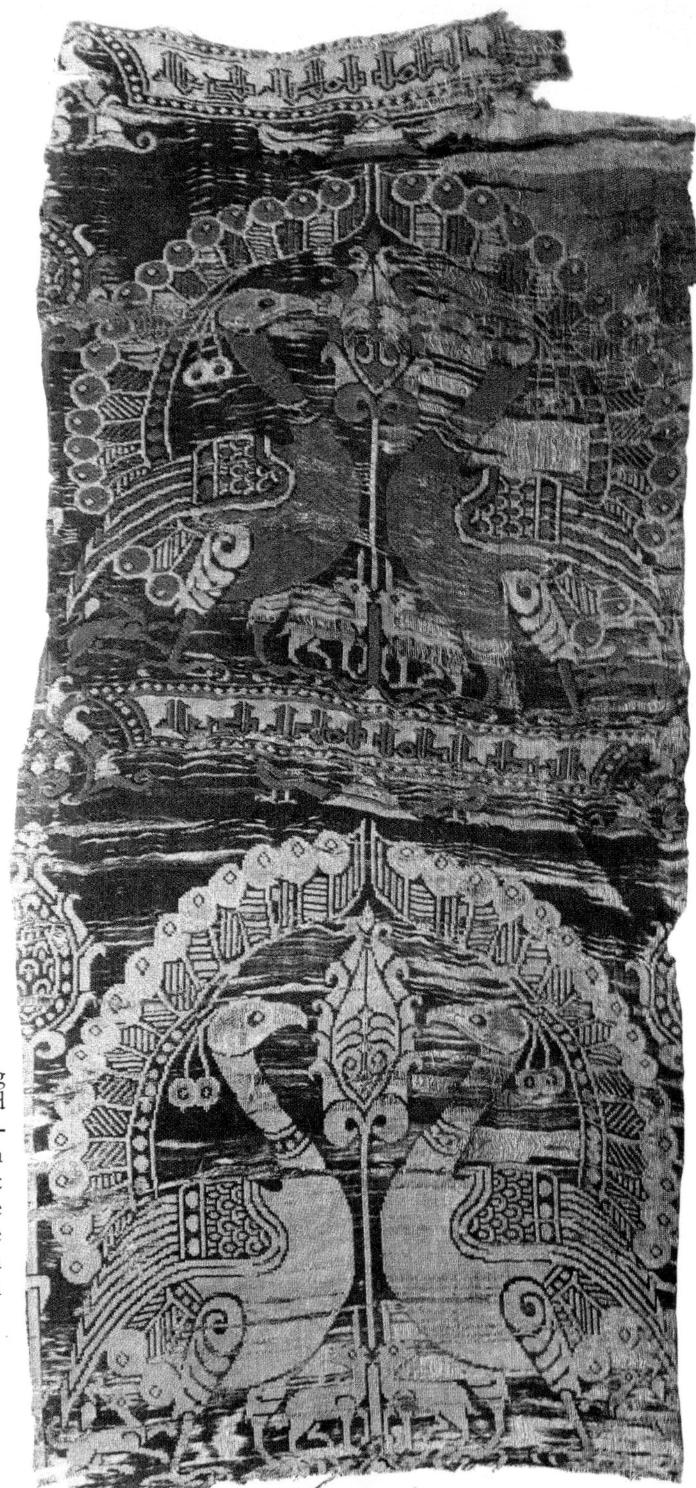

157 Woven silk bearing confronted peacocks and a kufic inscription. Together with fragments in the Victoria and Albert Museum and in Toulouse Cathedral, it is one of the finest pieces of Spanish textile weaving. Twelfth century

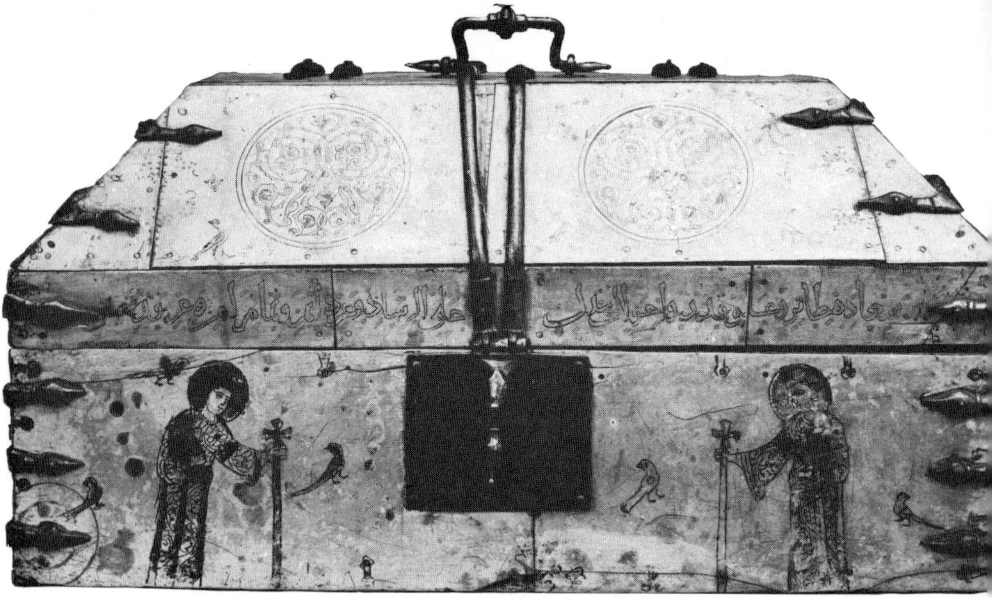

158 Front and back views of an ivory casket originally from the Cathedral in Bari. The decoration is painted – a characteristic of Sicilian work. The figures may be compared with those on the ceiling of the Palatine chapel at Palermo (*Ill. 82*). Twelfth century

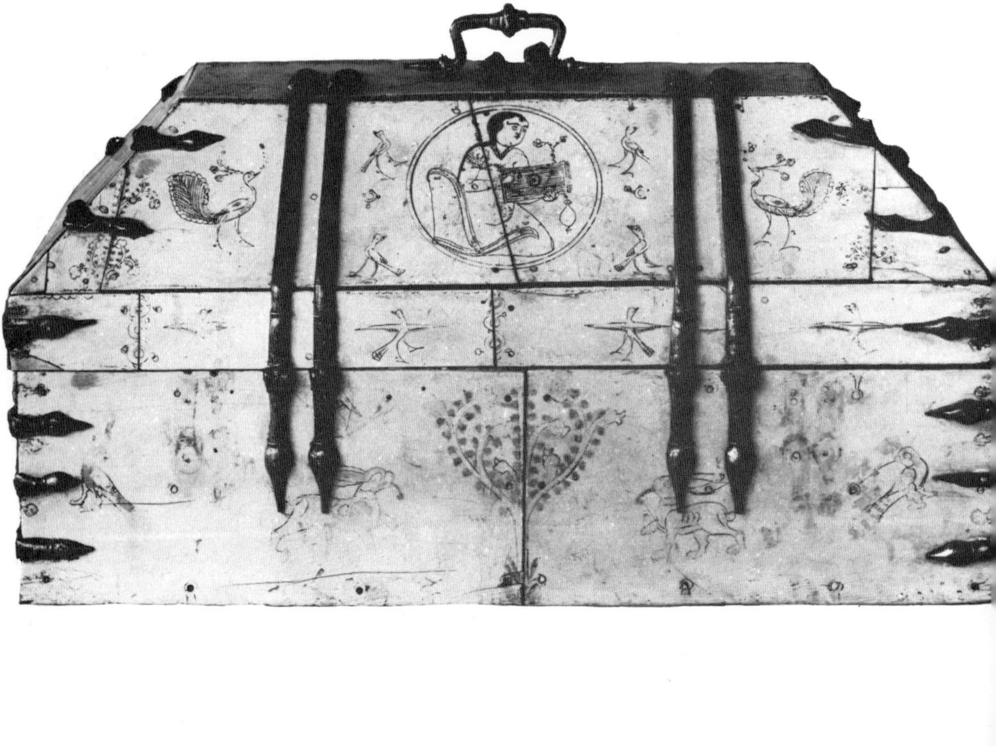

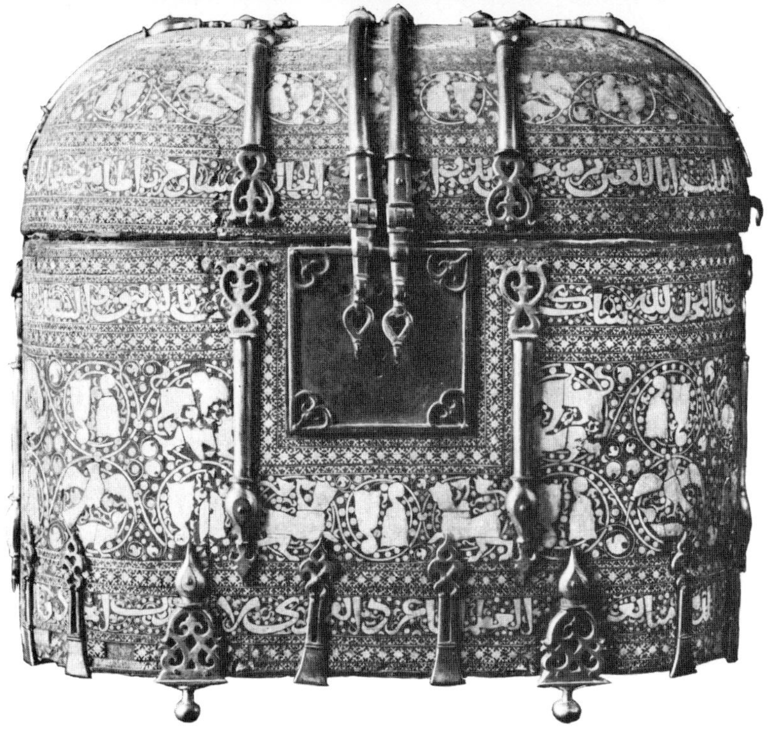

159 Ivory casket of the thirteenth century. The decoration is similar to that which appeared on such metalwork of the period

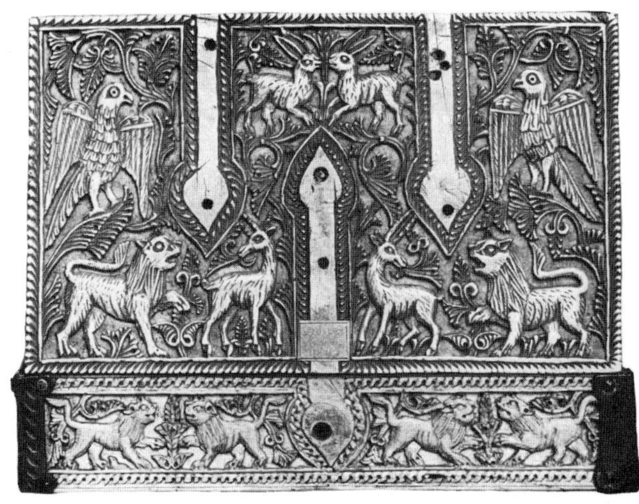

160 Ivory casket of the eleventh century with decoration in relief. It is not always easy to distinguish between Spanish and Sicilian ivories, but in general those with a deeply carved decoration may be assigned to Spain and those with painted decoration to Sicily

by craftsmen from Constantinople, the palaces, with their small, high rooms, arranged around a central square, must have been Islamic in inspiration. Links with Africa were maintained even after the arrival of the Normans; the ceiling of the Palatine chapel, though dated to 1154, is a wholly Egyptian work (see p. 84) and Muslim craftsmen were probably similarly employed elsewhere alongside the Byzantine ones – the Coronation Mantle, with its kufic inscription, affords firm proof of this. But the hey-day of Islamic art in Sicily was short-lived, and little of real consequence was done once the Norman kings were firmly established soon after the middle of the eleventh century.

CHAPTER NINE

The Seljuks of Rum

We have already seen how, in the eleventh century, the Seljuk Turks moved westwards from Central Asia under their leader Tügrül Beg and established themselves in Persia and Mesopotamia. Their advance westwards was pushed forward by Tügrül's son Alp Arslan until, in 1071, it was met by the Byzantine forces under the Emperor Nicephorus Phocas and, contrary, in Byzantine eyes, to all expectations, the Byzantines were roundly defeated in the notorious battle of Manzikert. Within a very short time the Seljuks had penetrated as far as Nicaea (Isnik), only fifty miles as the crow flies from Constantinople, and although they were driven out from this city in 1097, their hold on eastern and central Asia Minor was firmly established and was indeed gradually extended, so that by the early twelfth century most of Asia Minor was a Seljuk state. They remained in control for more than two centuries in spite of Mongol attacks in 1242, until eventually the centralized power disintegrated in the early fourteenth century. Firm government was again re-established by another Turkish family, the Ottomans or Osmanlis, around the middle of the fourteenth century. During the age we know as the Seljuk one, however, chieftains of other groups achieved semi or more or less complete independence in a number of areas; the most important of them were the Danişmends at Sivas. Generally speaking, however, the whole area enjoyed a period of firm, sound rule and considerable economic prosperity, and saw the development of a new and very distinctive art, which is usually known as that of the western Seljuks, or the Seljuks of Rum.

Their art owed a clear debt to the East, especially with regard to the plans of mosques and madrassas and the motifs which were used to decorate sculptures, pottery and mosaics. But the architecture though related to that of Persia was also very distinct. Buildings were almost invariably built in stone instead of brick, and craftsmen took

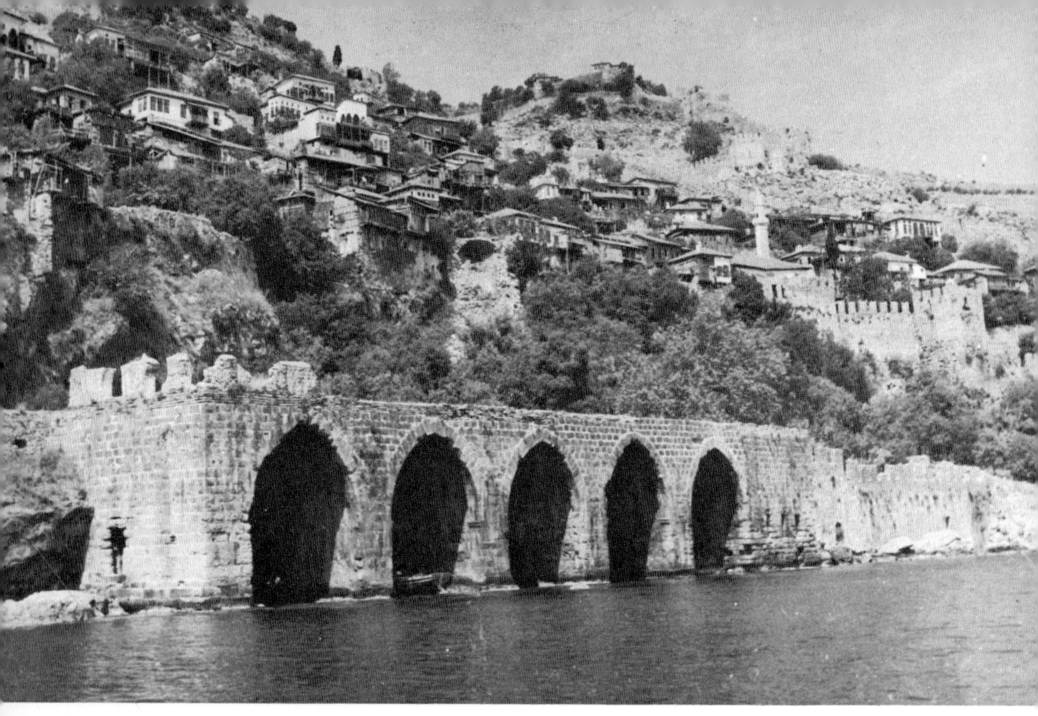

161 Covered berths for ships at Alanya, Turkey, built in 1228 for one of the Seljuk sultans. Nearly all the Muslim rulers were great patrons of religious works, but secular monuments are rare outside Turkey, and nowhere else is an example of naval architecture known

over certain techniques and learnt something with regard to style from the Byzantine world, first in the way of a direct inheritance from the captured and subjected territories, and later, when once Seljuk power was firmly established, by way of day-to-day trade and exchange. The two states seem to have coexisted on terms of reasonable friendliness and equality, in spite of the differences of faith; there were times indeed when the Byzantines preferred to maintain good relations with the Seljuks rather than with their fellow-Christians, the Crusaders. The very fact that this highland people, who had never seen the sea, built docks and covered berths for ships at Alanya (*Ill. 161*) attests the change that had been brought about in their make-up as a result of their contacts with an old-established Mediterranean power. But as one looks at the Seljuk buildings, it is their truly original character that most strikes one, and it is only after some probing that the debt that they owe to inspiration from elsewhere becomes apparent.

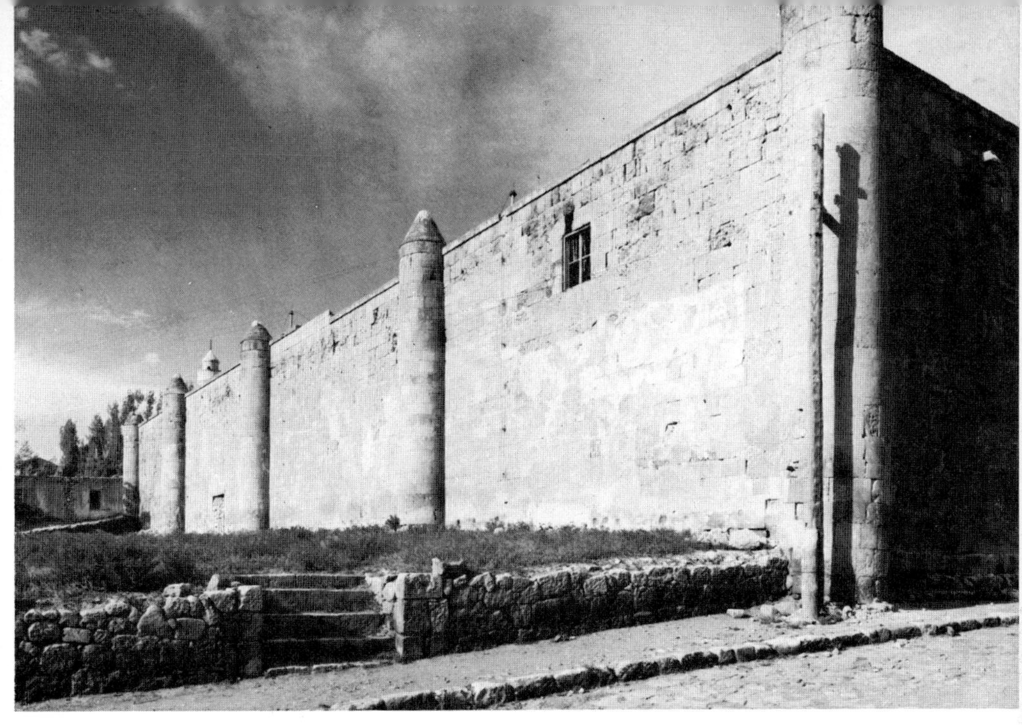

162 Han at Tercan, eastern Turkey. Twelfth century. The Seljuks and allied princes endowed Turkey with a number of magnificent hans, set at intervals of a day's journey apart along the more important trade routes

Though every part of the Islamic world was responsible for the production of works of art of virtually every type, there seem, as we look back today, to be certain especially outstanding arts that we can associate with particular areas or ages – glass with Syria, pottery and miniatures with Persia, or metalwork with northern Mesopotamia, for example – and if we were to follow up this line of thought it would certainly be architecture and architectural decoration that we would associate with the Seljuks of Rum. All over Asia Minor there survive to this day a mass of mosques and madrassas in a very distinctive style and boasting decorations either in carved stone or tile-work which are among the finest in all Islam; and there is one type of building that stands out especially, namely, the *han* or *caravanseray* (*Ill. 162*). These were set up at regular intervals along all the more essential trade routes, and are important not only because of the quality of the architecture and sculpture, but also because the Seljuks were the first to develop fine buildings planned

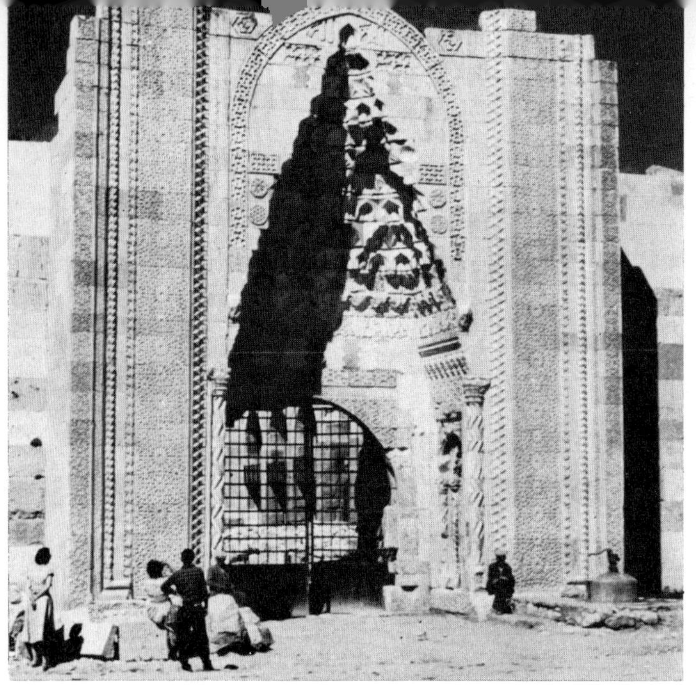

163 Portal of the Sultan Han on the Konya–Aksaray road. Many of the hans are of considerable size and great magnificence, and the Sultan Han is one of the finest. Begun 1229, completed 1236

especially for this purpose. Most of these hans are of considerable size, some are almost palaces, and they stood a day's journey, that is, about 30 kilometres, apart. A particularly impressive series survives along the road from Konya to Kayseri to this day. The one nearest to Konya shows the Syrian influence in its architecture, and in the use of stones of two colours for the voussoirs of the arches. In the best of the others, like Sultan Han near Sivas, the structure is all of dark grey stone and the decoration, usually confined to the entrance, is elaborately carved.

There are numerous variants in the details of the sculptured decorations, but in general the plan of the hans is the same: an outer wall enclosing a rectangular area, with a single entrance at the middle of one of the narrow ends (*Ill. 163*). Inside there were vaulted chambers on either side of the entrance and along the longer sides; at the opposite end to the entrance there was a great central hall, usually with a circular opening in the middle of its roof. A mosque was invariably included, small in size, but elaborately carved and decorated. It either stood alone in the centre of the court, or was situated at an upper level above the entrance. The finest of them is

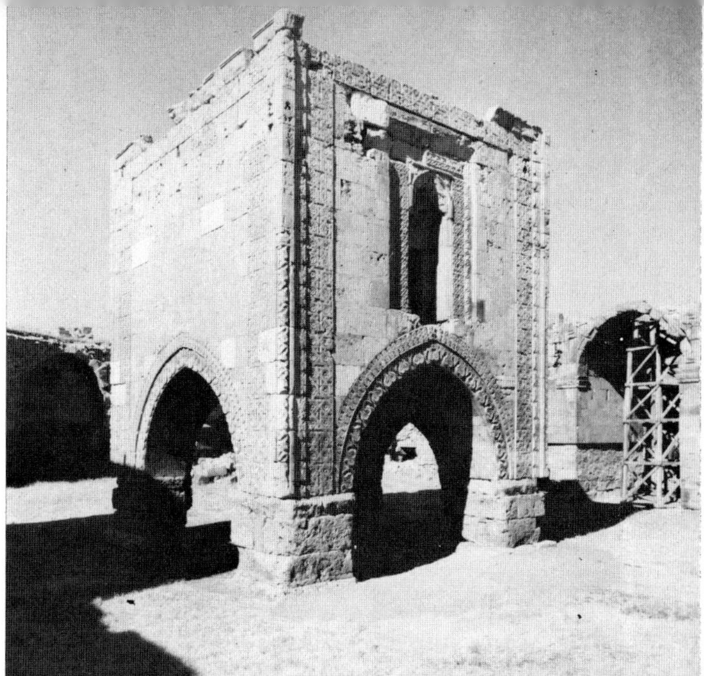

164 Mosque of the Sultan 'Palaz' Han on the Kayseri–Sivas road. 1229–36. The hans were not only provided with living quarters and stabling, but in each there was always a mosque. This was sometimes an independent structure and often situated over the entrance gate

probably that occupying the centre of the court of a great han near Sivas, one of the largest and most spectacular of the series (*Ill. 164*).

The largest of these hans, such as that near Sivas or the Sultan Han on the Konya–Kayseri road, provided food and even entertainment in the form of a band of musicians, for the visitors; in the smaller ones lodging and stabling only were available. But there was always security. One wonders sometimes why the Romans and Byzantines, who valued their roads and routes of communication so highly, never seem to have built caravanserays. Perhaps it is an indication of the security of the age. Under the *Pax Romana* of earlier times protection was not required, so the buildings were less solid, less defensive in character; in the Seljuk age, when the country was more disturbed, a fortress-like structure which was virtually unassailable except to prolonged attack, may well have been a prerequisite for trade. But the care and expense lavished throughout the twelfth and the thirteenth centuries on the construction of the hans, many of which stand miles away from any other inhabitation, does indicate the economic prosperity of the age and the lavishness of the patronage of the various sultans.

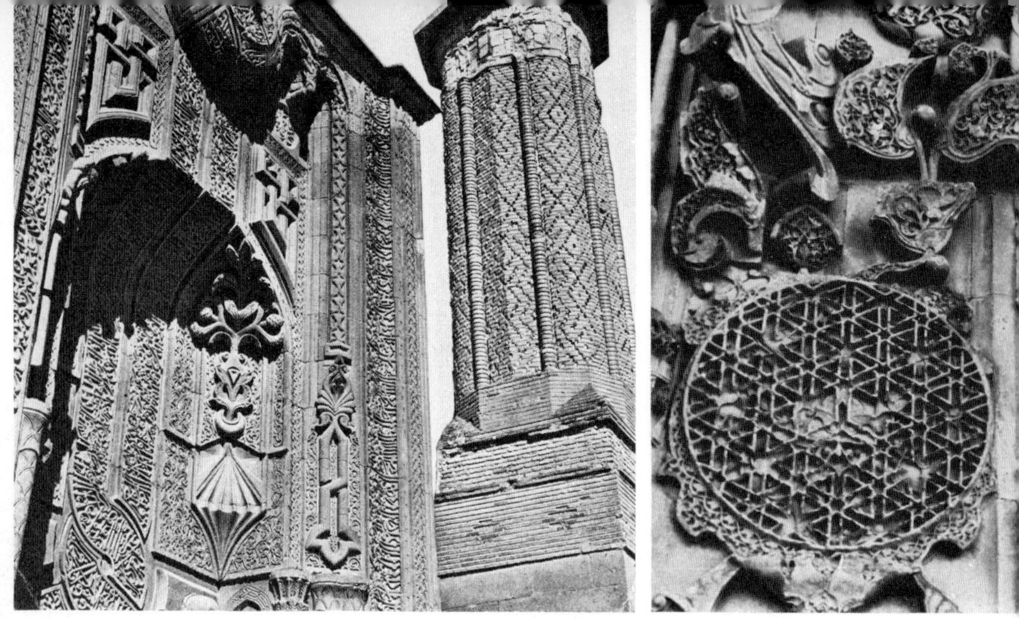

165 (*left*) Detail of sculptured decoration on the Ince Minare Madrassa at Konya. 1258

166 (*centre*) Detail of sculpture on the Ulu Cami at Divriği. 1228. The mosque is one of the finest and most ornate in Asia Minor

The entrance of the larger mosques and madrassas were very similar to those of the hans; that is to say, they consisted of tall doorways topped by pointed arches and very lavishly decorated with carvings. There was, however, a good deal of variation in style from area to area. At Konya script and interlacing patterns usually played an important role in the ornament (*Ill. 165*), but large-scale patterns sometimes based on floral designs and sometimes on geometric ones formed the basis of the compositions which the script or interlacings adorned. At Sivas (*Ill. 167*), under the patronage of the independent family which ruled there, the designs tended to be rather more classical and severe. At Divriği (*Ill. 166*), further to the east, much of the work was in high-relief, the intervening surfaces being adorned with intricate patterns in low-relief. At Erzurum there was greater reticence and the interior court of the great Çifte Minare Madrassa (*Ill. 168*) is plain except for a low-relief frieze bordering the arches and a similar decoration on two of the columns. This is indeed probably one of the most dignified of all the buildings in the Seljuk style in Anatolia.

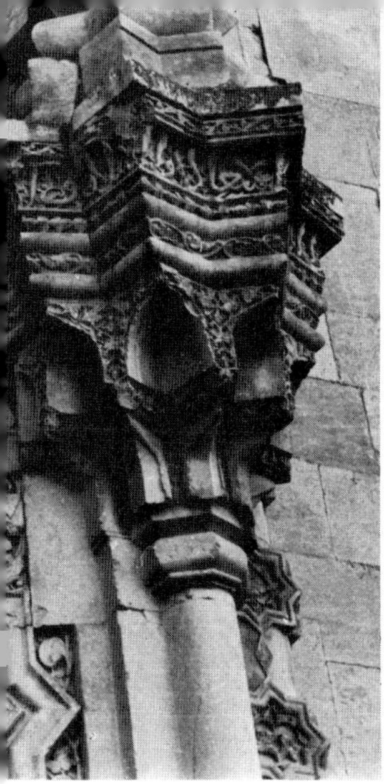

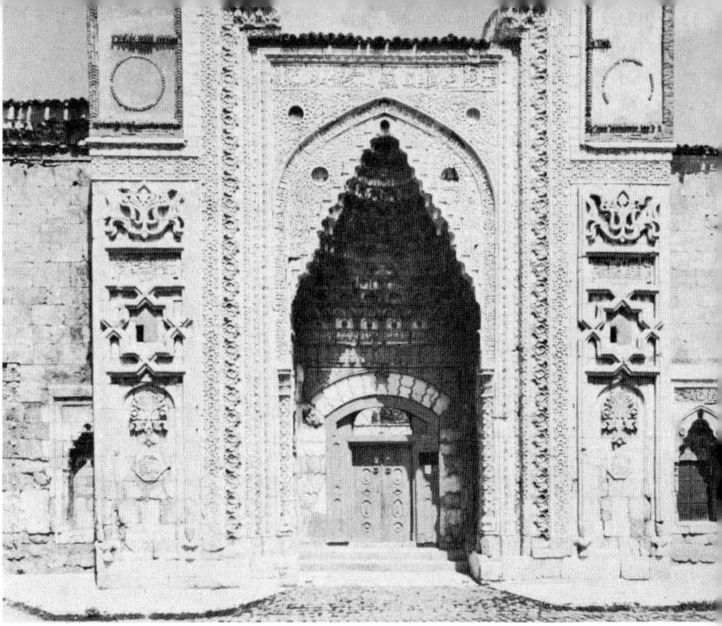

167 (*right*) Portal of the Gök Madrassa at Sivas. 1271–2. It might seem at first glance that the decoration is somewhat monotonous, but many local styles are quite distinct

168 (*below*) The Çifte Minare Madrassa at Erzurum. 1253. Here the carved decoration is more restrained and linear than in western Turkey

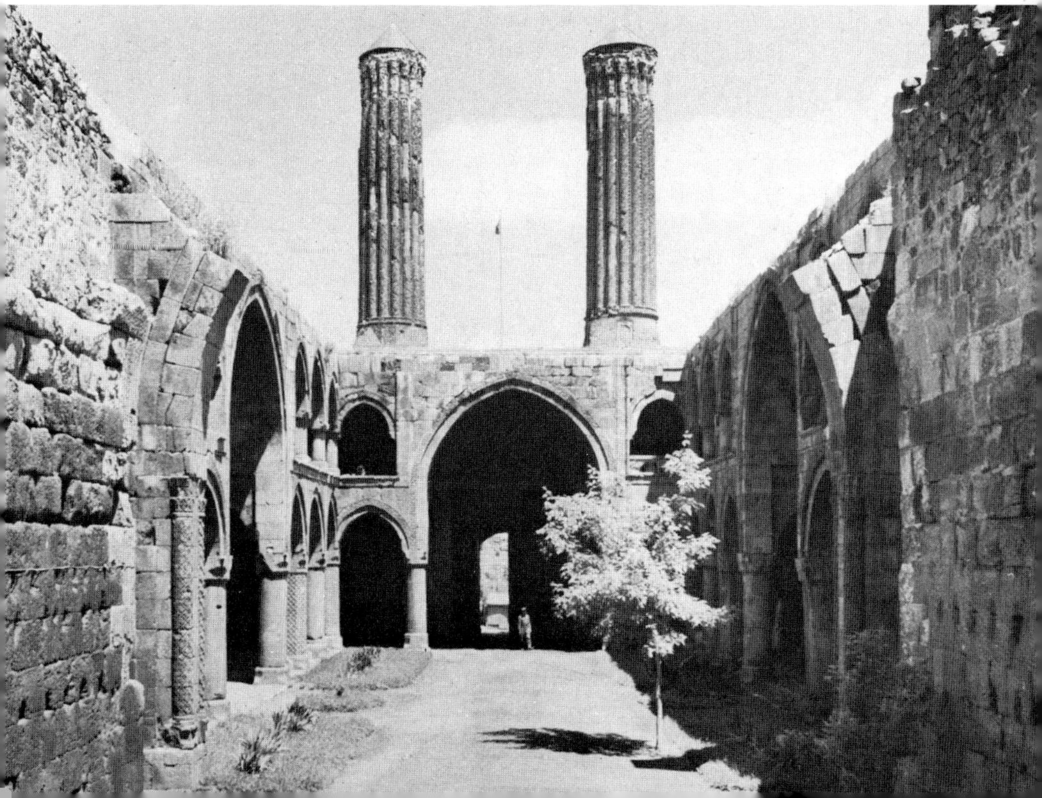

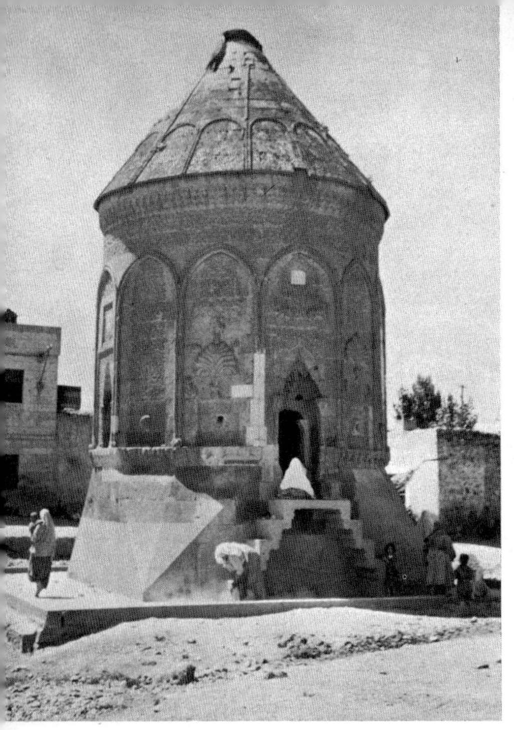

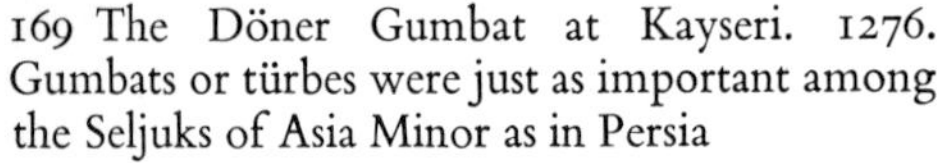

169 The Döner Gumbat at Kayseri. 1276. Gumbats or türbes were just as important among the Seljuks of Asia Minor as in Persia

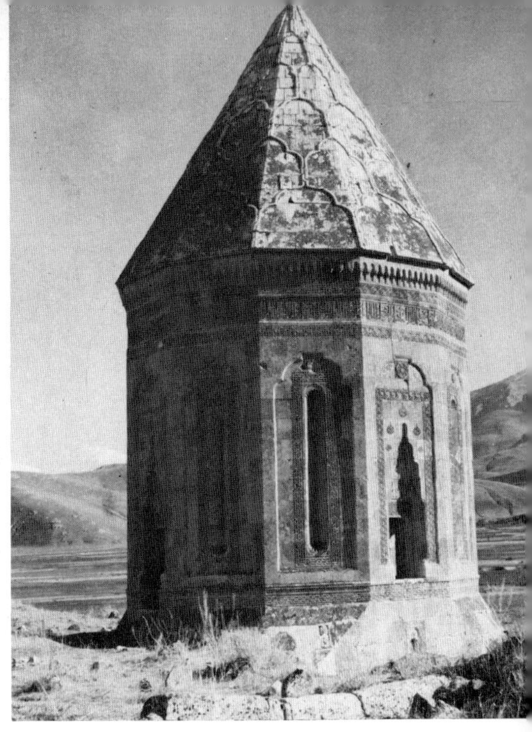

170 Gumbat built for Princess Hatuma in 1322 at Akhlat on the shores of Lake Van. This is one of the latest in date of the Seljuk gumbats

Apart from the great decorated entrances which served for hans, mosques and madrassas alike, the Seljuks of Rum were responsible for considerable developments in two other forms of architecture, the minaret and the *gumbat* or tomb (*Ill. 169, 170*). We have already seen with what importance these tomb structures were regarded by the eastern branch of the Seljuks in Persia; they were no less numerous in Anatolia, and a long series of examples exist all over the country. The star-shaped plan which produced such lovely results in Persia (see p. 61) was, however, discarded, and the more westerly ones were nearly always circular or polygonal on plan and were of stone rather than brick. There was usually an entrance to the upper chamber fairly high up on one side. An exception to the usual scheme, but a very impressive one, exists at Tercan in eastern Anatolia where the gumbat itself is enclosed by a massive circular wall, with an elaborately carved doorway (*Ill. 171*).

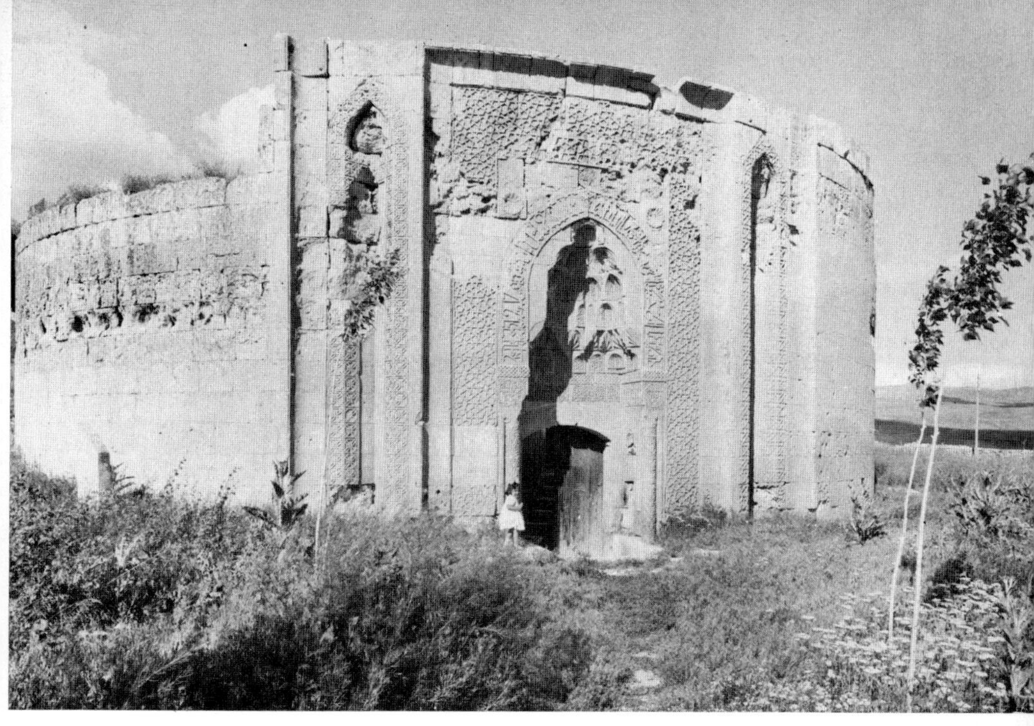

171 The Mama Hatun Gumbat at Tercan, eastern Turkey. The plan of this structure is unusual, for the gumbat itself is surrounded by a high wall

Though the mosques and madrassas, like the hans, were usually of stone, a few, like that at Beyşehir (*Ill. 173*), were partly of wood, while the minarets were more often built of brick. Perhaps structures in this material were found to be more resistant to earthquake shock. The bricks were usually set so as to produce an intricate geometric pattern on the surface; sometimes, as in the Çifte Minare at Erzerum, glazed tiles of black and blue were used in addition to the simple unglazed bricks. In this case their colour formed a delightful contrast with the brownish-red brick above and the dark grey stone of the main entrance façade below. Usually, however, the tile decoration was reserved for interiors. Minarets were usually single, but there were a few buildings where minarets were used in pairs to flank the entrance to the mosques, an outstanding example with twin minarets being the Çifte Minare Madrassa at Sivas (*Ill. 172*).

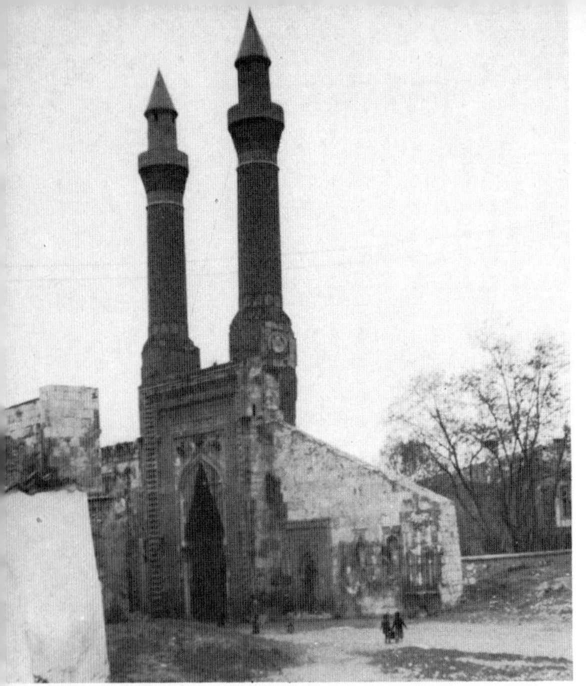

172 Façade of the Çifte Minare Madrassa at Sivas. 1271. These entrance fronts, flanked by twin minarets, are particularly impressive

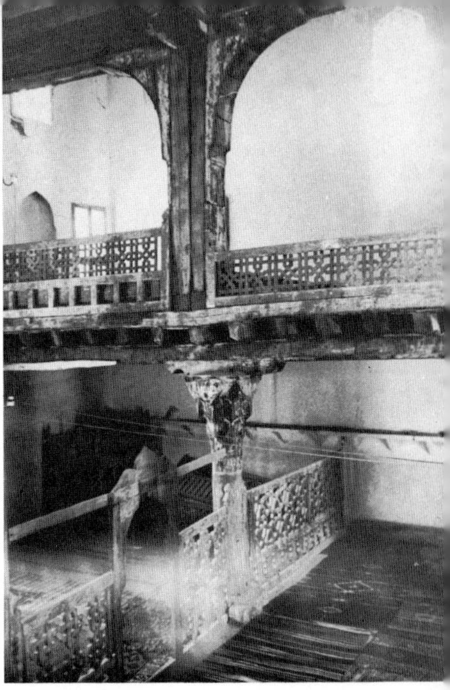

173 Interior of the mosque at Beyşehir. 1156–1220. Here wood has been used in place of stone

The finest examples of tile-work are to be found at Konya, the main capital of the whole Seljuk area. It would seem that it was here that the manufacture of glazed pottery was centred, and it was here certainly that the art of setting the tiles reached its highest perfection. The colours were limited to blue, white and black, and the tiles were set like great mosaic cubes to form intricate angular patterns. The large-scale designs on the doorways and the pendentives of the domes where star shapes, geometric interlace, script, and key patterns were favoured, are particularly effective (*Ill. 175*). Many of the motifs, especially the key patterns, savour strongly of the Far East; more so indeed than the carved decorations of the exteriors, where the angular Chinese-looking key pattern was less in favour. Sometimes the same tiles were used on a smaller scale to adorn mihrabs (*Ill. 174*), and they were set into the small stalactite niches of which the Seljuk craftsmen were so fond. These niches were usual both as an element of the stone sculpture and in plaster and woodwork.

174 (*opposite*) Detail of mosaic tile-work in the Sirçali Madrassa, Konya. 1243. The technique of cutting tiles to make up formal patterns was brought by the Seljuks from Persia. The actual ornament is often of a Central Asian or even Chinese character

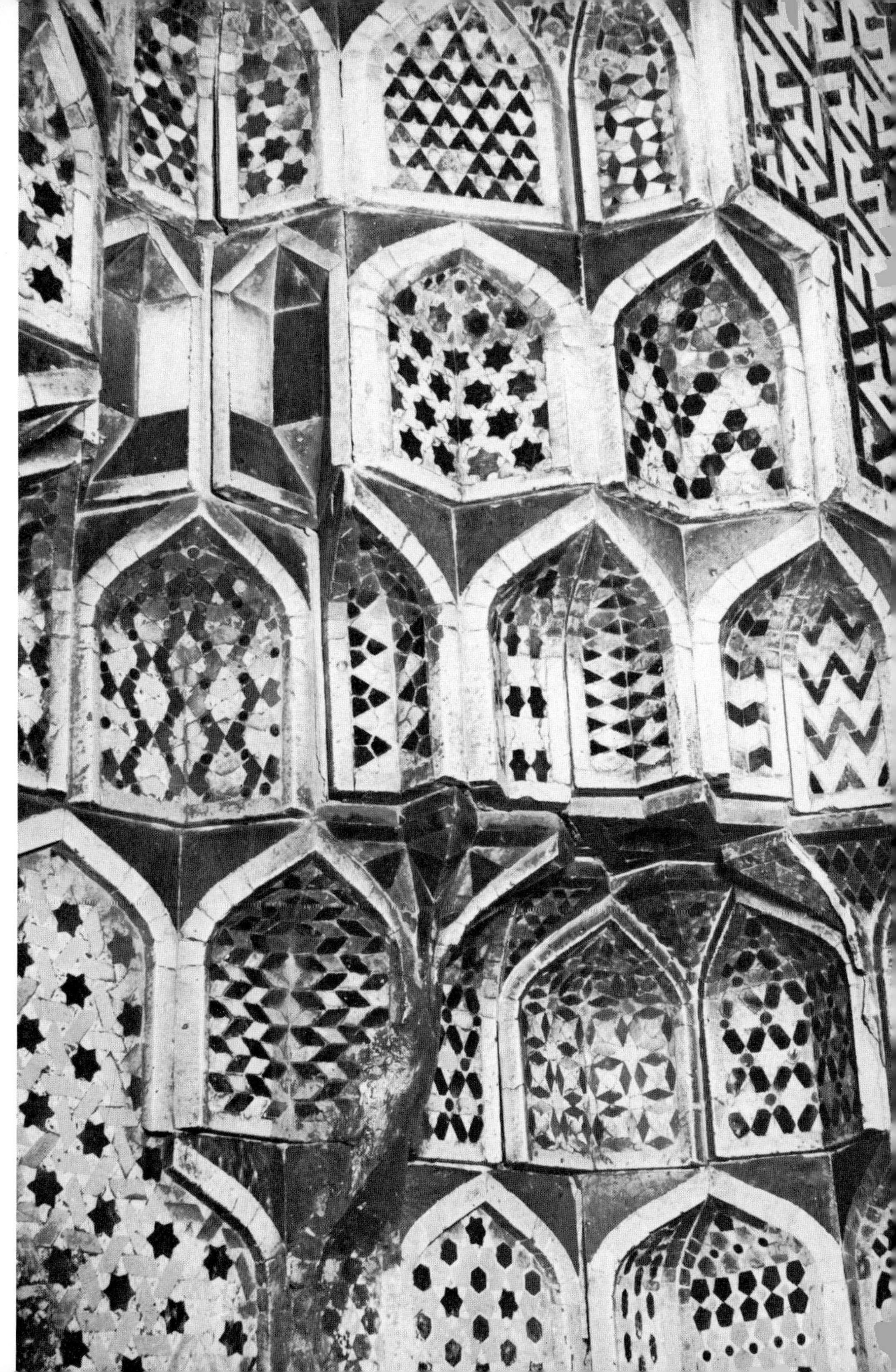

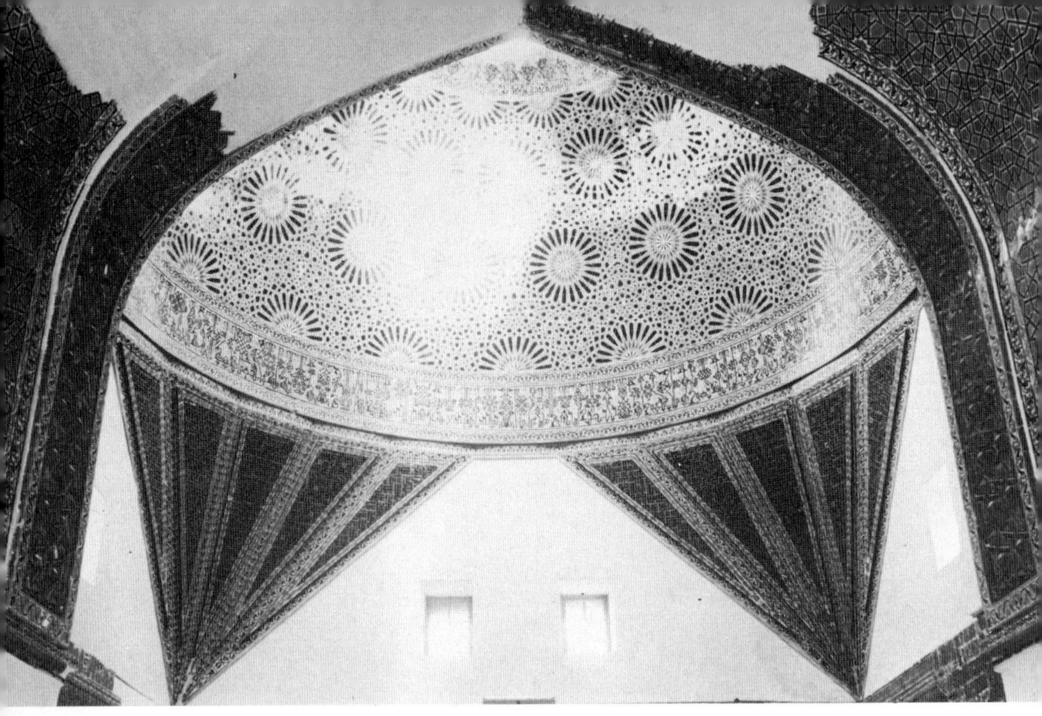

175 Dome of the Büyük Karatay Madrassa, Konya, showing tile mosaics. 1252. The colour scheme of this work was usually restricted to blue and black, but in some cases gold was used as well

The same over-all type of sculpture that we see on a large scale on the stone façades was also used on a smaller scale for woodwork: pulpits, doors, koran stands and so forth were all adorned in this way, and much of the work was not only of great technical skill but also of great beauty (*Ill. 177*). Some of the pulpits are still to be found in the mosques for which they were originally made; others are now in museums, notably the Ethnographical Museum at Ankara and the Museum at Konya, where the majority of the smaller Seljuk works of art have now been concentrated. Usually the star patterns which were so much favoured in the tile-work formed the basis of the designs, while the detail was filled in with rather effective inconsequence, as we see on a pair of doors at Konya (*Ill. 176*). Complicated geometric patterns seem to have intrigued and delighted the Seljuk artists, and as time went on the tendency towards complication increased.

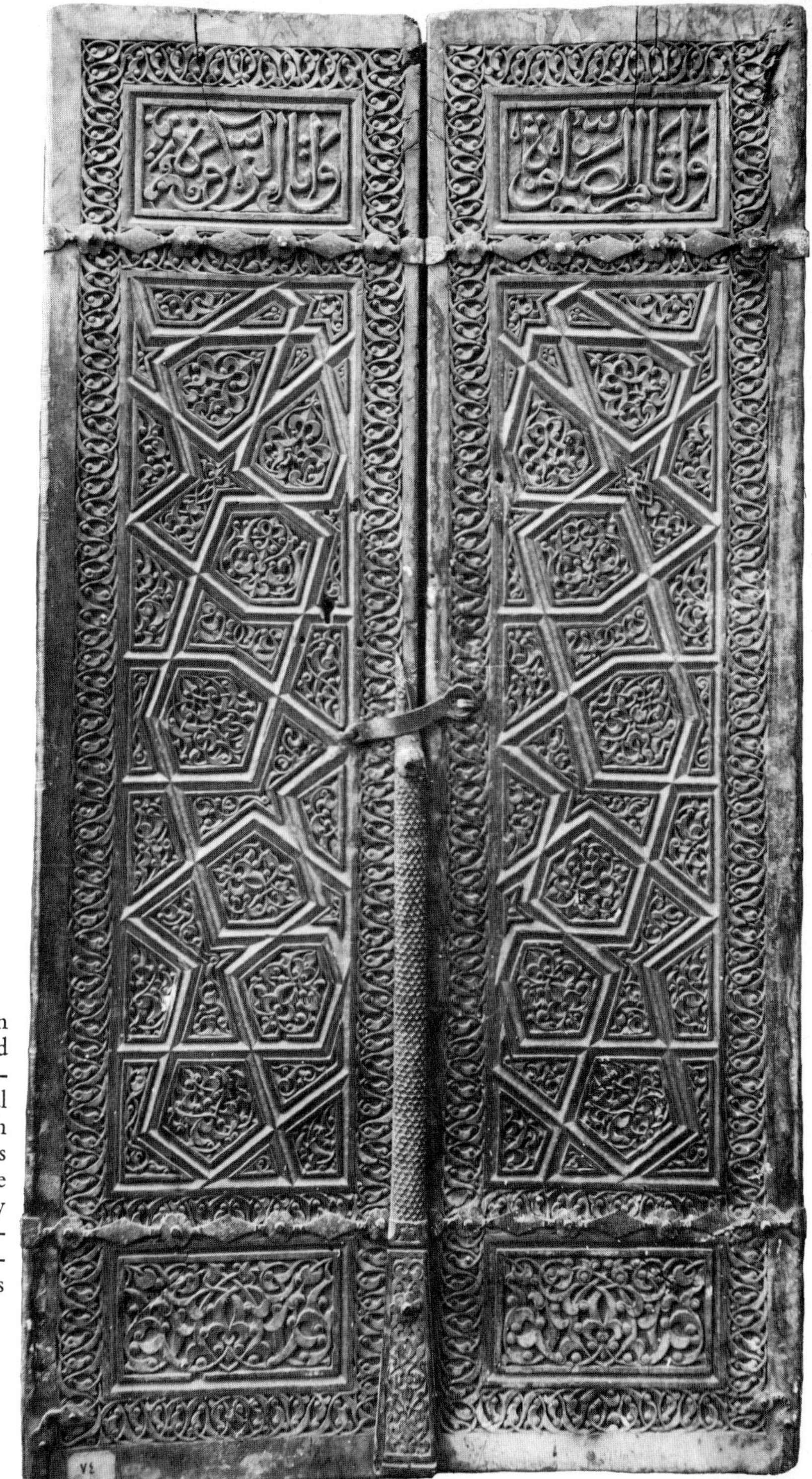

176 Wooden doors carved with a geometric and floral design. Twelfth century. Doors of this type once existed in nearly all the more important mosques, madrassas and hans

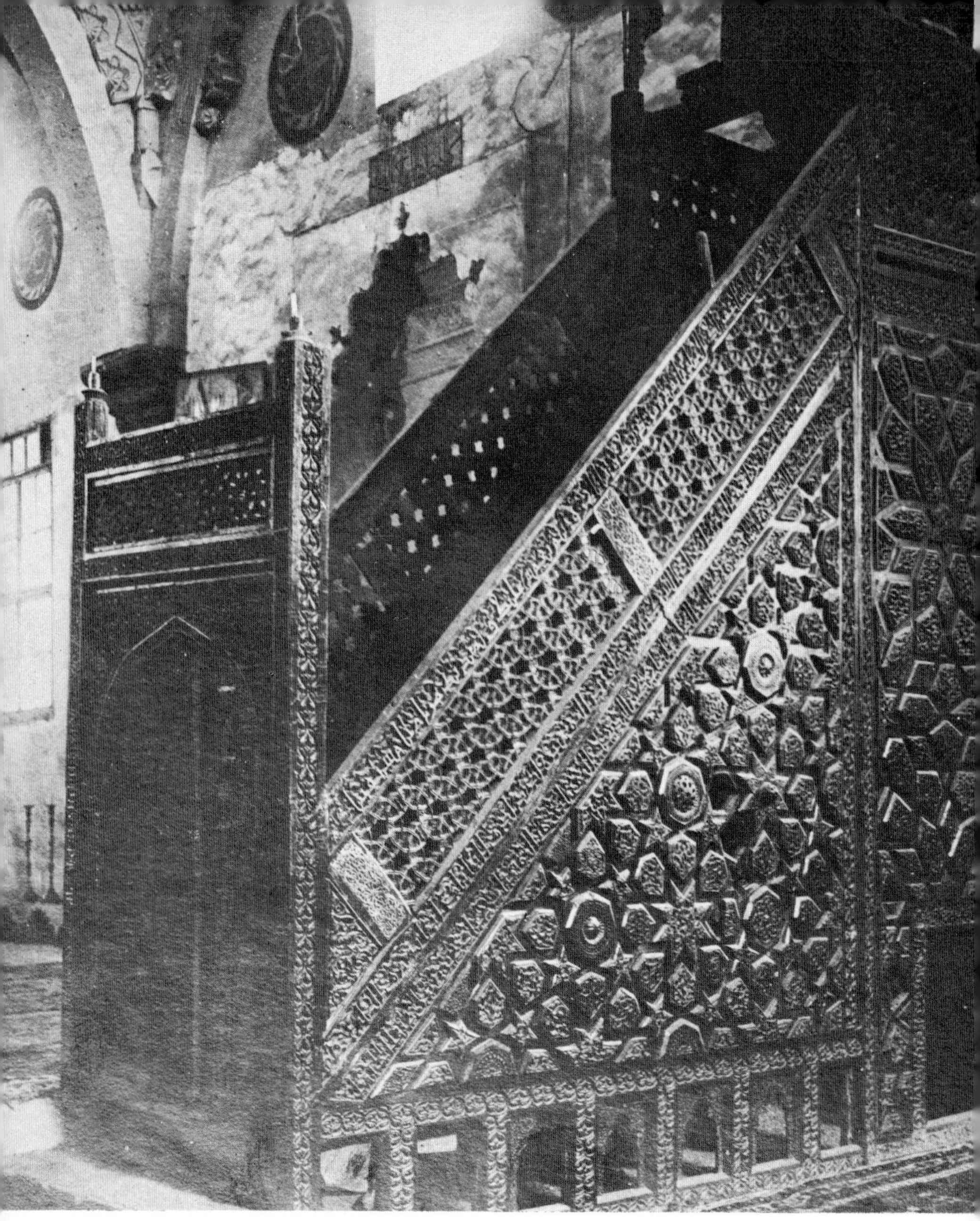

177 Carved mimbar in the Kebir Cami, Aksaray. Thirteenth century. The Seljuk mosques of Turkey are especially rich in carved woodwork. Good timber was available over most of Turkey and its availability must have stimulated the craft of wood carving

Not very many works on a really small scale have come down to us from Seljuk times, but the few that have serve to indicate the proficiency of technique and the high quality of the arts that were practised. In contrast to the blue and black tile mosaics used for the decoration of mosques, secular pottery, so far as we know, consisted of three main types: sgraffito wares, not unlike those of Persia, but related at the same time to Byzantine products; vessels of red body with rather intricate designs in blue above a white slip – the type is usually known as 'Miletus ware' – and painted tiles of octagonal or star shape with a figural decoration in red, gold, black and white, usually on a blue ground, not unlike the Minai style of Persia (see p. 68) (*Ill. 186*). In one type there was also a secondary decoration in lustre, which was achieved by firing for a second time at a lower temperature. Examples have come from Konya and a summer residence of the sultans at Kay Kubadabad near Beyşehir, and were used, so far as we know, only in the palaces. A few vessels seem to have been made in the same technique in addition to the tiles (*Ill. 185*). They represent the only type of luxury pottery, for the two other groups we have noted were strictly utilitarian, and the Miletus ware bowls hardly came into use before the thirteenth century. Their decoration was, however, by no means crude, even if their red bodies are hardly to be compared with high-class wares of Persia of the same period.

If we know little of Seljuk pottery, we know even less about their textiles, for there are very few woven stuffs that can be definitely assigned to this age; a silk at Lyons in the name of Kaykubad I, dated to 1218–19, is the most important of them. But one thing that is certain is that the Seljuk craftsmen produced carpets, and so far as is known at present, it is to them that must be assigned the institution of carpet manufacturing in Asia Minor which was to become of such immense importance in Ottoman times. A number of carpets which are with little doubt to be regarded as Seljuk were discovered still in use in the Ala'ed din Mosque at Konya (*Ill. 182*) early in this century. Others have been found at Beyşehir, which are now preserved either in the Mevlana Museum at Konya or the Türk ve Islam Müzesi at Istanbul (*Ill. 178–81*).

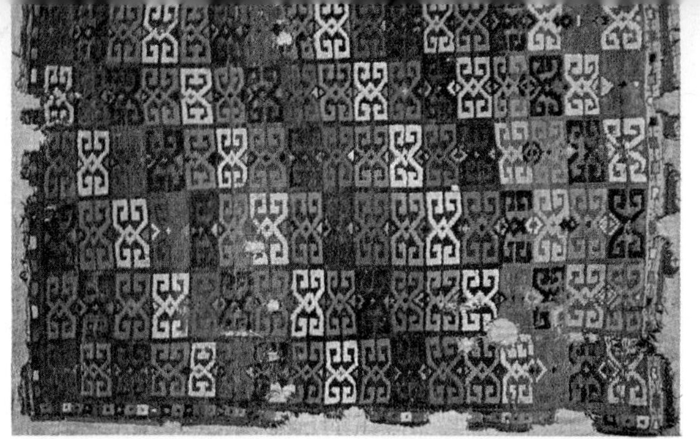

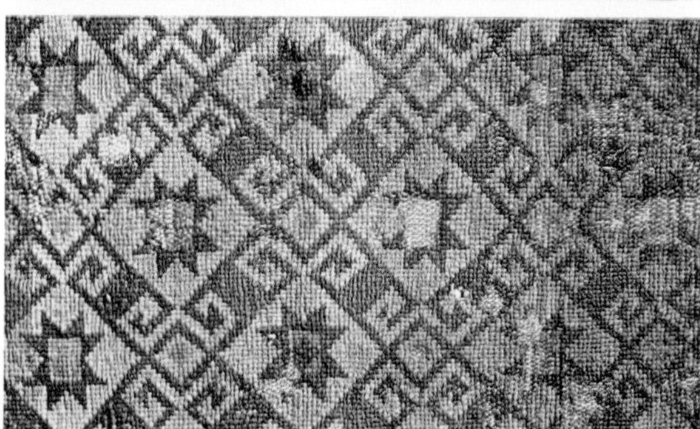

178–181 Woollen carpets of the Seljuk period. These are some of the earliest carpets known from Turkey and come from the Ala'ed din Mosque at Konya. Their decorations, essentially Seljuk in character, are associated with different regions. The prevailing colours are brown, ochre, red, blue, purple and green. (*Ill. 179*) is one of the most complete carpets and has a kufic inscription on the border. (*Ill. 180*) is based on stylized animals

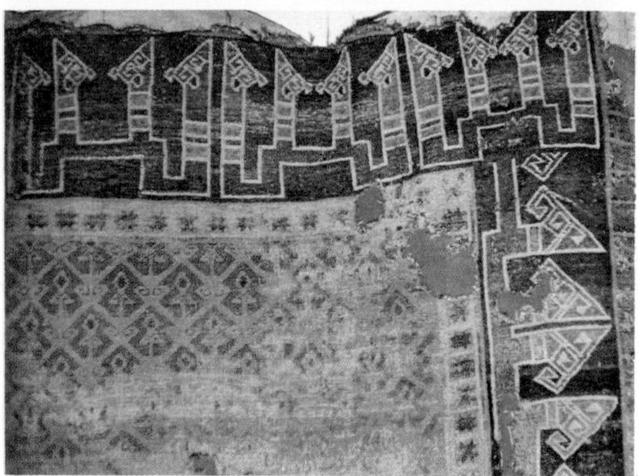

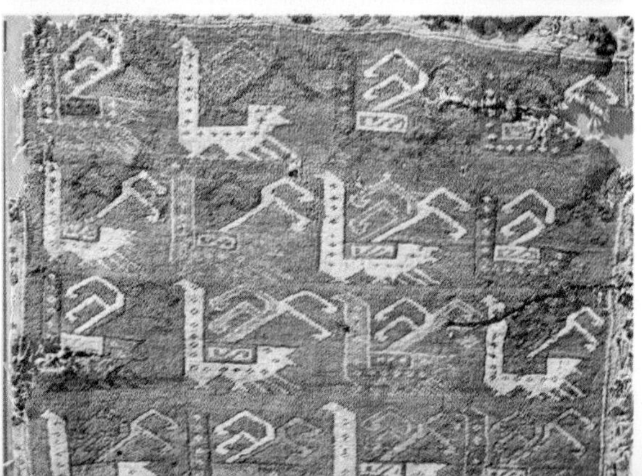

182 (*opposite*) Interior of the Ala'ed din Mosque at Konya showing how the carpets were spread on the floor

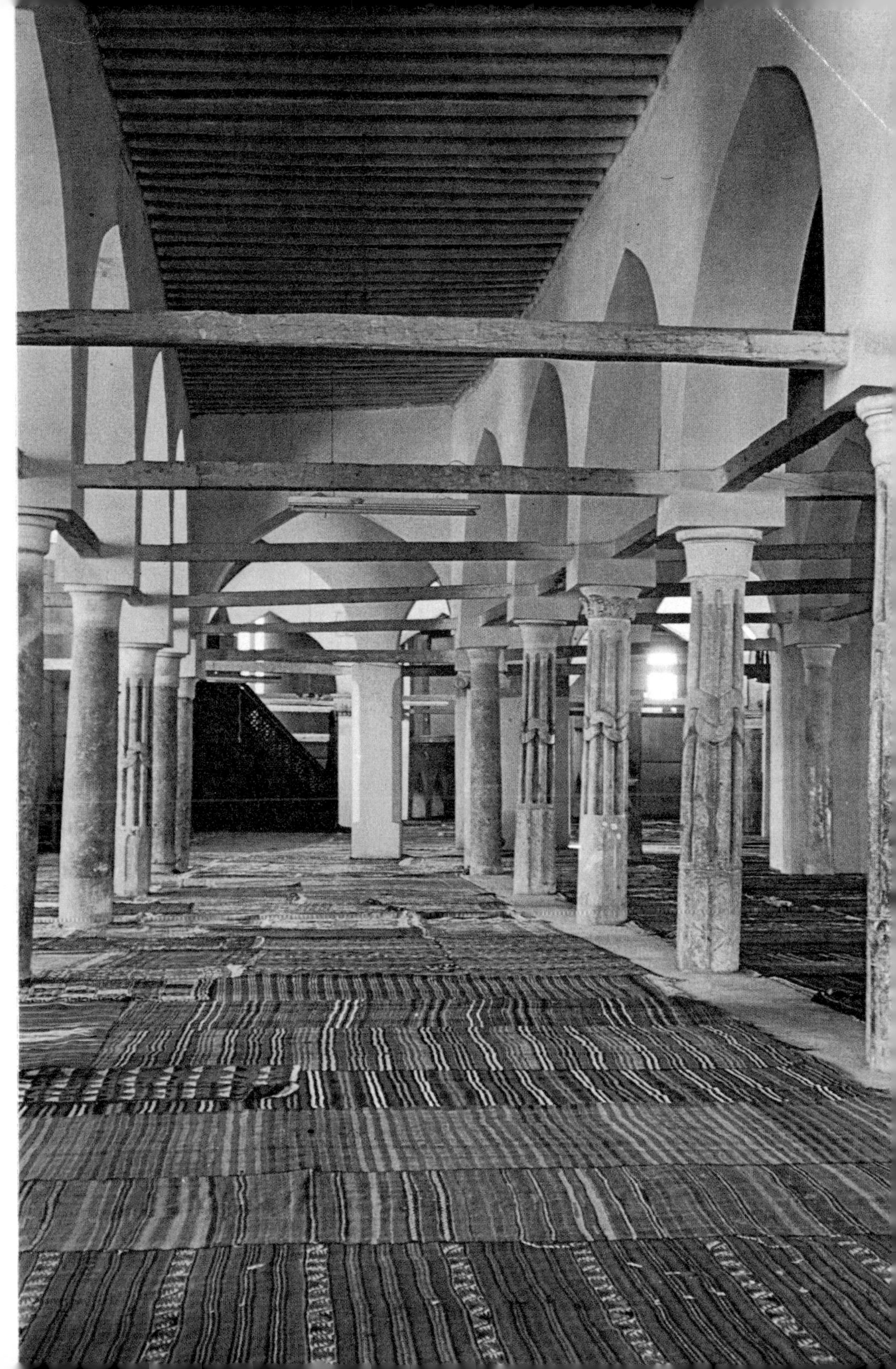

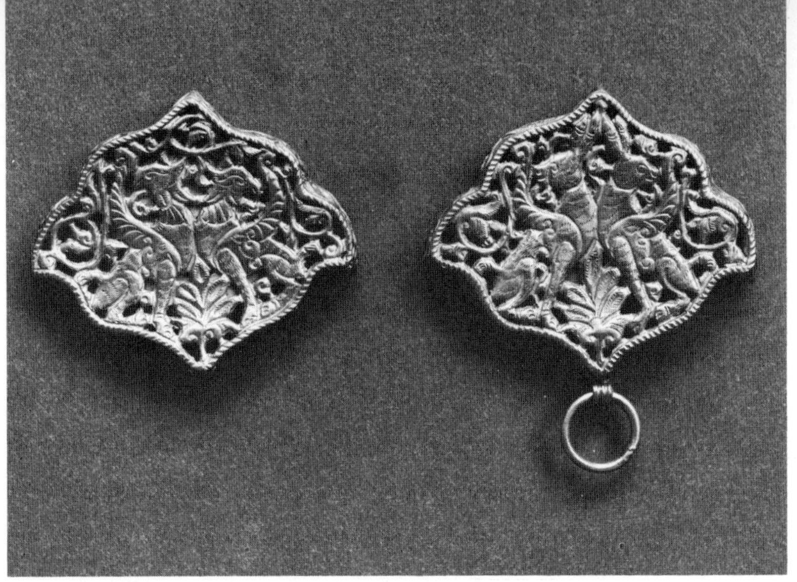

183 Gold buckles of the Seljuk period. The open-work decoration takes the form of a gryphon and a winged monster. *c.* 1236–46. Small-scale work of this type in this period is not very common

Some fragments found at Fostat in 1935 are also probably Turkish. All bear basically geometric decorations similar to those on the stonework and wood, but contrived perhaps with rather greater balance. The backgrounds are dark blue or red, the designs usually in yellow or light green and the geometric patterns, made up of lozenges, stars and similar motifs, or of kufic script, are particularly effective. Once more the designs attest the Asiatic origins of the Seljuks, while the fact that carpets seem to have constituted the most important branch of their textile industry, bears witness to the nomadic basis of their culture, for it was undoubtedly in nomadic society more than anywhere else that the carpet had a truly significant role to play.

The metalwork of the western Seljuks was perhaps rather less distinctive than the carpets, for such examples of the favourite Muslim types of spouted vessel, mortar or candlestick that we know are closely similar to those from Persia. They seem also to have liked ornaments and pieces of jewellery moulded or carved with small-scale patterns. But here the geometric forms which were so prominent in the other arts have given place to naturalistic ones, such as scrolls, birds or animals; the latter are often shown in pairs, either confronted or back to back, and seem to have been taken over from the sophisticated textiles that had been produced in Persia from Sassanian times onwards. The most characteristic type of Seljuk metalwork is a particular type of weight (*Ill. 184*), circular in form, flat on the under side, but with a design case in fairly high-relief on the top. These designs usually consisted of birds, surrounded by a border in the form of an inscription; very similar weights were made by the Seljuks in Persia, and they continued to be in use in subsequent times also. Belt buckles and other items of personal adornment were also popular (*Ill. 183*).

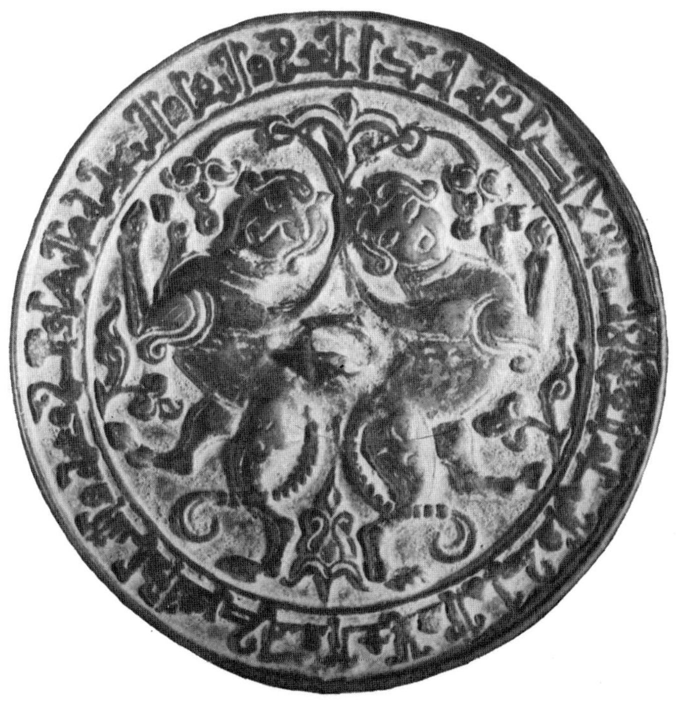

184 Bronze weight of the Ortokid period. Weights of this type, with relief ornament on the top, were common in Persia and Asia Minor alike. In most cases it is hardly possible to distinguish the products of the different areas

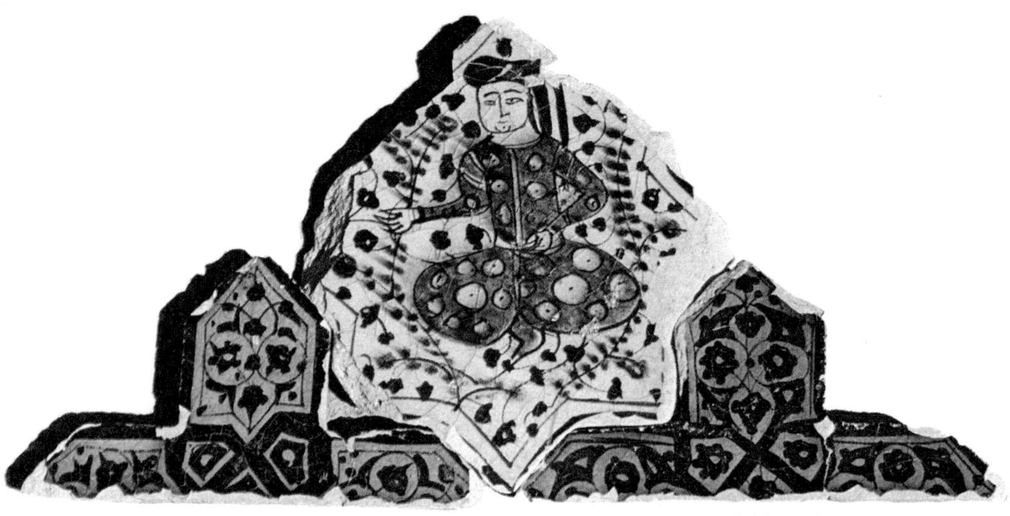

185 Group of tiles with painted decoration in gold, blue and black from Kay Kubadabad. Thirteenth century. A large number of fragments of tiles of this type were found during excavations of the Seljuk palace here.

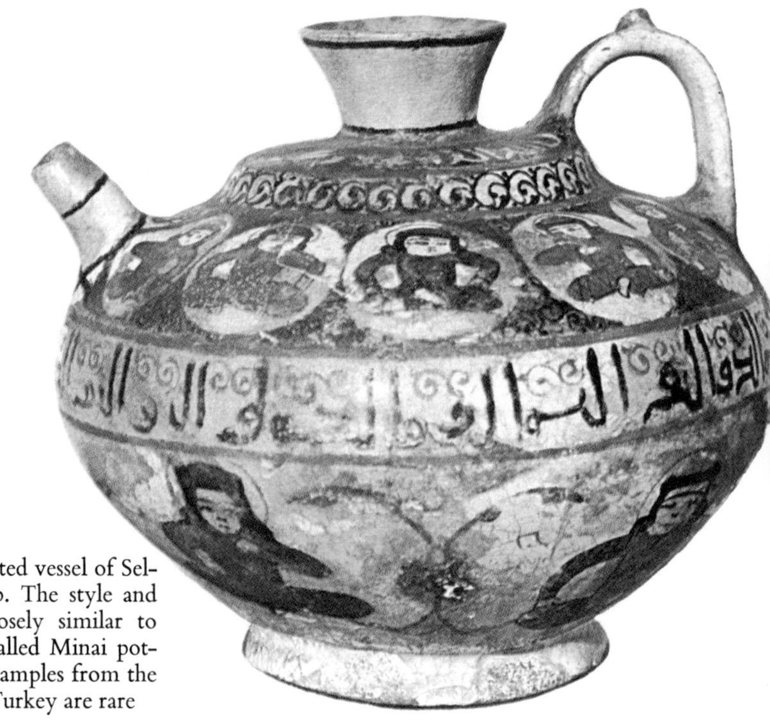

186 A small spouted vessel of Seljuk workmanship. The style and technique are closely similar to those of the so-called Minai pottery of Persia. Examples from the Seljuk period in Turkey are rare

CHAPTER TEN

The Ottoman Turks

It has sometimes been assumed that the Turks as a race have made but little contribution to art, and that the quality of the works produced under their patronage is to be attributed to the fact that they employed Persian, Armenian or Greek craftsmen. But the very distinctive character of Seljuk work, especially in architecture and sculpture, serves to disprove this. The deception becomes even more apparent when Ottoman art is examined, for it again is wholly original and distinct, owing in general but little to Persia, and even if the ideas that were to form the basis of Ottoman architecture were adopted from Byzantium, the basic theme was so developed that almost at once it became a distinctive style. Like Brahms' Variations on a Theme of Haydn, the variations constituted the work of art rather than the basic theme.

The Ottomans first appeared in Anatolia during the days of Seljuk rule, but with the decline in the power of the latter towards the end of the thirteenth century they gradually asserted their position under the leadership of Osman, and it was from his name that that of the group was derived. For this reason they were first known as the Osmanlis. In 1338 Osman's successor as leader, Orkhan, captured Bursa from the Byzantines, and soon after the middle of the century the Osmanli Turks were already established in Europe; in 1389 they defeated the Serbs at Kossovo. It was towards the West that their eyes were first directed, rather than towards the subordination of the other Muslim group in Asia Minor, but by 1400 they had secured the country behind them and were firmly enough entrenched in western Asia Minor and even in eastern Europe to be but little affected by the defeat of their armies at the hand of Tamerlane. Though their Sultan, Beyazid, was captured and taken off to Asia, his successor Muhammad had reunited Anatolia by 1405 and in 1422 Sultan Murad was at the walls of Constantinople, though it was not until 1453 that the Byzantine capital fell before the attack of Sultan Mehmed Fatih, or Muhammad the Conqueror as he is better known in the West. From then onwards the old Byzantium, the city which had defied all attacks since it was founded by Constantine I in 330, became their capital. It was to be embellished by many fine buildings, while the court was to prove a centre of patronage hardly surpassed even by its Christian predecessor. But the city was, in the long run, also to prove the undoing of the régime, for once the hard life of the military conqueror, once the rigours of the uplands, had been finally left behind, the old virility and energy that had inspired leaders and stimulated the activities of so many Turkish groups in their long pilgrimage across Asia declined, and, from the time of Süleyman I onwards (1520–66), it was no longer the drive of the rulers that kept the state in being but rather the fact that there were no more energetic rivals on the scene to supplant them. But even if the later Ottoman sultans showed little of the enterprise of the early conquerors, they were mostly great patrons of the arts, and much work of very fine quality was executed under their aegis.

The architecture – and for that matter, the pottery also – that they sponsored falls into two very distinct groups: that done prior to, or very soon after, the conquest of Constantinople, when Seljuk elements were to the fore, and that done after about 1500, when a wholly new style was developed in a way which would have been virtually impossible had the great Byzantine cathedral of Hagia Sophia not been there as a model. The main centre of development of the former style was Bursa, that of the second Constantinople, though there are fine examples of mosques in the second style elsewhere, including perhaps the finest of all the mosques that the Ottomans ever set up, that at Edirne, built for Sultan Selim II by the architect Sinan between 1570 and 1574 (*Ill. 187*). Here, as in all Sinan's mosques, the central dome was the essential point around which the structure was developed; in most of the works of his predecessors, though domes played a part, they were on a smaller scale and did not dominate the structure in quite the same way. The earlier style is typified by the Ulu Cami at Bursa, begun for Murad I (1359–89), but only finished about 1420 (*Ill. 188*). Though tile-work

187 (*right*) The mosque of Sultan Selim II at Edirne. 1570–4. It is perhaps the finest work of the architect Sinan, who was responsible for a great many buildings in the sixteenth century, for individual as well as imperial patrons

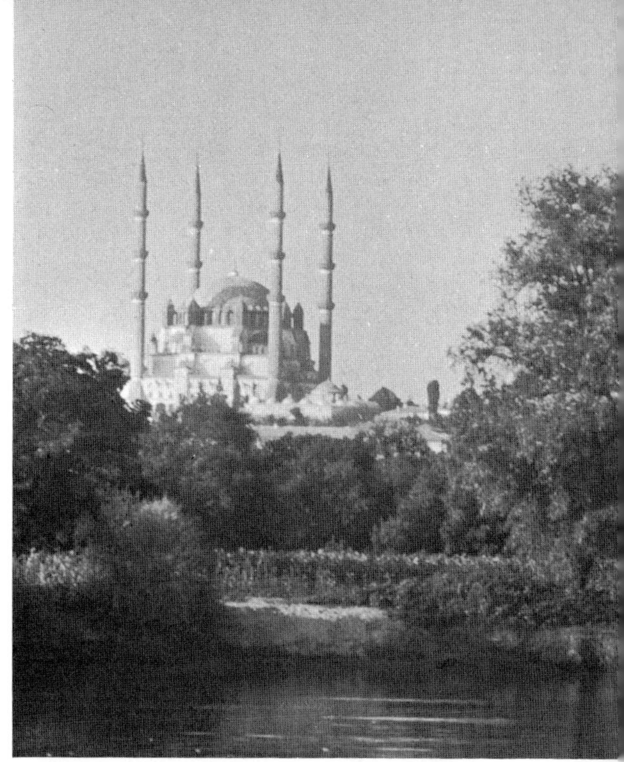

188 (*below*) The interior of the Ulu Cami, Bursa. 1359–1420. Before the Ottomans conquered Constantinople, their capital was established at Bursa on the Asiatic side of the Bosphorus. It is there that the most important examples of early Ottoman architecture are to be found

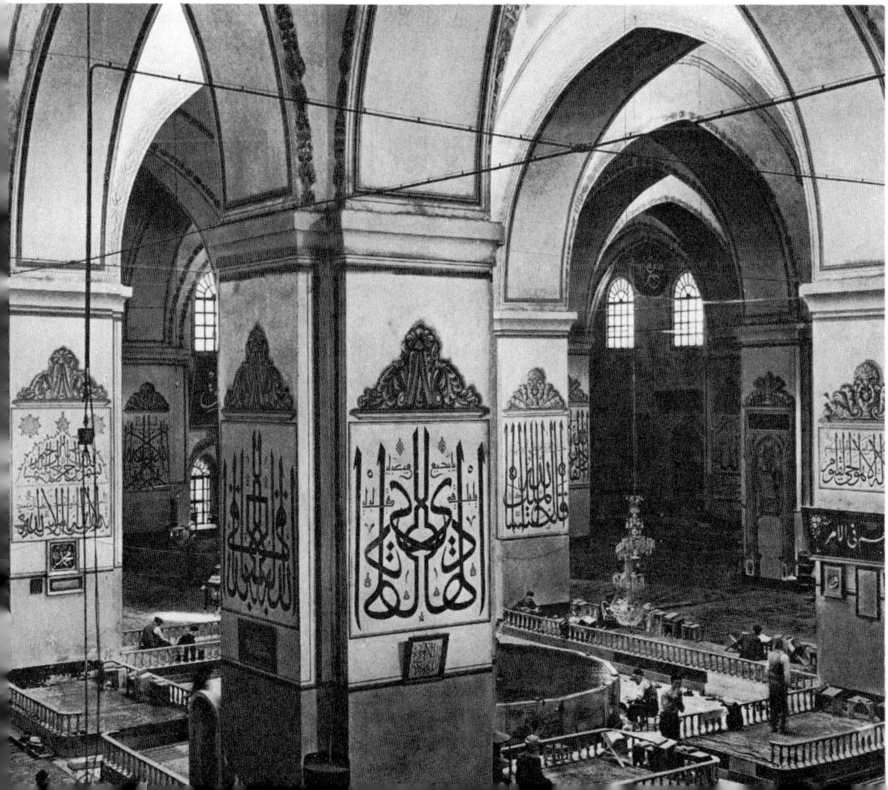

plays a part here and in other early Ottoman structures such as the Yeşil Cami at Bursa (1419–24) (*Ill. 189*) or the Çinili Kiosk (1472) at Constantinople (*Ill. 190*), or Istanbul as the Turks called it, the Ottoman approach to architecture was much more sober and restrained than the Seljuk, and the rich, lavish sculptures which were so loved in the earlier phase were in general avoided in the later; at best they took the form of very sober, restrained decorations in low-relief.

It has sometimes been held that the new style was essentially the invention of the architect Sinan, whom the Turks laud as their greatest genius and whom the Greeks claim as a compatriot. But though he was to bring the new style to fruition, the earliest of the mosques in which the central dome constituted the dominant feature was that of Sultan Beyazid II, built between 1500 and 1505 to the design of the architect Hayrüddin. It consists of a principal sanctuary with central dome on four piers, a mihrab at the centre of one wall, with the entrance opposite it; beyond the entrance is a great columned court, like an atrium, very similar to that which existed originally in front of Hagia Sophia. The mosque of Beyazid is unusual, however, in the great width of its entrance façade and in the length of the space which separates the twin minarets that delimit it on either side.

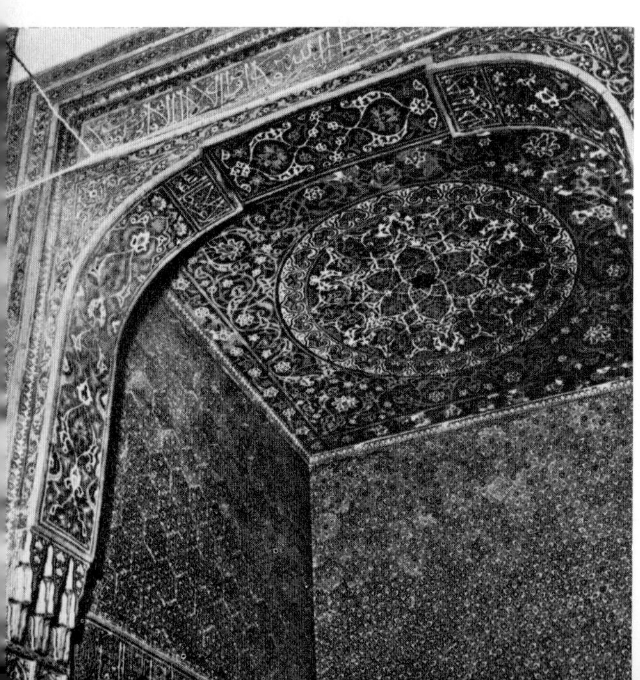

189 Tile decoration in the Yeşil Cami, Bursa. 1419–24. The decoration of the tiles still shows hints of the earlier Seljuk style. The painted square tiles developed by the Ottomans came later

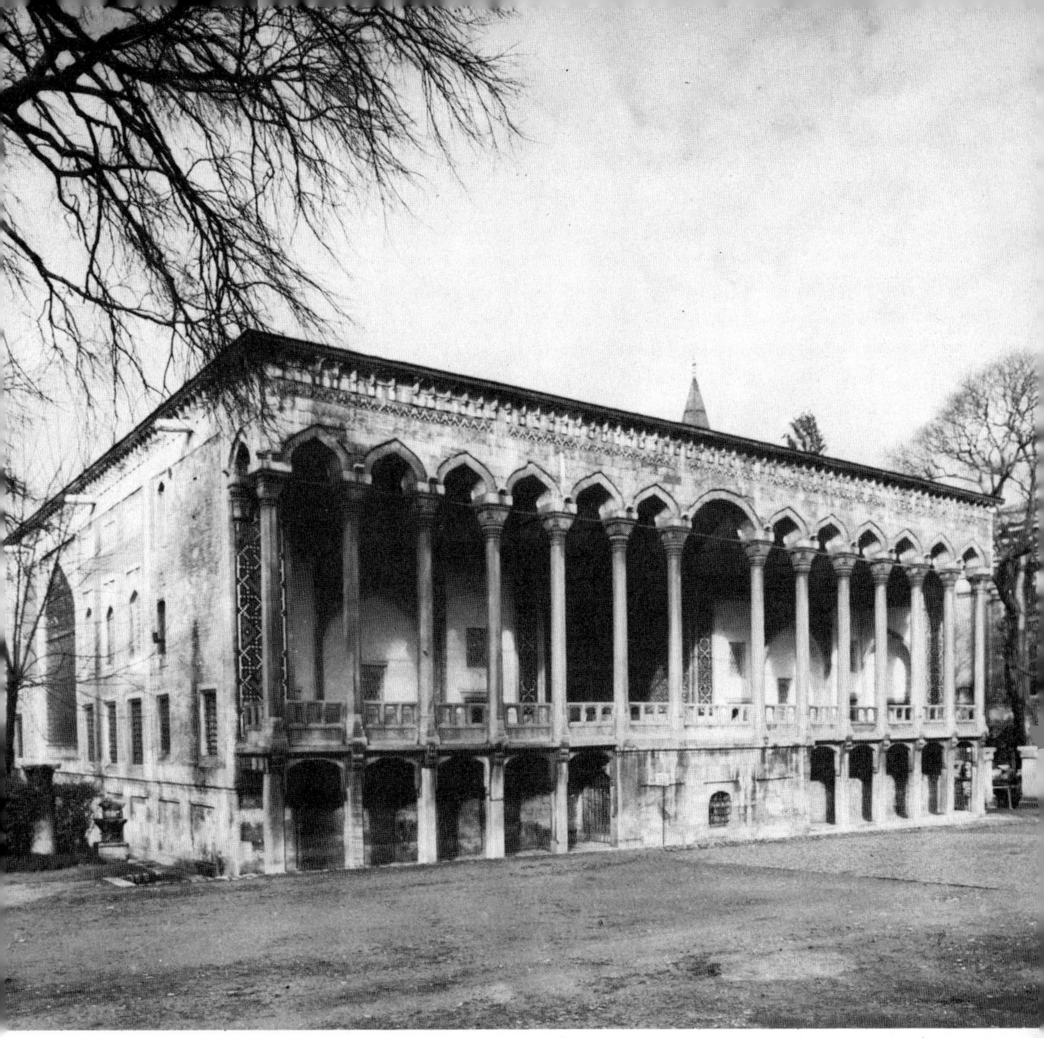

190 The Çinili Kiosk is the earliest example of Ottoman building still extant in Istanbul and its tile decoration, and to some extent its architecture, are closer to work at Bursa, than later monuments in Istanbul

Even if the glory of the first variation on the theme of Hagia Sophia must go to Hayrüddin, it was Sinan who was to carry the idea forward. He completed the Şehzade Mosque, which he liked to call a work of his years of apprenticeship, in 1548, as a fairly simple variant of the plan of Hagia Sophia. It was followed by a long series of other works – as many as eighty-one mosques are recorded, apart from madrassas, libraries and other buildings. The earlier ones were

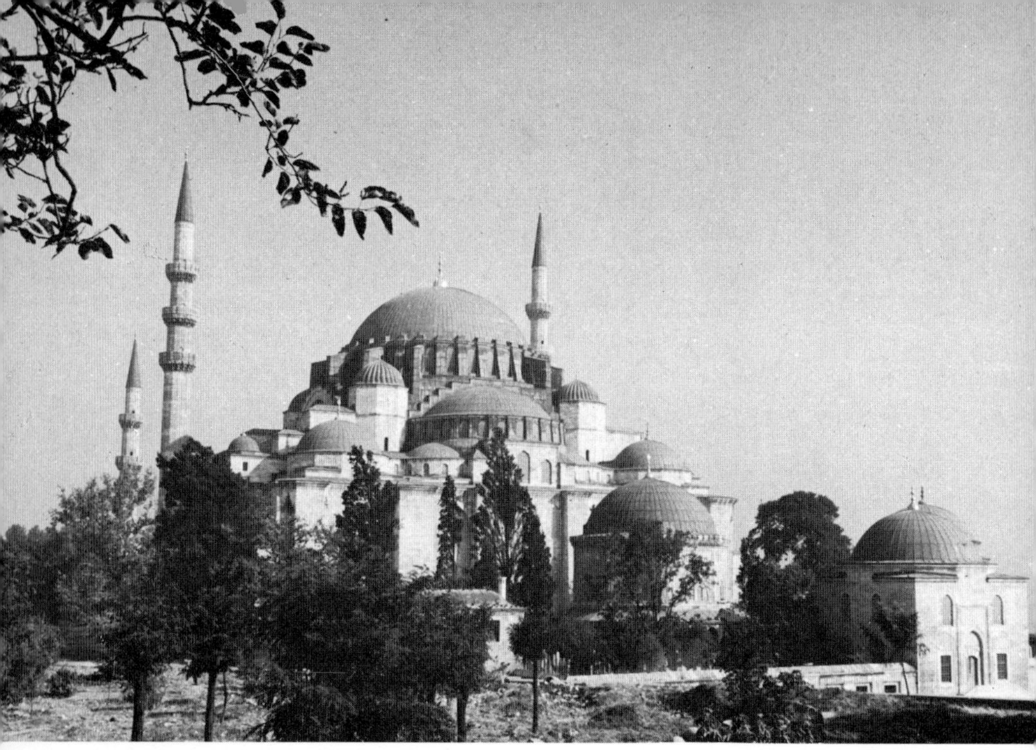

191 The Süleymaniye Mosque, Istanbul. Built by Süleyman the Magnificent and designed by Sinan. This is to be counted as the finest of Sinan's works in Istanbul. It has four minarets and their situation, at the four corners of the forecourt, is unusual. 1550–7

built under the patronage of the great Sultan Süleyman – 'Süleyman the Magnificent', as he was usually called – the later ones for Sultan Selim II.

The most famous and probably the most beautiful is the mosque of Sultan Süleyman in Istanbul (1550–7), which stands in a superb position dominating the Golden Horn (*Ill. 191, 192*). Its great dome is supported on four square piers, and it has four minarets, two flanking the entrance and two at the extremity of the atrium-like forecourt. The architect himself, however, is said to have regarded the mosque of Sultan Selim at Edirne as his most perfect and mature work.

In the mosque of Sultan Süleyman, as indeed was the case with all the larger mosques, there were numerous subsidiary buildings, for in most cases a school or college was associated with the main foundation, living quarters were provided for the students and for

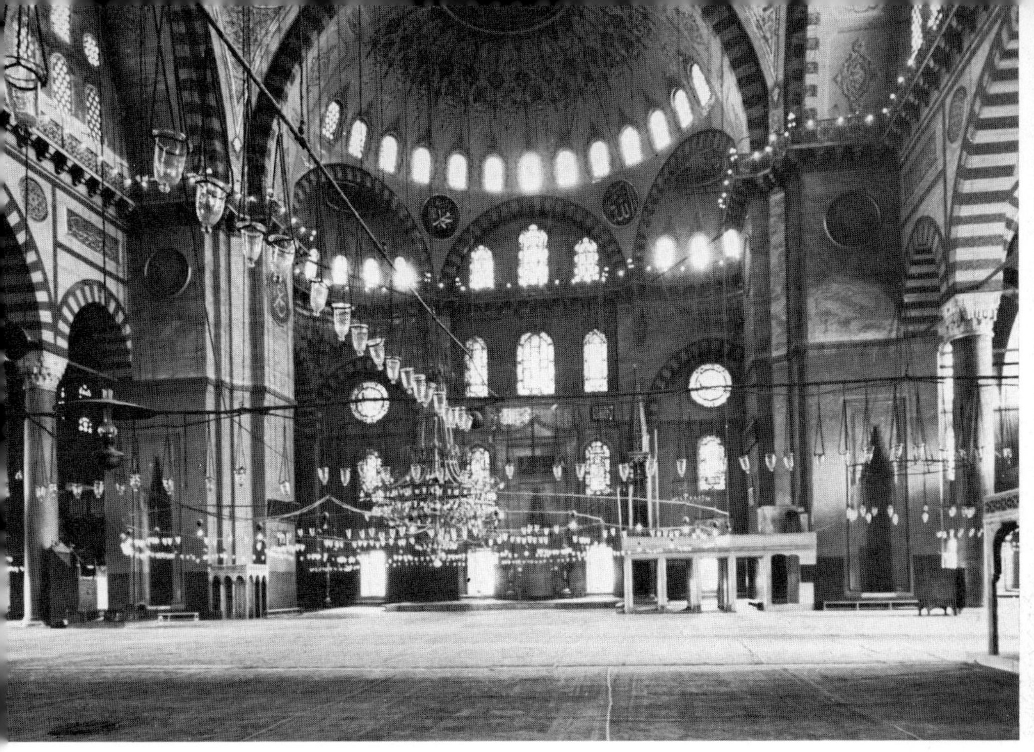

192 Interior of the Süleymaniye Mosque, Istanbul. 1550–7. The interior is the most spacious of all the mosques in the capital and owes as clear debt to Justinian's Hagia Sophia, which was turned into a mosque after the Turkish conquest

those who served in the mosques; often too there were rooms in which the sultan could rest or hold court, and sometimes there was even a bazaar quarter associated with the larger mosques. Close by, the mosques, türbes or mausolea were built – there are a whole series of imperial ones close to Hagia Sophia, but those of Sultan Süleyman and his consort Roxelana stand to the south-east of the Süleymaniye Mosque are among the most beautiful (*Ill. 194, 195*).

The ideas that Sinan perfected served as the theme for nearly all the mosques built thereafter, but in many of the later buildings the proportions were often rather less perfect than in the work of the master. Thus in the mosque of Sultan Ahmed (1609) (*Ill. 193, 196*) the piers that hold up the dome are somewhat clumsy and heavy, though outside its six tall minarets give it a lightness and delicacy which is truly outstanding, and the lovely tiles adorning its interior have

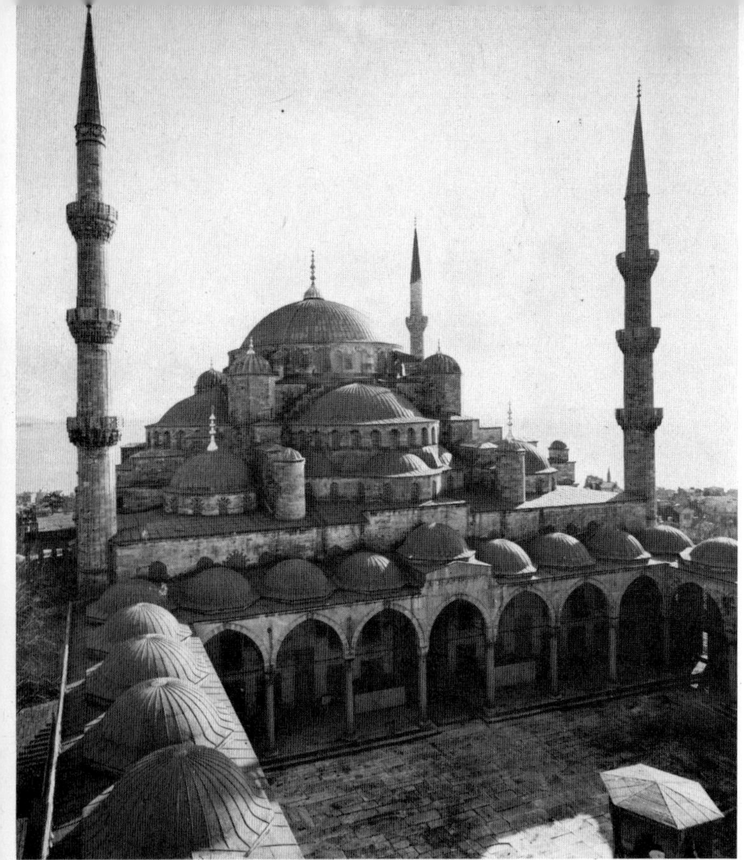

193 The mosque of Sultan Ahmed, Istanbul. 1609–16. The six minarets, one at each corner of the building, and two more at the extremity of the forecourt, are unique. Their slender, pencil-like form is particularly effective

given to it the name by which it is most usually known today, 'The Blue Mosque'. But the purist would regard them as decadent, and attractive though the over-all effect is, the details of the tile-work perhaps lack something of the quality of the earlier work, as we see it in Süleyman's türbe (*Ill. 194*) or in certain smaller mosques like Sinan's Sokollu Mehmet Pasha (1571) or Rüstem Pasha (*c.* 1550), both of which are veritable tile museums (*Ill. 197–200*).

The nature of these tiles is quite distinct. First the old idea of mosaic work, where tiles of two colours were cut out and set together to form a pattern, so popular with the Seljuks, had disappeared, as had that of the alternating star-shaped and octagonal tiles decorated in lustre which the Seljuks brought from Persia.

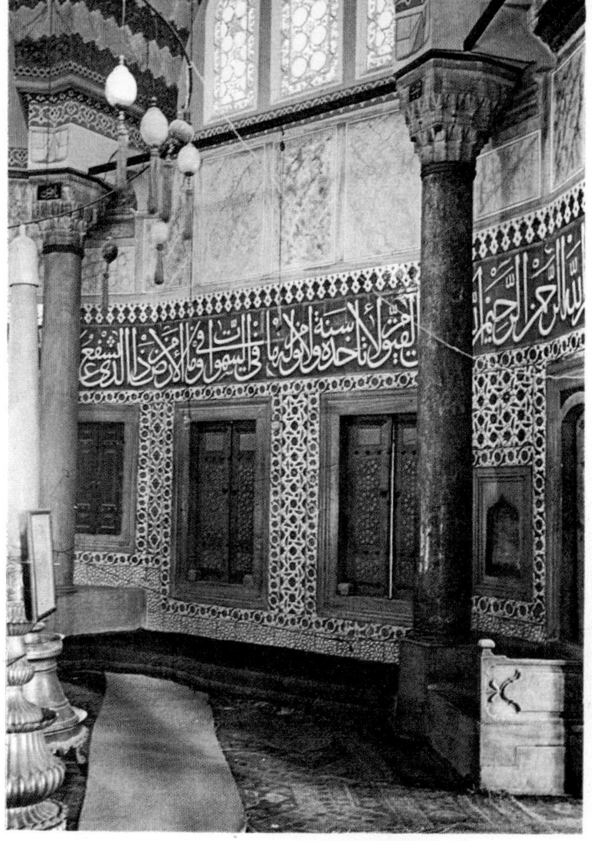

194 The interior of the mausoleum of Sultan Süleyman, Istanbul. 1566. Both this and the mausoleum of his favourite wife, Roxelana, stand close to the Süleymaniye Mosque. The form is derived from that of the gumbat, so popular in Seljuk times

195 Detail of the tile-work in Sultan Süleyman's mausoleum. These tiles are typical of the work of the Isnik potters at their best and are among the finest in Istanbul. The designs were painted on the tiles and the glaze added above, a technique quite distinct from that which prevailed in Seljuk times

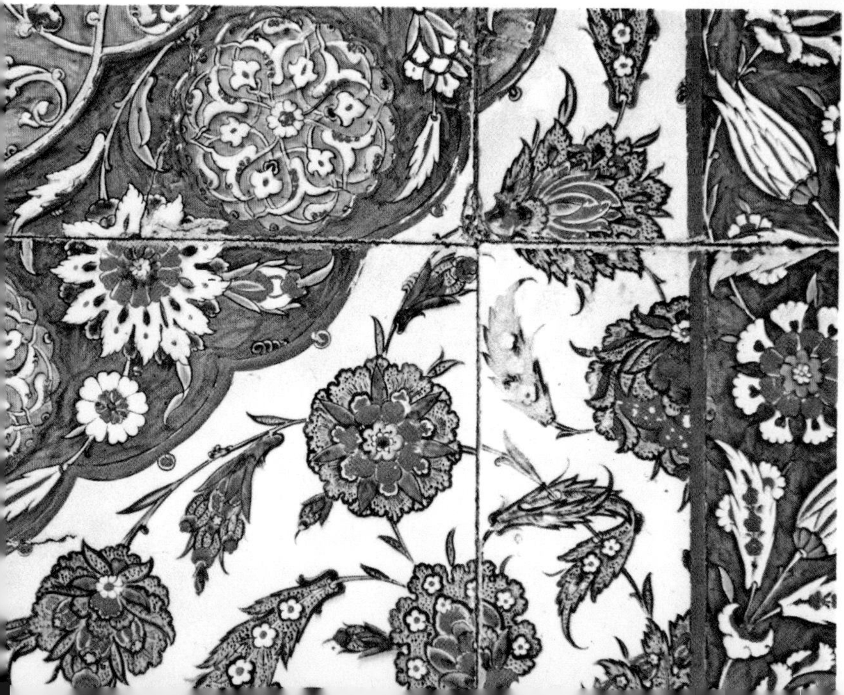

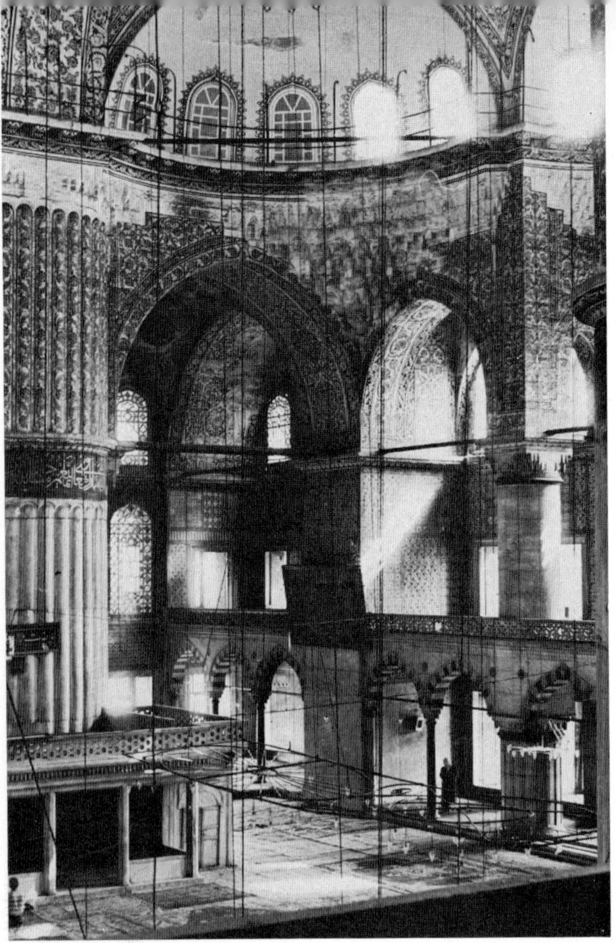

196 Interior of the mosque of Sultan Ahmed. 1609–16. The tile-work is predominantly blue and for this reason has been given the name 'Blue Mosque' by which it is often called, although the effect is perhaps somewhat monotonous in contrast to some of the buildings of the previous century

Instead the tiles of the Ottomans were square or rectangular, and fitted together in fours or even greater numbers to form elaborate large-scale panels, bearing an adornment of flowers and scrolls in various colours. The body was usually of a fine white paste, the designs done in deep blue, green, lilac, aubergine and a characteristic upstanding tomato red, usually against a white, sometimes an azure ground. The colours were themselves vitrifiable pastes, but were covered by a transparent glaze of uniform colour. The introduction of the technique has sometimes been attributed to Persian craftsmen brought back by Selim I when he captured Tabriz in 1514. There is certainly some similarity as regards colour and design with the so-called Kubachi wares of Persia (see p. 244), but there are also marked differences, and the suggestion of a Persian origin is not wholly convincing, for the technique, the nature of the decoration, and the style of its rendering developed very rapidly along quite distinctive lines under the patronage of the Ottomans, and the pottery soon became one of the most individual and outstanding of the arts of the Islamic world.

The most important centre of production was the town of Isnik, the Byzantine Nicaea, and the factories there seem to have been equally concerned with the manufacture of both vessels and tiles, for the techniques of the two are identical. Wares of both types were widely exported, but the finest tiles were mostly made for Istanbul, and it is in the mosques and the royal palace there that the best examples are preserved. But from the point of view of pottery, the products must be studied as a whole, for the same workmen and designers were responsible for tiles and vessels alike.

The products of Isnik have been divided into three primary groups: an earlier, dating from about 1490 to 1525, an intermediate, most important from 1525 to 1535, and a late, from 1550 or thereabouts until the beginning of the eighteenth century. Thereafter the main centre of activity moved to Kütahya, where a new and distinct style was developed.

During the first of these periods the decorations were restricted to blue and white (*Ill. 201*); the glazes were thin and fine, the shapes of the vessels followed metal prototypes, and the tiles were comparatively restricted in scope; there are some examples in the mosque of Murad II at Bursa. The second phase, sometimes described as the 'Damascus style' (*Ill. 203*), which was characterized by a more varied palette, several shades of blue and a lovely sage green predominating, while from about 1540 manganese brown was also often added. Flowers like bluebells or carnations formed the main motifs of decoration; sometimes the effect was rather Chinese, at others it was more original, as for instance in a very distinctive group where a mass of thin scrolls in blue cover the surface. This group is usually known as 'Golden Horn ware' (*Ill. 202*). It was at one time associated with Istanbul, but it now seems likely that all the examples were made at Isnik.

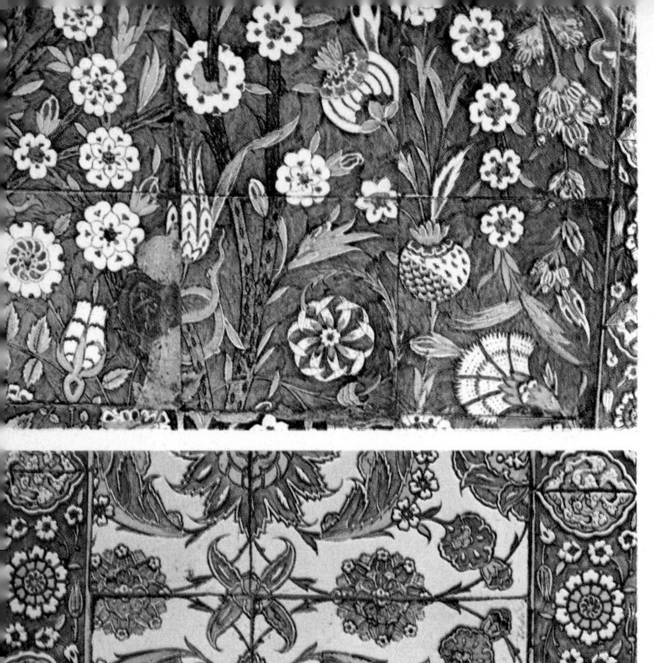

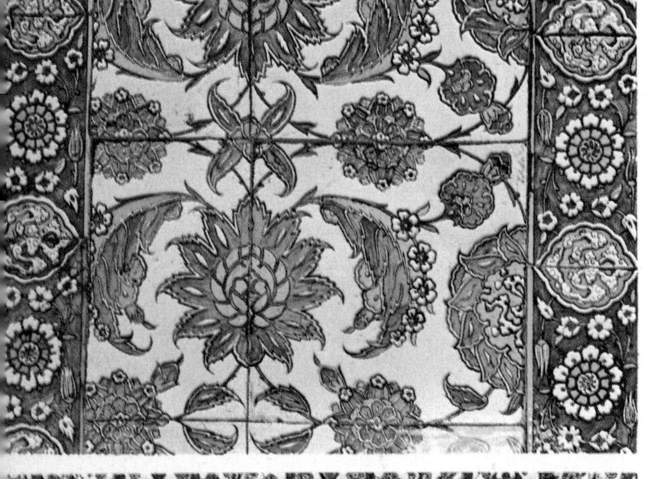

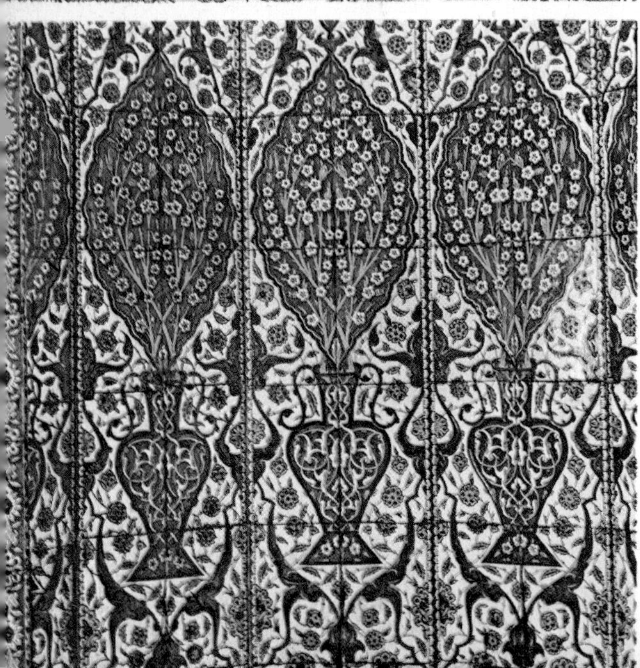

197, 198, 199 (*left*) Details of tile-work in the mosque of Rüstem Pasha, Istanbul. *c.* 1550. The mosque was built for one of Sultan Süleyman's grand viziers by Sinan, and its tile decorations are both very extensive and of outstanding quality. Virtually all the wall space inside the mosque and within the porch is tiled

200 (*opposite*) Tiled mihrab in the mosque of Sokollu Mehmet Pasha, designed by Sinan for an independent patron. The mosque is a building of great beauty, perhaps Sinan's finest small-scale work. Its tiled mihrab is unsurpassed even by the tiles of the mosque of Rüstem Pasha or Sultan Süleyman's mausoleum. 1571–2

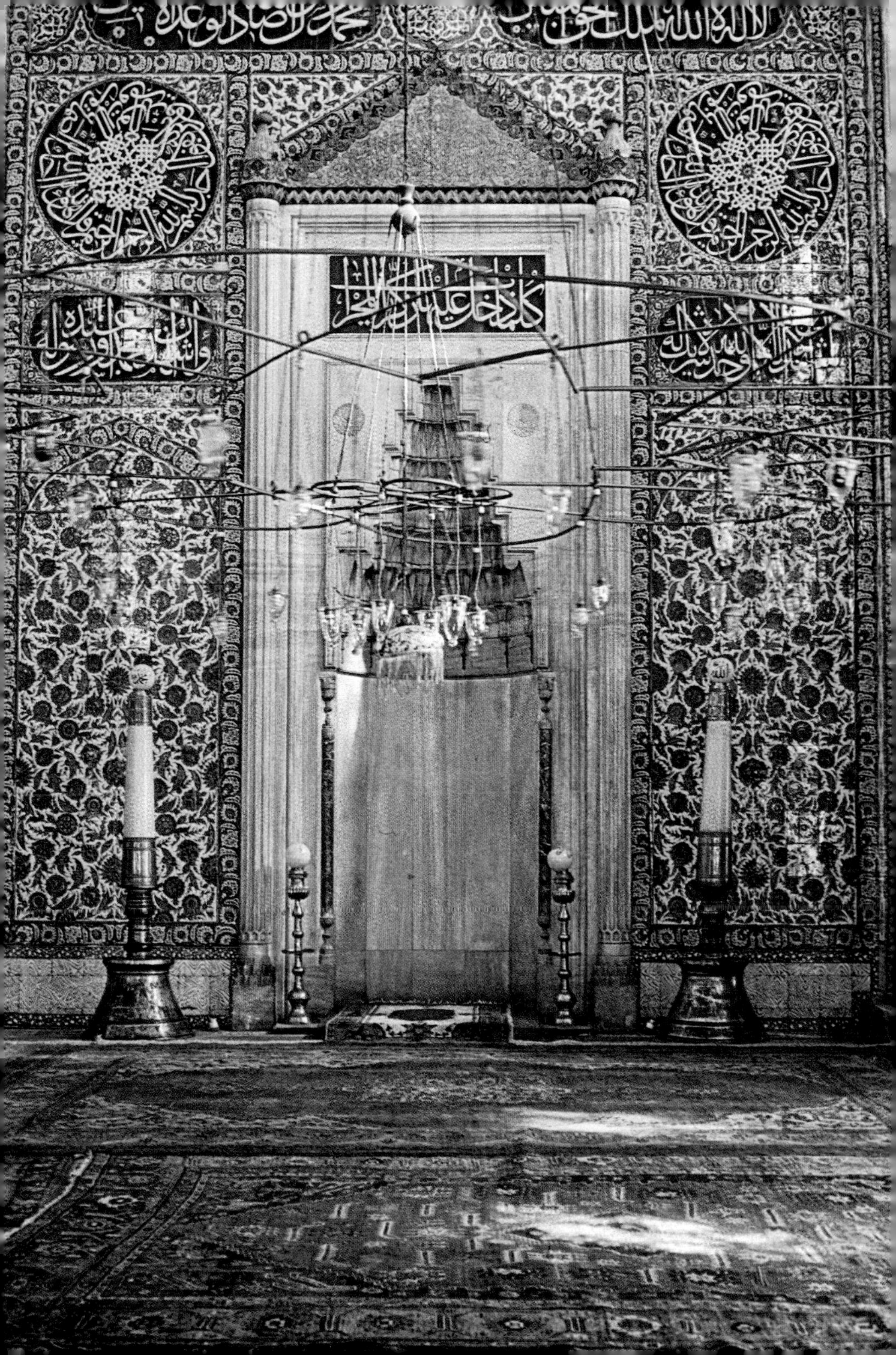

The third group of Isnik ware is the most important of all. It is that often called the 'Rhodian', though Rhodes was never a centre of manufacture. It is characterized by a new technique of underglaze painting and by a greater variety of colours, especially the use of the so-called 'Armenian bole', which produced a brilliant tomato red when fired; it stood up in slight relief under the glaze (*Ill. 206*). Tulips also became one of the most favoured motifs. Vessels seem to have formed a by-product of the tile industry, and many of them are extremely beautiful, while the tiles remain quite unequalled. Some of the finest examples are to be found in the mosques of Rüstem Pasha (1550) and Sokollu Mehmet Pasha (1571) at Istanbul as well as in the Saray (*Ill. 204*) and in other mosques of the early seventeenth century, such as the Sultan Ahmed mosque (1609–16). When these tiles were being made some three hundred workers were employed at Isnik; by 1649 only nine were working there and by the beginning of the next century the industry was nearly extinct. A few workers were collected together in about 1724 at Istanbul and a factory established on the spot where the Blachernae palace had stood, near to where the land walls met the Golden Horn, and work was continued there, the old Isnik designs being reproduced in a thin rather niggling manner. Later in the eighteenth century the best work was done at Kütahya. The most distinctive products of these potteries were small vessels – dishes, jugs or objects in the shape of eggs which were fixed on to the cords suspending lamps or candelabra to prevent mice from consuming the oil or eating the candles (*Ill. 207*). Red, black, blue, green and bright yellow were the favourite colours and the designs were usually finicky and linear. Many of the potters seem to have been Armenians or Greeks, and the vessels often bear inscriptions in these languages. Tiles with Christian subjects were also made, examples of which are preserved in the Armenian cathedral at Jerusalem.

201 (*above*) Bowl belonging to the earlier period of Isnik ware, *c.* 1510. The Isnik potters were as proficient at producing vessels as they were at making tiles

202 (*below*) Bowl of a group usually known as 'Golden Horn ware', *c.* 1545. Once it was believed that these were made on the Golden Horn, but it is now generally accepted that they came from Isnik

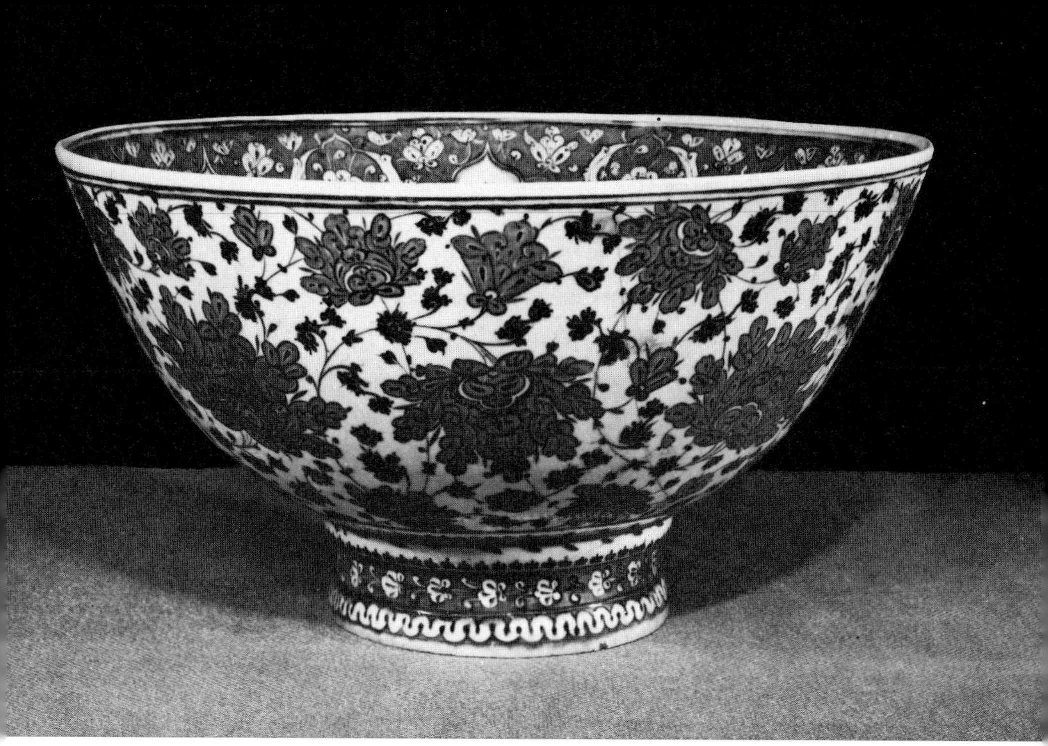

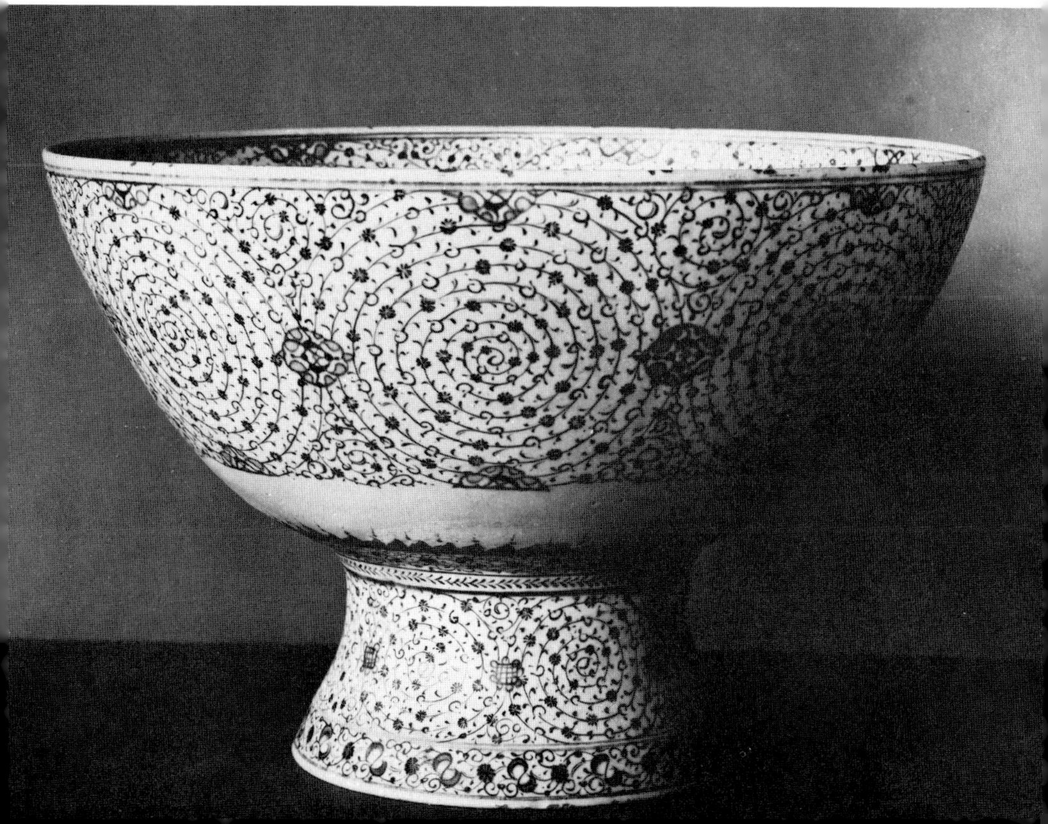

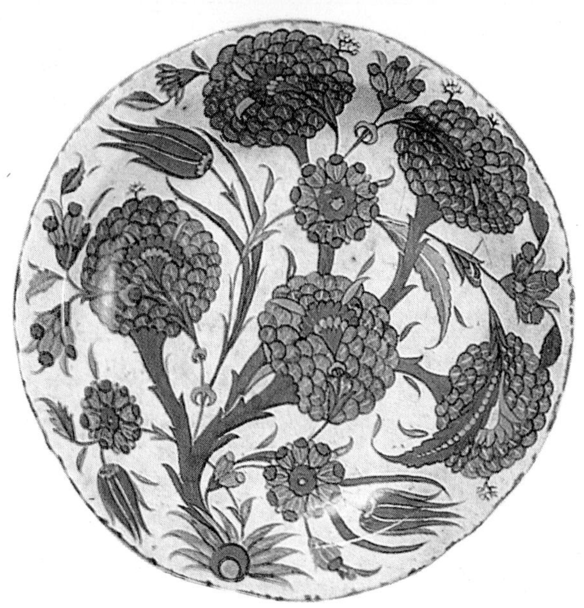

203 Large dish of Isnik ware, dating from *c.* 1545. These lively floral designs, in which tulips and carnations play a prominent part, were characteristic of much of the best Isnik ware

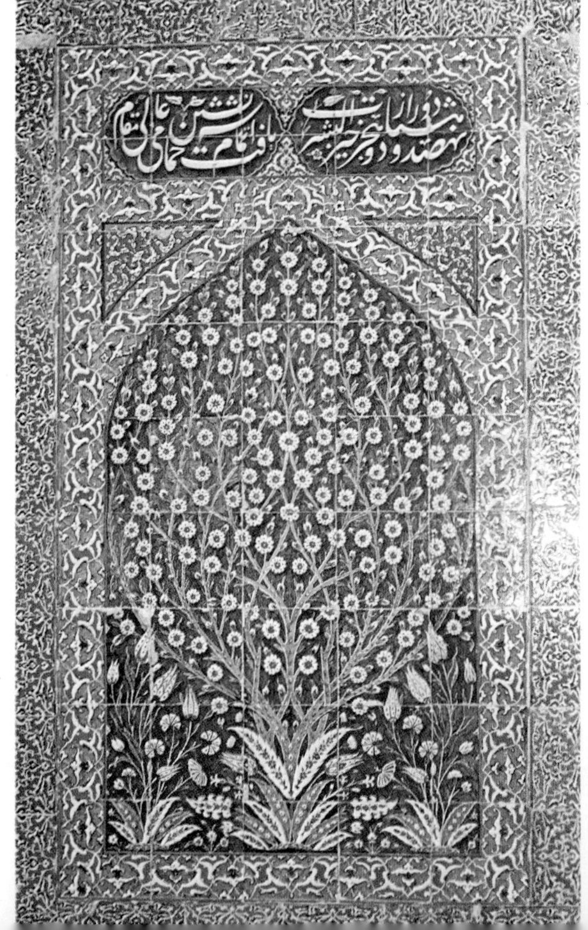

204 Tile panel in the Saray, Istanbul. Mid-sixteenth century. Tiles were used for the decoration of religious and secular buildings, without much distinction of character. Much of the finest work is to be found in small rooms of the imperial harem

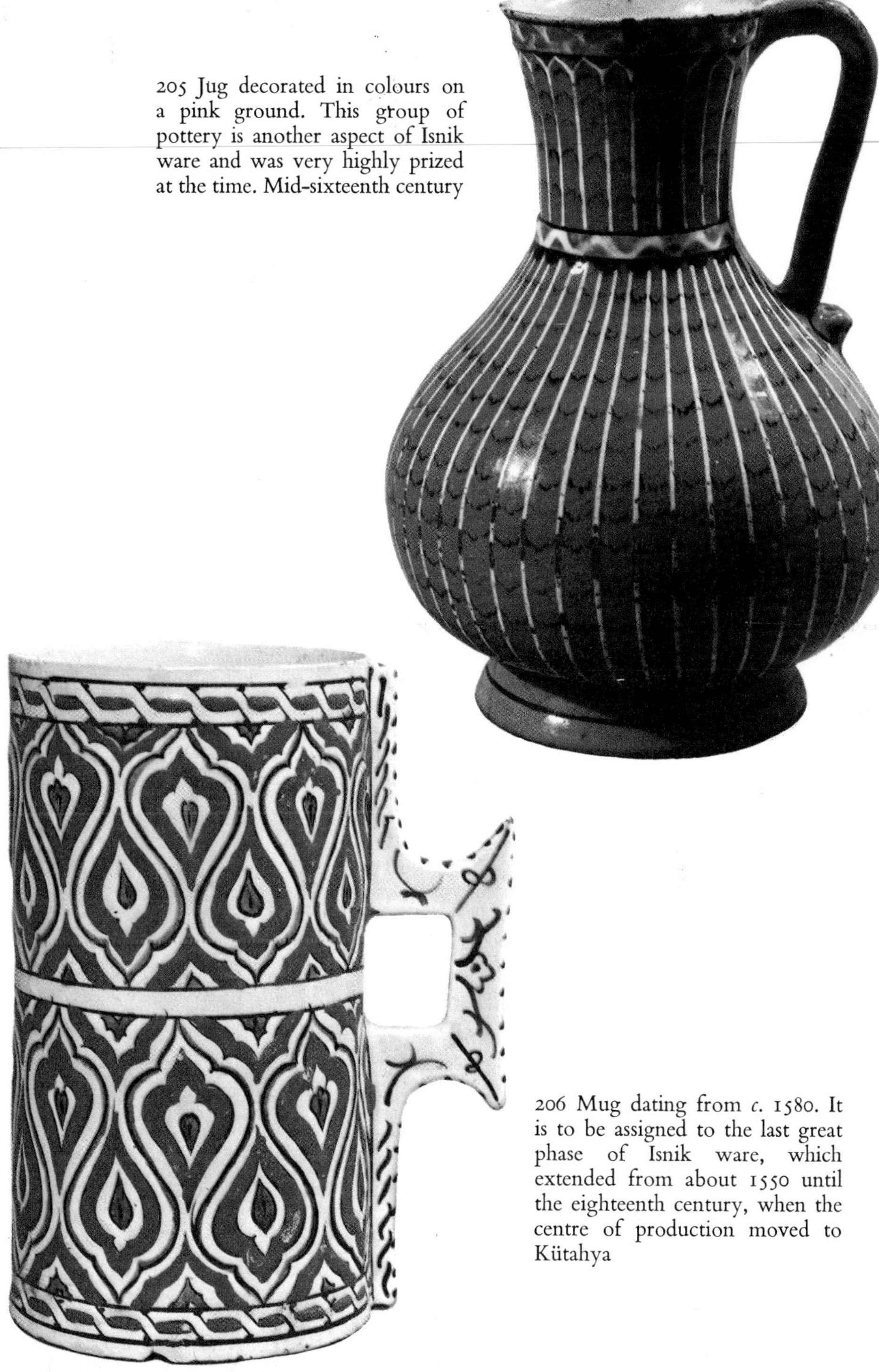

205 Jug decorated in colours on a pink ground. This group of pottery is another aspect of Isnik ware and was very highly prized at the time. Mid-sixteenth century

206 Mug dating from *c.* 1580. It is to be assigned to the last great phase of Isnik ware, which extended from about 1550 until the eighteenth century, when the centre of production moved to Kütahya

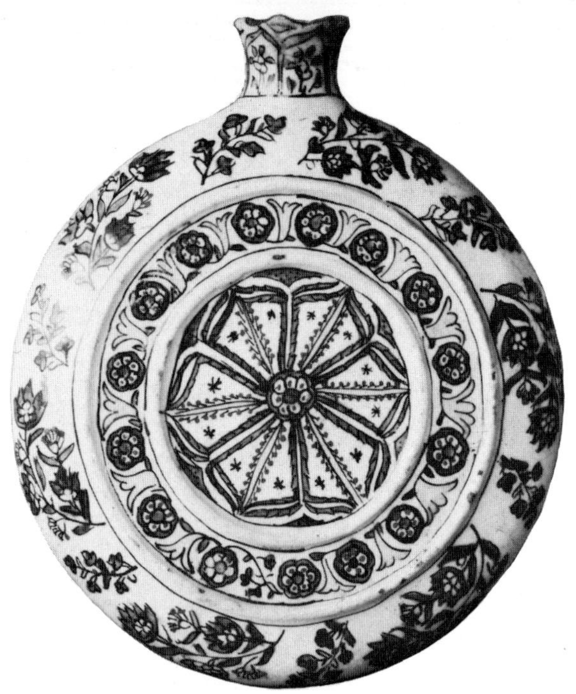

207 Flask of blue and white Kütahya ware. The small-scale, almost finicky design is characteristic of this type of pottery, which in the eighteenth century to a great extent supplanted that of Isnik

In addition to these luxury wares, all characterized by their fine white bodies, their brilliant, highly fired glazes and their rich colours, plainer wares, with red (*Ill. 205*) or buff bodies and simple decorations were also usual. On one group glazes of several colours were made to intermingle so that they give a marbled effect. On another dots and lines on a thick white slip were used alone below cream and green glazes; on another, of later eighteenth- and nineteenth-century date, spirited designs of boats, trees, mosques and so on were painted on to bowls and dishes, thick and coarse perhaps, but none the less pleasant and attractive. But they represent peasant rather than fine art, and can hardly be classed alongside the best work of Isnik.

Many of the same floral motifs that we see on the Isnik pottery were also used on the silk textiles, another luxury product which was developed along similarly distinctive lines as the pottery. The textile industry was centred at Bursa and the silk weavers or the makers

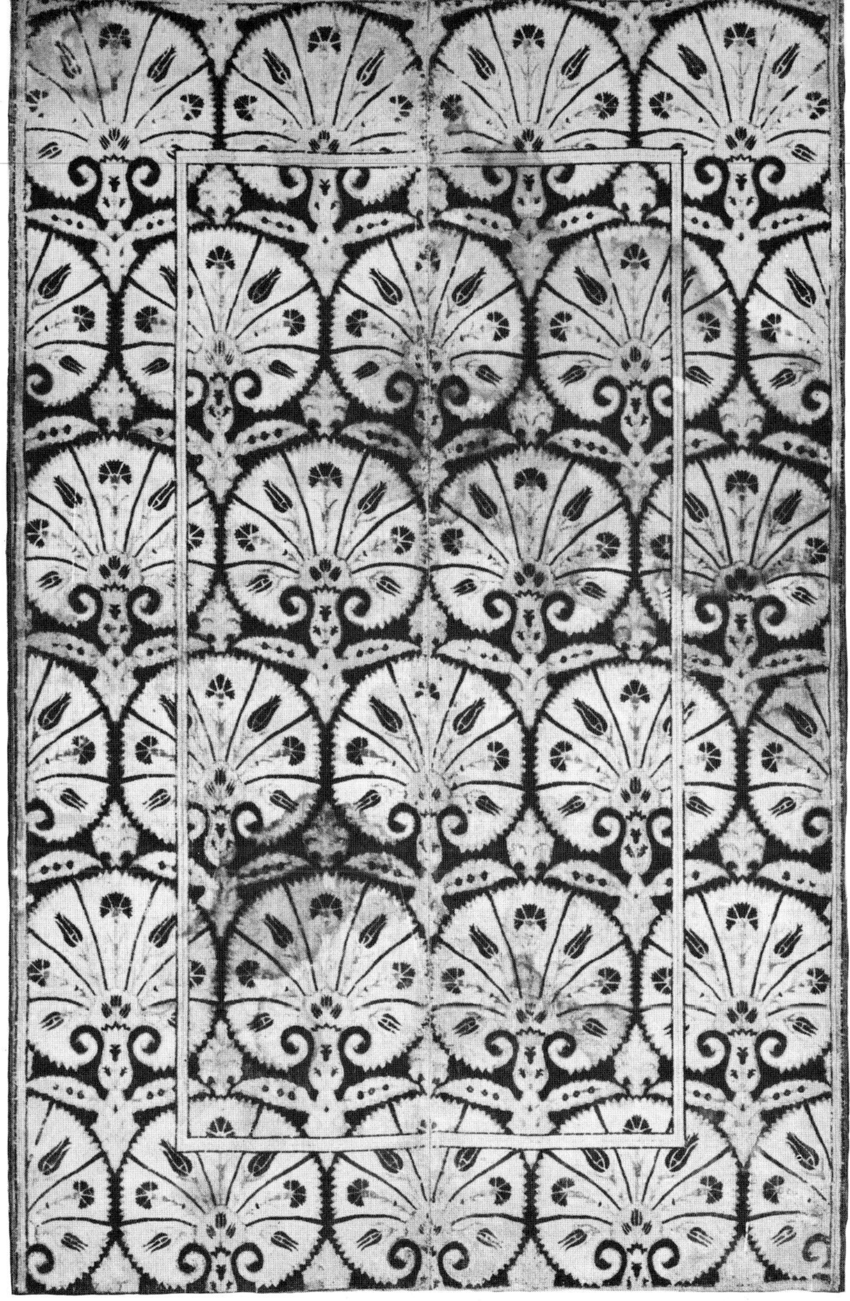

208 Crimson velvet brocade of the sixteenth century. Woven silks and velvets of superb quality were produced in large quantities for the Ottoman sultans, most probably at Bursa. They were highly prized and their style is most distinctive

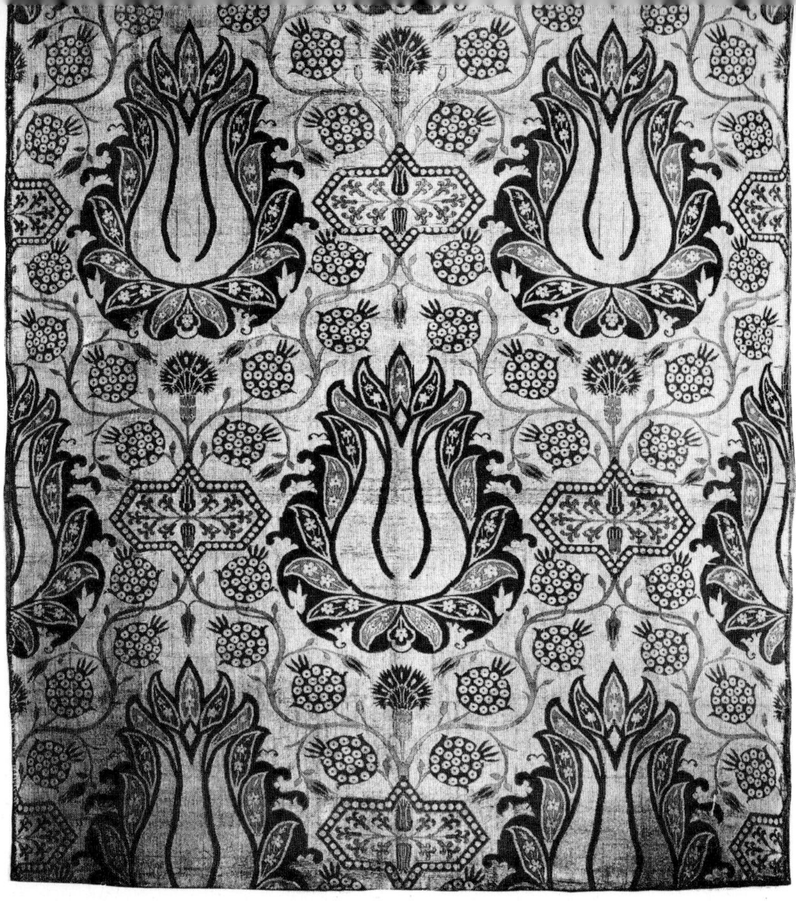

209 Woven silk of the sixteenth century. The designs are always formal, sometimes even geometric, and in this the Turkish textiles contrast markedly with the Persian ones, where naturalism prevailed

of velvets produced for the Ottoman sultans work which was in its way just as superb as that which had been done for the Byzantine emperors before them ever since the cultivation of silk was first introduced to the West by Justinian (*Ill. 209*). Bursa seems to have been the main centre in early times, but there is evidence to suggest that there were looms producing very similar silks on the Island of Chios; the only distinction seems to be that the weaving done there was rather less tight, and with time the stuffs tended to fray more easily. Silks and brocades (*Ill. 208*) were in great demand to provide hangings, covers and, above all, the rich court costumes, and the

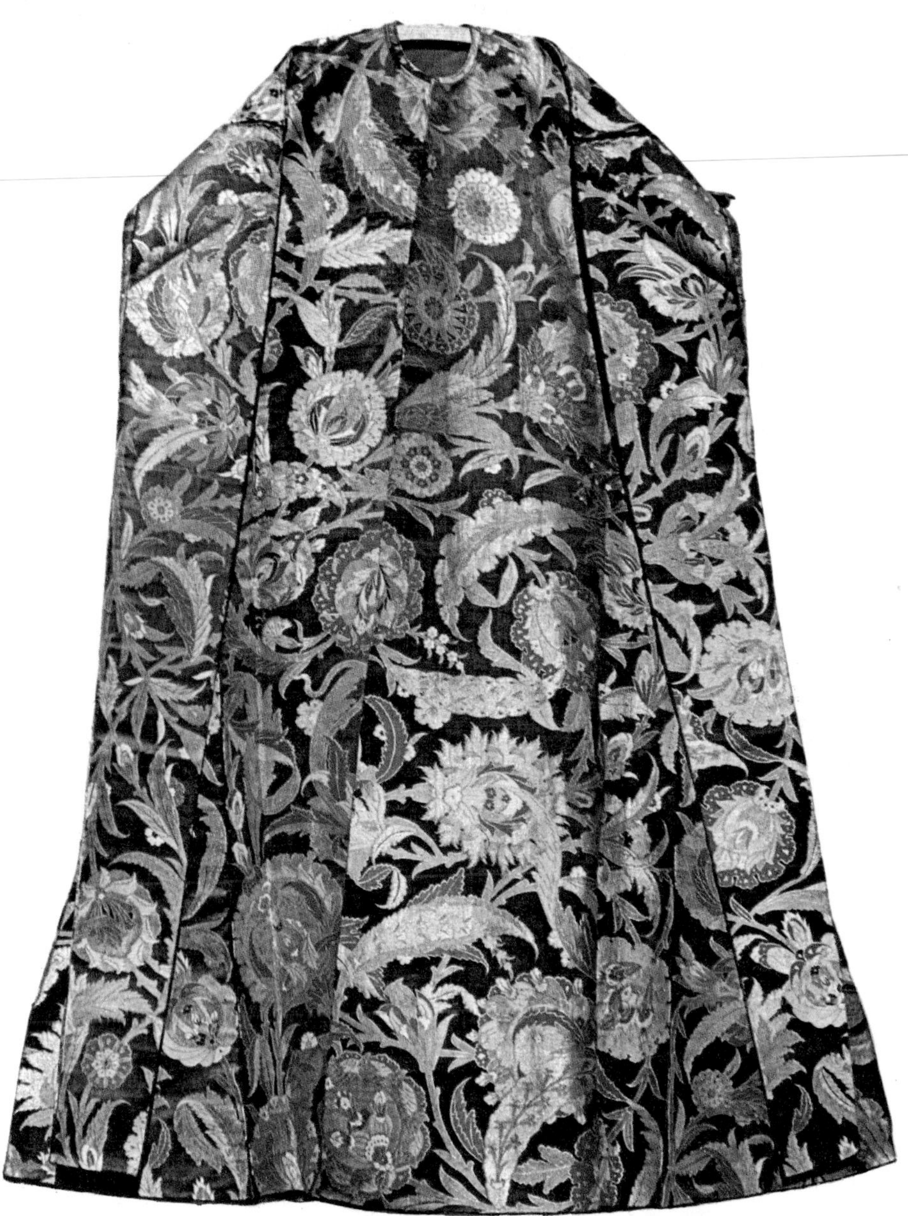

210 Silk costume, said to be that of Beyazid II (1481–1512). Many of the costumes of the sultans are preserved in the Saray at Istanbul, but the attributions are somewhat doubtful and the silk of which this one is made would seem to be later in date than this particular sultan

demands of the palace must have been enormous. Receipts and other documents relating to their manufacture still survive in the archives of the Saray at Istanbul; also preserved are rolls of silk which have never been used, and the costumes worn on state occasions by many of the sultans (*Ill. 210*). Red, blue and yellow were the most usual colours for the ground, with elaborate floral designs in red, blue, black and gold. One of the favourite patterns was made up of a repeat of two stripes and three dots; it was perhaps a conventionalized reproduction of the leopard skins which had formed a part of the royal costume in the early days when the Turks were still nomads in the uplands of Asia.

The silks were no doubt also used as coverings for the sofas and divans which constituted the main furniture of the Turkish interiors, but even more prized for this purpose were the lovely silk velvets, made probably at Bursa and in later times also at Skutari, on the Asiatic coast opposite Istanbul. These too are also of quite outstanding quality, but their designs tend to be more formal, for they were more often made not as continuous strips, to be cut to shape for costumes, but as rectangular pieces of set size. But strips were also made, for velvets were sometimes used for making costumes, more especially the short-sleeved waistcoats which were worn under the long silk robes.

Superb though the Turkish silks and velvets are, they are perhaps less famous in the West than the rugs and carpets. Unlike the silks and velvets, which were made in factories under the patronage of the sultans, the carpets represent a peasant industry, which was developed independently in various regions of Anatolia. The earliest examples followed on from those of Seljuk times, and bore similar angular patterns, but stylized birds and animals soon began to be used, and animal carpets which are Turkish rather than Persian are to be found in European paintings of the fifteenth and following centuries. These furnish the most important evidence regarding the problems of chronology. The oldest actual Ottoman rug that is known is probably one of the Ushak type dated to 1584 (*Ill. 211*). From the next century onwards examples became numerous enough to make possible a system of classification which permits the distinc-

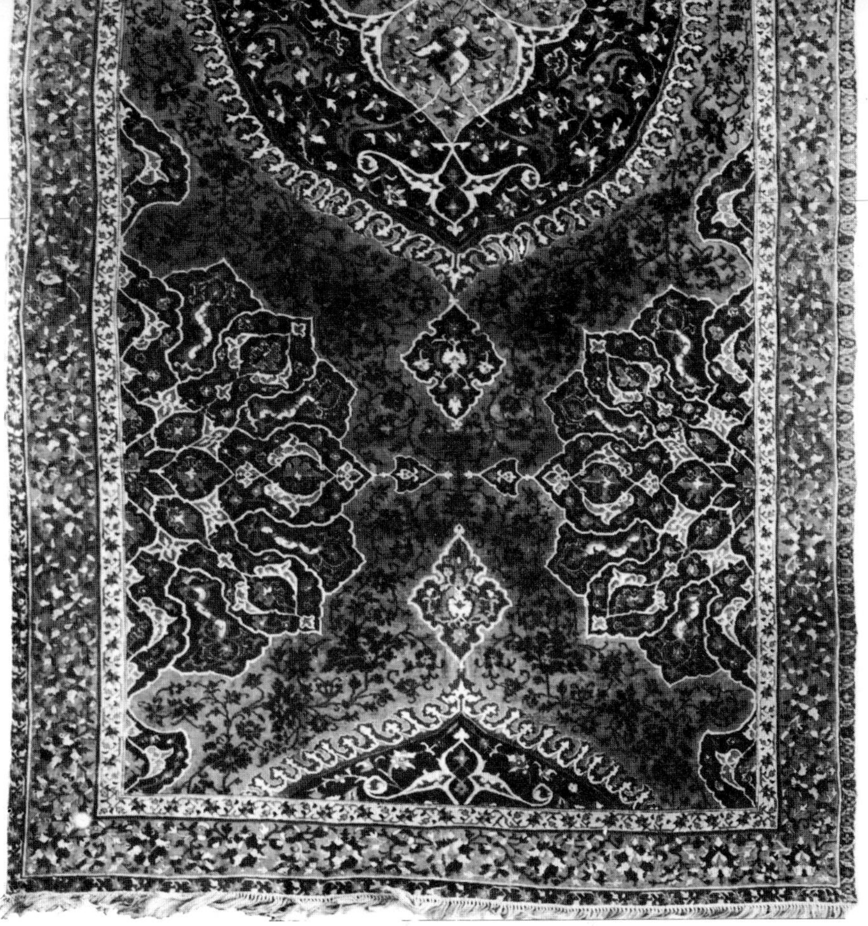

211 Carpet of Ushak type. Late eighteenth century. In contrast to the silks and velvets, which were all essentially 'court' products made in centralized workshops, the rugs were all made in the villages, and represent a peasant art

tion of a number of individual local types. The most famous of them are those associated with Ushak, Bergama, Gördes, Kula, Ladik, and Kirşehir. In each of these regions is to be found an individual type of design and a particular colour scheme, though the so-called 'Gördes ("Gordian") knot' was universally employed in Turkey (see p. 252). Most of these products took the form of rugs; the large-scale carpets, so common in Persia, were less favoured in Turkey, and the so-called 'Turkey carpet' was a comparatively late innovation. They were normally made of wool and cotton, though specially rich rugs for court use were sometimes of silk.

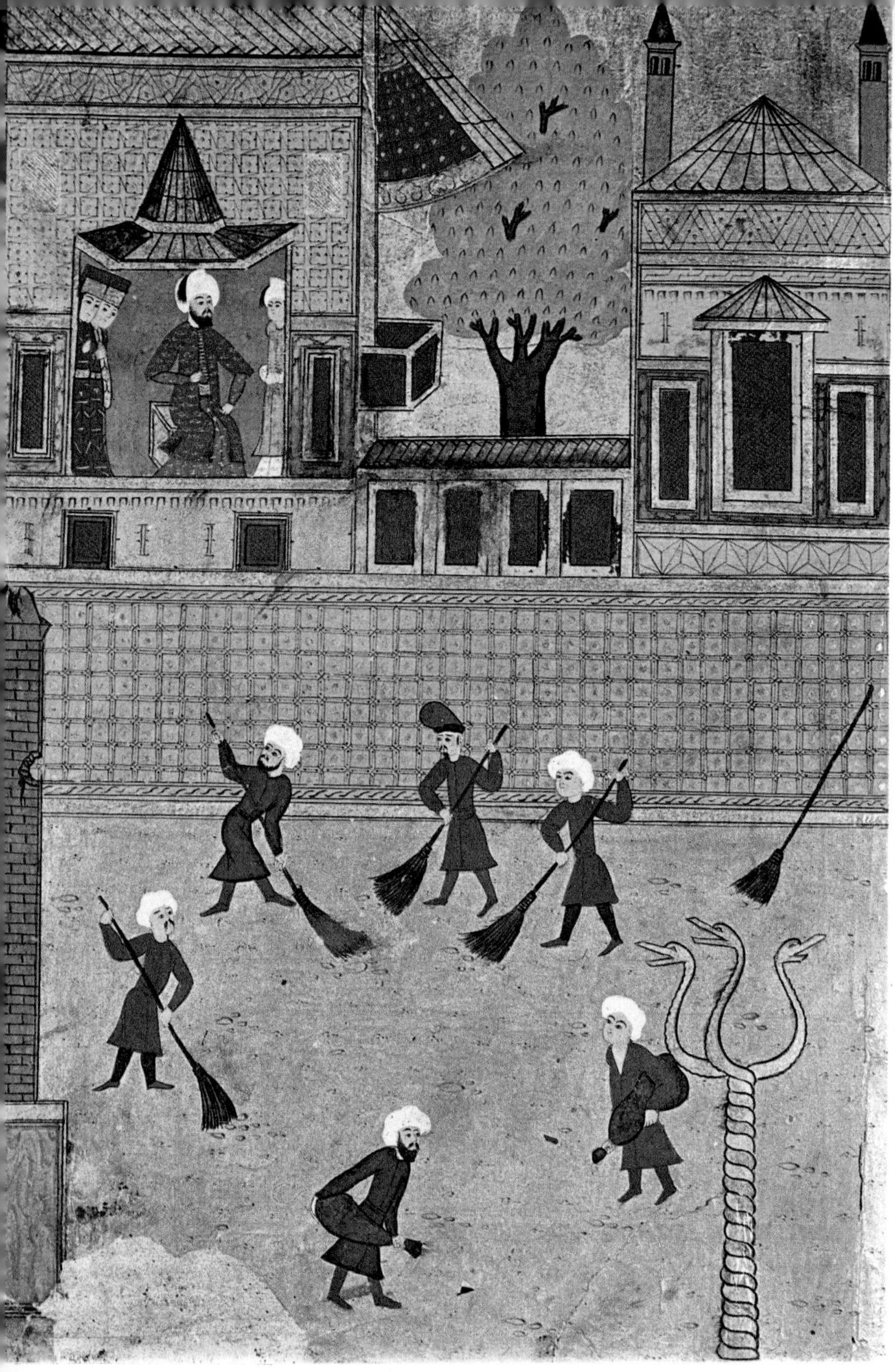

212 Sweepers performing in the Hippodrome. This is a leaf from a manuscript known as the *Surnama* of Murad III (1574–95) which depicts parades of the various workers' guilds in the Hippodrome in Istanbul

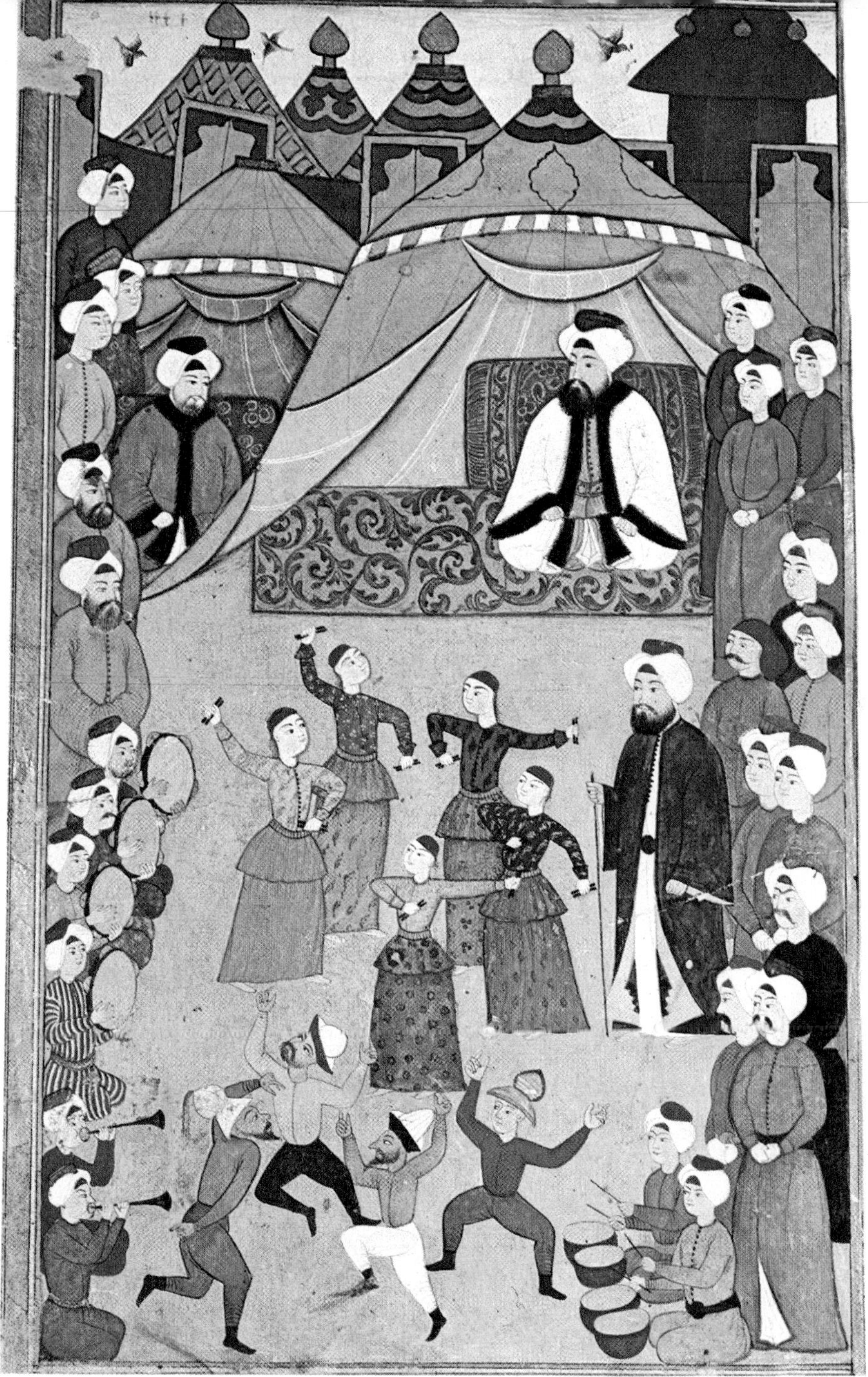

213 The sultan watching dancers and comedians in the Hippodrome. This leaf from the *Surnama* of Ahmed III (1703–30) contrasts markedly with the poetic, imaginative painting in Persia at the same time, with its clear-cut, practical art

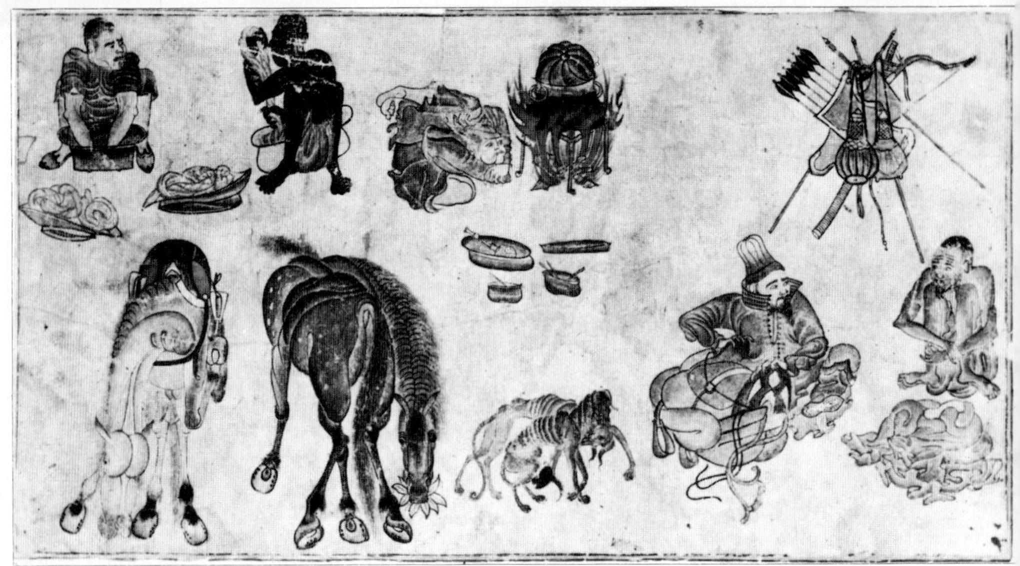

214 Illustration of a nomadic encampment from the 'Album of the Conqueror' by the Turkish painter, Siyah Kalem. In the treatment of perspective, especially in this work, his work contrasts strongly with that of his Persian contemporaries

One further branch of Ottoman art remains to be considered – the painting. Once again scholars of the past have tended to regard this art as a poor reflection of the Persian, but although painters were brought from Persia by many of the sultans and though a good deal of work was done in Turkey in imitation of the Persian, with its search for a sort of idyllic dream-world, a great deal was also done in a style which was wholly Ottoman. In the fifteenth century it was characterized by a forcefulness and realism which was totally absent in Persian art of the same time, as can be seen, in the very striking illustrations that fill the so-called 'Album of the Conqueror' in the Topkapi Library in Istanbul. Two artists of great ability worked on this book; one, Ahmed Musa, was responsible for a series of Koranic scenes of great originality and daring, in that he truly depicted the Prophet's features; the other, Mehmet Siyah Kalem, executed some truly remarkable figures of men and animals in a style that owed much to China, but which was also essentially personal (*Ill. 214*). His work represents some of the most accomplished in all Islamic painting. Later the heritage of these styles is to be seen in the delightful illustrations of particular events which are to be found in the so-called *Hünernama*, 'Lives of the Sultans', or *Surnama*, 'Books of Festivals', where daily scenes are shown in a naïve yet most expressive manner. In one of these books, the *Surnama* of Murad III, the various trades are depicted parading in the Hippodrome at Constantinople before the sultan (*Ill. 212*). In another, done as late as the eighteenth century, dancers and comedians are shown before Ahmed III (1703–30) (*Ill. 213*). In others battle scenes, firework displays, and sports are shown. This art, essentially Turkish in character, is far removed from that of the enchanting dream-world of Persia. It is a virile, male art, full of life and action, in which love and romance have little part to play. It is only thanks to the publication of material in the Saray at Istanbul in very recent years that we have got to know something of it, but what we now know serves finally to dispel the old ideas of Turkish ineptitude in the visual arts.

One can hardly leave Turkey without a word as to the last phase of art at Istanbul, the Turkish baroque. It is perhaps not a great style, nor can it be termed a truly Islamic one, but it has great charm, and the decorative paintings that adorn some of the rooms of the Harem or a few of the old wooden houses that survive on the banks of the Bosphorus deserve to be rescued from the neglect which they have fallen into during the last century.

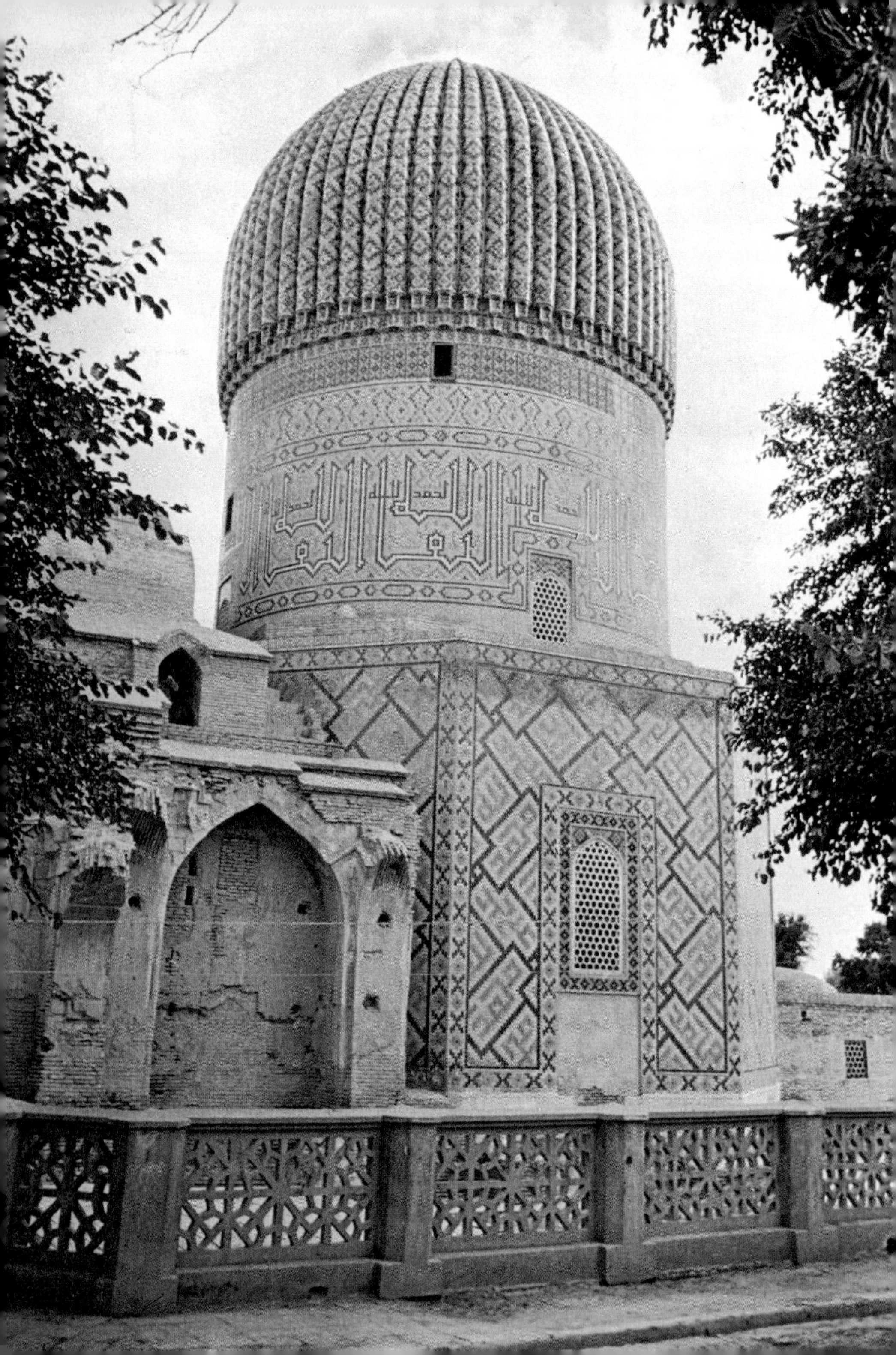

CHAPTER ELEVEN

Persian Art: the Later Fourteenth and Early Fifteenth centuries

Just as the great quattrocento was in many ways the most outstanding and certainly the one most dominated by Italy in the story of Renaissance art in the West, so was the period between about 1370 and 1500 the most outstanding in Persia, even though its beginning was marked by a phase of conquest under Tamerlane which was little less violent than that of the first Mongol eruption under Hulagu. But if there were destructions, they were less widespread than in the thirteenth century, and Tamerlane was almost as outstanding as a patron of architecture and the arts as he was as a conqueror. The example he set was followed by his successors, nearly all of whom were active and enlightened patrons. The superb Gawhar Shad at Meshad thus dates from between 1405 and 1418 and most of the buildings at Herat belong to the first quarter of the fifteenth century. Work was also done at Balkh, Shiraz and in numerous others places.

It was, however, primarily in his beloved Turkistan that Tamerlane's own patronage was most active, and it is there that some of the finest mosques of the age around 1400 are to be found; it was there, too, at Samarkand, that he was buried. His mausoleum, the Gur Emir (*Ill. 215*), finished in 1434, is one of the world's most perfect buildings, and there are a series of other mosques and mausolea there which are little less superb. Most of them are distinguished, as are other buildings of the age like the mosque at Herat, by a new type of dome, lobed and slightly bulbous, but of great beauty. The use of tile-work on the exteriors was also greatly extended, so that whole façades, even the domes themselves, came to be decorated. It would seem that these tiles were all made locally, close to the buildings for

215 The mausoleum of Tamerlane, the Gur Emir, at Samarkand. 1434. Tamerlane the Mongol may have been the scourge of much of the Islamic world, but he was also a great patron of art and his beloved Samarkand benefited considerably by his hand

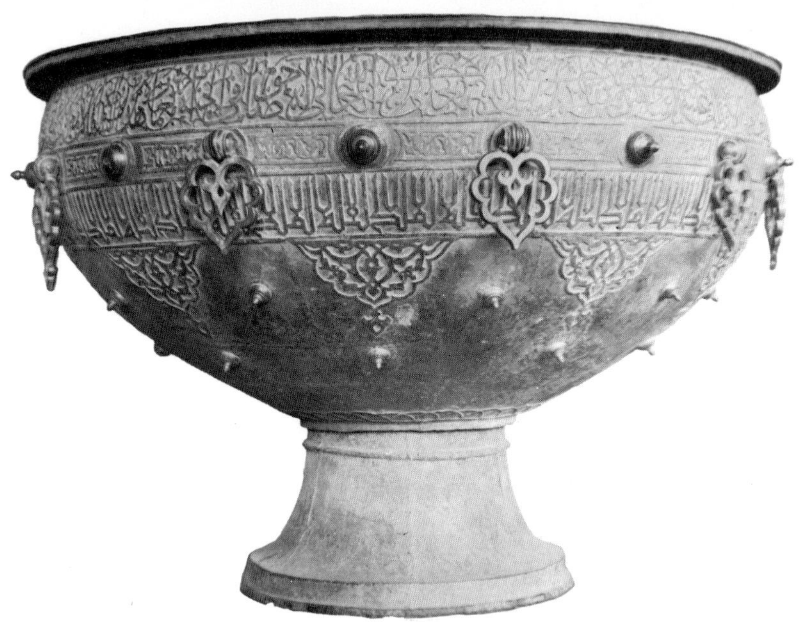

216 This vast bronze cauldron weighing about two tons was made for Tamerlane in the early fifteenth century in Samarkand. No larger or finer piece of Islamic metalwork exists

which they were intended, and that craftsmen were brought to the various places for the purpose; in this way the close similarity of work in places very far apart from one another is to be explained.

The tile decoration set the keynote against which the other arts were developed. It is one of unusual richness and brilliance. Textiles were woven in numerous centres throughout Persia and most favoured were rich silks and sheeny satins (*Ill. 218*), in the manufacture of which gold and silver threads were profusely used. In pottery the Sultanabad wares of the previous century were elaborated, and attempts were made to imitate the brilliance of Chinese blue and white of the early Ming style (from 1368). Again the centres of manufacture were widespread throughout the country, although Varamin was perhaps the most important of them. In glass the same taste for the delicate and exquisite was displayed (*Ill. 217*), while in metal some of the work was truly magnificent; no finer example was probably ever made than the great cauldron of Tamerlane from Samarkand, now in the Hermitage (*Ill. 216*).

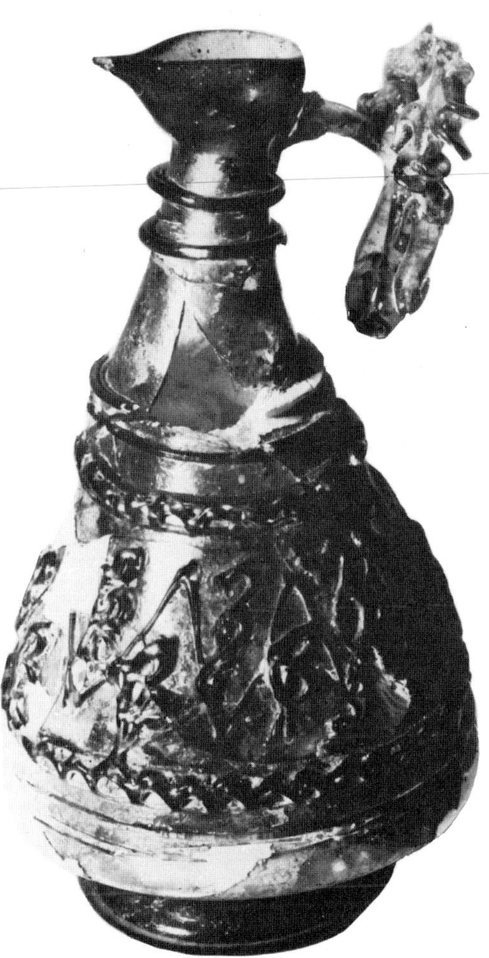

217 Glass bottle with ornament in relief. The glass of Syria and Egypt was perhaps more famous than the Persian, but recent discoveries have shown that Persian work was also very fine, especially in the later periods

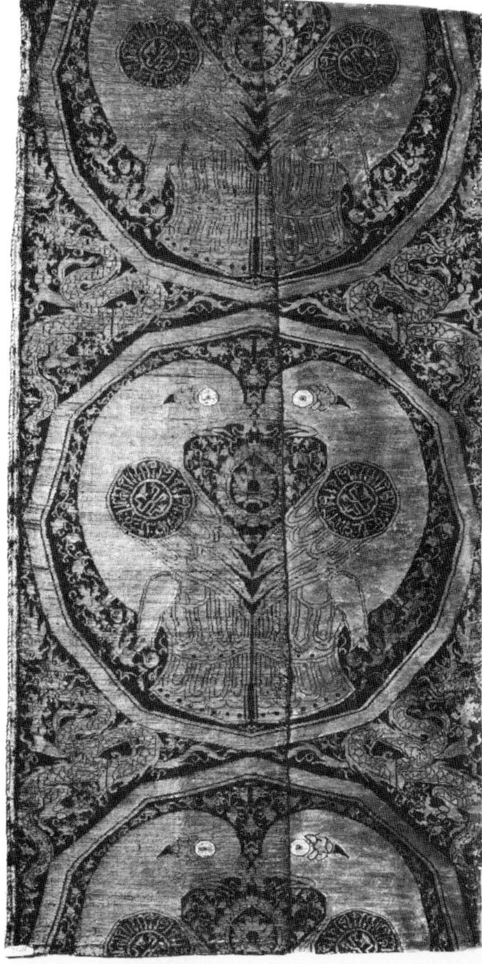

218 Persian satin of the fourteenth century. Persia was from earliest times an important centre of textile weaving, but some of the finest of its products are to be assigned to the later fourteenth or fifteenth centuries

It was, however, in the miniature paintings that the art of this age reached its height. Here a style which was wholly and completely Persian had developed out of the mixed styles of the Ilkhan period, and though work of great quality was done in the second half of the fourteenth century, it was really thanks to the enthusiasm of Tamerlane and his descendants that the most important developments took place. Under Tamerlane himself Samarkand was certainly an important centre, and there are records of garden pavilions adorned with frescoes and of exquisite painted textiles that were admired there. However, no paintings which can actually be assigned to Samarkand survive. It is to other centres like Shiraz and Herat that we must turn for actual examples, while rather later Tabriz again became significant, and there was probably an important school at Isfahan.

The work of Shiraz (*Ill. 219*) is to be distinguished by its brilliance of colouring, by a love of gorgeous landscapes, by the frequent inclusion of freely drawn bird and flower motifs in the margins, and by the faces of the figures with their rounded contours, fine lines, narrow eyes, and rather characteristic sideward glances. The system of vertical perspective, where the various figures were shown one above the other and where such things as carpets or ponds appeared flat upon the pages, was adhered to, though a new aid to producing perspective effects seems to have been universally adopted in out-of-door scenes by the time of the origin of the Shiraz school, which took the form of the inclusion of a hill in the background. Thus scenes were frequently staged on what appears to be the edge of a precipice, and the horizon was indicated by a sudden drop in the landscape. Figures in the extreme background look as if they were climbing up the inevitable hill behind, their heads and shoulders appearing over the imaginary horizon. Sometimes again they were shown emerging from behind a little hill which fills one corner of the picture.

The earliest Shiraz manuscript so far known is a *Shah-nama* in Istanbul dated to 1370. More impressive and typical, however, are two volumes of epics, dated to 1397, in the British Museum and the Chester Beatty collection. The complete maturity of the school appears in an anthology in the Gulbenkian collection done for

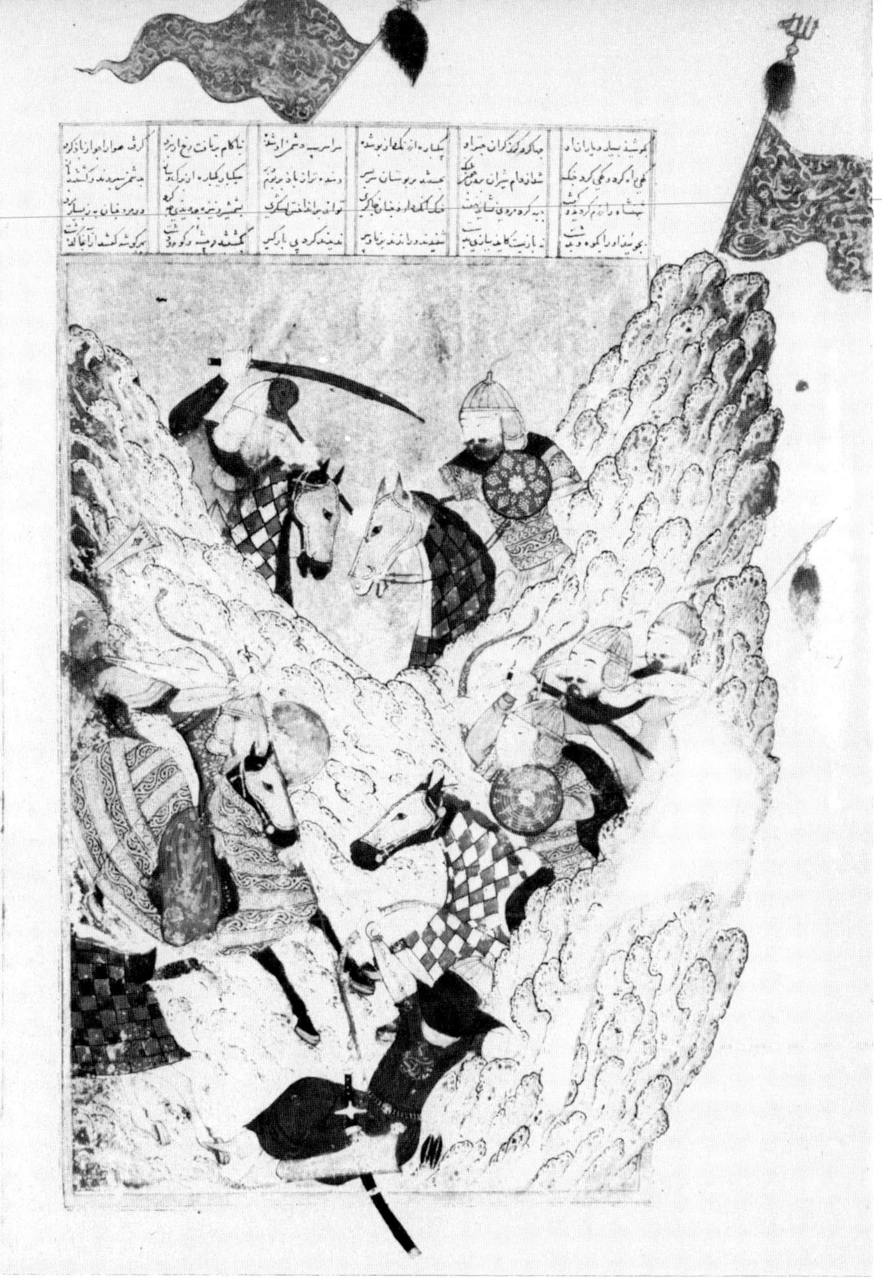

219 Leaf from a manuscript dated 1398 showing a battle between Tamujin and the Emir of Cathay. It is typical of the supremely delicate style that was developed in Persia in the latter part of the fourteenth century (Shiraz School)

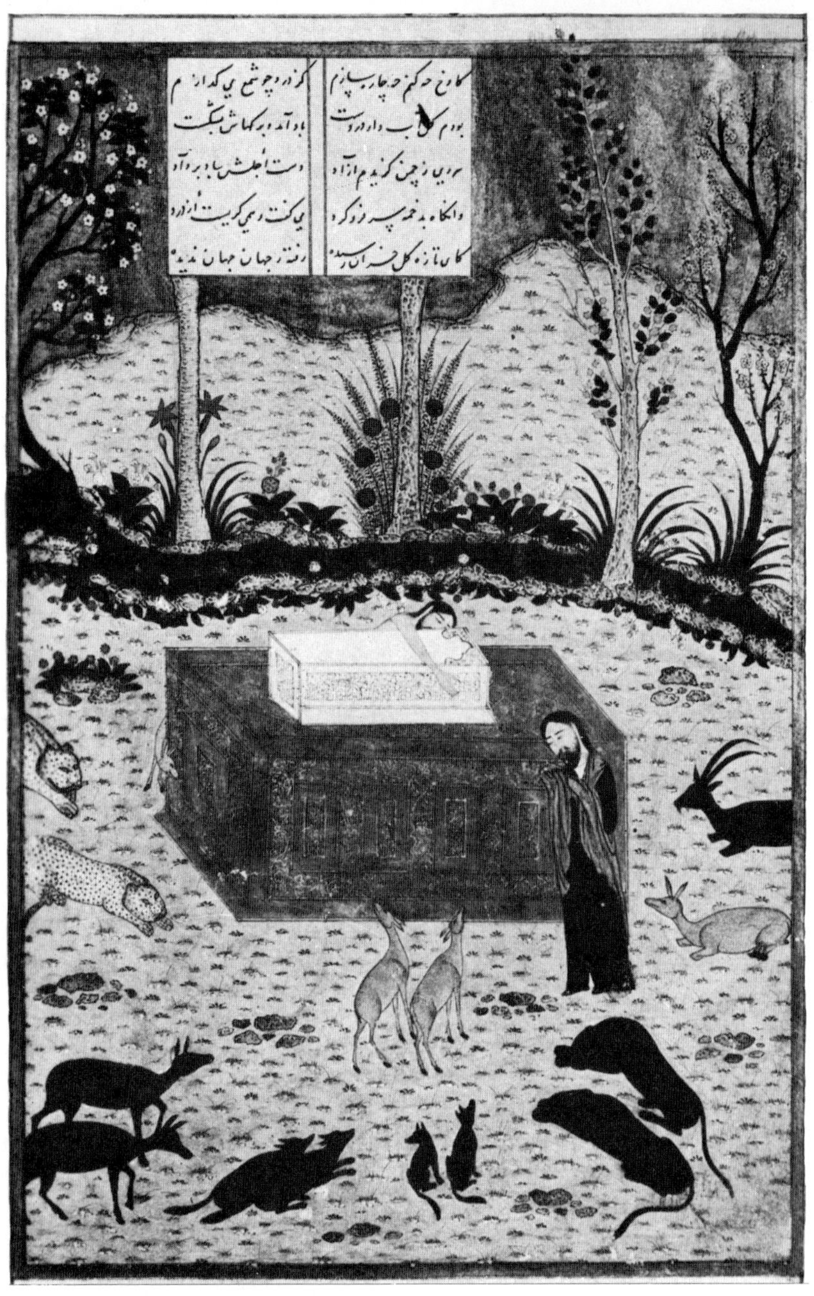

220 Leaf from a manuscript written for Iskander Sultan at Shiraz in 1410. The subject, Majnun at Laila's tomb, is part of the famous love story particularly popular in Persia at the time

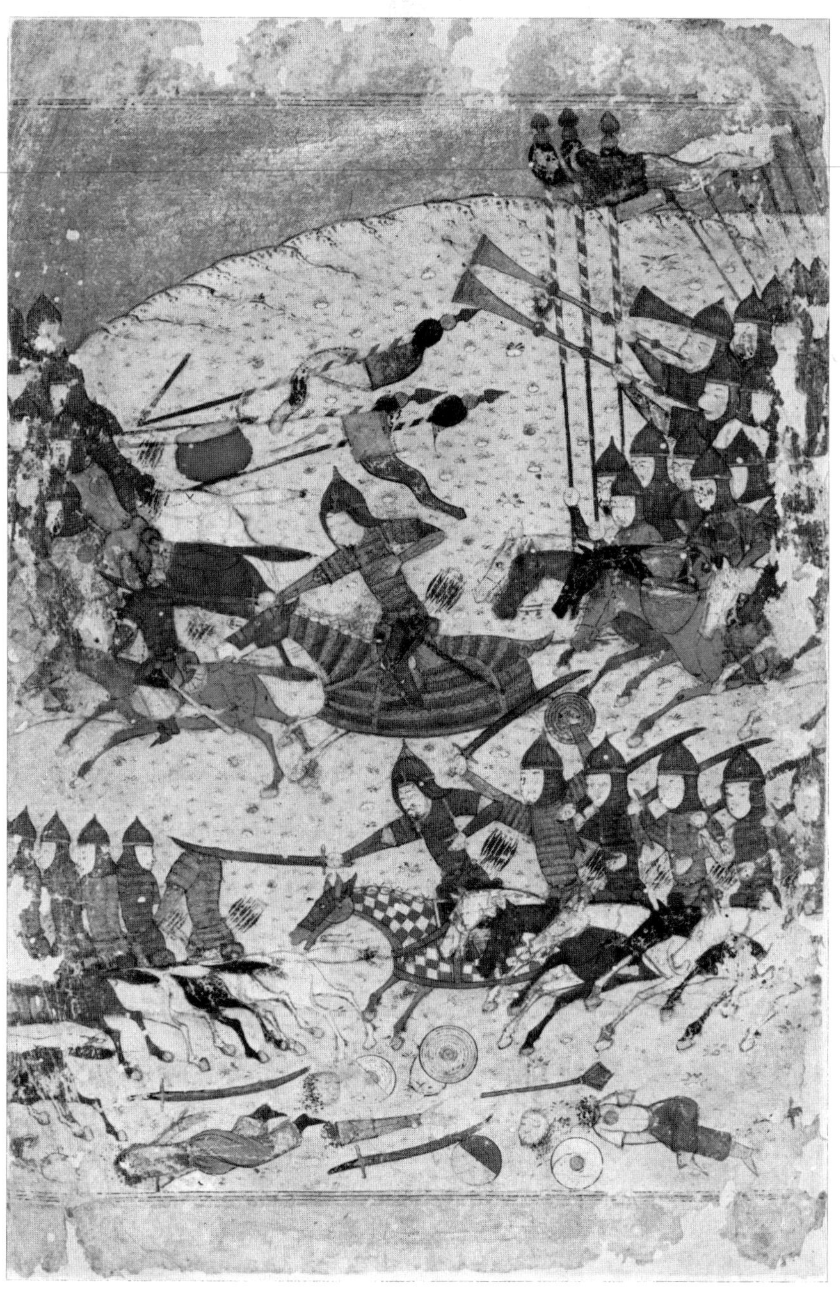

221 The defeat of Pir Padishah and Sultan Ali by the army of Shah Rukh. A page from a lost manuscript of Hafiz i Abru's *History*, perhaps executed at Herat for Shah Rukh himself

Iskandar Sultan in 1410 (*Ill. 220*). Several different artists certainly worked on this volume, amongst them the calligrapher Muhammad Husayn, whose name we meet again ten years later in an Anthology of the Poets executed for Prince Baysunghur, and now at Berlin. The colour scheme of the miniatures in the Gulbenkian volume is rather cold, yet they are strong and forceful, as well as full of delightful decorative detail. Many of them cover double pages. A copy of Fables of Bidpai, *Kalila wa Dimna*, at Teheran, was also probably done for Iskandar Sultan just before his deposition in 1414.

Tamerlane's eldest and most important son, Shah Rukh (1404–47), was, however, established at Herat, and the school which he founded only came to an end with the sack of the town in 1507. Shah Rukh himself was serious and sober in outlook, and was mainly responsible for the production of histories, like the *History* of Hafiz i Abru (1420–30). The scene (*Ill. 221*) showing the defeat of Pir Padishah of Astarabad and Sultan Ali, chief of the Sarbadars, a brigand people of Khurasan, is remarkable as a nearly contemporary representation of a historic event. Shah Rukh's forces were commanded by Amir Sa 'id Khwaja, who is shown beheading an enemy as he leads his charging troops. The trumpets, standards, and raised and threatening swords, create a feeling of victorious movement and defiant conquest. The figure-drawing of the miniature owes something to the school of Shiraz.

Shah Rukh's gay son Baysunghur Mirza (d. 1433), on the other hand, favoured works in a lighter vein and it was under his patronage that the Herat school reached its fullest development. Its work was characterized by an even greater love of descriptive detail than at Shiraz, the figures were usually rather small, the work was exceptionally delicate and the colouring softer and deeper than that of Shiraz. Very particular shades of orange and red were habitually used. Chinese motifs such as the *kilin* or stylized cloud-form were almost invariably present, though there was nothing Chinese in the actual style.

222 Illustration from a manuscript of a *Shah-nama* done for Baysunghur Mirza in 1430, which is an outstanding work of the Herat school. This represents an account being given to Luhrasp of the disappearance of Kay Khusraw

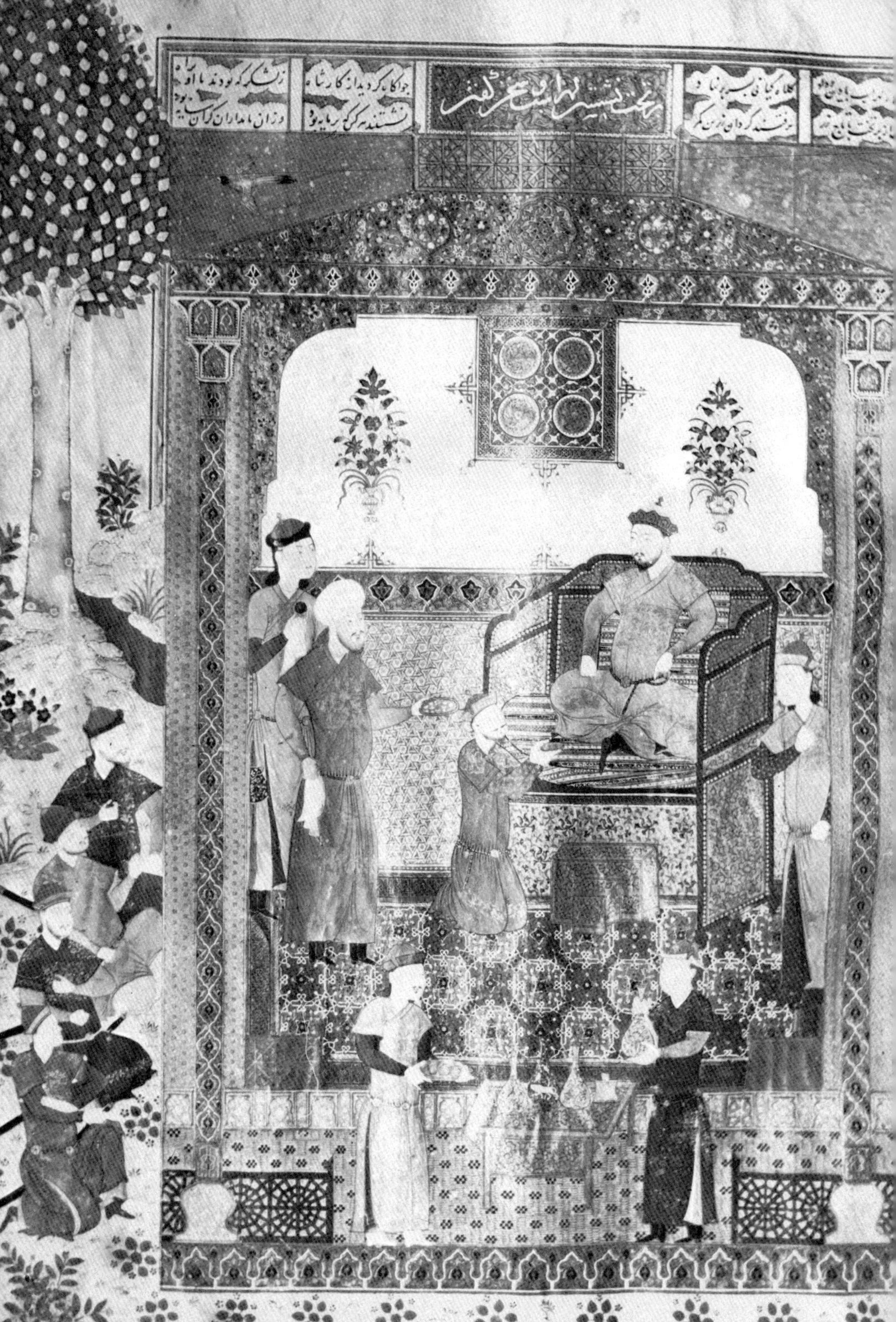

One of the most outstanding examples of the school is a *Shah-nama* now in the Gulistan Palace at Teheran, which was done for Baysunghur in 1430 (*Ill. 222*). The scene where Kay Khusraw's disappearance is related to Luhrasp is wholly characteristic, both in the beauty of its colour and the elaboration of its detail. Another quite enchanting miniature is that of Humay and Humayun in China, now in the Musée des Arts Decoratifs, Paris (*Ill. 223*). The artist shows little intellectual curiosity, but the symbolic decorative basis of Persian painting is here fully apparent and the result is particularly successful. The flowers shine in the brilliance of daylight while the stars are out in the sky; realism is combined with symbolism; the artist is completely unbounded by the practicality of naturalism, yet his approach remains completely comprehensible.

Except for the *Shah-nama*, the books which were most familiar in the Abbasid and Mongol periods were now less popular and various new works came into prominence such as the *Khamsa* or Five Poems of Nizami, the *Bustan* of Sadi, or the 'Joseph and Zulaykha' of Jami. In most copies one or two scenes only were selected for illustration, and usually it was the most popular scenes which were chosen, so that we have a great number of examples of certain well-known events like Bahram Gur hunting the wild ass, and many fewer examples of the less popular scenes. Yet there is no monotony in this, for the merit of the painting lay in the rendering, not in the invention of new themes. What may be termed 'the handed down model' was almost as sacred a precept of the arts as in the Buddhist world, and we see something of the same outlook in Byzantium where once more the merit of a painting lay in the artist's capacity to breathe new life into something hallowed by time. The outlook was thus quite distinct from the energetic inquiring spirit of the West where curiosity and a search for the new dominated the outlook.

In a few very rich volumes nearly all the scenes of each story were illustrated, and there is probably no more sumptuous example than

223 The arrival of Prince Humay and his reception by Princess Humayun in the garden of the Emperor of China. Leaf from a poem by Khawadju Kirmani done in Herat, 1291–1352, for Baysunghur Mirza

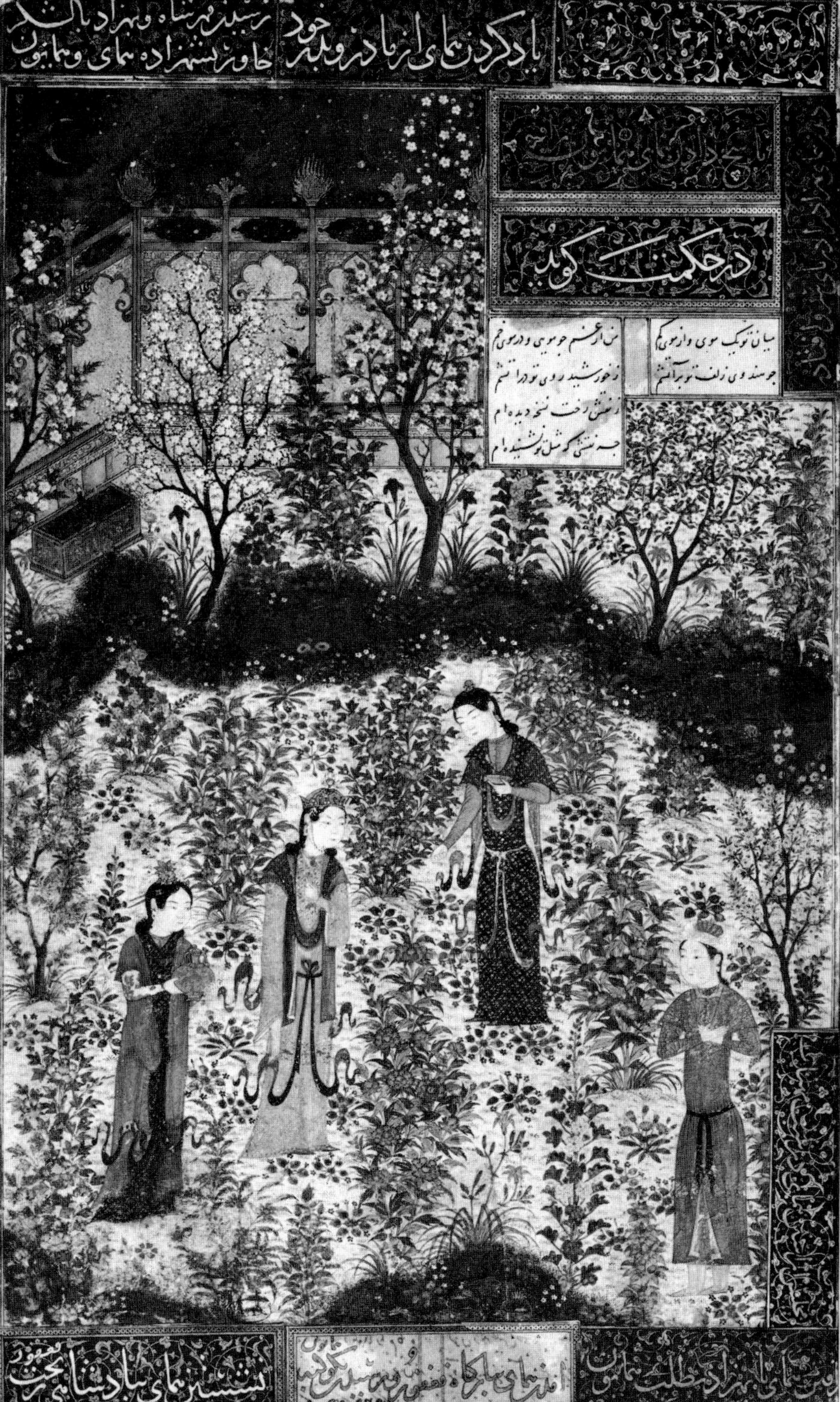

a *Shah-nama*, now in the Library of the Royal Asiatic Society, London. It contains twenty-three miniatures, and was done for another of Shah Rukh's sons, Muhammad Juki, around 1440. More than one man probably worked on it, and some of the miniatures are more expressive than others; yet all are of really outstanding quality. One of the most moving illustrates the death of the Paladins in the snow (*Ill. 224*). A few faithful followers had accompanied Kay Khusraw to the mountains where he went to end his life; the king warned them that a storm was approaching and told them to return, but before they could leave their master the snow overwhelmed them and they all perished. In the illustration they are shown seated beside a pool, while behind the ominous snow clouds gather in the sky. Binyon writes of this: 'The huddled bewilderment of the doomed Paladins, crouching coldly by the desolate mountain stream, is wonderfully expressed in the illustration.' One might add that the soft heaviness of the snow clouds has probably never been more effectually rendered and the Oriental acceptance of the inevitability of fate is conveyed with striking success.

What is perhaps the most characteristic feature of the second half of the fifteenth century, however, is the fact that then certain painters began to sign their works. One of the first to do so was Ruh-Allah Mirak, who did two rather stiff pages inserted in a later Nizami dated about 1496 and now in the British Museum. Others are known, but the most famous of all was Bihzad, who was born somewhere about 1440 and died not long after 1514. His style was more intense, more dramatic, than that of many of the painters of the age, and he was obviously more interested in individuals and their character and in the affairs of everyday life than were most of his contemporaries, who were content to live in an enchanting dream-like world of their own. From 1468 until 1506 Bihzad was at the head of the Herat Academy and his chief patron, Mir Ali Shir Nevai, was a friend of the Sultan Husayn Bayqara (1470–1506), who also patronized the work of the artist, as did his successor, the barbarous Muhammad Khan Shaybani. It was at Herat that most of his work was done, though after 1506 he was taken to Tabriz, whither the capital was moved by the new sultan, Shah Ismail, founder of the Safavid dynasty.

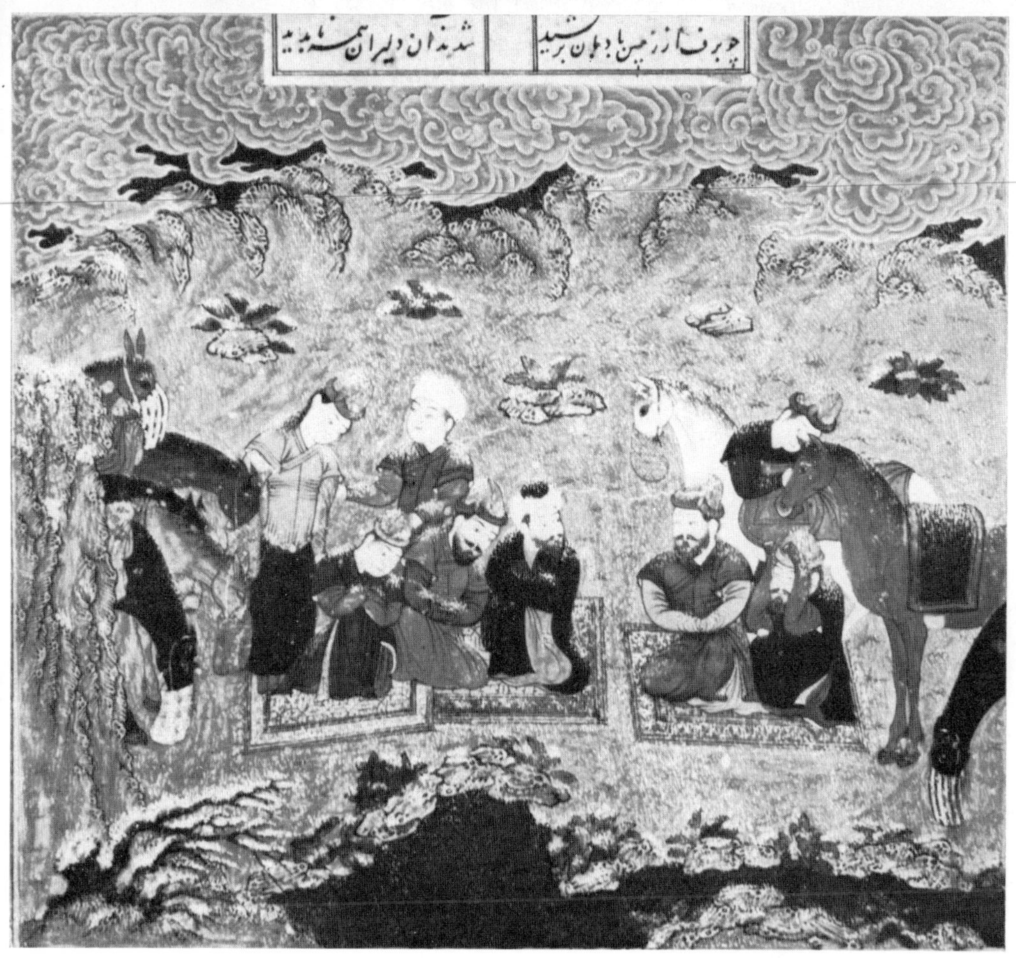

224 Illustration from a *Shah-nama* done at Herat about 1440. It contains a large number of illustrations of very high quality. Here a group of Paladins are shown seated by a pool

There he brought new fame to the old school which had never ceased to function, even if Shiraz and Herat were more important.

The problem of attribution is very complicated in the case of Bihzad, partly because he had numerous pupils who followed him closely, and partly because his style came to be regarded during his lifetime as the very acme of painting, and collectors of the period who wished to show their appreciation of a particular work would write under it 'Worthy of Bihzad' or just 'Bihzad' by way of praising it. Or again the collectors of the next half-century would very frequently attribute paintings to Bihzad much as canvases were in the eighteenth century assigned to Raphael, though the scholarly examination of style that can be given today shows that neither attribution can be relied on. Hence the signatures can but seldom be accepted, and it was only in a very few instances that the master himself signed his work. When he did so, the signature was usually put in the most obscure of places. For example, in a miniature showing King Dara with his herdsmen in a copy of Sadi's *Bustan* at Cairo (1488–9), the miniature is signed in minute letters on the king's quiver (*Ill. 225*). The signature reads, 'work of the slave Bihzad'. The theme of this illustration was a popular one; the king had mistaken his herdsman for an enemy and was about to draw his bow when the man stopped him and reproved him for not knowing his servants by sight. The double frontispiece of this book, which is not actually signed, must also be by the master.

Signatures which can be relied on also appear on miniatures in a *Gulistan* in the Rothschild collection of 1486, and in two *Khamsas* in the British Museum dated 1493 and 1494 (*Ill. 229*). A portrait, in Teheran, of Sultan Husayn in a garden, dated 1495, is also to be assigned to him. Though no signatures are present, a *Zafar-nama* or 'History of Tamerlane' in the Garrett collection may also be attributed to Bihzad on stylistic grounds. It contains six large double page miniatures, and was written in 1467 for Sultan Husayn Bayqara, but the miniatures were probably added around 1490. This was quite a common practice in Islamic painting, for the calligrapher usually left blank pages which were afterwards filled in by the illustrator. The scene showing the construction of the Great Mosque of Samarkand is full of the vivid energy which characterizes Bihzad's work. Another page (*Ill. 227*), showing an assault on a fortress, is again typical and illustrates the capture of the Christian fortress of the Knights of St John which took place about 1402. Tamerlane is said to be the figure on horseback on the right; his troops are crossing the moat by a temporary bridge.

In addition to the scenes in books Bihzad was also responsible for a number of single studies of individuals or animals, and though his

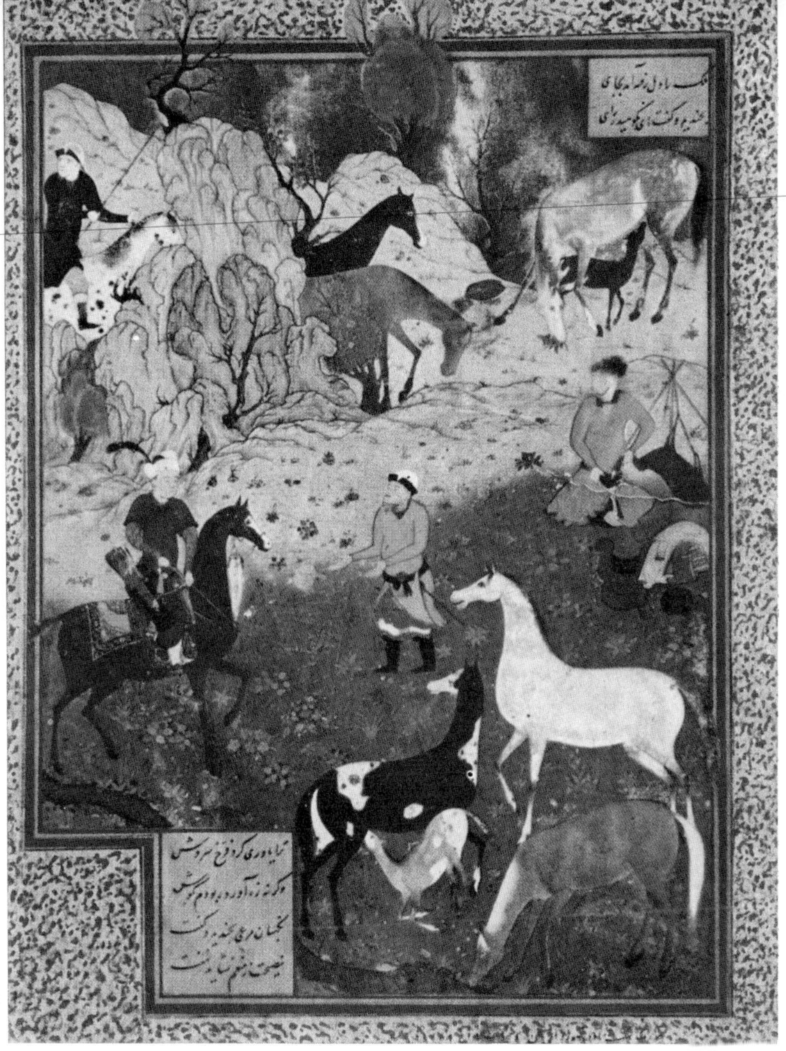

225 This illustration of King Dara and his herdsmen from Sadi's *Bustan* is a signed work of the great painter Bihzad. *c.* 1489

portraits were not as powerful as his other work they are not by any means negligible. One, now in the Freer Gallery, which is signed and usually accepted as by him, depicts a young man painting (*Ill. 226*). It was for long believed that this was copied by Bihzad after an original by Gentile Bellini, who was in Constantinople in 1479 and 1480, but there is little real evidence to support this claim.

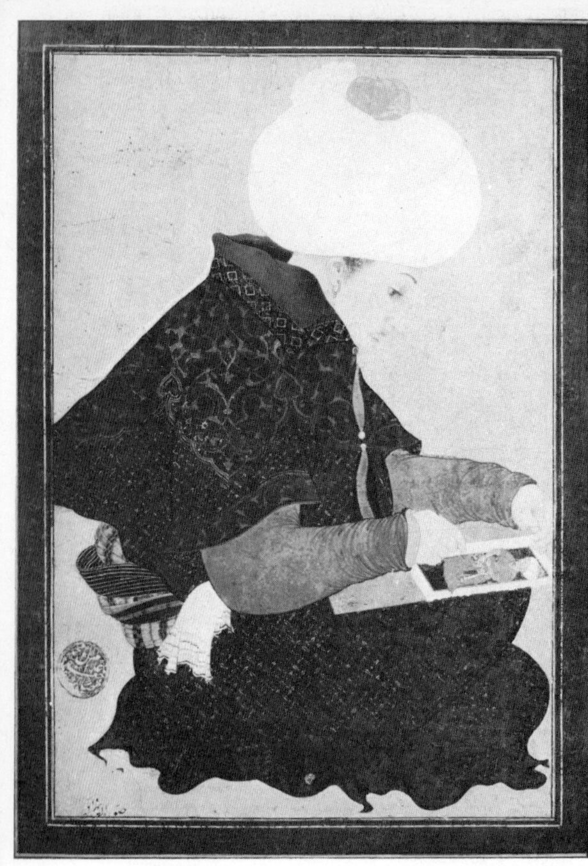

226 Portrait of a painter in Turkish costume. It was at one time thought to be a copy made by Bihzad of a painting by Bellini, but this theory can hardly be accepted. Persian, late fifteenth century

The picture's principal interest lies rather in the fact that it is one of the first portrait miniatures that we have; in the next century these studies of individuals were to become one of the favourite themes of the Persian painter.

The paintings of the earlier years of the sixteenth century all owe a great debt to Bihzad; many of the artists had been his pupils, and so great was his fame, so definite his style, that he exercised a very widespread influence. Indeed the new school of Tabriz which was established by Shah Ismail to a great extent owed its development to the foundations laid by Bihzad. We know many of its masters by name – a number of them collaborated in the production of a magnificent copy of Nizami's works done for Shah Tahmasp between 1539 and 1543 and now in the British Museum.

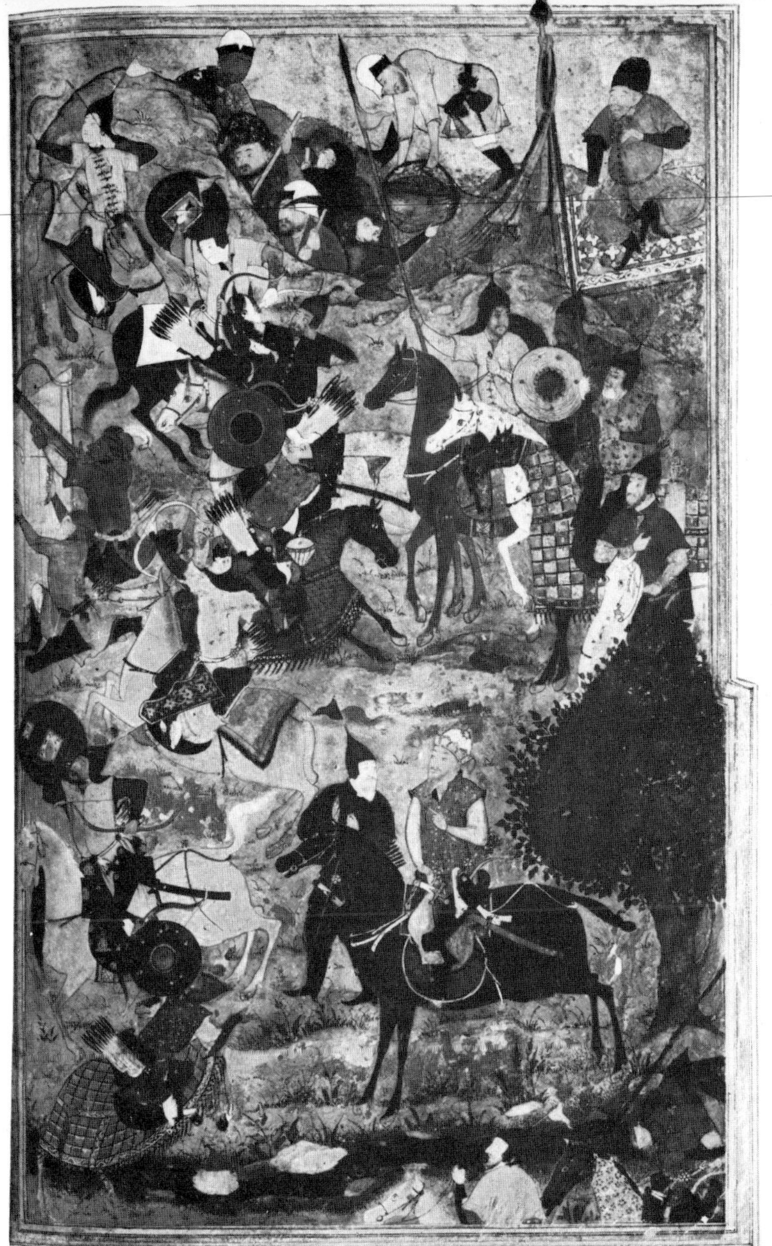

227 Illustration from a *Zafar-nama* (life of Tamerlane) showing part of the capture of the fortress of the Knights of St John at Smyrna. The miniatures are almost certainly by Bihzad and done at Herat *c.* 1490

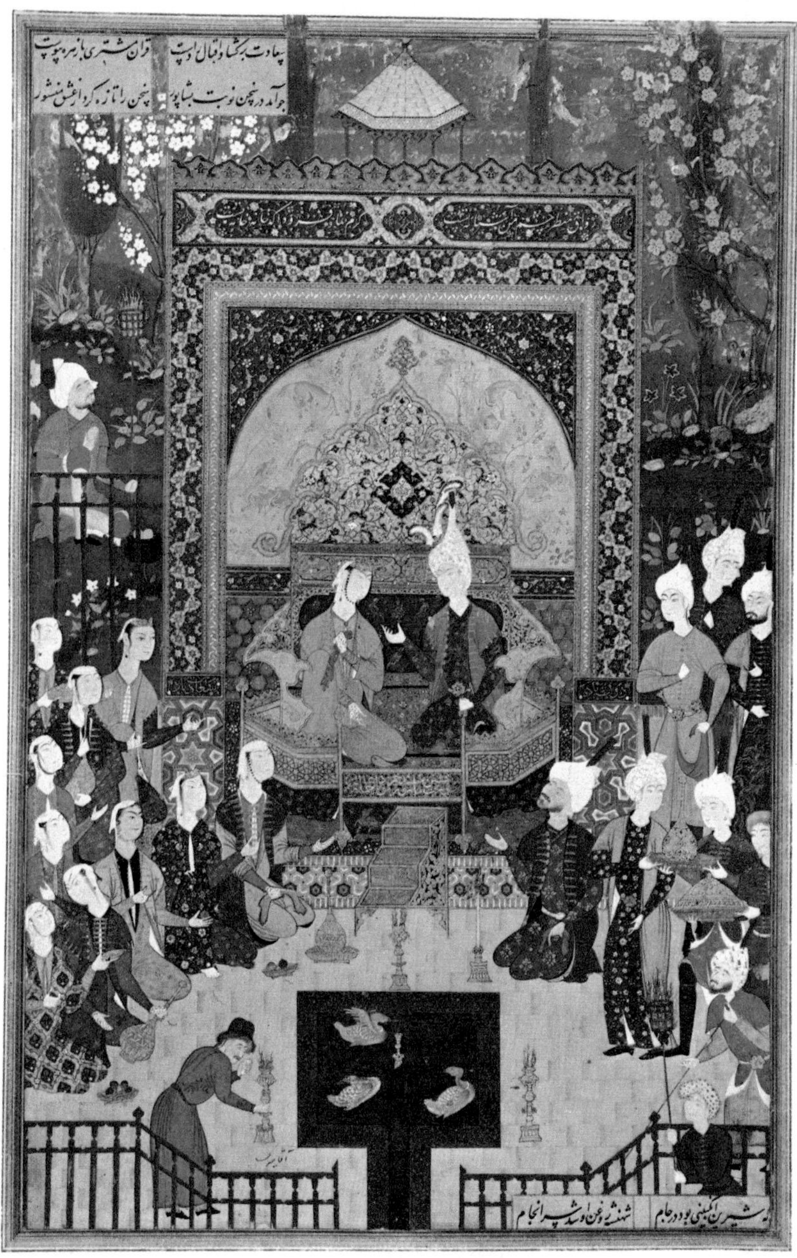

228 Illustration from a *Khamsa* of Nizami showing Khusraw and Shirin sitting at night listening to stories told by Shirin's handmaidens

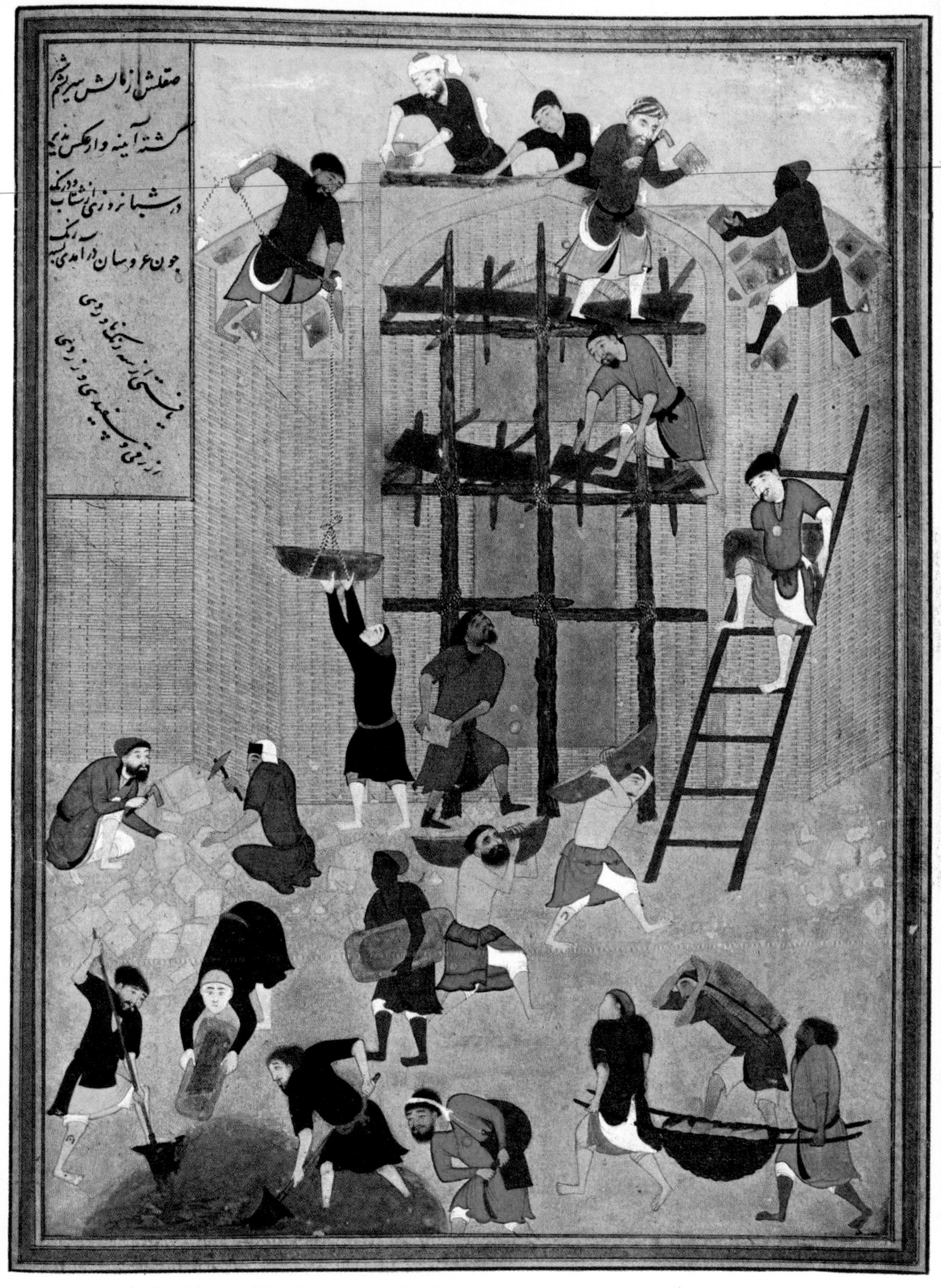

229 The building of the famous castle of Khawarnaq from Nizami's *Khamsa*. The manuscript was illustrated about 1494 and the miniatures are the work of Bihzad

It is a book of outstanding quality and richness, containing seventeen miniatures of the greatest beauty though four of them were added at a later date. Mirak, Mirza Ali, Mir Sayyid Ali and Muzaffar Ali all did miniatures for it, in addition to painters whose names we do not know. Of the scenes that are not definitely attributed, one of the most delightful shows an old woman complaining to Sultan Sanjar (*Ill. 230*); she comes to the king and tells him that she has been robbed by one of his soldiers; the king replies that he is much too busy to attend to such trivialities, and she answers him: 'What is the good of going out to war when you can't even keep your soldiers in order!' A delightful Eastern illustration of the intimate relation existing between a king and his subjects. Kuehnel thinks it may have been done by Sultan Muhammad. Perhaps the rather fussy, tumbled rocks that fill the background are to be regarded as characteristic of his style – they were later to become usual in Indian painting.

Of the painters known by name whose work appears in the British Museum Nizami, the most important, was probably Aga Mirak who came from Isfahan and had worked also at Herat. His style was rather more decorative and rather less humanistic than that of Bihzad, but he was certainly a great exponent of the more decorative manner. A magnificent Ascension of the Prophet in the British Museum Nizami has been attributed to him on stylistic grounds and it is certainly characteristic of his manner. More definitely to be attributed to him is the painting of Khusraw and Shurin sitting together at night listening to stories told by Shurin's handmaidens (*Ill. 228*). In this finely detailed and delicate miniature the couple are seen framed by a beautifully tiled façade and surrounded by attendants. Yet another by Mirak shows Anushirvan and his vizier at a ruined palace. They hear the owls hooting in the ruins and the vizier translates their conversation, one of which says that he can offer his mate a magnificent ruined tower as her marriage portion; the other replies that if the king continues his wars one thousand ruined homes would soon be available. The storks, the deer feeding in the ruins, the flowers

230 An old woman complaining to Sultan Sanjar from a *Khamsa* of Nizami done for Shah Tahmasp. 1539–43. The work is by a number of different painters but the master responsible for this miniature is not known by name

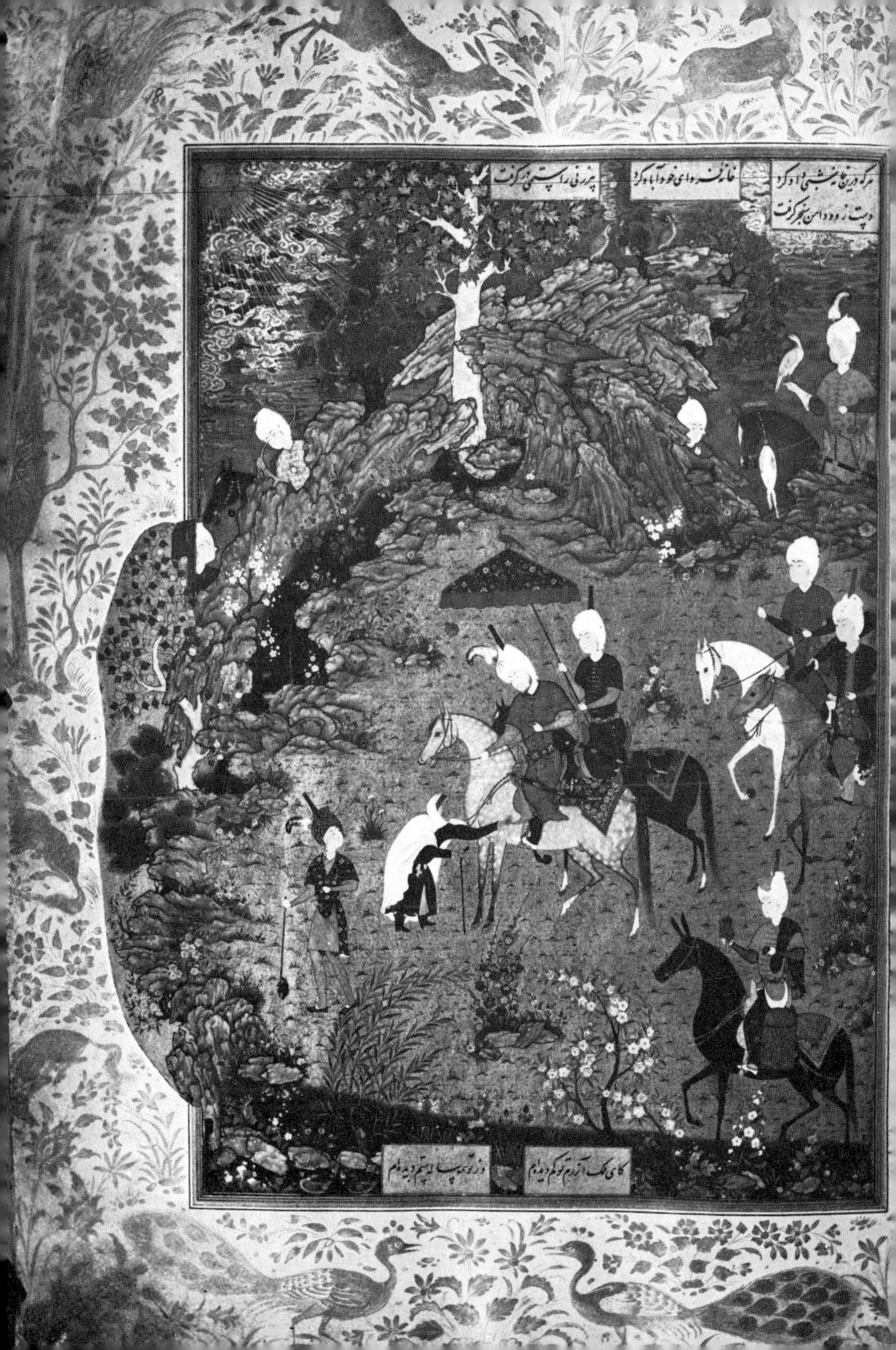
هر که درین خانه شبی داد کرد
خانه فردای خود آباد کرد
پیرزنی را ستمی در گرفت
دست زد و دامن سنجر گرفت
کای ملک آزرم تو کم دیده‌ام
وز تو همه ساله ستم دیده‌ام

by the stream, all have the brilliant detail of a Vermeer, combined with a delightful charm and phantasy that is essentially Persian. This was a very favourite subject, but Mirak's rendering is probably the finest of all that have come down to us. The scene was especially well suited to his particular capacities. The painting is signed by the artist upon the wall of the ruined mosque.

Another fine page in the British Museum Nizami is the work of Mir Sayyid Ali, son of a painter who brought him as a youth to Tabriz to study under Bihzad. His work in the Nizami, characterized by a penetrating interest in the country and its everyday life, illustrates one of the scenes from the love story of Majnun and Laila, an old-established tale rewritten by Nizami, telling how Majnun is made mad by his love for Laila. Their marriage is impossible because of the circumstances and he flees to the desert and makes friends with the animals. Longing to see Laila, he persuades an old woman who is exhibiting a madman in order to earn her living to let him change places with her performer. The woman brings Majnun in chains to Laila's tent (*Ill. 231*), but on seeing his beloved, Majnun becomes mad himself and rushes away in a frenzy. The scene was a favourite one and the poem seems to have been one of those most often copied at this stage. Its popularity is probably to be accounted for to a great extent by the deeply religious mystical outlook of the Persians, the story symbolizing the longing of the soul for some ultimate spiritual power. In human relationships this ardent longing could never be fully satisfied. In another painting in this volume Majnun is shown at the Kaaba in Mecca, a final turn to faith at the end of his career.

Mir Sayyid Ali went in 1550 to Kabul and then to Delhi, where he was responsible to a great extent for founding the important Indo-Persian school of painting. His style, before he left, was a distinct one, and quite a few paintings can be assigned to him with considerable probability, more especially some in an album in the Cartier collection. His manner may have changed in India, for taken

231 An illustration from the same *Khamsa* as *Ill. 230* by the painter Mir Sayyid Ali who had been an apprentice of Bihzad in his youth. In 1550 he went to Kabul and then to Delhi. This picture shows Majnun being brought by a beggar woman to Laila's tent

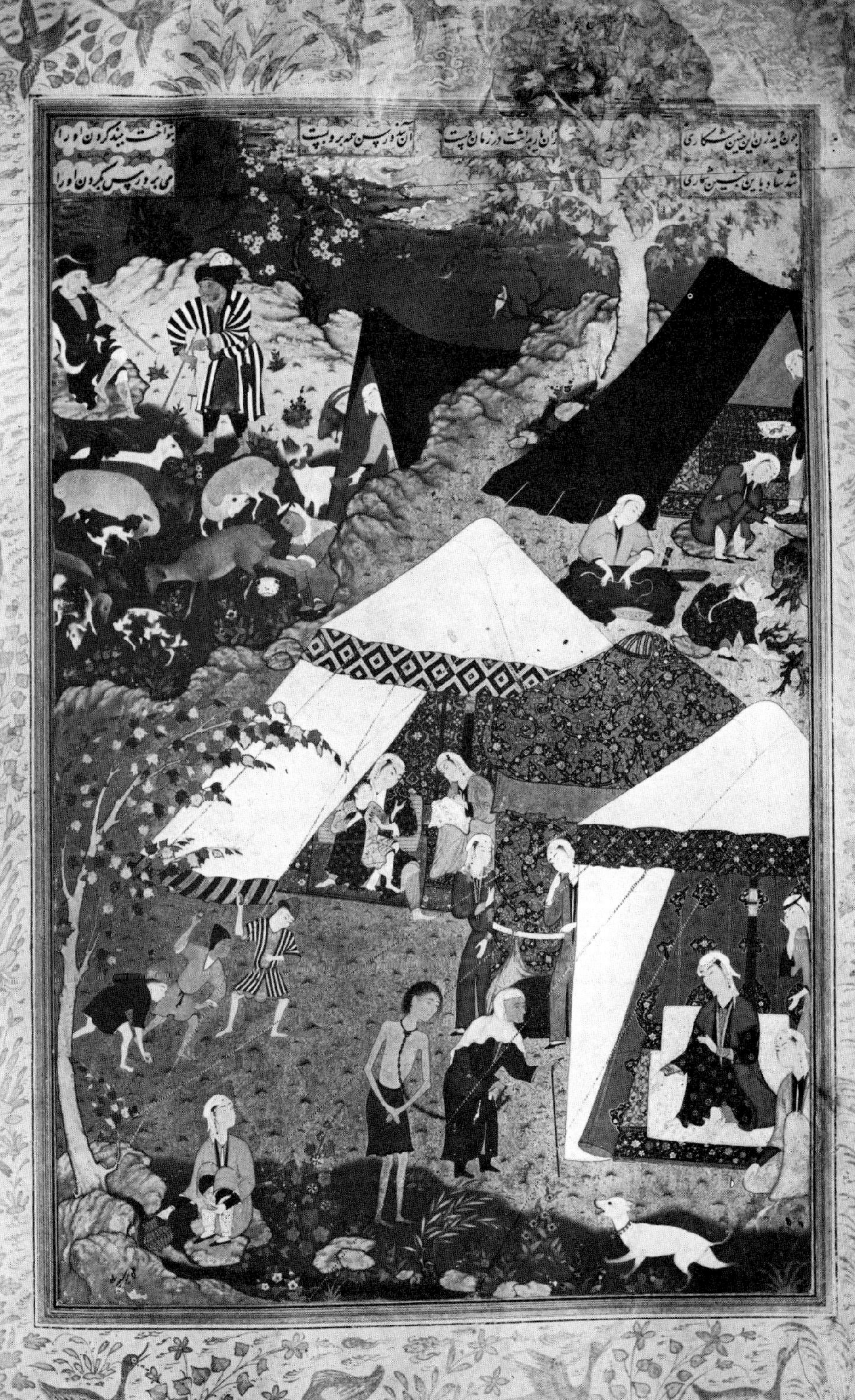

as a whole Indian work developed along the lines of realism and the painters there took a greater interest in portraiture and actuality than did their Persian colleagues, leaving the dreamland and mysticism of Persia far behind.

Mir Sayyid Ali is probably to be distinguished from another painter with a rather similar name whose work also appears in the British Museum Nizami, namely, Mirza Ali. He was a native of Tabriz and was especially noted as a designer of arabesque ornament. He was responsible for illustrating another of the incidents from the story of Khusraw and Shirin, in which the portrait of Khusraw is shown to Shirin, Princess of the Armenians, by Khusraw's best friend (*Ill. 232*). A further scene, where Khusraw listens to a lute, is probably also to be attributed to him. Kuehnel also assigns to him the delightful double-page miniature of Joseph and the Ladies of Egypt in a *Khamsa* of 1522 at Teheran. He is to be distinguished from another miniaturist, Muzaffar Ali, who was responsible for painting a delightful scene from the Legend of Bahram Gur in the British Museum Nizami. This man was a pupil of Bihzad, who died soon after Shah Tahmasp in 1576. The theme of Bahram Gur is perhaps the most popular of all that were illustrated at this time, and it is to be found on textiles, on pottery or on metalwork just as often as in book illustrations.

Of the other painters of this era, mention must be made of Shayk Zada, a pupil of Bihzad, of whose work only one signed miniature, formerly in the Cartier collection, survives; of Abd al-Aziz, who executed a portrait in one of the albums in the Saray at Constantinople; of Abd as-Samad, who went as a young man to India, and of Siyavush the Georgian. The latter moved to Turkey where he worked for Süleyman the Magnificent. Afterwards he usually signed himself Rumi, a word in common use in the Islamic world to designate the region formerly controlled by the Byzantine Empire. Vali Jan was another painter who began his life at Tabriz and later moved to Istanbul, while Kamal of Tabriz, one of the pupils of Mirza Ali, is to be distinguished primarily on the grounds of the

232 Miniature from the same *Khamsa* as *Ill. 230* by the painter Mirza Ali. He is probably to be distinguished from Mir Sayyid Ali, though the names are similar. Here the portrait of Khusraw is shown to Shirin

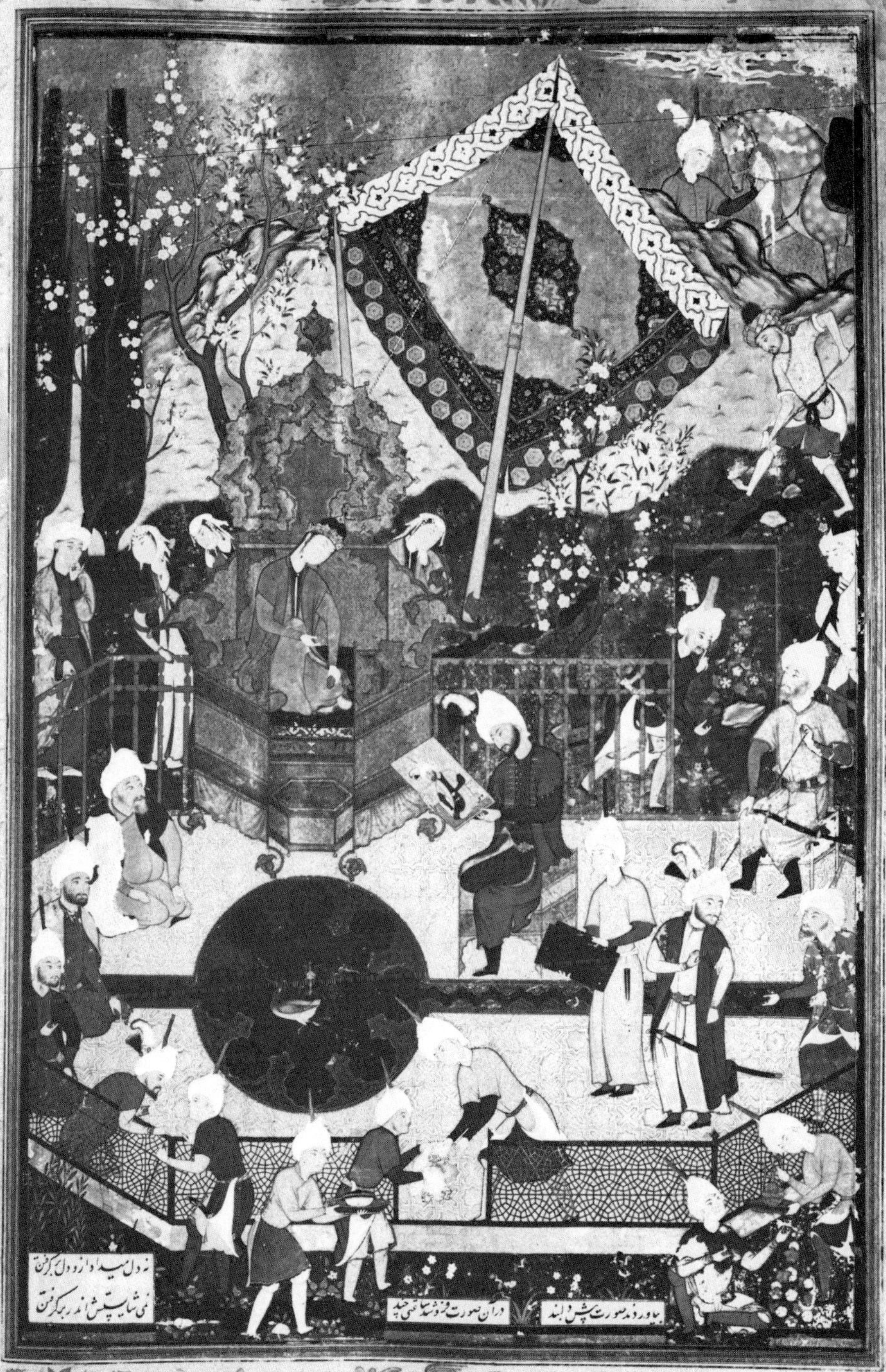

gracious, delicate, rather calligraphic quality of his work. The end of the Tabriz school was marked by Muhammadi, who flourished about 1580. His works were again individual, in that they are full of vivid life. He liked to depict open-air scenes, and his figures were usually shown jumping, capering or running. His more static manner is illustrated by a fine drawing of himself now at Boston.

Most of these men were centred on Tabriz. Herat, however, remained important until about 1534, in spite of being sacked by the Uzbegs in 1507. Thereafter its role was eclipsed by Bokhara. In the later part of the previous century work of a rather coarse type had been produced there under local patronage, but the school began to grow in importance around 1525. It was, however, not until the arrival there of artists from Herat in the 'thirties that any real distinction was achieved. Even so Bokhara remained conservative, and the experiments in composition, to be seen in a search for a multiplicity of planes, and a love of rather full scenes and tall figures, which had been introduced by Bihzad, never found much favour north of the Oxus, where the figures tended to be dumpy, and where strong primary colours were admired.

The same was probably true of other local schools at this time, such as that of Qazvin. Work continued at Shiraz, where decorative backgrounds were much in favour and where the figures or themes of the main painting often overlapped on to the borders. But on the whole, work of the middle of the century tended to be somewhat stereotyped, and it was not until the last quarter that any real developments of consequence took place. Then, under the patronage of Shah Abbas (1587–1629), there arose that tender, delicate, even exquisite style of Persian art which is perhaps more familiar today than any other. The old historical romance declined in popularity, the full illustrative scenes so typical of the Herat and Shiraz schools were forsaken, and studies of single figures or delicate pastoral scenes where landscapes played a major role became more popular. A delicate drawing of two oxen ploughing or a peasant at work satisfied the tastes of this new age more completely than one of the spirited combats or the enchanting adventures of the *Shah-nama*, where action or an event had the principal role to play.

CHAPTER TWELVE

The Later Safavid Age

Though the Safavid dynasty was established as early as 1502 – it was to survive until 1736 – there was, as we have seen, no very marked break in art in the years just after 1500, and it was really only with the transference of the capital from Qazvin – which had for a time succeeded Tabriz – to Isfahan in 1598 by Shah Abbas (1587–1628) that the true Safavid style in art was fully developed. Though there is a fine mosque there, the city of Qazvin has little to offer the visitor in comparison with Isfahan, which is still entirely redolent of the spirit of the age of its last great patron, and literally teems with monuments of Safavid art. The great Masjid-i-Jami and many other buildings also do, it is true, go back to earlier times, but the extensive open area which now forms the centre of the city, the Maydan-i-Shah (*Ill. 233*), was laid out as a polo ground by Shah Abbas, and he grouped a whole series of new buildings around it. The most important of them are the Masjid-i-Shaykh Lutfullah (1602–3) (*Ill. 234*) and the Masjid-i-Shah (1612–13) (*Ill. 235*) in the religious sphere, and in the secular the Ali Kapu (*Ill. 236*), the Chagar Bagh (1598) and the Chihil Sutun (*Ill. 237*) palaces, their roofs supported on tall wooden columns. The bridge of Allahverdi Khan (*c.* 1600) (*Ill. 238*) some distance away must also be noted. Happily nearly all these buildings are in a good state of repair; all are rich and ornate, and the lovely tile-work on the domes and entrance façades of the mosques serves to indicate the spirit of luxury and delight which characterized the age. All is colour, delicacy and beauty, and the tone that was set by the architecture was borne out by the other arts. The metalwork showed a new inventiveness and imagination so far as the forms were concerned; the textiles were rich and of astonishing technical excellence; the tiles bright and gorgeous and admirably in tune with the buildings which they decorated, while glass vessels of great delicacy and originality were also made.

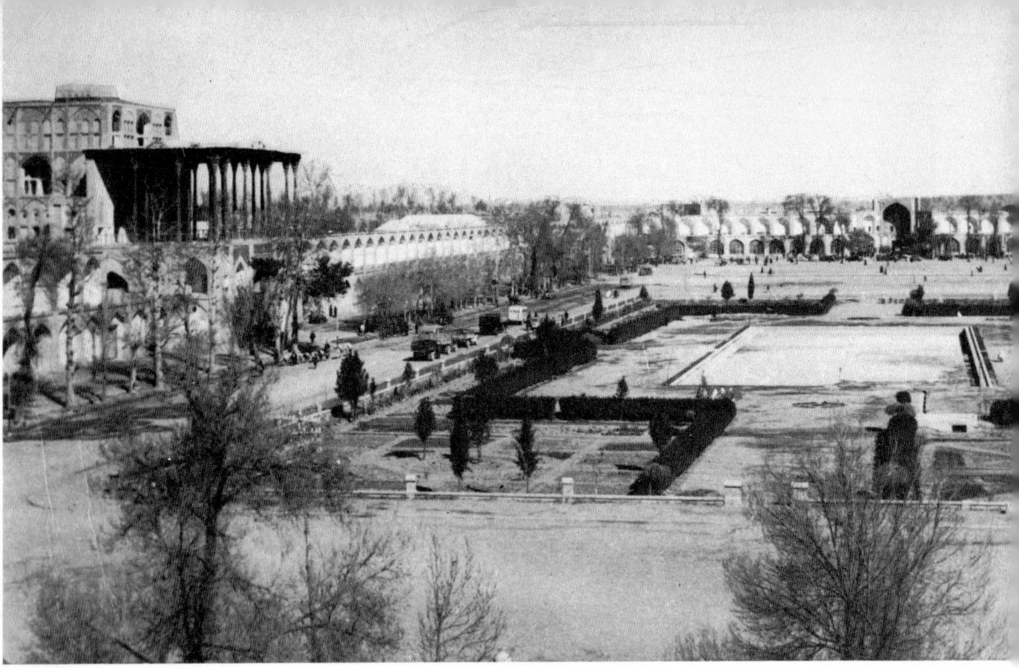

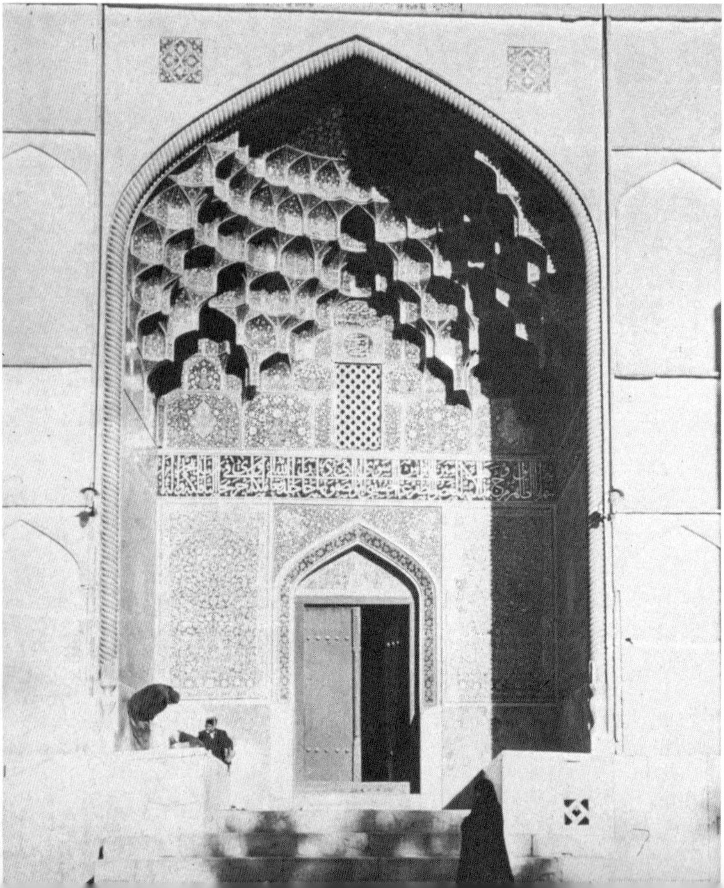

233 (*above*) View of the Maydan-i-Shah, Isfahan, from the Masjid-i-Shah. The Maydan was laid out as a great polo ground by Shah Abbas and surrounding it were built many of Isfahan's

234 (*below*) Portal of the Masjid-i-Shaykh Lutfullah at Isfahan. 1602–3. Its tiled entrance and dome are of great beauty and it is to be counted among one of the finest works of the great Safavid period

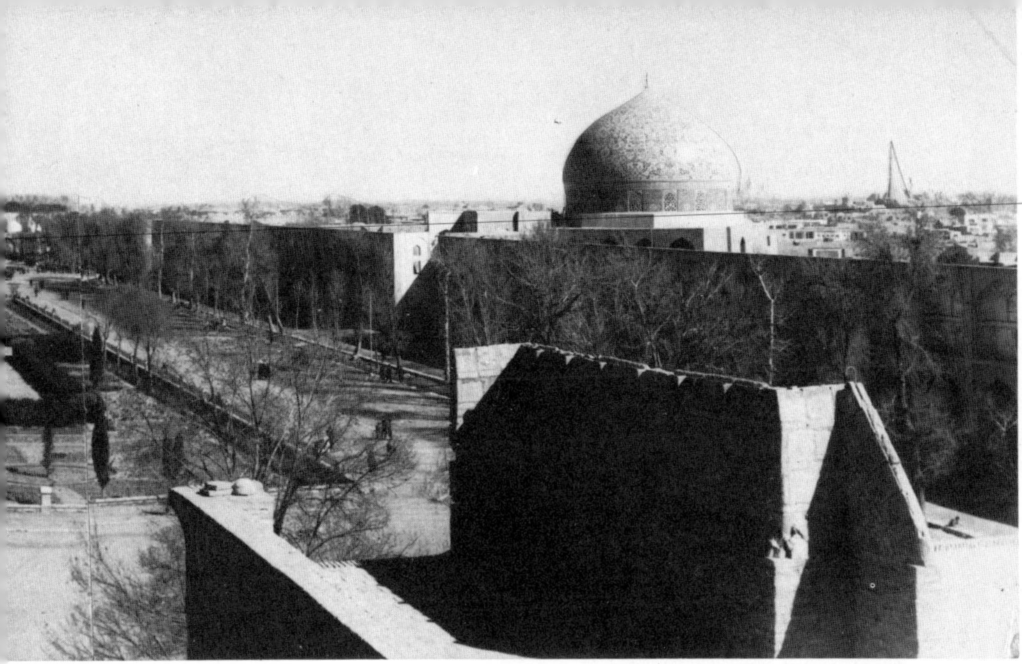

ıost important build-
ıgs. The Ali Kapu can
e seen on the left,
pposite is the Qaisa-
yeh, the entrance to
e 'Royal' Bazaar, and
the right stands the
utfullah mosque

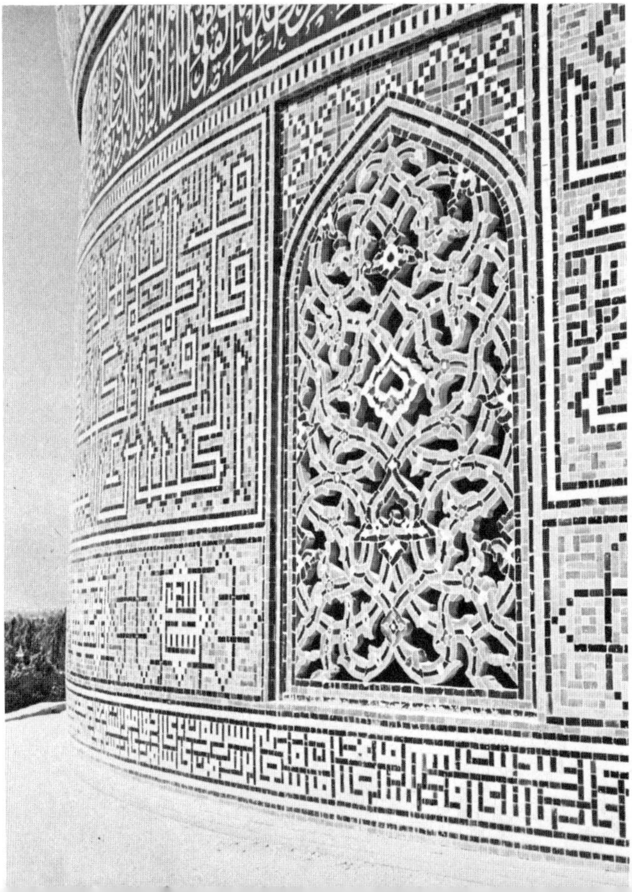

235 The drum of the dome of the Masjid-i-Shah mosque, Isfahan (1612–13), shows the richness and wealth of the tile-work of this period

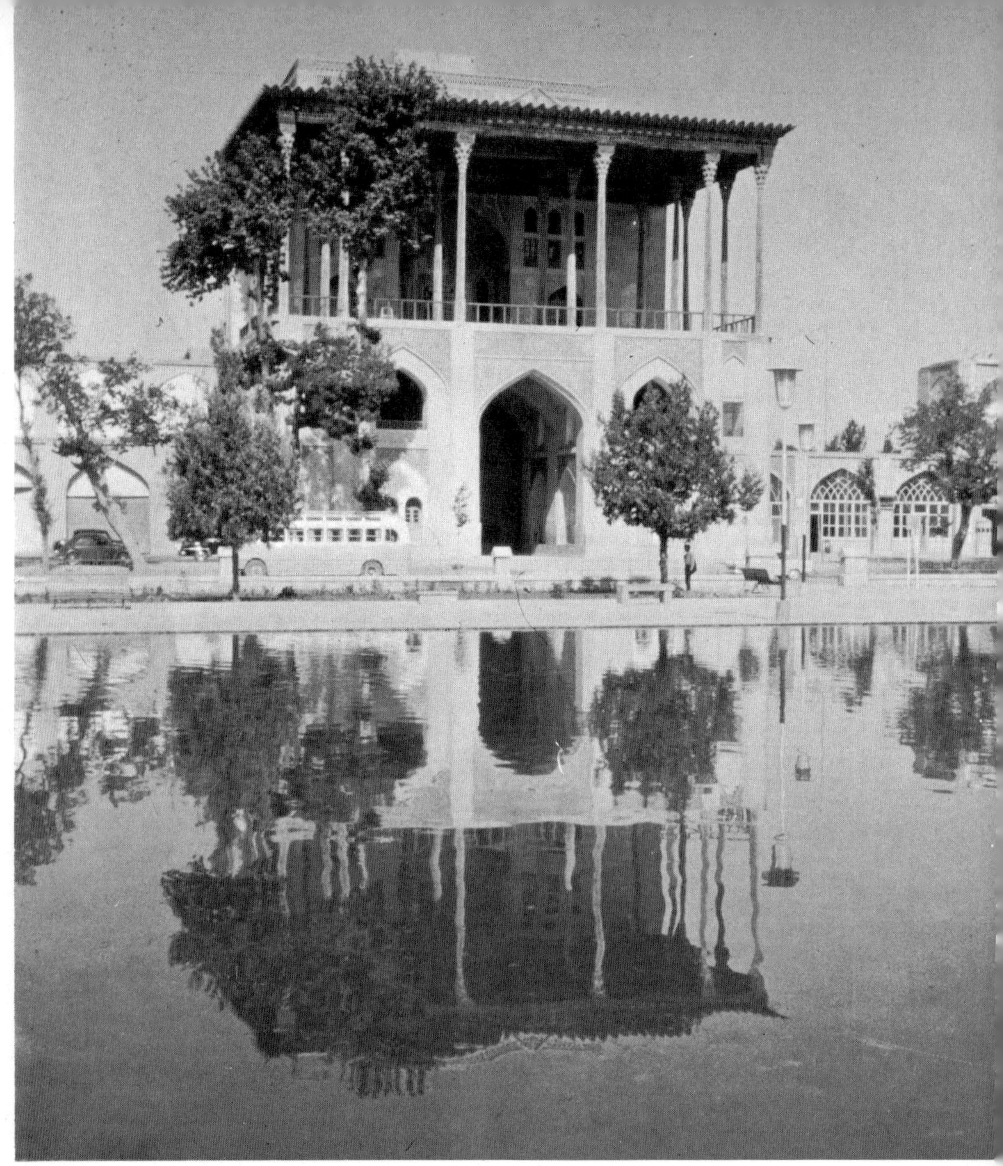

236, 237 (*above*) the Ali Kapu; (*above right*) the Chihil Sutun, Isfahan, *c.* 1598. Shah Abbas built several palaces, all close together, but in contrast to the mosques and religious structures they are mainly built of wood, and their tall slender columns are especially delightful

238 (*below right*) Allahverdi Khan Bridge, Isfahan. Built by order of Shah Abbas by one of his viziers as an extension of the promenade of the Chagar Bagh, it is a most impressive bridge. Built soon after 1600

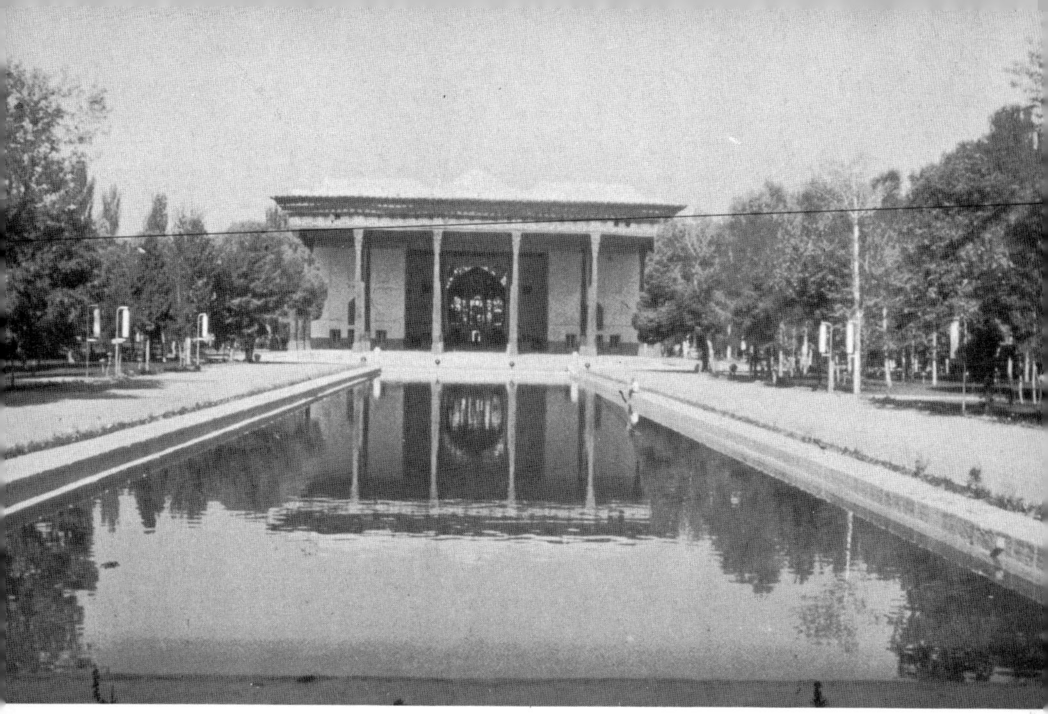

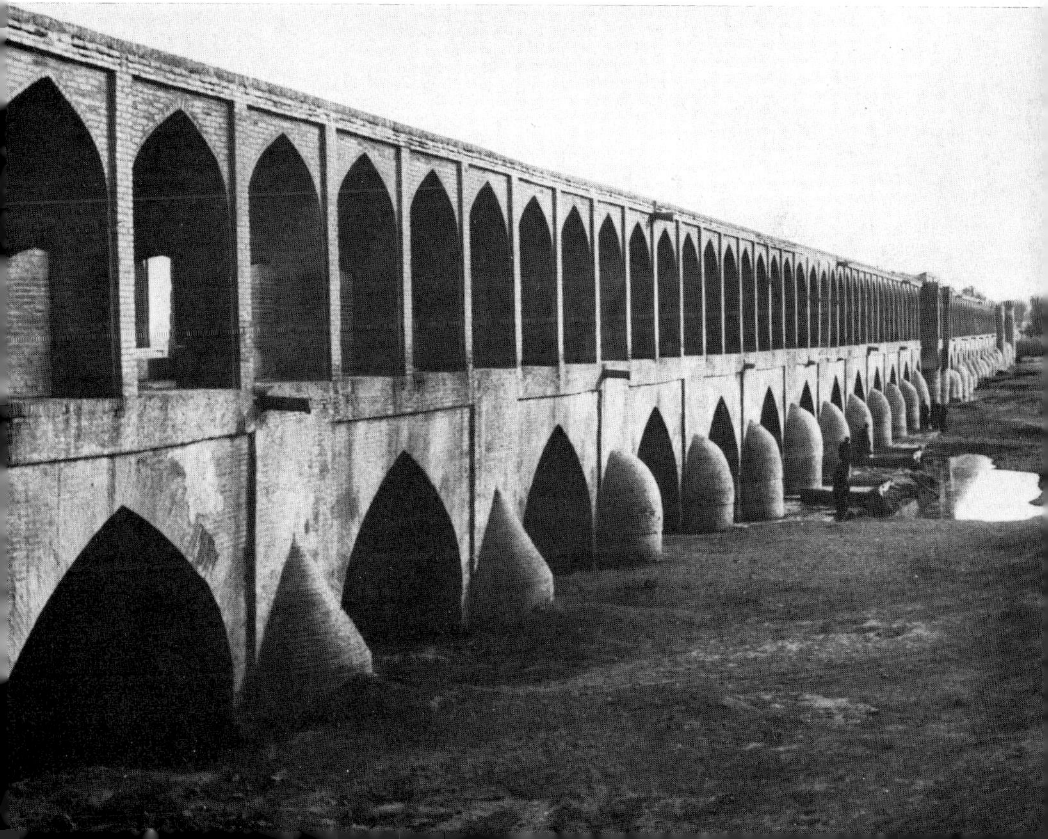

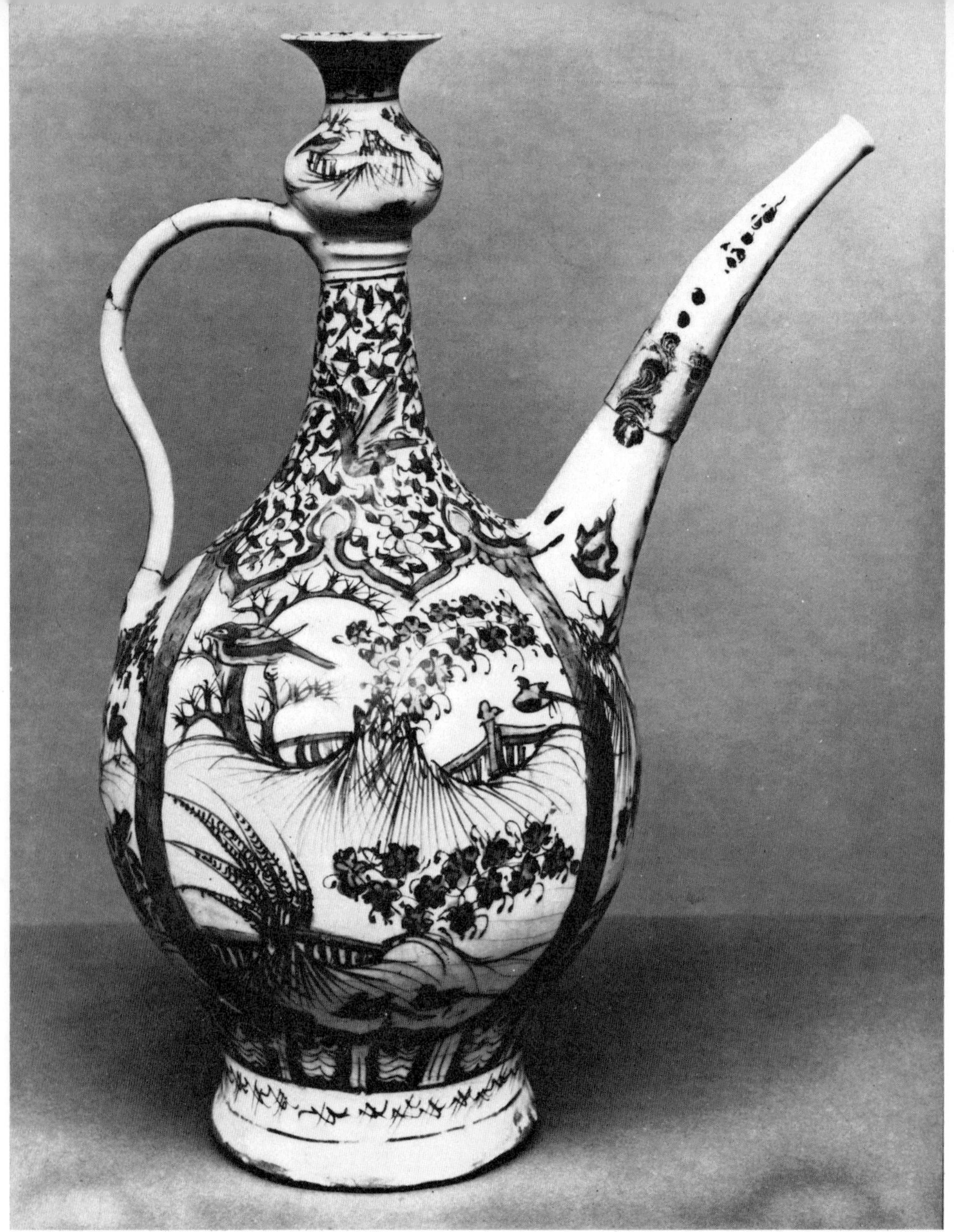

239 Ewer with decoration in blue under a white glaze. The intention of the potter was clearly to imitate Chinese blue-and-white, both with regard to the decoration and in the body of the vessel itself which is semi-porcelain

The tile-work of the age follows on the lines established several centuries before, in the days of the Seljuks, although tiles with a painted design tended to replace those done in the old mosaic technique as the age proceeded. In the manufacture of vessels on the other hand, though fine lustre was still in favour, a number of fresh techniques were introduced and the majority of the potters sought new and distinct ends, the principal aim being to produce wares as near to Chinese prototypes as possible, both with regard to the body – the result was a sort of semi-porcelain – and with regard to decoration – which was either inspired by Ming blue-and-white or by celadon (*Ill. 239*). Again the vessels were usually of very elaborate shapes, many of them not ideally suited to pottery. In fact, admiration of the Chinese and the search for elaboration and originality tended to dull the natural taste of the potters, so that the instinctive feeling for form and decoration which had been so prominent in the earlier ages was no longer in control. There is no disputing the quality of the ceramics of this age, but they were intended to serve as decoration rather than for use; it is an art of the *grand atelier*, not of the individual, and as such fails to attract our sympathy today as readily as the more spontaneous, though in some ways clumsier works of earlier times. There is a great room in the Teheran Museum devoted to the pottery of this type – most of it comes from the Ardebil shrine. Vessels formed an essential part of the decoration of the palaces of Isfahan; in one of them, the Ali Kapu, a room was entirely surrounded by shelves shaped to hold a mass of elaborate jugs and ewers. It delights the guides who show one around, and is truly ingenious, but must be counted a curiosity rather than a work of art.

One family of pottery at this age does, however, stand out because of its rather simple and wholly spontaneous character. It is that which we know as Kubachi, and is represented almost entirely by large plates or dishes, with a rather thick white body, bearing a polychrome under-painted decoration (*Ill. 240*). The glazes are thick and are distinguished by a characteristic crackle. Flowers, scrolls and similar motifs, and sometimes the busts of human figures, done in a style like the drawings of the age, constitute the decoration. The

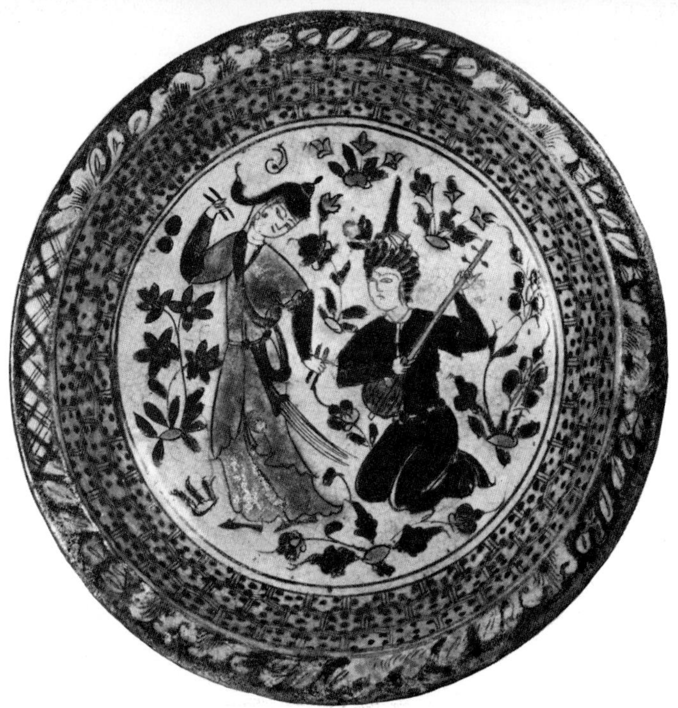

240 Earthenware dish of the type known as Kubachi, *c.* 1550. Most of the potteries made for the court were in the Chinese style, but one type, that known as Kubachi ware, is more Persian in character

designs were mostly done in black, blue, green, brownish-red and yellow, against a cream-coloured ground. The colouring is not unlike that of the later Isnik potteries of Turkey, but the designs are more flowing and the colours less brilliant, so that the general effect is less grand but gentler and more poetic.

A relationship between the Turkish and the Kubachi pottery has been suggested, but if it existed at the outset it was certainly not maintained, and the two types developed along distinct lines. The Kubachi ware was, however, shorter-lived, and so far as we know its production was more limited and its distribution restricted; its association with the region of Kubachi in north-west Persia is probably quite fortuitous; for some reason vessels of the type seem to have been treasured and preserved by the local inhabitants. The earliest piece we know is dated to 1469, and it would seem that the ware went out of production fairly early in the seventeenth century.

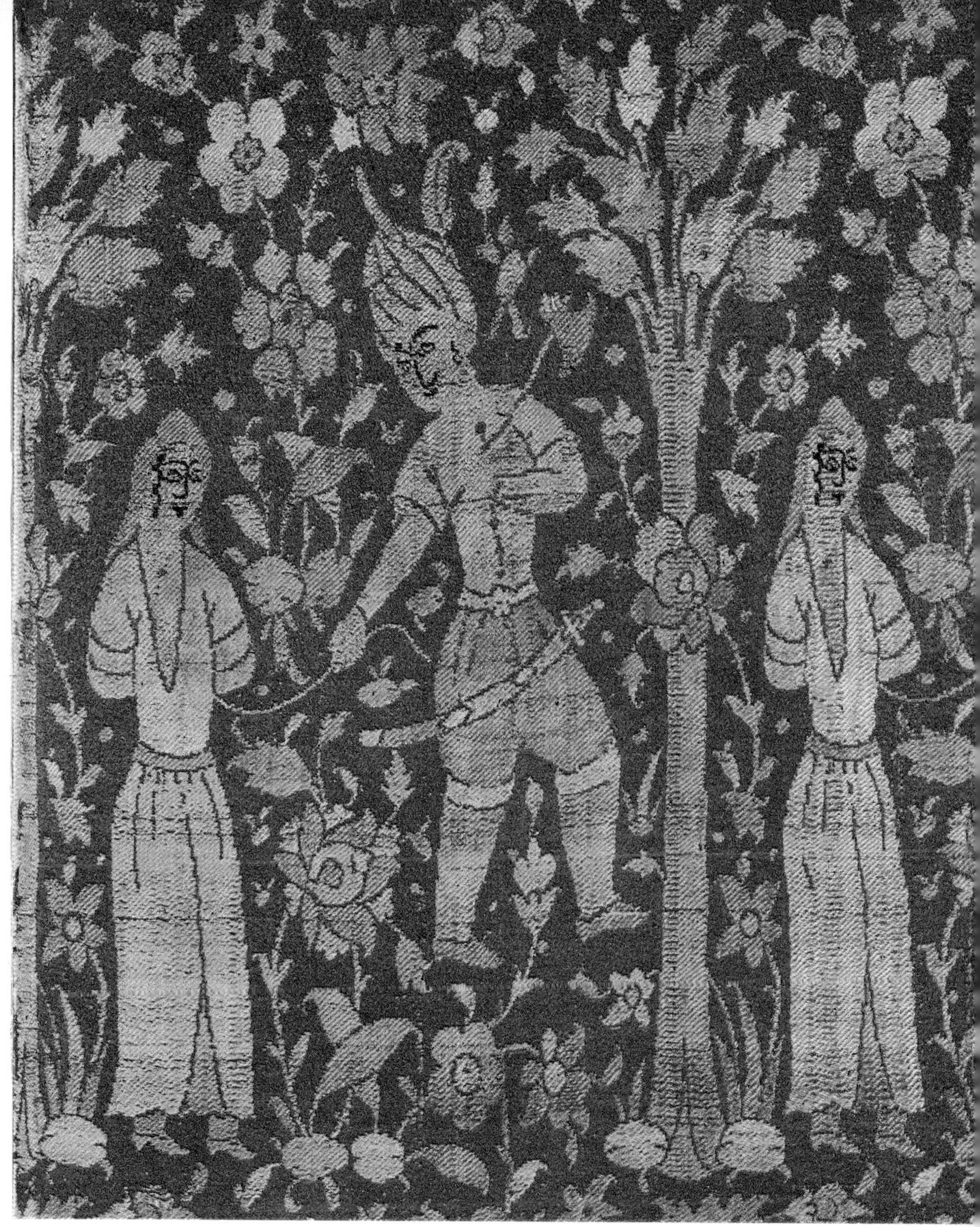

241 Silk textile with warriors leading prisoners. Late sixteenth century. Silks and brocades at this time were often adorned with figural themes inspired by illustrations of manuscripts

If the pottery of the age, apart from the Kubachi, tended to be somewhat derivative, the same is not true of the textiles, for it is to the Safavid period that some of the finest of Persian silk weaves and velvets are to be attributed. It is true that here too the formal designs of earlier times were discarded, and a whole new repertory closer to that of the miniature painter than to that of the designer was adopted, but the weavers seem to have known how to make best use of these designs, and while the pottery of the age seems rather over-sophisticated, like a Louis XV drawing-room, the textiles lose none of the old basic grandeur, yet add to it new delights of colour and technical excellence (*Ill. 242*). Some of them bear decorative designs, where birds and small animals combine with the foliage to delight the observer, in a riot of rich colour, where gold and silver threads play a significant part; on others the same tales that inspired the miniaturists were illustrated, with almost the same subtlety and feeling. Indeed, the best of the miniature painters often turned to designing the patterns for the textile weavers. One of them, Ghiyath by name, worked mainly at Yazd, but Kashan and Isfahan were also important centres of silk weaving.

The silks (*Ill. 241*) are often so like the miniatures that they can be dated very accurately by comparing them with the comparatively numerous dated examples of the latter art. But they were not necessarily made in the same places, for though Yazd and Kashan were important centres of textile weaving, the best miniatures were at first produced in centres like Bokhara, Samarkand or Shiraz, where schools had been established over a long period, and subsequently in the capital cities, first Tabriz and Qazvin and then Isfahan. The miniature paintings that were done in Isfahan after the transfer of the capital thither took on an entirely new character. Portraits and single figures of ladies, boys, lovers or dervishes now became more common than scenes, and line drawings more usual than paintings. The large head-dresses worn by the men serve to distinguish the work of the period, and the costumes quite often showed the influence of Europe. Some of the painters were even sent to study in Rome, but the manner of the West was never in any sense fully assimilated, as it was at rather a later date in India.

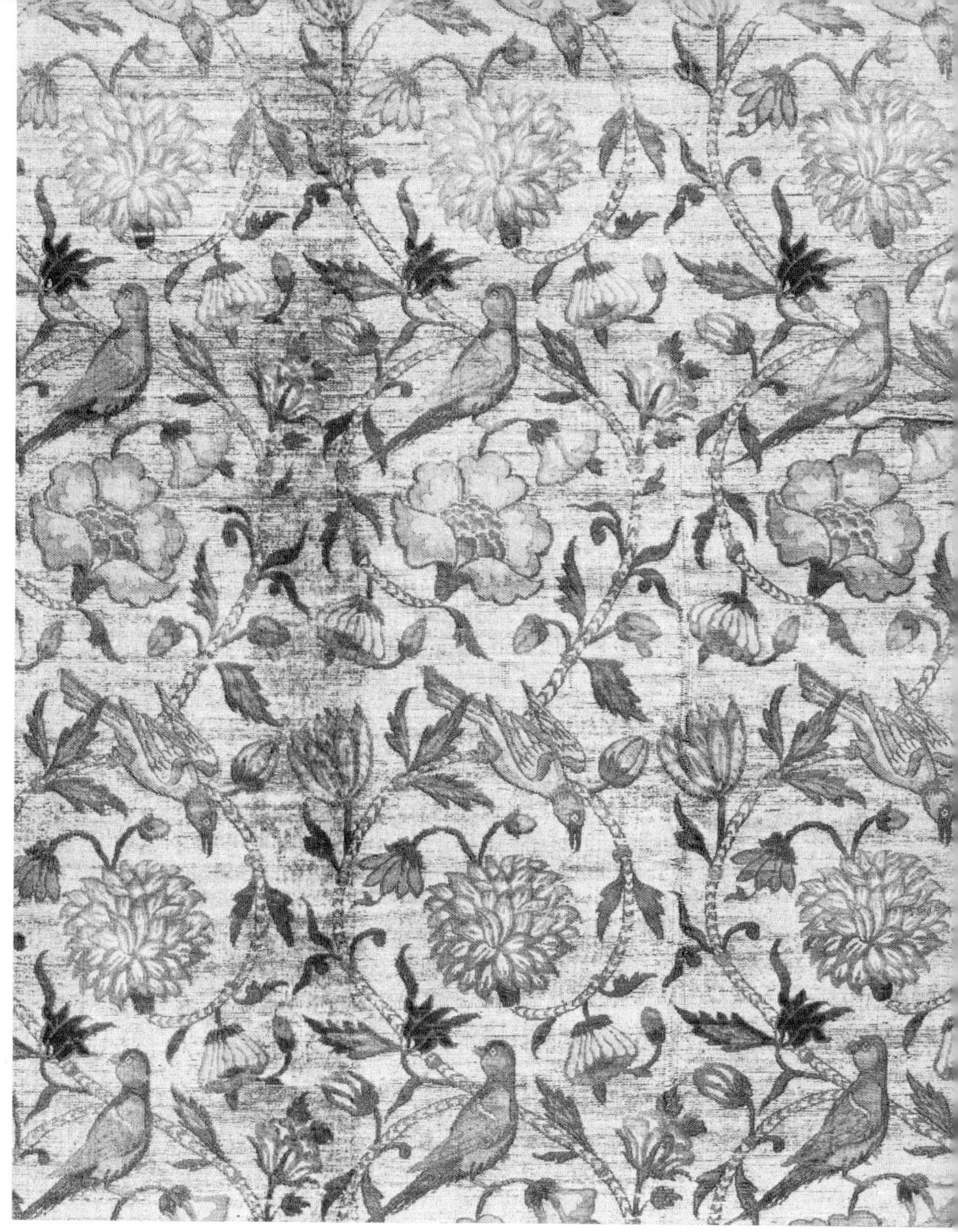

242 Brocade with birds and flowers. Brocades of this type were much in favour in Safavid times, and the products of the Persian looms were both numerous and of outstanding quality

The most famous painter of the age, Riza-i-Abbasi, was an outstanding figure. As with Bihzad, his work and signature were both copied and forged; moreover, there seem to have been at least three other painters of the name of Riza living at much the same time, who worked in a closely similar style. The most important of these, Aga Riza, is a name which we find in attributory inscriptions only, and not in holographic signatures. Kuehnel thinks it is just another designation for Riza-i-Abbasi, though other authorities regard him as a separate individual, as for instance Martin. But Martin confuses him with a calligrapher by the name of Ali Riza, who died in 1573–4, whereas the painter lived well on into the seventeenth century. The second painter of the name was Muhammad Riza of Tabriz, who went to Constantinople. The third Aga Riza-i-Murid is more distinct; he worked both in Persia and India. A fourth painter, Muhammad Riza Mashadi, may also have been different from Riza-i-Abbasi.

As for Riza-i-Abbasi's work, Kuehnel cites a list of authentic and mostly dated pieces which provides us with a sure basis on which to found our conception of his style. He was a great master of line and his drawings (*Ill. 243*) have a delicacy and exquisiteness which, though much imitated, was never really equalled in the work of others of the period, delightful though it often is (*Ill. 244*).

In addition to the book illustrations, some large-scale wall-paintings have also been preserved. They are delightful in themselves and also help to give some idea of the wall-paintings which were, according to the records, being produced long before the period of Shah Abbas. Like the drawings and miniatures, they sometimes show the influence of western Europe and some of the wall-paintings at Isfahan even included the portraits of European travellers who visited Persia at the time. Most important are those in the Ali Kapu and the Chihil Sutun.

After the middle of the seventeenth century a definite decline set in so far as painting was concerned, and though much quite attractive

243 Drawing showing three hunters in a landscape by Riza-i-Abbasi. Mid-sixteenth century. Riza-i-Abbasi was the most famous artist of this century and favoured line drawings and naturalistic subjects to illustrative themes which were so popular a century earlier

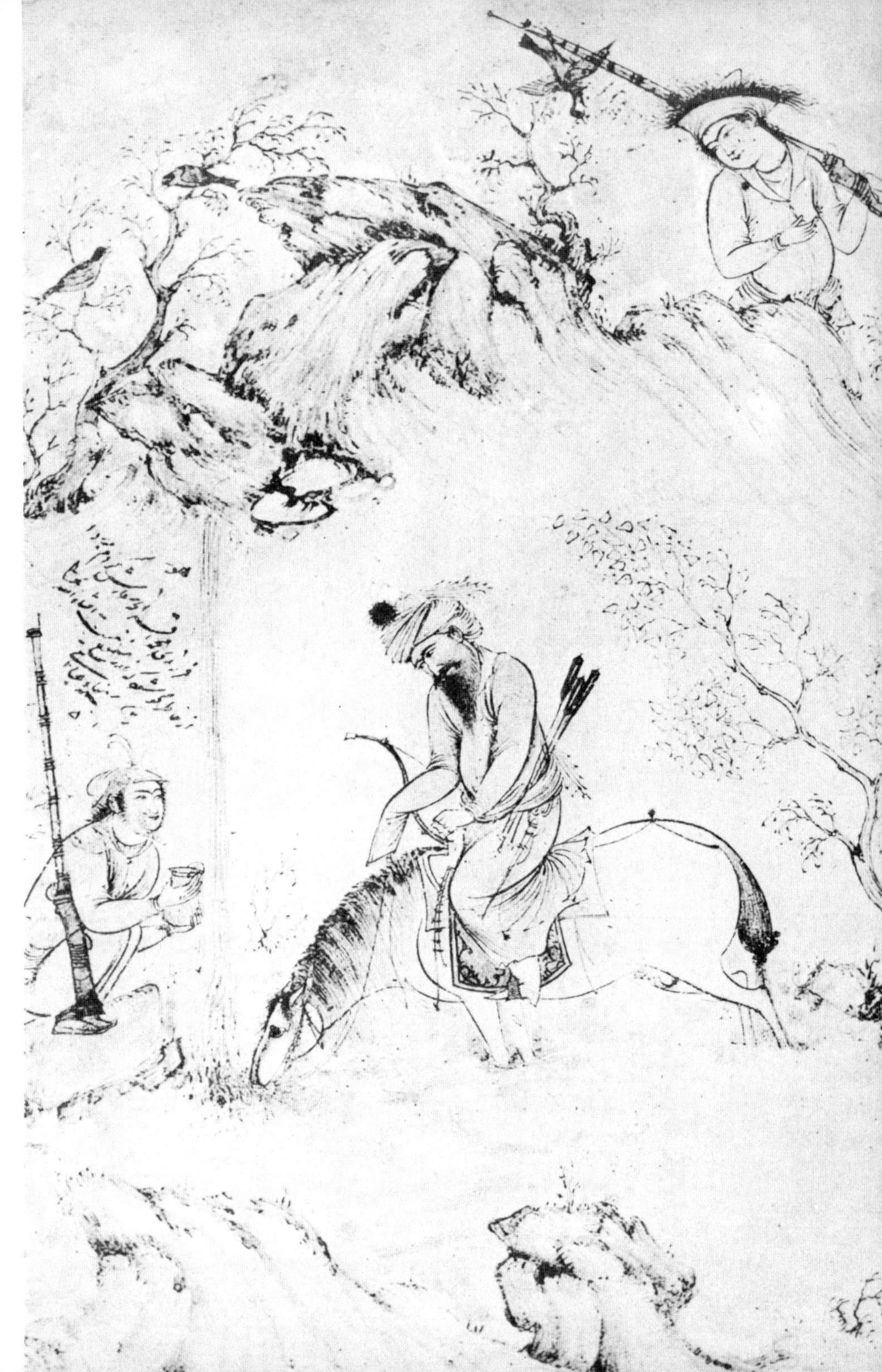

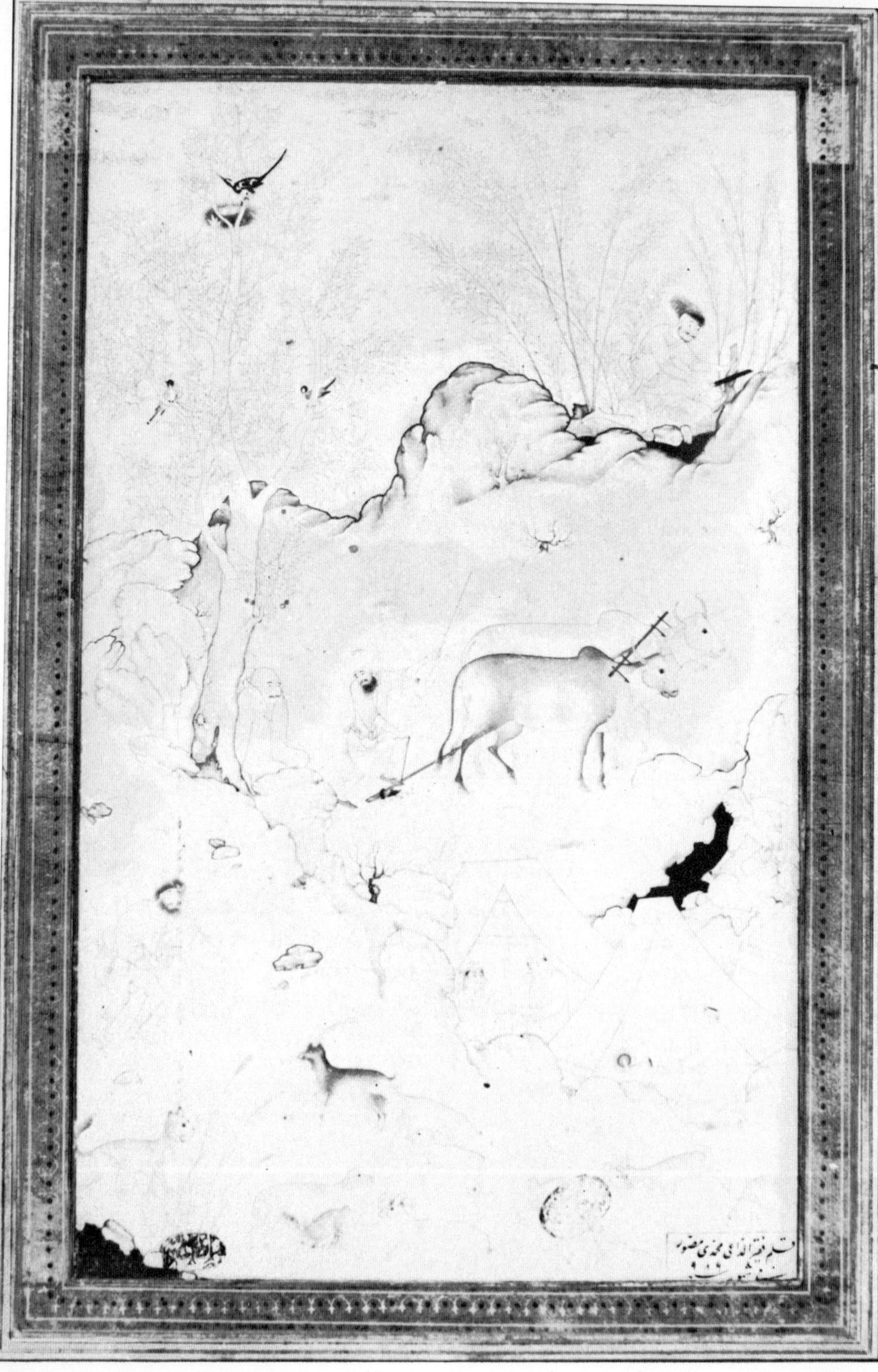
رقم فقیر الداعی محمدی مصور

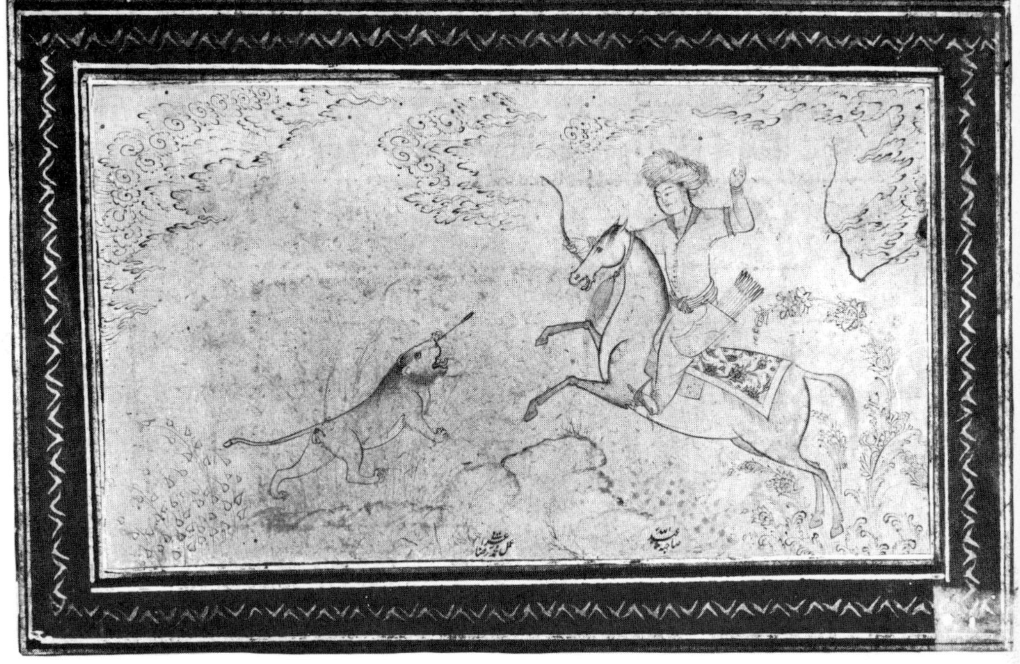

245 Drawing of a lion-hunter by Muhammad Riza Iraqi. Although Riza-i-Abbasi was the last of the really great masters, good work even if of a limited nature, continued to be produced in the seventeenth century

work was produced for another century or so, the majesty and glory of Persian painting was at an end. Only here and there, as for instance in some of the work of Muin Muzaffar, the best of Riza-i-Abbasi's pupils, did the style rise above mediocrity. A rather delightful portrait by him of his master (*Ill. 246*) may be cited. He lived all through the seventeenth century and works by him dated as far apart as 1638 and 1707 are known. Another artist, Muhammad Shafi, was Riza-i-Abbasi's son; he is known mainly as a flower painter, though he also did some portraits of his father.

But if the art of painting saw a certain decadence, that of carpet weaving seems to have come into its own more at this period than at any other, thanks to some extent to the greatly intensified demand

244 Drawing of oxen ploughing, in the style of Riza-i-Abbasi. Simple subjects of this kind, as well as drawings of beautiful girls and youths, characterize the taste of the later sixteenth and seventeenth centuries

which opened up as a result of trading contacts with the West. By the seventeenth century a large number of centres were involved in carpet production, and what had once been virtually a court preserve had become a national industry of great extent and importance. Once again the miniatures come to our aid in the problem of dating, for the painters loved to depict carpets with the greatest care and precision. Indeed, it is to the miniatures that we have to turn for our information as to the early history of carpet weaving, for with one exception early examples are non-existent. The one exception is a well-preserved knotted carpet of an essentially Persian type from a Scythian burial at Pazyryk in the Altai of about 500 BC; it is now in the Hermitage Museum at Leningrad. But from about the middle of the sixteenth century the carpets that survive are comparatively numerous, and the expert can be reasonably sure as to where and when examples were made, though classification of older carpets in Persia is more often made on the basis of design rather than on that of locality. Thus it would be more usual to speak of a 'garden', 'floral', 'animal', 'vase' or 'medallion' carpet of the seventeenth century than of one from Tabriz, Sine, Farahana or Kashan. Only after the mid-eighteenth century does a distinction according to locality become possible. But the so-called Sine knot was universally employed in contrast to the Gördes knot of Turkey.

The Persian carpets vary from small prayer rugs to carpets of immense size, like the superb Ardebil carpet (*Ill. 247*) in the Victoria and Albert Museum, which dates from 1540. The material most generally used was wool, but the warps were sometimes of cotton. A series of specially rich carpets, where silk was used for the pile instead of wool, are known as 'Polish carpets'. They were made and used in Persia itself, but seem to have been especially valued in Poland, and were exported thither from Persia in quite large numbers in the later sixteenth and earlier seventeenth centuries. Most of the best-preserved examples came from Poland and so gave a name to the group.

246 Portrait of Riza-i-Abbasi by his pupil Muin Muzaffar, dated 1676. Realist drawings of the period were often of very high quality and even the minor masters produced exquisite line drawings

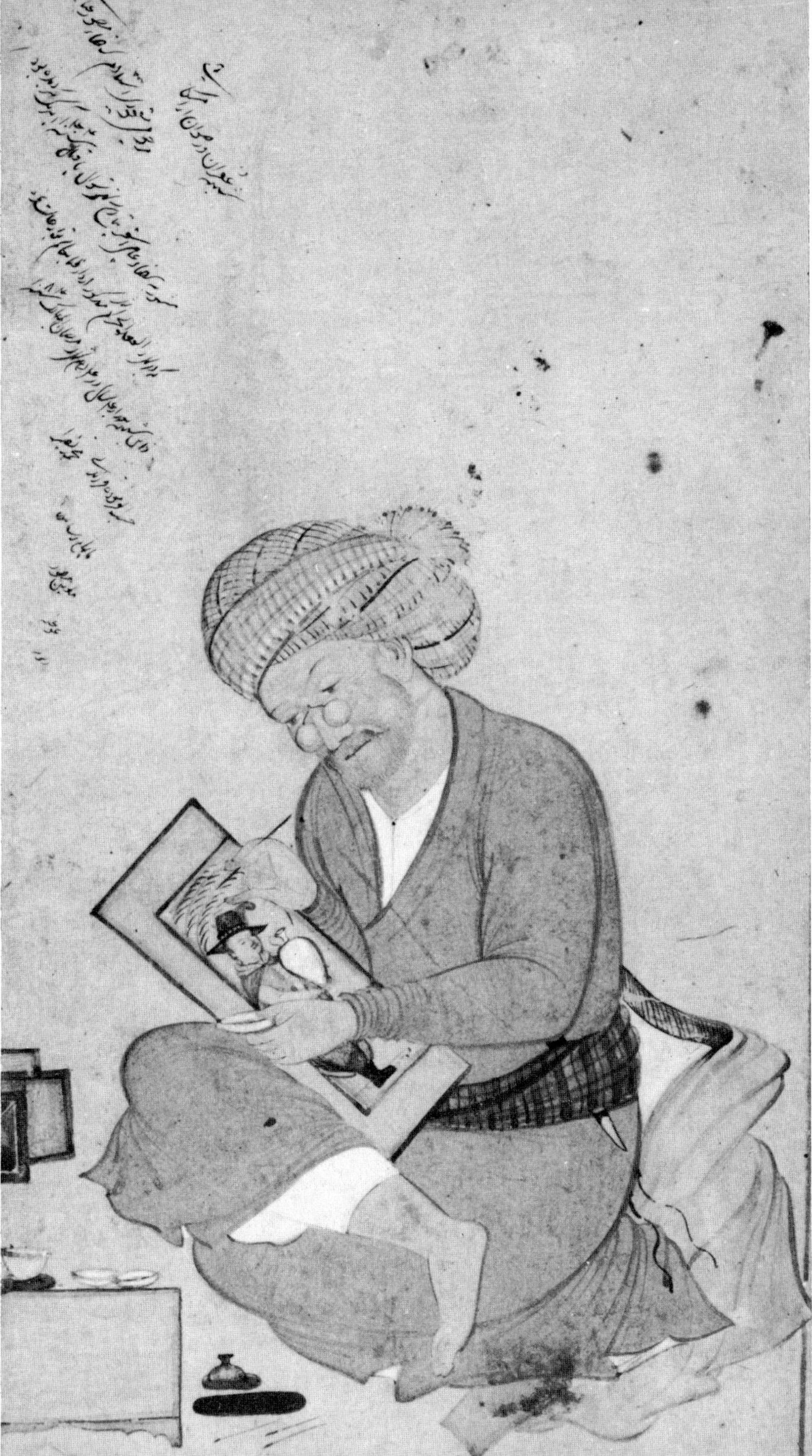

The carpets really mark the end of our story. Long after the superb potteries, the fine metalwork, the glorious silks and the enchanting miniatures had ceased to be produced, carpets and rugs which were of the first artistic quality were being made in Persia, in Turkey, and in the region between the two, where a distinctive type usually known as Caucasian, was woven (*Ill. 248, 249*). With their severe, geometric patterns, these belong neither to Persia, where the designs were suave and poetic, nor to Turkey, where, in spite of a marked degree of stylization, motifs that were basically naturalistic were still most often employed. The severe geometric abstractions of the Caucasian carpets is something quite distinct from either, and represents the last survival of the purely non-representational arts of the nomad world of Central Asia which we encountered in the tile-work of the Seljuk age and in some of the early pottery or the textiles of Turkey.

It was a style wholly opposed to the naturalism of Hellenistic art, which dominated at the outset in Umayyad Syria, and distinct too from the basically representational, even if stylized art, of the Sassanians which left so important a legacy in Abbasid Mesopotamia and in Persia. But the role of the non-representational style of inner Asia exercised an influence as time went on which was little less important. The tile mosaics of the Seljuks, the interlacing designs of the end pages of the korans, the marble closure slabs of Egyptian architecture all owe a debt to this art, and if, at the end of this survey, the elements that went to form the art of Islam may be enumerated, the non-representational art of middle Asia must share the glory with the legacy left on the one hand by Hellenism and on the other by the Sassanians. It was the blend of these all influences that produced Islamic art, the patronage of the diverse rulers that nurtured it, and the genius of the individuals, few of them giants, but all endowed with great sensibility, that made its flowering possible. We know but few of these men by name, and we know still less of their personalities and their lives. Like the Paladins in the Snow (*Ill. 224*)

247 Detail of the Ardebil carpet originally from the mosque of Ismail Shah, Ardebil. 1540. The carpet is probably the largest ever to have been made in Persia, and its workmanship is of quite outstanding quality

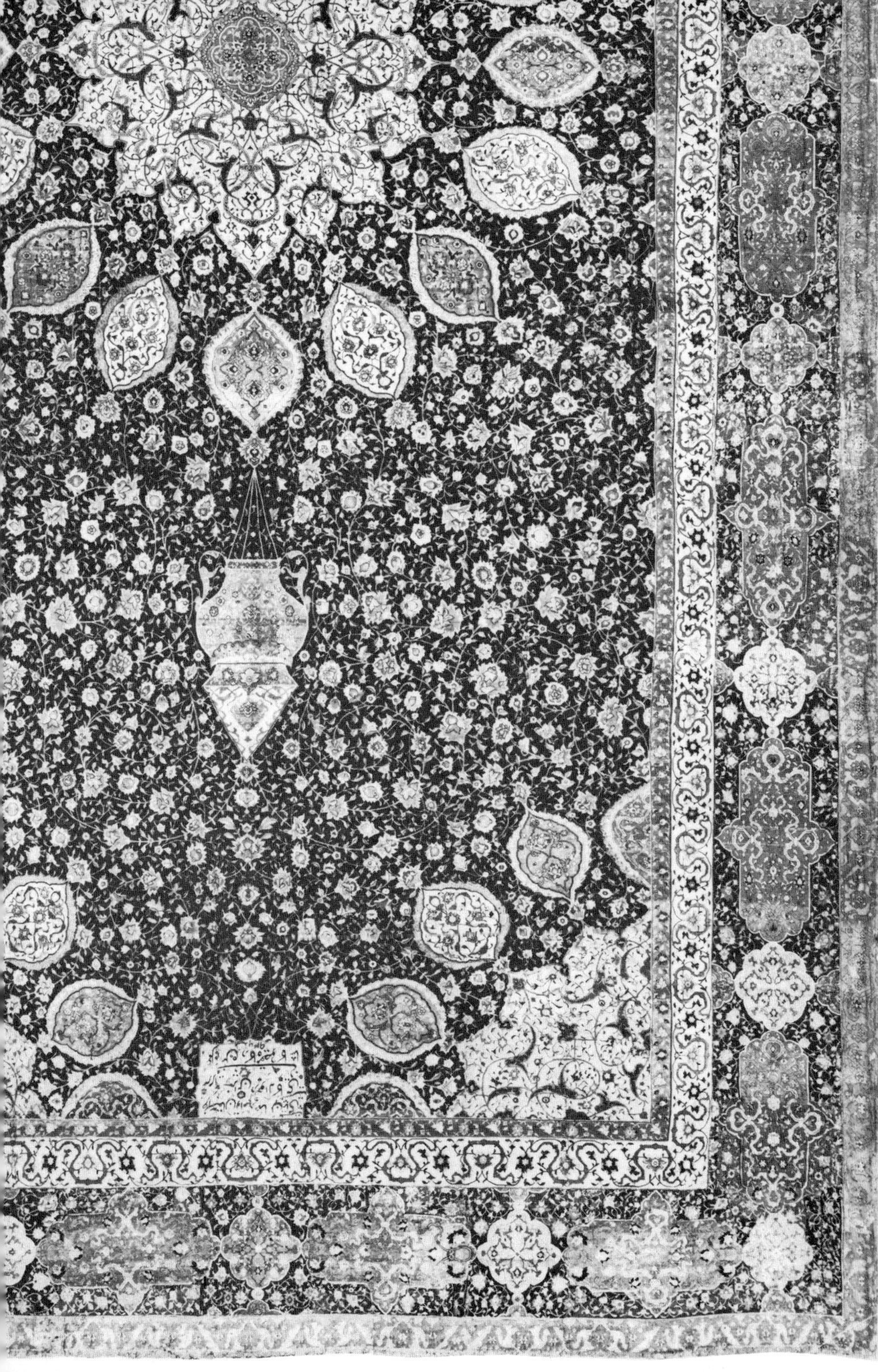

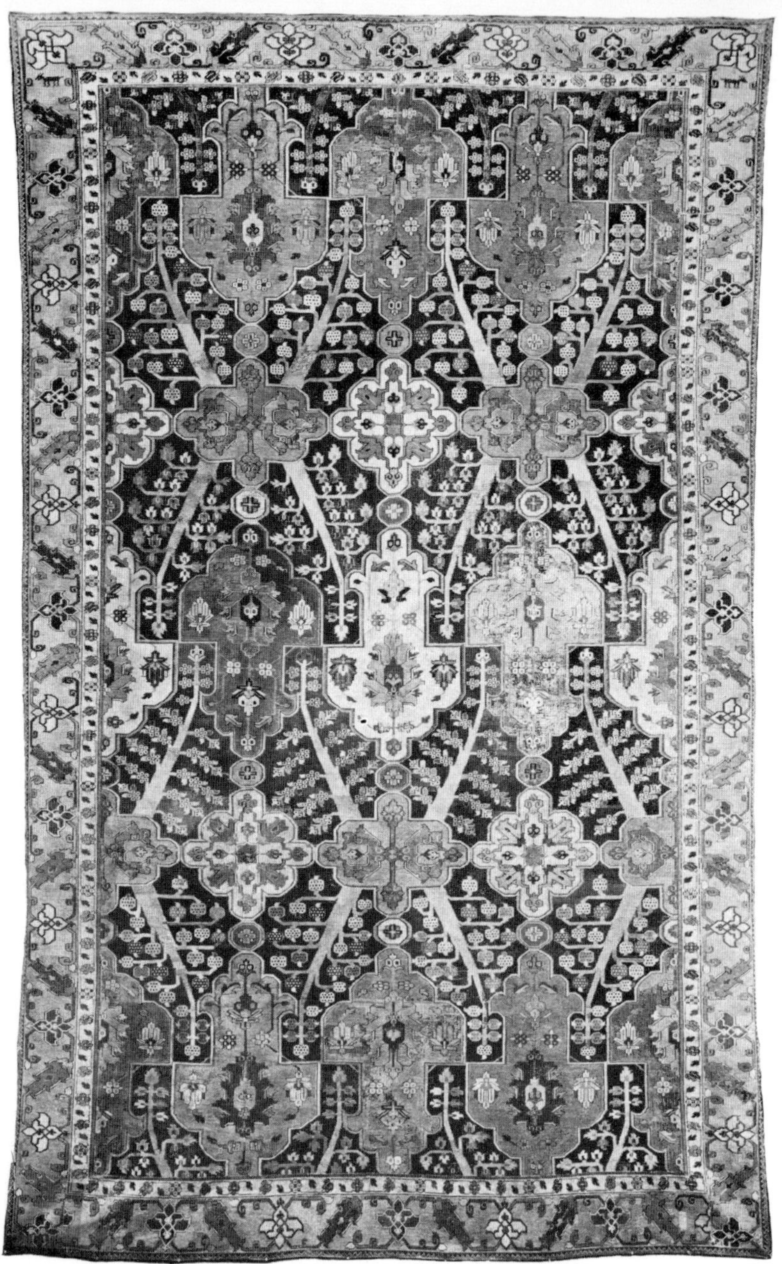

248 Carpets with geometric designs of this type were mostly made in the north-west of Persia. Classification is usually made on the basis of the design

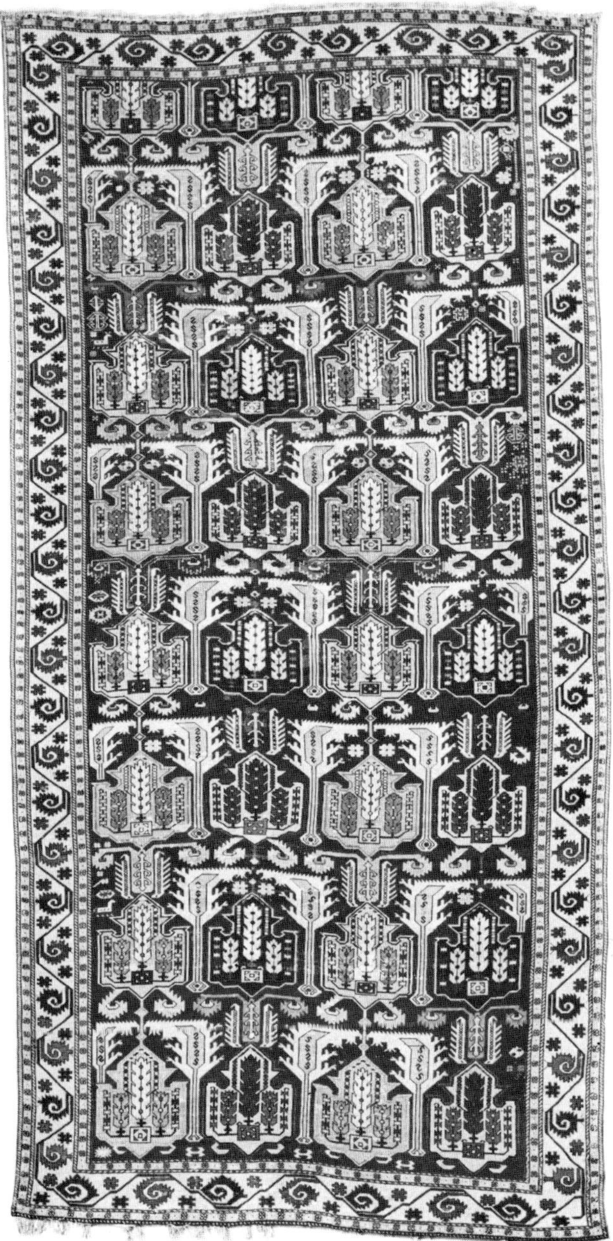

249 Carpet of the type known as 'Caucasian'. It is a particularly fine example of the type and is dated to the early eighteenth century

they are patient, mute, fatalistic; their fame, their names, rested in the hand of Allah, the all-merciful. There they were in safe keeping. But their works, or some of them, have remained a joy and delight, even a source of inspiration, to those of a different age and a different faith. May the reproductions that appear in this book serve to bring them before a wider circle, and show that the great concern with self and self-expression which so much obsesses the artists of today in the West is not necessarily to be regarded as an essential in the production of good art.

Bibliography

Table of Dates

Maps

List of Illustrations

Index

Bibliography

The bibliography has in the main been confined to monographs of a general character in English, French and German. The titles of a few recent articles have, however, also been included when they contain important additions to our general knowledge of the arts or to basic theories and their development. Further information of a detailed character can be found in the full bibliography compiled by K. A. C. Creswell, *A Bibliography of the Architecture, Art and Crafts of Islam, to 1st January 1960*. The American University at Cairo, 1961.

General

CRESWELL, K. A. C. *A Short Account of Early Muslim Architecture*, London, 1958.
A most useful summary

DIEZ, E. *Die Kunst der islamischen Völker*, Potsdam, 1917.
A most useful general outline in German, but rather out-of-date

DIMAND, M. S. *A Handbook of Mohammedan Decorative Arts*, New York, 1930, new editions 1944, 1958.
Limited to material in the Metropolitan Museum, New York, otherwise the most complete survey in English

KOECHLIN, R. and MIGEON, G. *Cent Planches d'art musulman*, Paris, 1929.
Fine colour illustrations

KUEHNEL, E. *Die Islamische Kunst*, A. Springer, Handbuch der Kunstgeschichte, VI, Leipzig, 1929.
One of the best summaries in German
– *Islamische Kleinkunst*, Berlin, 1925.
A useful survey of the minor arts

MARÇAIS, G. *L'Art musulman*, Paris, 1926.
Small, but up-to-date and well illustrated, especially useful for North Africa

MIGEON, G. *Manuel d'art musulman*, 2 vols. Paris, 1927.
The best general work on the subject

PINDER-WILSON, R. *Islamic Art* – 100 Plates in colour, London, 1957.
No text, but good colour illustrations

SALADIN, H. *Manuel d'art musulman*. I. *L'Architecture*, Paris, 1907.
The only small and complete handbook of the architecture, but now not easy to procure

Chapter One

CRESWELL, K. A. C. *Early Muslim Architecture*, vol. I, Oxford, 1932.
The most complete work on the subject

HAMILTON, R. W. *Khirbat al-Mafjah*, Oxford, 1959.
An up-to-date monograph

SCHLUMBERGER, D. 'Deux Fresques Omeyyades', *Syria*, XXV, 1946.
Basic publication of important material

Chapter Two

BELL, G. M. L. *Palace and Mosque at Ukhaidir*, Oxford, 1914.
Basic publication of an important monument

CRESWELL, K. A. C. *Early Muslim Architecture*, vol. II, Oxford, 1940.

LANE, A. *Early Islamic Pottery, Mesopotamia, Egypt and Persia*, London, 1937.

SARRE, F. and HERZFELD, E. *Die Ausgrabungen von Samarra*, Berlin. I. Herzfeld. *Der Wandschmuck*, 1913; II. Sarre. *Die Keramik*, 1925; III. Herzfeld. *Die Malereien*, 1927; IV. Herzfeld. *Geschichte der Stadt Samarra*, 1948.
Basic publication of an excavation of outstanding importance

Chapter Three

POPE, A. U. *A Survey of Persian Art*, 6 vols. Oxford, 1939.
Contains articles by numerous prominent authorities on their special subjects

SHEPHERD, D. G. and HENNING, W. B. 'Zandaniji identified', *Aus der Welt der Islamischer Kunst* – Festschrift E. Kuehnel, Berlin, 1959, p. 15.

Valuable new evidence on the classification of textiles

WILKINSON, C. and others. 'Excavations at Nishapur', *Bulletin of the Metropolitan Museum*, New York, XXX, 1930, XXXII, 1932, XXXIII, 1933, XXXVII, 1942.
An important excavation, but a fuller publication, better illustrated, is still awaited

Chapter Four

Egypt

CRESWELL, K. A. C. *The Muslim Architecture of Egypt*, vol. I, 939–1171, Oxford, 1952.
The fullest and most complete work on the subject

MEYER, L. A. *Saracenic Heraldry*, Oxford, 1932.
A penetrating study of a subject unique to Egypt and Syria

North Africa

CRESWELL, K. A. C. *The Muslim Architecture of Egypt*, vol. I, Oxford, 1952.

KUEHNEL, E. *Maurische Kunst*, Berlin, 1924.
A most useful summary

MARÇAIS, G. *Manuel d'art musulman (Tunisie, Algérie, Maroc, Espagne, Sicile)*, Paris, 1926.
– *L'Architecture musulmane d'occident*, Paris, 1955.
A useful survey

TERRASSE, H. *L'Art hispano-mauresque des origines au XIIIe siècle*, Paris, 1932.
The fullest work on the region

Chapter Five

ETTINGHAUSEN, R. *Arab Painting*, London, 1962.
Up to date, informative, stimulating and beautifully illustrated

LANE, A. *Early Islamic Pottery, Mesopotamia, Egypt and Persia*, London, 1937.

OTTO-DORN, K. 'Türkisch-Islamisches Bildgut in der Figurenreliefs von Achthamar' in *Anatolia* VI, University of Ankara, 1961.
A very penetrating and provocative essay

RICE, D. S. *Le Baptistère de St Louis*, Paris, 1953.
– 'Studies in Islamic Metal Work' in *Bulletin of the School of Oriental and African Studies*, Vol. 14, pt 3; vol. 15, pt 1–3; vol. 17, pt 2, 1952–55.
The most authoritative writings on metalwork

SARRE, F. and HERZFELD, E. *Archäologische Reise im Euphrat- und Tigris Gebiet*, Berlin, 1911–12.
A full survey of an important region

Chapter Six

LANE, A. *Later Islamic Pottery, Persia, Syria, Egypt, Turkey*, London, 1960.
A most useful survey

POPE, A. U. *A Survey of Persian Art*, Oxford, 1939.

Chapter Seven

ALY BAGHAT BEY and MASSOUL, F. *La Céramique musulmane de l'Egypte*, Cairo, 1930.
A basic publication of the Fostat material

CRESWELL, K. A. C. *The Muslim Architecture of Egypt*, vol. II, Oxford, 1959.

ETTINGHAUSEN, R. *Arab Painting*, London, 1962.

LANE, A. *Later Islamic Pottery, Persia, Syria, Egypt, Turkey*, London, 1960.

Chapter Eight

MARÇAIS, G. *Manuel d'art musulman*, Paris, 1926.

TERRASSE, H. *L'Art hispano-mauresque des origines au XIIIe siècle*, Paris, 1932.

Chapter Nine

GABRIEL, A. *Monuments turcs d'Anatolie*, Paris, 1931–34.
– *Voyages archéologiques dans la Turquie orientale*, Paris, 1940.
Both very fully illustrated basic surveys

RICE, T. TALBOT, *The Seljuks*, London, 1961.
A most useful general account

Chapter Ten

ETTINGHAUSEN, R., IPSIROGLU, N. S. and EYUBOGLU, S. *Turkey – Ancient Miniatures*, UNESCO, 1961.
A useful text, exploring new ground; fine plates

GLUECK, H. *Die Kunst der Osmanen*, Leipzig, 1922.
A standard work

LANE, A. *Later Islamic Pottery, Persia, Syria, Egypt, Turkey*, London, 1960.

RIEFSTAHL, R. M. *Turkish Architecture in south-western Anatolia*, Harvard, 1931.
A well-written survey of a little known region

Chapters Eleven and Twelve

ARNOLD, SIR T. *Bihzad and his paintings in the Zafar Namah*, MS, London, 1930.
Brief note on paintings of exceptional quality

BINYON, L. *The Poems of Nizami described*, London, 1928.
A charming and penetrating study

BINYON, L., WILKINSON, J. V. S. and GRAY, B. *Persian Miniature Painting*, Oxford, 1933.
A full and most useful survey

BINYON, L. and WILKINSON, J. V. S. *The Shah Namah of Firdausi*, London, 1931.
A useful and well-illustrated account of one of the most important of all Persian books

GRAY, B. *Persian Painting*, London, 1961.
A useful, beautifully illustrated survey

GUEST, G. D. *Shiraz Painting in the Sixteenth Century*, Washington, 1949.
A useful study of a limited field

POPE, A. U. *A Survey of Persian Art*, Oxford, 1939.

Table of Dates

The Central area

632–661	Orthodox caliphs in Arabia. The Age of Expansion
661–750	The Umayyad caliphs, with capital at Damascus
750–1258	The Abbasid caliphate, with capitals at Baghdad and Samarra
877 onwards	Syria mainly under the control of Egypt

Egypt

641	Muslim conquest of Egypt
641–868	Governors appointed by Umayyads and Abbasids
868–904	The Tulunid dynasty
935–969	The Ikhshidids
969–1171	The Fatimids
1168–1250	The Ayyubids
1252–1517	The Mamluks
1517–1805	Egypt under the control of the Ottoman Turks

North Africa

669–800	Governors appointed by the Umayyads and Abbasids
789–985	The Idrisids of Morocco
800–909	The Aghlabids of Tunis
900–972	The Fatimids
972–1148	The Zayrids of Tunis
1056–1147	The Almoravids of Morocco
1130–1269	The Almohads
1228–1534	The Hafsids of Tunis

Spain

710–712	Arab conquest
713–750	Governors appointed by the Umayyads of Damascus
756–1031	The Umayyads of Cordova
	Thereafter Spain was either divided among numerous minor rulers or under the control of North Africa

Sicily

827–878	Conquered by the Aghlabids of Tunis
909–1071	Under control of the Fatimids

Persia

638–640	Arab conquest
661–820	Governors appointed by the Umayyads and Abbasids
819–1055	The Samanids in Transoxiana and northern Persia
820–874	The Tahrids in Khorasan
864–1032	The Alids in Tabaristan
868–903	The Saffarids
879–930	The Sajids in Azerbaijan
1037–1194	The Seljuks, who unite Mesopotamia and most of Persia under their rule
1077–1231	The Shahs of Khwarazm in Khiva
1136–1225	The Ildeghizids, Atabegs of Azerbaijan
1148–1287	The Salgharids, Atabegs of Fars
1148–1339	The Hazaraspids, Atabegs of Luristan
1127–1262	The Zangids, Atabegs of upper Mesopotamia
1101–1231	The Ortakids, Atabegs of Diyarbakir
1206–1353	The Ilkhans
1313–1393	The Muzaffarids of Fars, Kerman and Kurdistan
1369–1500	The Timurids
1378–1469	The Kara-Kuyunli of Azerbaijan
1428–1599	The Shaibanids of Transoxiana
1502–1736	The Safavids

Afghanistan

711	Arab conquest of Sindh
962–1186	The Ghaznavids
1100–1215	The Ghorids
1526–1857	The Mogul emperors

Turkey and Asia Minor

1071	Seljuks win battle of Manzikert
1077–1327	The Seljuks of Rum
1300–1924	The Ottoman or Osmanli Sultans, with capital at Bursa 1326, and at Istanbul (Constantinople) from 1453

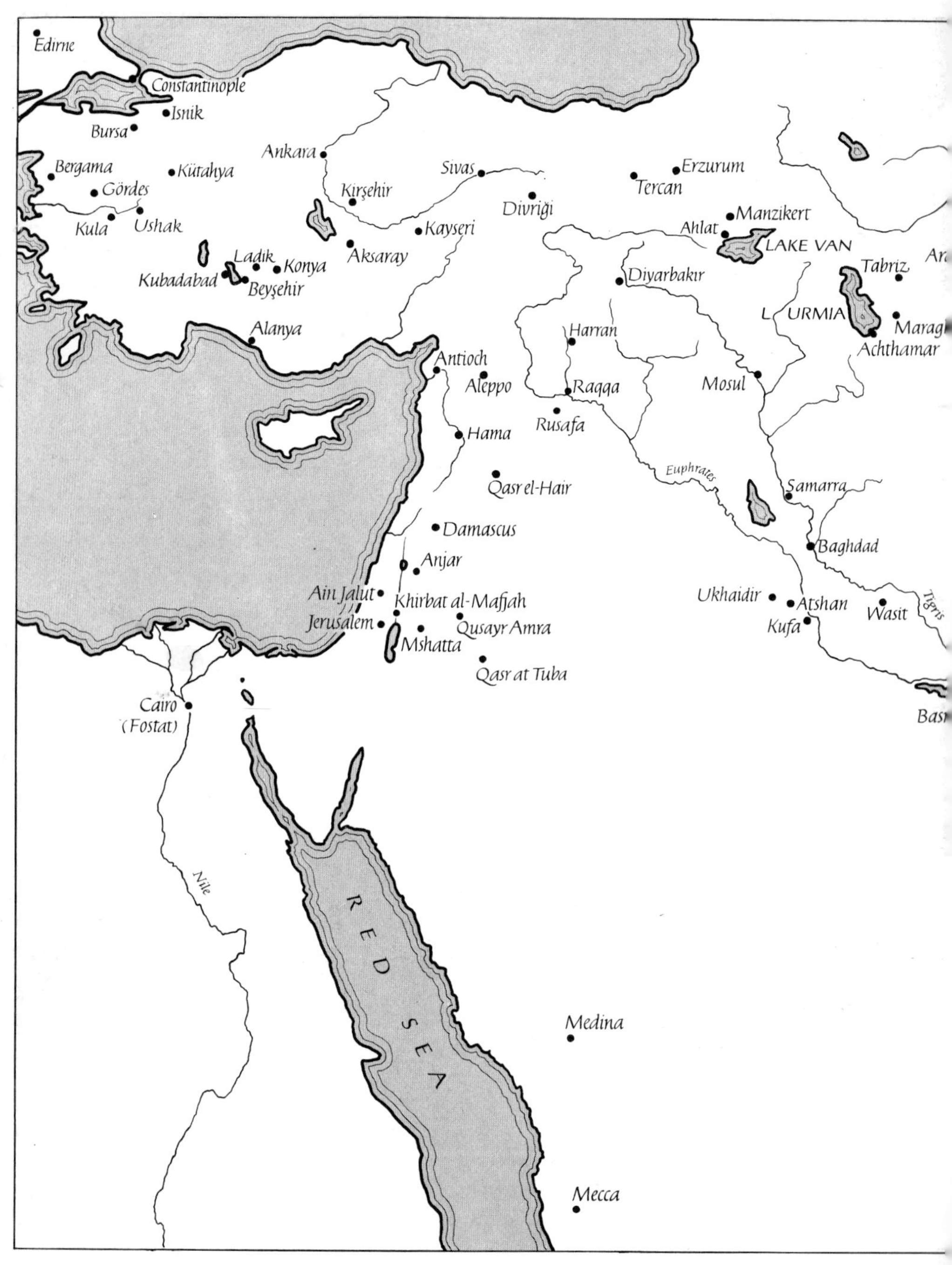
Edirne
Constantinople
Isnik
Bursa
Bergama
Kütahya
Gördes
Kula
Ushak
Ankara
Kirşehir
Sivas
Divriği
Kayseri
Aksaray
Ladik
Konya
Kubadabad
Beyşehir
Alanya
Erzurum
Tercan
Manzikert
Ahlat
LAKE VAN
Diyarbakır
Tabriz
L URMIA
Maragh
Achthamar
Harran
Antioch
Aleppo
Raqqa
Mosul
Rusafa
Hama
Euphrates
Qasr el-Hair
Samarra
Damascus
Baghdad
Anjar
Ain Jalut
Khirbat al-Mafjah
Ukhaidir
Atshan
Wasit
Tigris
Jerusalem
Qusayr Amra
Kufa
Mshatta
Qasr at Tuba
Cairo
(Fostat)
Nile
RED SEA
Medina
Mecca

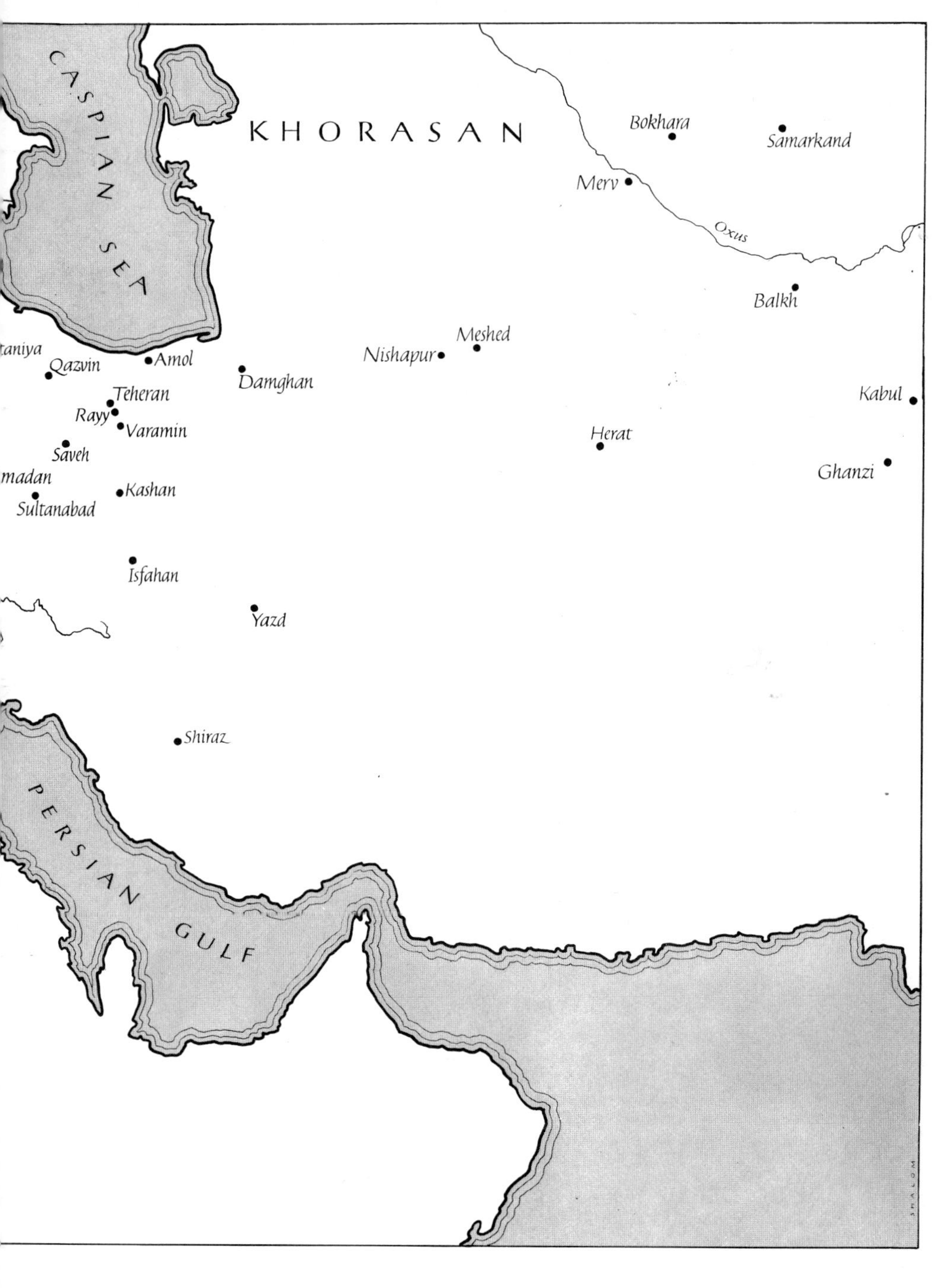
CASPIAN SEA
KHORASAN
Bokhara
Samarkand
Merv
Oxus
Balkh
Meshed
Nishapur
taniya
Qazvin
Amol
Damghan
Teheran
Rayy
Varamin
Kabul
Herat
Saveh
madan
Ghanzi
Kashan
Sultanabad
Isfahan
Yazd
Shiraz
PERSIAN GULF

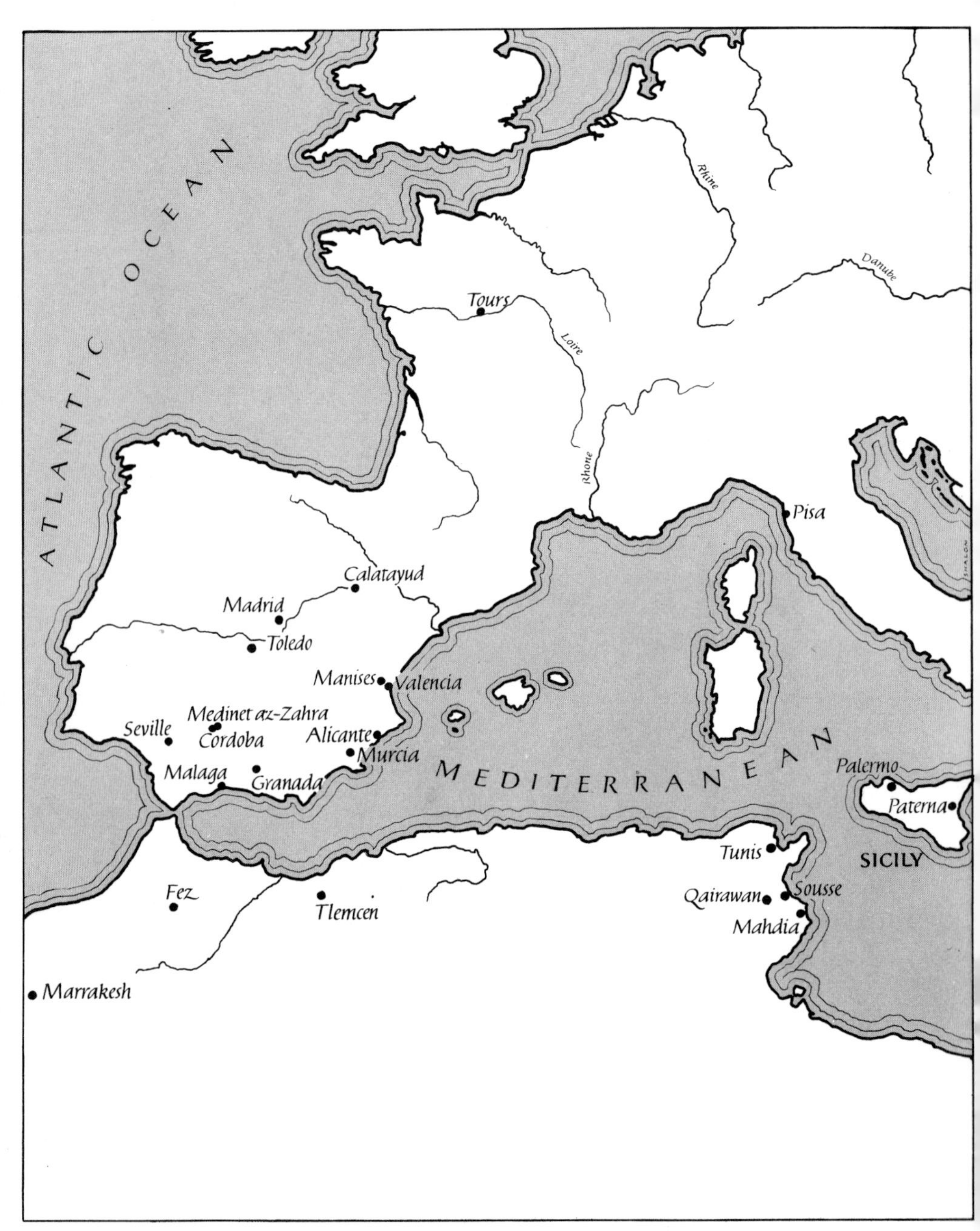

ATLANTIC OCEAN
Rhine
Danube
Tours
Loire
Rhone
Pisa
Calatayud
Madrid
Toledo
Manises
Valencia
Medinet az-Zahra
Seville
Cordoba
Alicante
Murcia
Malaga
Granada
MEDITERRANEAN
Palermo
Paterna
SICILY
Tunis
Qairawan
Sousse
Mahdia
Fez
Tlemcen
Marrakesh

List of Illustrations

The author and publishers are grateful to the many official bodies, institutions and individuals mentioned below for their assistance in supplying original illustration material.

22 Ukhaidir; Court of Honour, north side. Abbasid Period, *c.* 780. Photo: D. Talbot Rice.

23 Wall-painting; Dancers. Harem of the Jausaq Palace, Samarra. Reconstruction of original in the Çinili-Kiosk, Istanbul. Abbasid Period, 833–41. Photo: Staatliche Museen zu Berlin.

24 Stucco decoration; Style A. Samarra. Abbasid Period, ninth century. Photo: Staatliche Museen zu Berlin.

25 Stucco decoration; Style B. From private house, Samarra. Abbasid Period, ninth century. Photo: Staatliche Museen zu Berlin.

26 Stucco decoration; Style C. From private house, Samarra. Abbasid Period, ninth century. Photo: Staatliche Museen zu Berlin.

27 Great Mosque and minaret (*Malwiya*), Samarra. View from the north. Photo: Staatliche Museen zu Berlin.

28 Plan; the Great Mosque, Samarra.

29 Embroidery; Peacocks, lions and other animals in roundels. Silk. Mesopotamian, tenth–eleventh century. Photo: Museum of Fine Arts, Boston.

30 Wooden panels; Takrit, ninth century. Photo: Cook.

31 Jar cover; Barbotine ware. Unglazed pottery. Susa, ninth century. Wm. Rockhill Nelson Gallery, Kansas City. After A. U. Pope, *A Survey of Persian Art.*

32 Bowl; Samarra ware. Blue painted under cream-coloured glaze. Samarra, ninth century. H. 2½″ (6.5), diam. 8⅛″ (20.5). Photo: Staatliche Museen zu Berlin.

33 Dish; Glazed relief ware. Kufic inscription in green lustre is a distich by Muhammed ibn Bashir: 'Despair not even if your seeking is long. That you will see an issue when you seek the end of patience.' Diam. 8½″ (21.5). Photo: Courtesy, Trustees of the British Museum.

34 Bowl; Stylized eagle. Painted gold and brown lustre. Samarra, ninth century. H. 3¼″ (8.3), diam. 6½″ (16.7). Photo: Staatliche Museen zu Berlin.

35 Tiles; From the mihrab, the Great Mosque, Qairawan. Dark brown lustre. Baghdad, *c.* 862. Photo: Roger Wood.

36 Mimbar; Great Mosque, Qairawan. Carved wood. 862. Photo: Roger Wood.

37 Courtyard of the Mosque of Ibn Tulun, Cairo, showing ablutions fountain to the left, and minaret in background. 876–9. Photo: A. F. Kersting.

38 Stucco decoration; Soffit of pointed arch. Mosque of Ibn Tulun, Cairo. 876. Photo: C. F. Mohammad.

39 Tarik-khana mosque, Damaghan, central Persia. Interior view. 750–86. Photo: J. Powell.

40 Ornamental brickwork (detail); Dome setting. Mausoleum of Ismail the Samanid, Bokhara. *c.* 907. Photo: J. Powell.

41 Mausoleum of Ismail the Samanid, Bokhara. Exterior view. *c.* 907. Photo: J. Powell.

42 Stucco decoration; Detail of pillar and arch soffit. Masjid-i-Jami, Nayin. *c.* 960. Photo: Olga Ford.

43 Bowl; Falconer. Painted in black, green and yellow on white ground. Nishapur, tenth century, 12¼″ × 4¾″ (31 × 12). Collection Foroughi, Teheran Museum. Photo: Edmund Wilford.

44 Bowl; Decoration in red bole and dark brown on cream ground. Nishapur, tenth century. Diam. *c.* 10″ (25.5). Royal Scottish Museum. Photo: Tom Scott.

45 Bowl; Decoration in black on cream ground. Samarkand or Nishapur, tenth century. Diam. *c.* 6″ (15.0). Royal Scottish Museum. Photo: Tom Scott.

46 Dish; Earthenware covered with white slip, painted with brown kufic inscription: 'Knowledge, the beginning of it is bitter to taste, but the end is sweeter than honey.' Samarkand, ninth–tenth century. Diam. 14½″ (37). Louvre. Photo: A. C. Cooper.

47 Plate; Siege of a castle. Silver, carved and engraved and partially gilded. Late or post-Sassanian. Diam. 9⅜″ (23.7). Photo: State Hermitage Museum, Leningrad.

48 Cauldron; Equestrian figure of armed warrior and two eagles. Rim decorated with horses and lions. Cast bronze. Daghestan, twelfth or early thirteenth century. H. 2′ 1″ (63.4). Photo: Victoria and Albert Museum, Crown copyright.

49 Textile; Elephants and kufic inscription: 'Glory and happiness to the Commander Abu Mansur Bukhtakin, may God prolong his prosperity.' Silk on cotton woof. Formerly in the church of St-Josse, Pas de Calais. Khorasan, tenth century. H. 20¼″, (51.0) L. 36″ (61.5). Louvre. Photo: Giraudon.

50 Textile; stylized confronted lions and dogs. Silk eighth–ninth century. N. Persia or Soghdia. Photo: Victoria and Albert Museum, Crown copyright.

51 Brickwork; Rabat-i-Malik, Persia. Second half of the eleventh century. Photo: A. U. Pope, *A Survey of Persian Art.*

52 Tower of Masud III, Ghanzi, Afghanistan. 1099–1115. Photo: J. Powell.

53 Minaret, Jam, Afghanistan. Built by Ghiyath ad-din Muhammad. Ghurid dynasty, 1163–1203. Photo: J. Powell.

54 Courtyard of the Masjid-i-Jami, Isfahan. 1088. Photo: J. Powell.

55 Small dome; Masjid-i-Jami, Qazvin. 1113. Photo: A. U. Pope, *A Survey of Persian Art.*

56 Ribbed vaulting (detail); Dome chamber, Masjid-i-Jami, Isfahan. 1088. Photo: A. U. Pope, *A Survey of Persian Art.*

57 Stucco decoration (detail); Gumbat-i-Alaviyan, Hamadan. Second half of the twelfth century. Photo: A. U. Pope, *A Survey of Persian Art.*

58 Gumbat-i-Qabus, Persia. Built for the Emir Shamas al-Ma'ali Qabus. 1006. Photo: J. Powell.

59 Tomb tower of Mumina Khatun, Nakhechivan. 1186. Photo: A. U. Pope, *A Survey of Persian Art.*

60 Drawing; Tents seen by the Friar William of Rubruquis on his visit to Mongolian court in 1253. After de Bergeron, *Journey of Rubruquis.*

61 Bowl; Splash-glazed ware. Foliate and scroll pattern, incised decoration under yellow and green glaze. Persian, eighth–ninth century. Diam. 11⅝″ (30.0). The Logan–Patten–Ryerson Collection. Photo: Courtesy, The Art Institute of Chicago.

62 Bowl; Bird with lions and stags against background of hatched lines. Red earthenware, decoration engraved through white slip under clear glaze. Persian, ninth–tenth century. H. 2½″ (6.5), diam. 7¾″ (19.5). Photo: A. C. Cooper.

63 Bowl; Human-headed quadruped and floral scrolls. Earthenware, covered with white slip, engraved and glazed green. Gabri. Eleventh century. Diam. 9⅞″ (25.0). Photo: A. C. Cooper.

64 Bowl; Aghkand ware. Duck among sprays and scrolls, zigzag border. Red earthenware with white slip, painted green, brown and purple, under cream-coloured glaze. Eleventh century. H. 3⅝″ (9.0), diam. 11″ (28.0). Photo: A. C. Cooper.

65 Dish; Prince Khusraw discovers Shirin bathing. Scalloped upright sides and narrow grooved rim. Signed Sayyid Shams ad-din al Hasani. Kashan. *c.* 1210. Diam. 13⅜″ (33.5). Photo: Courtesy, Smithsonian Institution, Freer Gallery of Art, Washington DC.

66 Dish; Rider. White earthenware, painted in brownish-gold lustre with light blue glaze on reverse. Rayy, late twelfth century. Diam. 14¾″ (37.5). Brangwyn Collection. Photo: Victoria and Albert Museum, Crown copyright.

67 Bowl; Amol ware. Decoration in pale green and thin sgraffito. Persian, twelfth–thirteenth century. Diam. *c.* 8″ (20.0). Author's collection. Photo: John Webb.

68 Dish; Labaki ware. Dancers and hyenas. Decorated in relief and coloured glazes. Persian, twelfth century. Diam. 16″ (39.3). Photo: National Gallery of Victoria, Melbourne.

69 Bowl; Minai ware. Confronted riders. White earthenware, painted in colours and gold on opaque white glaze. Rayy, late twelfth–early thirteenth century. Diam. 8½″ (21.5). Photo: Victoria and Albert Museum, Crown copyright.

70 Flask; Spouted, painted with black designs under türquoise glaze. Persian (Kashan), thirteenth century. Photo: Teheran Museum.

71 Tray; Inscribed: 'Everlasting honour.' Engraved bronze, traces of gilding. Persian, twelfth–thirteenth century. H. 2 $\frac{11}{16}$″ (7.0), diam. 18¾″ (48.0). Photo: Victoria and Albert Museum, Crown copyright.

72 Incense burner; Signed: Ali ibn Muhammad as-Salihi (?). Bronze pierced engraved and inlaid with copper. Persian, twelfth century. L. 18½″ (47). State Hermitage Museum, Leningrad. Photo: S. C. R. Photo Library.

73 Kettle; Signed: Muhammad ibn 'Abd al-Wahid and Masud ibn Ahmad. Bronze, inlaid with enamels. Herat, 1163. State Hermitage Museum, Leningrad. Photo: S. C. R. Photo Library.

74 Central dome of the Great Mosque, Cordova. 961–8. Photo: Mas, Barcelona.

75 The Great Mosque, Cordova. View of the Sanctuary from the Palmas Door. Left, the mihrab. Photo: Mas, Barcelona.

76 Stucco decoration; Arch spandrals. Palace of Abd er-Rahman III (912–961), Medinet az-Zahra. Photo: Mas, Barcelona.

77 Ivory casket; made for Princess Subh, mother of a son to Caliph al-Hakim II. 964. Formerly in the Cathedral Treasury, Zamora. Photo: Museo Arqueologico Nacional, Madrid.

78 Textile (detail); the so-called Veil of Hisham. People, lions, birds and quadrupeds in medallions. Kufic inscription bears name of Hisham II. Silk and gold. Formerly at Church of San Estaban de Gormaz. 976–1012. Academy of History, Madrid. Photo: D. Ramoz.

79 Courtyard, Great Mosque, Qairawan. View looking SE. 836–62. Photo: Courtauld Institute of Art.

80 Dome in front of the mihrab, Great Mosque, Qairawan. 836–62. Photo: Roger Wood.

81 Minaret, Great Mosque, Qairwan. View looking NW. Photo: A. F. Kersting.

82 Painting; Detail from ceiling of the Cappella Palatina, Palermo. Photo: John Webb.

83 Wall-painting; Seated figure. From a bath near Cairo. Eleventh century. Photo: Museum of Islamic Art, Cairo.

84 Nilometer, Rhoda Island, Cairo. After K. A. C. Creswell, *Muslim Architecture in Egypt* II.

85 Mosque of al-Azhar, Cairo. West *iwan* of the courtyard. Founded 970. Photo: A. F. Kersting.

86 Stone carving; Mosque of al-Hakim, Cairo. 990–1013. Photo: C. F. Mohammad.

87 Wooden doors; From Mosque of al-Azhar, Cairo. Presented by al-Hakim in 1010. Photo: Museum of Islamic Art, Cairo.

88 Mihrab of al-Afdal; from Mosque of Ibn Tulun, Cairo, Stucco, 1094. Photo: C. F. Mohammad.

89 The Bab el-Futuh, Cairo. Photo: A. F. Kersting.

90 Ewer; Squatting lions and ibex inscribed with the name of Caliph al-Aziz. Carved rock crystal. Fatimid, 975–96. St Mark's Treasury, Venice. Photo: O. Böhm.

91 Bowl; A Coptic priest with censer. Signed by the potter Sa'ad. Earthenware painted in copper-toned lustre on opaque white glaze. Probably found at Luxor. Fatimid, first half of the twelfth century.

Diam. 8⅞″ (22.4). Photo: Victoria and Albert Museum, Crown copyright.

92 Jar; Earthenware painted yellow lustre on opaque white glaze. Fostat. Fatimid, first half of the twelfth century. H. 12⅛″ (30.8). Photo: Victoria and Albert Museum, Crown copyright.

93 Gryphon; eagle-headed, lion-bodied aquamanile or fountain. Bronze. Fatimid, eleventh century. H. (1.50 m.) Campo Santo, Pisa. Photo: Anderson.

94 Textile; the so-called Veil of St Anne. Detail of a facsimile made in 1850. Photo: Courtesy, Cathedral Treasury, Apt.

95 Stone mihrab, Mosul. Photo: Director-General of Antiquities, Baghdad.

96 Manuscript; From a koran possibly by Ali ibn-Hilal, called Ibn al-Bawwab. Paper. Baghdad, *c.* 1000. (Ms 1431, fol. 7 v.) 7″ × 5¼″ (17.7 × 13.5). Photo: Chester Beatty Library, Dublin.

97 Oliphant; Ivory. Fourteenth century. L. *c.* 23″ (58.5). Royal Scottish Museum. Photo: Tom Scott.

98 Manuscript; The physician Andromakhos watching labourers at work. Book of Antidotes (*Kitab ad-Diryaq*), Pseudo-Galen. Probably N. Iraq, 1199. (Ms arabe 2964, fol. 22.) 5½″ × 8⅜″ (14.0 × 21.0). Photo: Bibliothèque Nationale, Paris.

99 Dish; Engraved with the name of Alp Arslan. Silver. Rayy, 1066. Photo: Courtesy, Museum of Fine Arts, Boston.

100 Talisman Gate, Baghdad (detail). Built 1221, destroyed 1917. After F. Sarre and E. Herzfeld.

101 Manuscript; Dioscorides and a student. *De Materia Medica* of Dioscorides. N. Iraq or Syria, 1229. (Ms Ahmed III, 2127.) 5¼″ × 6¾″ (13.5 × 17.4). Topkapi Saray Muzesi, Istanbul. Photo: Wim Swaan.

102 Manuscript; Frontispiece to Book of Songs (*Kitab el Aghani*) of Abu'l Faraj al-Isfahani. Feyzullah Ef. (2nd vol.) 1217. Millet Kütüphanesi, Istanbul. Photo: Wim Swaan.

103 Manuscript; The plant Atraghalus and a hunting scene. *De Materia Medica* of Dioscorides. Baghdad. 1224. (Ms 3703, fol. 29 r.) 6¼″ × 7¾″ (16.0 × 19.3). Süleymaniye Library, Istanbul. Photo: Wim Swaan.

104 Manuscript; the king of the hares interviews his subjects. Fables of Bidpai (*Kalila wa Dimna*). Probably Syrian, second quarter of the fourteenth century. (Ms arabe 3467, fol. 70.) 6½″ × 7″ (16.3 × 17.9). Photo: Bibliothèque Nationale, Paris.

105 Manuscript; Half-naked old man talks to Abu Zayd and his companions. Assemblies (*Maqamat*) of al-Hariri. (Ms arabe 3929, fol. 54 v. St Vaast.) Late thirteenth century. 3½″ × 7¼″ (9.2 × 18.8). Photo: Bibliothèque Nationale, Paris.

106 Manuscript; A sermon in the mosque. Assemblies (*Maqamat*) of al-Hariri. Probably Syrian, 1222/3. (Ms arabe 6094.) 6¼″ × 4⅛″ (15.7 × 20.5). Photo: Bibliothèque Nationale, Paris.

107 Manuscript; The Eastern Isles. (39th *Maqama.*) Assemblies (*Maqamat*) of al-Hariri. Painted by Yahya ibn Mahmud al-Wasiti. Baghdad, 1237. (Ms arabe 5847, fol. 121 r. Schefer Hariri.) 10¼″ × 11″ (25.9 × 28.0). Photo: Bibliothèque Nationale, Paris.

108 Manuscript; The Standard Bearers of the Caliph's Guard. (7th *Maqama.*) Assemblies (*Maqamat*) of al-Hariri. Painted by Yahya ibn Mahmud al-Wasiti. Baghdad, 1237. (Ms arabe 5847, fol. 19 r. Schefer Hariri.) 10¼″ × 11″ (25.9 × 28.0). Photo: Bibliothèque Nationale, Paris.

109 Dish (detail); Bears name of Ortokid Prince Süleyman ibn-Daud of Isn-Kaifa (reigned 1114–44). Bronze and enamel. Ferdinandeum, Innsbruck. Photo: D. S. Rice.

110 Ewer; Inscribed: 'made by Shuja ibn Mana of Mosul.' Inlaid brass. Mosul, 1232. H. 12″ (30.5). Blacas Collection. Photo: Courtesy, Trustees of the British Museum.

111 Manuscript; Two bears. Morgan Bestiary, *Manafi al-Hayawan* of Ibn Baktishu. Margha, 1298. (Ms 500 fol. 24.) 13⅜″ × 9⅝″ (33.5 × 24.5). Photo: Courtesy, Trustees of the Pierpont Morgan Library.

112 Manuscript; Phoenix. Morgan Bestiary, *Manafi al-Hayawan* of Ibn Baktishu. Margha, 1298. (Ms 500 fol. 55.) (13⅜″ × 9⅝″) (33.5 × 24.5). Photo: Courtesy, Trustees of the Pierpont Morgan Library.

113 Manuscript; The Temptation. Chronology of Ancient Peoples of al-Biruni. Tabriz, 1307–8. (Ms Arab 161 fol. 48 v.) 12½″ × 7½″ (32.0 × 19.2). Photo: Edinburgh University Library.

114 Manuscript; The Prophet Jeremiah. Universal History of Rashid al-Din. Tabriz, 1307–8. (Ms 20 fol. 13 v.) 17¾″ × 13¼″ (45.0 × 33.7). Photo: Edinburgh University Library.

115 Manuscript; Embassy to the court of the Negus of Abyssinia. Universal History of Rashid al-Din. Tabriz, 1307–8. (Ms 20 fol. 52 r.) 17¾″ × 13¼″ (45.0 × 33.7). Photo: Edinburgh University Library.

116 Manuscript; Battle scene. Universal History of Rashid al-Din. Tabriz, 1307–8. (Ms 20 fol. 124 v.) 17¾″ × 13¼″ (45.0 × 33.7). Photo: Edinburgh University Library.

117 Manuscript; Jonah and the Whale. Universal History of Rashid al-Din. Tabriz, 1307–8. (Ms 20 fol. 23 v.) 17¾″ × 13¼″ (45.0 × 33.7). Photo: Edinburgh University Library.

118 Manuscript; Bahram Gur killing the Dragon. *Shah-nama* of Firdausi (formerly known as 'Demotte Shah-nama'). Persia, fourteenth century. 16″ × 11 9/16″ (40.5 × 30.0). Mrs Grace Rainey Rogers Fund. Photo: Cleveland Museum of Art, Cleveland, Ohio.

119 Manuscript; The Bier of the Great Iskander. *Shah-nama* of Firdausi (Demotte). Tabriz, 1330–6 (No. 38.3). 9 13/16″ × 11″ (25.0 × 28.0). Photo: Courtesy, Smithsonian Institution, Freer Gallery of Art, Washington DC.

120 Manuscript; Rustem dragging the Khakhan of China from his elephant. *Shah-nama* (Book of Kings) of Firdausi. Mongol, late thirteenth century. Photo: Courtesy, Museum of Fine Arts, Boston.

121 Manuscript; (*above*) Bulgars bathing in the Volga, (*below*) Tibetans adoring a new-born child. Book of Marvels of the World. Baghdad School, 1388. (Supp. Per. 332 fol. 194 v.) Photo: Bibliothèque Nationale, Paris.

122 Bowl; Birds and foliage. Decorated in underglaze colours of blue. Persia (Sultanabad district), fourteenth century. H. 4″ (10.0). Photo: Courtesy, Trustees of the British Museum.

123 Bowl; Fluted sides, dark blue, turquoise and black. Persian (Kashan), first half of the fourteenth century. Diam. 8¼″ (12.0). Sir E. Hitchcock Collection. Photo: Victoria and Albert Museum, Crown copyright.

124 Mausoleum of Uljaitu Khodabende Shah, Sultaniya. Exterior view. Begun 1305. Photo: D. Talbot Rice.

125 Mausoleum of Uljaitu Khodabende Shah, Sultaniya, Interior view. Begun 1305. Photo: D. Talbot Rice.

126 Double minaret, Isfahan. Late fourteenth century. After A. U. Pope, *A Survey of Persian Art.*

127 The citadel walls, Tabriz. Photo: Mme Th. Ullens de Schooten.

128 Masjid-i-Jami, Varamin. Built 1325–6. After A. U. Pope, *A Survey of Persian Art.*

129 Bowl; Two fish. Engraved and painted with coloured glazes. Raqqa, thirteenth century. National Museum, Damascus. Photo: Director-General of Antiquities, Damascus.

130 Vase; Dark painted under clear glaze. Raqqa, thirteenth century. National Museum, Damascus. Photo: Director-General of Antiquities, Damascus.

131 Horseman; pottery figurine with coloured glazes. Raqqa, thirteenth century. National Museum, Damascus. Photo: Director-General of Antiquities, Damascus.

132 Bowl; Sgraffito decoration. Fostat, thirteenth century. Photo: Benaki Museum, Athens.

133 Bowl; Brown and yellow sgraffitto ware. Red earthenware white slip with yellow transparent glaze. Egyptian, fourteenth century. H. 8″ (20.3), diam. $11\frac{1}{2}$″ (29.4). Photo: Victoria and Albert Museum, Crown copyright.

134 Mosque lamp; With three quotations from the Koran and a dedication to the Mamluk Sultan Beybars II. Glass painted in enamel colours. Syrian, early fourteenth century. Cairo. H. $11\frac{3}{8}$″ (28.5), diam. 10″ (25.5). Photo: Victoria and Albert Museum, Crown copyright.

135 Mosque lamp; Made for Sayf ad-Din Tuquz-timur, Assessor of Sultan an-Nasir Muhammad. Syrian, 1340. Photo: Courtesy, Trustees of the British Museum.

136 Carved wooden panel. Thirteenth century. National Museum, Damascus. Photo: Dir.-Gen. of Antiquities, Damascus.

137 Basin; Bears name of Sultan an-Nasir Muhammad. Copper inlaid with silver and bronze. Egypt, early fourteenth century. Diam. $21\frac{1}{8}$″ (53.6). Photo: Courtesy, Trustees of the British Museum.

138 Basin; so-called Baptistry of St Louis. Copper inlaid with silver. Mamluk, fourteenth century. Louvre. Photo: Archive Photographiques.

139 Manuscript; A Water Clock. Treatise of al-Jazari on *Automata*. Mamluk, thirteenth century. Photo: Courtesy, Museum of Fine Arts, Boston.

140 Manuscript; The physician awakening, discovers a party in his house. Banquet of the Physicians (*Risalat Da'wat al-Atibba*) of al-Muktar ibn al-Hasan ibn Butlan. Probably Syrian, 1273. (Ms A. 125 Inf. fol. 35 v.) $4\frac{1}{2}$″ × $6\frac{1}{2}$″ (11.6 × 16.5). Photo: Biblioteca Ambrosiana, Milan.

141 Manuscript; Two seated figures Assemblies (*Maqamat*) of al-Hariri. Mamluk, 1237. (Add. Ms 22.114 fol. 96.) $10\frac{1}{2}$″ × $7\frac{3}{4}$″ (26.7 × 19.8). Photo: Courtesy, Trustees of the British Museum.

142 Manuscript; Enthroned Prince. Assemblies (*Maqamat*) of al-Hariri. Probably Egyptian, 1334. (A.F. 9 fol. 1 r. frontispiece.) $8\frac{3}{4}$″ × 7″ (12.2 × 17.5). Photo: Nationalbibliothek, Vienna.

143 Mosque of Beybars, Cairo. North-west entrance. 1260–77. After K. A. C. Creswell, *Muslim Architecture in Egypt* II.

144 Interior of the tomb chamber, Mosque of Qala-un, Cairo. 1279–90. Photo: A. F. Kersting.

145 Minaret; Madrassa of Sultan an-Nasir Muhammad, Cairo. 1294–1340. Photo: C. F. Mohammad.

146 The dome of the Tomb Mosque of Qaitbay, the Eastern Cemetery, Cairo. 1463–96. Photo: A. F. Kersting.

147 Mosque lamp; Blue, black and turquoise. Turkish (Isnik), 1549. H. 15″ (38.0). From the Dome of the Rock, Jerusalem. Photo: Courtesy, Trustees of the British Museum.

148 Cushion cover (detail); Embroidered silk on linen. Egyptian, seventh–eleventh century, 23″ × 17″ (58.5 × 43.3). Photo: Victoria and Albert Museum, Crown copyright.

149 The mihrab chamber, the Great Mosque, Tlemcen. Photo: Mas, Barcelona.

150 The Court of Lions, Alhambra, Granada. Nasrid, fourteenth century. Photo: Olga Ford.

151 Minaret of the Qutubiya mosque, Marrakesh. Almohad, twelfth century. Photo: Olga Ford.

152 Rabat Gate, Marrakesh. Late twelfth century. Photo: Edmund Wilford.

153 Dish; polychrome ware. Fifteenth century. Rabat Museum. Photo: Edmund Wilford.

154 Dish; Hispano-Mauresque ware. Tin-glazed earthenware with lustre decoration in gold and blue. Valencia, early fifteenth century. Photo: Victoria and Albert Museum, Crown copyright.

155 Textile; The Tapestry of the Witches. Stylized birds and monsters. Hispano-Arabic, twelfth century. Archaeological and Artistic Museum, Vich (Barcelona). Photo: Mas, Barcelona.

156 Coronation Mantle of the Holy Roman Empire; probably made for Roger II. Shows lions attacking camels. Embroidered with gold and coloured silks on red twill. Kufic inscription shows that the mantle was made 'in the Royal Workshop of the capital of Sicily in the year 528 of the *Hegira*.' 1134. Diam. 9′ 10½″ (3.42 m.). Photo: Kunsthistorisches Museum, Vienna.

157 Textile; Confronted peacocks and kufic inscription. Hispano or Siculo Arabic, twelfth century. H. 9¾″ (24.8), L. 5⅞″ (14.7). Musée de Cluny. Photo: J. Hyde.

158 Casket (front and back views); Figures of two saints, a seated musician, a swan and animals. Wood covered with ivory, decorated in outline and gilded. Naskh inscription: 'The happiness of a bird and the height of esteem and conditions which point to the proper guidance and everlasting glory and may the ending be perfect and may glory endure.' Siculo-Arabic, twelfth century. Formerly in the Cathedral, Bari. Photo: Victoria and Albert Museum, Crown copyright.

159 Casket; Friezes of inscription, people and animals. Wood encrusted with ivory. Siculo-Arabic (?), thirteenth century. Palazzo Reale, Cappella Palatina, Palermo. Photo: Alinari.

160 Casket; Decorated with animals amongst foliage. Ivory. Hispano-Mauresque, tenth–eleventh century. H. 1⅛″ (3), L. 3½″ (9). Louvre. Photo: Archive Photographiques.

161 The naval arsenal, *tersane*, Alanya. Built of brick, 1228. L. 187′ (57 m.). Photo: Press Broadcasting and Tourist Department, Ankara.

162 The Han, Tercan. Exterior view. Twelfth century. Photo: J. Powell.

163 Portal of the Sultan Han on the Konya–Aksaray road. Built 1229, completed 1236. Photo: David Wilson.

164 The Mosque of Sultan 'Palaz' Han on the Kayseri–Sivas road. Built 1230–40. Photo: D. Talbot Rice.

165 Detail of carving and brick work; Ince (Slender) Minare Madrassa, Konya. Built by Abdulla Oğlu Kelük in 1258 as theological college. Photo: D. Talbot Rice.

166 Carving (detail); North portal of the Ulu Cami, Divriği. Built by Ahmet, son of Ibrahim of Tiflis and Khurramshah, son of Muhid of Ahlat, 1228. Photo: V. Gordon.

167 Portal; Gök (Blue) Madrassa, Sivas. Founded by Vizier Sahip Ata and built by Abdulla Oğlu Kelük in 1271–2. Photo: J. Powell.

168 The Çifte or Hatuniye Madrassa, Erzurum. Interior view. Built by Huand Hatun, daughter of Ala'ed din Kaykubad II. 1253. Photo: J. Powell.

169 The Döner Gumbat, Kayseri. Built for Princess Shah Cihan Hatun. 1276. Photo: Gerard Bakker.

170 Mausoleum; Built for Princess Hatuma, on the shore of Lake Van, between Van and Achtavan. 1322. Photo: J. Powell.

171 Mausoleum; The Mama Hatun Gumbat, Tercan. Built by Muffadal the Cross-eyed of Ahlat. Photo: J. Powell.

172 Façade; The Çifte (Double) Minare Madrassa, Sivas. Founded by the Vizier Şemseddin Juwaini. 1271. Photo: D. Talbot Rice.

173 Interior of Mosque at Beyşehir, showing wooden structure. 1156–1220. Photo: D. Talbot Rice.

174 Mosaic tiles (detail); Mihrab of Sirçali Madrassa, Konya. 1243. Photo: D. Talbot Rice.

175 Mosaic tiles; Detail from dome and pendentives, Büyük Karatay Madrassa, Konya. Deep blue and gold. 1252. Photo: Olga Ford.

176 Wooden doors; Carved with geometric and floral patterns. Twelfth century. Ethnographical Museum, Konya. Photo: D. Talbot Rice.

177 Mimbar; Carved wood. Kebir Cami, Aksaray. Thirteenth century. Photo: D. Talbot Rice.

178 Carpet (detail); woven wool. Thirteenth century. Türk ve Islam Müzesi, Istanbul. Photo: Olga Ford.

179 Carpet (detail); Ethnographical Museum, Konya. Photo: Olga Ford.

180 Carpet (detail); Stylized plant pattern, dark red on light red. Grey-blue on black border with kufic inscription. 17′ × 9′ 4″ (5.20 × 28.5 m.). Türk ve Islam Müzesi, Istanbul. Photo: Olga Ford.

181 Carpet (detail); Stylized animal pattern. Thirteenth century. Ethnographical Museum, Konya. Photo: Olga Ford.

182 Ala'ed din Mosque, Konya. Interior view. Built by Kiliçarslan II, 1156–1220. Photo: Olga Ford.

183 Gold buckles; Gryphon and rabbit-headed, winged creatures. *c.* 1236–46. 3″ × 2⅜″ (7.5 × 6). Photo: Staatliche Museen zu Berlin.

184 Bronze weight; human-headed gryphons. Ortokid period. Cabinet des Médailles. Photo: Bibliothèque Nationale, Paris.

185 Tiles; Star-shaped and painted and glazed. Kubadabad, thirteenth century. Karatay Madrassa (Ceramics) Museum, Konya. Photo: Olga Ford.

186 Spouted vessel; Figures of men of Uygur appearance. Ethnographic Museum, Ankara. Photo: Olga Ford.

187 Mosque of Selim II, Edirne. Designed by Sinan, built 1570–4. Photo: Gerard Bakker.

188 Ulu Cami, Bursa. Interior view. 1359–1420. Photo: Thames and Hudson Archive.

189 Tile-work (detail); Yeşil Cami, Bursa. 1419–24. Photo: Thames and Hudson Archive.

190 Çinili Kiosk, Istanbul. Originally part of the New Palace of Mehmet the Conqueror. 1472. Photo: D. Talbot Rice.

191 Süleymaniye Mosque, Istanbul. Exterior view. Built by Süleyman the Magnificent, designed by Sinan. 1550–7. Photo: Olga Ford.

192 Süleymaniye Mosque, Istanbul. Interior view. Built by Süleyman the Magnificent, designed by Sinan. 1550–7. Photo: J. Powell.

193 Mosque of Sultan Ahmed (The Blue Mosque), Istanbul. Exterior view. Designed by Mehmet Aga. 1609–16. Photo: J. Powell.

194 Mausoleum; Sultan Süleyman the Magnificent, Istanbul. Designed by Sinan. 1566. Photo: Olga Ford.

195 Tiles (detail); Mausoleum of Süleyman the Magnificent, Istanbul. Turkish (Isnik), sixteenth century. Photo: Olga Ford.

196 Mosque of Sultan Ahmed (The Blue Mosque), Istanbul. Interior view. Designed by Mehmet Aga. 1609–16. Photo: Olga Ford.

197 Tiles (detail); Rüstem Pasha Mosque, Istanbul. 1550. Turkish (Isnik), sixteenth century. Photo: Olga Ford.

198 Tiles (detail); Flower patterns on deep blue background. Rüstem Pasha Mosque, Istanbul. 1550. Turkish (Isnik), sixteenth century. Photo: Olga Ford.

199 Tiles (detail); Deep blue, green on white. From mihrab of Rüstem Pasha Mosque. Istanbul. Photo: Olga Ford.

200 Mihrab; Sokullu Mehmet Pasha Mosque, Istanbul. 1571–2. Photo: Olga Ford.

201 Bowl; Painted in shades of blue. Turkish (Isnik), *c.* 1510. Diam. 18″ (45.7). Photo: Victoria and Albert Museum, Crown copyright.

202 Bowl; 'Golden Horn ware'. Painted greenish-black, blue and turquoise. Turkish (Isnik), *c.* 1540–50. Diam. 16¾″ (42.5). Photo: Victoria and Albert Museum, Crown copyright.

203 Dish; Painted olive-green, blue and turquoise with black outlines. Turkish (Isnik), *c.* 1540–50. Diam. 14¾″ (37.5). Salting Collection. Victoria and Albert Museum. Photo: John Webb.

204 Tiles; panel from the Harem in the Topkapi Saray, Istanbul. Turkish (Isnik), sixteenth century. Photo: Olga Ford.

205 Jug; Painted in black, white and blue on salmon-pink ground. Turkish (Isnik), second half of sixteenth century. H. 11½″ (29). Salting Collection, Victoria and Albert Museum. Photo: John Webb.

206 Mug; Painted red, blue and black outline under opaque white glaze. Turkish (Isnik), 1570–1600. H. 7¾″ (19.5). Salting Collection, Victoria and Albert Museum. Photo: John Webb.

207 Flask; Polychrome blue and white. Turkish (Kütahya), eighteenth century. H. 7¾″ (19.5). Photo: Victoria and Albert Museum, Crown copyright.

208 Textile; Crimson velvet brocade. Turkish, sixteenth century. Photo: Benaki Museum, Athens.

209 Textile; woven silk. Turkish (Bursa), sixteenth century. Photo: Benaki Museum, Athens.

210 Costume of Sultan Beyazid II (1481–1512). Long-sleeved upper Kaffan. Flowers and leaves on deep brown ground. Topkapi Saray Museum. Istanbul. Photo: Olga Ford.

211 Carpet; Wool. Gördes knots with two shoots of wool weft on wool warps. 104 knots to sq. in. Turkish (Ushak), sixteenth century. 17′ 4″ × 8′ 2″ (5.27 × 2.49 m.). Photo: Victoria and Albert Museum, Crown copyright.

212 Manuscript; Sweepers in the Hippodrome, Istanbul. *Surnama* of Murad III (1574–95). (No. 339) 11¾″ × 12¼″ (30 × 31). Topkapi Saray Library, Istanbul. Photo: Wim Swaan.

213 Manuscript; Sultan watching dancers and comedians in the Hippodrome, Istanbul. *Surnama* of Ahmed III. 1703–30. Topkapi Saray Library, Istanbul. Photo: Wim Swaan.

214 Painting; Nomad encampment. 'Album of the Conqueror.' Mehmet Siyah Kalem. Turkish, fifteenth century. H. 6¾″ (16.7). Topkapi Library, Istanbul. Photo: John Webb.

215 Mausoleum of Tamerlane, the Gur Emir, Samarkand. 1434. Photo: J. E. Dayton.

216 Cauldron of Tamerlane. Bronze. Samarkand. 1399. Weight *c.* 2 tons, diam. 7½′ (2.45 m.). Photo: State Hermitage Museum, Leningrad.

217 Glass bottle; Ornamented in relief with elaborate handle. Fourteenth century. Teheran Museum. Photo: Director-General of Antiquities, Teheran.

218 Textile; Birds on black ground enriched with gilt thread. Satin. Persian, fourteenth century. Staatliche Museen, Berlin (West). Photo: W. Steinkopf.

219 Manuscript; Battle of Tamujin with army of Cathay. *Garshasp Nama.* Persia (Shiraz School), 1398. (Or. Ms 2780 fol. 49 v.) 10″ × 6½″ (2.5 × 16.5). Photo: Courtesy, Trustees of the British Museum.

220 Manuscript; Majun at Laila's tomb. Persian Anthology, written for Iskander Sultan. Persian (Shiraz School), 1410. 10¾″ × 5″ (27.7 × 17.8). Photo: Fundação Calouste Gulbenkian Museu.

221 The defeat of Pir Padishah and Sultan Ali by the army of Shah Rukh. A detached page from a lost manuscript of the *History* of Hafiz i Abru, *c.* 1420. (Victoria and Albert Museum, E. 5499–1958.) Photo: Victoria and Albert Museum, Crown copyright.

222 Manuscript; Kay Khusraw's disappearance related to Luhrasp. *Shah-nama* for Baysunghur. Herat, 1430. Photo: Imperial Library of the Gulistan Palace, Teheran.

223 Manuscript; Prince Humay and Princess Humayun in the garden of the Emperor of China. Leaf from a poem of Khwadju Kirmani. Herat, 1291–1352. (Ms No. 3727.) Photo: Musée des Arts Decoratifs, Paris.

224 Manuscript; Paladins by a pool. *Shah-nama*. Herat School, 1440. (Or. Ms 239 fol. 428.) 11¼″7×¾″ (28.5×19.7). Photo: Courtesy, Trustees of the British Museum.

225 Manuscript; King Dara and his herdsmen. Sadi's *Bustan*. Herat School (?), 1489. Photo: National Library, Cairo.

226 Painting; Portrait of a painter in Turkish dress. Colour and little gold. Signed. Persian, late fifteenth century. 7⅜″×5″ (18.8×12.7). Photo: Courtesy, Smithsonian Institution, Freer Gallery of Art, Washington D C.

227 Manuscript; The Capture of the fortress of the Knights of St John, Smyrna. Miniature by Bihzad or atelier. Life of Tamerlane (*Zafar-nama*). Herat, 1467. (T.L. 6. 1950 fol. 449 v.) Courtesy, John Garrett Library, Johns Hopkins University of Baltimore. Photo: Walters Art Gallery, Baltimore.

228 Manuscript; Khusraw and Shirin listening to night singers. *Khamsa* of Nizami. Persian, 1539–43. (Or. Ms 2265 fol. 66 v.) 14½″×10″ (36.9×25.5). Photo: Courtesy, Trustees of the British Museum.

229 Manuscript; Building of the fort of Khwarnaq, by Bihzad. *Khamsa* of Nizami. Persian, 1494. (Or. Ms 6810 fol. 154 v.) 9½″×6¾″ (24.0×17.0). Photo: Courtesy, Trustees of the British Museum.

230 Manuscript; Old woman complaining to Sultan Sanjar. *Khamsa* of Nizami. Tabriz, 1539–43. (Or. Ms 2265 fol. 18 r.) 14½″×10″ (36.9×25.5). Photo: Courtesy, Trustees of the British Museum.

231 Manuscript; Majnun in chains brought by a beggar woman to Laila's tent. Miniature by Sayyid Ali. Tabriz, 1539–43. (Or. Ms 2265 fol. 157 v.) 14½″×10″ (36.9×25.5). Photo: Courtesy, Trustees of the British Museum.

232 Manuscript; Portrait of Khusraw shown to Shirin by Shapur. Miniature by Mirza Ali. Tabriz, 1539–43. (Or. Ms 2265 fol. 48 v.) 14½″×10″ (36.9×25.5). Photo: Courtesy, Trustees of the British Museum.

233 Maydan-i-Shah, Isfahan. General view. Photo: Lawrence Lockhart.

234 Portal; Masjid-i-Shaykh Lutfullah Mosque, Isfahan. Photo: Mme Th. Ullens de Schooten.

235 Drum of the dome of the Masjid-i-Shah, Isfahan. 1612–13. Photo: Edmund Wilford.

236 Ali Kapu Palace, Isfahan. General view. Photo: E. Ashcroft.

237 Chihil Sutun Palace, Isfahan. General view. Photo: E. Ashcroft.

238 Allahverdi Bridge, Isfahan. Built *c.* 1600. Photo: Lawrence Lockhart.

239 Ewer; Painted blue under white. Persian, early eighteenth century. Photo: Victoria and Albert Museum, Crown copyright.

240 Dish; Earthenware with polychrome painting. N. Persian (Kubachi), *c.* 1550. Diam. 12½″ (31.8). Photo: Victoria and Albert Museum, Crown copyright.

241 Textile (detail); Armed man leading woman prisoner among palm trees in flowering garden. Silk. Persian, late sixteenth century. H. 78½″ (1.98 m.), L. 23½″ (58.6). Victoria and Albert Museum, Crown copyright. Photo: John Webb.

242 Textile; Birds and flowers. Brocade of silver with design in soft coloured silks. Persian, seventeenth century. Photo: Metropolitan Museum of Art (Rogers Fund, 1926), New York.

243 Drawing; Three hunters and a landscape by Riza-i-Abbasi. Persian, late sixteenth

century. Formerly in the Cartier Collection, Paris. After, A. U. Pope, *A Survey of Persian Art.*

244 Drawing; Landscape with scenes of labour and oxen ploughing. Safavid, *c.* 1578. $10\frac{1}{4}'' \times 6\frac{5}{8}''$ (26.0 × 16.0). Photo: Giraudon.

245 Drawing; A mounted lion-hunter by Muhammad Riza Iraqi. Persian, *c.* 1600. (Or. Album 23610.) $6\frac{7}{8}'' \times 3\frac{3}{4}''$ (17.5 × 9.5). Photo: Courtesy, Trustees of the British Museum.

246 Drawing; Portrait of Riza-i-Abbasi by Muin Muzaffar. Persian, 1676. (No. 96 G.) Photo: Princeton University Library.

247 Carpet (detail); the so-called Ardebil carpet. From the Mosque of Ismail Shah, Ardebil. 340 knots per sq. in. Persian, 1540. 37′ 9″ × 17′ 6″ (11.52 × 5.34 m.). Photo: Victoria and Albert Museum. Crown copyright.

248 Compartment rug; Three rows of various shapes filled with flowers and trees. Caucasian, seventeenth century. 16′ 1″ × 8′ 11″ (4.90 × 2.72 m.). Photo: Philadelphia Museum of Art.

249 Compartment rug; Pattern of large bell-shaped flowers and angular saw-edged leaves. Wool. Caucasian, eighteenth century. Photo: Benaki Museum, Athens.

Index

Figures in italics refer to illustrations